SOUTH OF NORMAL

MY YEAR IN PARADISE

NORM SCHRIEVER

Some names and identifying details of people described in this book have been altered to protect their privacy.

South of Normal: My Year in Paradise
By Norm Schriever
1. Biography & Autobiography : Adventurers & Explorers 2. Travel : Special Interest - Adventure 3. Humor : General
ISBN: 978-1-935953-49-4

Cover design by Lewis Agrell
Interior design by Stephanie Martindale

Printed in the United States of America

Authority Publishing
11230 Gold Express Dr. #310-413
Gold River, CA 95670
800-877-1097
www.AuthorityPublishing.com

DEDICATION

Thanks for all of the support and love from my family, Angelika, my mother, Ferdinand, my father, R.I.P., Barbara, my sister, Sean, Colin, Ryan, and Madeline. A shout out to the DePinos—Mitch D and Fun Lisa, Jackson and Amelia, Glen Fu, Mrs. D, and Johnny D, R.I.P. Much love always to the Holthoffs—Lily, Joseph, R.I.P., Marcus, and Daryl, and to the whole Fuller family.

To Stephanie Chandler at Authority Publishing—the real brains and muscle behind the operation. Two literary influences I respect who took the time to help: Ben Hamper of *Rivethead* and M. Rutledge McCall of *Slipping into Darkness*. Sherrie Larolo Matusza and Alison Fineman Seidenfrau, thanks so much for your guidance.

Big ups to Adam Ambrecht for the artwork, Lauren Bretschenieder Flynn, Jessika Morrison for your edits. Jaime Lee, the cake was a hit! Tom Huynh and Leonard Row for the awesome photography. Thomas Dodson, thanks for your help and *pura vida*. Camille Elizabeth, thanks for spreading the word.

My old friend, Dylan Bruno, and Emmeli Bruno, Damien and Odin, Jason Sheftell, Shock G from Digital Underground, Liza Brown Somilleda, the Immortal Reilly, Melissa Hart, Tatum Reilly, Phil Rigney - my bro who was there when it all started, Stephen White and fam, Kyle McGee and fam, Mike Mercurio and fam, Dan Schuman, Luis Diego and fam, Diamond Dave Aaronson, awesome Danica Ratkovich thanks X2. Special thanks to Joey Famous and Big Mike Fabish for showing up and surviving the most interesting first 24 hours ever. Uri Carrazco, one love, bro! Bella Carrazco and Cashy Classy. Judah, Tank, and Brian Boyd. Jason Matthews, Jodi Martinez and fam, Adam Groth and fam, Beth Helmsin and Brad Harris, my peeps

Paul Duncan and Tracey Strong, Fidel and Steve, Heath and Amy, Nydia "NiniHead" and KK, Sugar Ray Schiavone, Gee, Mey Mey, Gina Mangulli Moran, Ron Carrano, and Scott Jackson. Sean Dolan, Brian Dolan, Ed and Bruce Crowder, Joena Russel, Chris Foster and fam. The amazing ML and Pete Kmeto. Carlye Leann, thanks for a crash in O Town! Lucinda and Vanessa Aguilar. Thanks for the support to my new friends like Jasmine, Krysta, Chris, Chivaughn, Tamara, and Heather.

The University of Connecticut and the Sigma Chi fraternity.

A special prayer of healing goes out to the families in my sister's town, Newtown, Connecticut.

Pura vida to my Tamarindo peeps: Cyn Castro, Flower Saborio, Jon Phillips at Bar One, Steve Rowland, Sandra, Dayana and Marcela, Derek Furlani, the Loonies Carla and Craig, Bernard, "the paparazzi of Tama," Avellino, Ivan, mi *hermano loco*!, Fernando from Villareal, Sarita "don't threaten me with a good time" Gillis. Sarah Long. Sarah Jordan, Alyssa Nitsche, Big Derrick, the Danes Louisa and Thor, Kelly Zak and Rafa at Kelly's Surf Shop, Reina Ramirez, Mishele Vargas, Jaime Peligro at the book store, Cristiano, the best bartender in the world, Lt. Colonel Tripp, Francisco and fam at Botella de Leche, Fatima, Christopher, Adrianna Barrantes, my Playa Coco crew, Melissa, Michelle, and Monique Oye, Shirley, Puna, Grace, Magally, Hazel, Yoisi, Rusty at Rusty's Pizza. Hector, thanks, budddddyyyyy. And last but not least, a blind dog named Motta.

In Nicaragua—"*dale duro*" to Eddy Centeno—thanks for watching my back, hermano, my roomie, Meghan Armbrecht, and yes, Morgan too, Tommas "old people look at hills" Coldrick, Adam "my main man in Tottinham" Williams, and the Panda Mon!, Blake Cash and Trevor Gibbs—thanks for everything at Banana Hamacas, Carmen, Jeiner, Sean Dennis, my homie "Big Wave" Chris Madden, the wild card Johnny Goldenberg, Alis Acuna, Ruth for the Spanish lessons, my buddy, Omar, Dickie at Maderas Village, DeWitt Foster the Black Tsunami, Fabiola, Captain Zach, Gretchen Escobar, Towe, Cory and Mandy, Elsi, Ruth, Marvel, Lindsay "The Big Lind" Laverty, Charles Davis, Shorylann, and my amiga Marta. A special thank you to Gaspar and family. Suertes y saludos, Nica, you have my heart.

Barrio Chino, San Juan del Sur: "*Jamas Nos Venceras*,"—"We will not be conquered."

CONTENTS

FOREWORD

Norm Schriever, that dude rocks a typewriter! This is my first and only chance to write a foreword for a book, and I never imagined that it would be the opening line. But what the hell, he is unconventional, and I am a bit weird.

It has been 15 years since I heard Norm's voice or seen his ugly mug. Who woulda guessed he'd have turned into such a solid young man? Did I say young? Yes, I did. I guess I suffer from the same self-delusion most 40-year-old guys do.

Norm and I were great friends when we were younger. We lost touch after high school, walking our separate paths, but then we had a chance meeting again through an old friend. It's rare to pick back up at the exact same place you left off, but I'm so happy we did. And so glad to have been surprised by the copy of Norm's first book, *Pushups in the Prayer Room*, that he signed and left for me after his recent visit to my house.

We had a lot to catch up on: I graduated from MIT with a degree in Environmental Engineering, worked an office job for two weeks, then promptly quit. Instead, I packed my dream wagon and traveled the States as a ski bum. I fell in love in Utah (both with the state and a girl), got my heart trampled (only by the girl), and moved on.

Through a weird turn of events, I ended up as an actor. I made about 14 movies and have done over 150 episodes of network television. I've been fortunate enough for acting to fund my true passions in life...exploration, adventure, and endeavoring to scratch that ever-present itch of curiosity.

I've driven across the U.S. at least twelve times, hiking, biking, and camping. I had a small hut on the beach in Baja for five years, where I learned to surf and speak bad Spanish. I've traversed almost every inch of coastal Central America, at night tying a hammock in front of the home of some big-hearted local family who offered to feed me, but in the process taught me about true happiness. I drove from Los Angeles to Denali, climbing and skiing mountains the whole way. With Crocs Shoes and UNICEF, I was welcomed into an Indian reservation in the central highlands of Panama to donate thousands of pairs of shoes to families in need.

I married a woman from Sweden, and that is where we spend our summers with our two children and her huge family. I've even learned enough of the language so that my own family will never be able to plot against me!

These days I spend much of my leisure time underwater, free-diving and spearfishing for healthy, wild-caught, sustainably harvested fish for my family to eat. At night I dream about the experiences I've had in the habitat of predator and prey.

But the accomplishment I'm most proud of is my role as husband and father, and I'm reminded every day to look at the world through the curious eyes of a child.

So, when I had the chance to read Norm's writing and learn what he had been up to for the last 15 years, it struck me…struck me that each of us who walks this earth does it with a different agenda, with a different motivation. Some do it to take, some to conquer, some to run, and some do it to give.

And then there are a very few who do it to truly learn. To learn with vigor and enthusiasm, to eat up every experience like it is the best one that exists. Because those who have humbled themselves to the vastness of this world and the brevity of our stay upon it have learned that each moment we share has the power to be the best, the worst, or the most meaningless one we've ever had…our choice. But it is, in fact, the pinnacle of our existence because it is the only one that actually exists. Everything else is just a memory or an idea that hasn't yet seen the light of day.

Norm travels with respect, with love, wide-eyed as if each and every human being is the master of something and with luck they might impart a small piece of that mastery to him. With each human connection, he's evolved and helped those he's touched to do the same. Truly, that is how we should all live.

That is why I recommend you read his work, because Norm has learned what I always say, "Those who haven't failed will never know the limits of their potential because they have been too lazy to strive beyond them." He is not lazy. He has striven. And he is one of the few who is learning his true potential.

Norm has succeeded and Norm has failed, but most of all he has been courageous enough to face the world head-on. He has allowed it to eat him whole, emerging from the fires forged into a better man. By granting the conch to every human he has met, Norm has become a man who has something valuable to share with the rest of us. Some of us who, after hours and miles of walking through a jungle lost in desperation, have shaken a family awake in the middle of the night in their *palapa*, asking for food and shelter, and some who couldn't imagine that act.

I see his work as much more than a fun romp around the darker corners of the world, narrated by a dude whose distinct sense of humor and unique slant on life illuminate its vibrant complexion. I also see it as an inspiration for those who have walked more modest paths, who haven't ventured as remotely, for people who may have only walked their safe backyards and sidewalks out front…

His writing shows us that in our similarities we are all unique. We have as much to learn as we have to teach, we are strongest in moments of weakness, and we succeed the most when we allow ourselves to fail.

I am so glad that Norm found his way back into my family's life, and that I have had the opportunity to swap stories with him face to face. I urge him to keep on rockin' the typewriter, so the rest of the world can learn and share by reading, without having to actually see his face that was destined for radio!

Congratulations are due to Norm for completing his second book, *South of Normal*. I hope you enjoy it as much as I did.

-Dylan Bruno
Actor, adventurer, and longtime friend.

INTRODUCTION

Some people come south to die. You can see it in their eyes—they've given up, wishing only to live out their last years in the tropics with a beer in hand and as few people in their affairs as possible. Some come south to save their lives, to rekindle their joy in the sunlight that sets them on fire every dawn. Others migrate toward the equator to surf, to dance, or to escape the frozen winters of their homelands. As for me, perhaps I moved to Costa Rica for all of those reasons? Or maybe I went south to simply *be,* maybe for the first time in my life.

This book is a simple expat story, a tale of a regular guy who was stupid or crazy enough to peer through the keyhole of his normal existence and give it all up for what he saw. It's not about the United States; I've tried to resist making political statements (and believe me, that was difficult), nor is it about Costa Rica. I don't claim to have solutions to society's problems or any secret koans of wisdom to share with you. In the grand scheme of things I'm just another traveler, one of the many adventurers who can't stand to sit still as the big, wild unknown beckons. There are a lot of backpackers, expatriates, and *Ticos* out there who could write better books. They are the *real* adventurers, the ones we should pay tribute to, but the only difference is that I have big ears and carry a pen.

This is merely a humble story about human beings living their lives together, trying to do the best that they can. Sometimes we did well, but sometimes we couldn't wait until the sun went down so we'd get another chance the next day. All I hope to accomplish with this book is to make you, the reader, think a little more, and feel something. But if I had to choose one, I'd like to make you feel something.

The fact that I'm documenting my time in Costa Rica makes a lot of people nervous. I've received concerned inquiries, subtle warnings, and even a death threat. Some of the people involved prefer I keep silent and just pretend that none of this ever happened. To them I will gently explain that this also happens to be the truth, the truth I lived through, and I refuse to apologize for that. But I am no one's judge; we're all guilty and innocent in some way in this story because we're all flawed human beings, especially me. I hold no ill will and sincerely wish everyone the best, even if it's obvious they don't reciprocate that sentiment. I excluded or softened a lot to protect people, keeping in mind they had to go on living their lives wherever they were in the world, especially in that wonderful little fishbowl called *Tamarindo.*

Even my own family and friends look at me funny, questioning when I'm going to settle down and get a regular job and walk the easy path. They scratch their heads at why I'd do something that makes no logical sense. Maybe after reading this they'll understand better. I think the transparency of my journey makes a lot of people uncomfortable because it makes them question whether they're kings and queens or merely pawns on the chess-board of their own lives. Good.

What I've done with my life still makes no logical sense to me, either. It's contrary to every human instinct of comfort, safety, and the pursuit of material gain. So why do I do it? In short, it's the legacy I have to leave the world. I can't *not* do it. After you discover that, little else matters along the way.

But let's turn to the pragmatic for a moment. How exactly *does* one end up a broke and happy writer living in Tamarindo, Costa Rica? It was a process equal parts research, planning, and the dice game of chance. Certain things went wrong for me in the United States at precisely the right time, which led me to take a hard look at my life and take a vacation in Tamarindo one December. When I returned home I couldn't get back on the hamster wheel of work and stress and bullshit no matter how hard I tried. So I decided to unplug from my life in the States and move south to chase my dream of writing a book. I did just that, and from there the jungle swallowed me up.

Oh, and I forgot to mention I also knew someone down in Tamarindo, an old friend nicknamed Pistol. And his girlfriend, Theresa, too.

Ahhh, Tamarindo. Even saying your name makes me smile. We've been through some crazy times together for sure, huh? Sometimes it was so wild I didn't believe my own eyes. But I promise you I wouldn't change a thing.

As you read on, it may sound like I went through a lot of struggles, and I did, but I've come to realize most of the real struggles were inside of me. There was a lot of good in Tamarindo and a lot of the other thing, too, just like anywhere—like in our hearts. But as you read this, please keep in mind we were all living in a postcard, by the beach, that beautiful woman, the ocean, at our side. The tide came in and the tide went out, and there was always laughter...

But enough of the small talk. Let's start the show. Buckle up and wave your regular life goodbye, because we're about to head...South of Normal.

In the interests of making life in a Spanish-speaking country more readable, I italicized those words spoken by Costa Ricans (Ticos) and native Spanish speakers, whether they were speaking English or Spanish.

CHAPTER 1

PRISON

The walls of the prison looked smaller than in my dreams. The first thing I thought about was how easy it would be for him to escape. The rain-worn concrete was crumbling in sections, and in some places only a chain link fence topped with barbed wire separated the grounds from the surrounding jungle. But even if he could break free, where the hell would he go? I looked around: nothing but snake brush and sugarcane plantations for miles. Clapboard shacks with outhouses, garbage burning in the front yards, barking dogs and skinny cows. One dirt road in or out. He'd get macheted by a local or go crazy with mosquito bites before he made it far.

"Hey—you ready?" Gary said, climbing out of the driver's seat of the truck and stretching. "Let's get in and get the fuck out—I want to be in Tamarindo by two."

"Yeah sure, Gary, let me just put my stuff away." I wiped the sweat off my face with a hand towel, recently stolen from the Hilton across from the airport. I put my backpack on the floor of the TrailBlazer and covered it with a yellowed *Tico Times* newspaper.

"So tell me again how this works?" But he was already halfway to the main gate.

"Just grab your passport," he yelled back. "We check in and go back to his cell. I've been here two or three times. It's nothing."

"Oh, okay. Yeah, let's do it. Think you can help me with all of his stuff?" But he didn't hear, or chose to ignore me, so I loaded up with plastic bags and walked after him, crossing the dead-end dirt road to the front of the prison. Costa Ricans in their Sunday best clothing milled about, making a feeble attempt to form organized lines. Those who stood in the sun covered their heads with pieces of cardboard or magazines. Every one of them stopped and looked at us when we walked up. Every one. Two gringos dropped into an ant farm of 300 poor Ticos.

Gary didn't appear to be self-conscious at all as he jostled his way into line.

"In here, in here. Come on, keep up," he said to me. He was skinnier than I'd expected and his head was shaved, unlike his picture on Skype. He looked pale and worn out, dark circles around his eyes. His shirt struck me as funny, a red mesh tank top like the pinnies we used to wear in junior high gym class. But who the hell was I—the fashion police? Maybe that's what people wore when visiting their friend in a Costa Rican prison. And going with him sure was a lot better than having to visit alone.

"Okay, this is it. Have your passport ready and hang tight." We picked a line seemingly at random and waited, packed in with fat mothers and their teenage daughters in tight jeans, holding grocery bags and pillows. Jesus, it was hot. I wiped down my forehead and neck again, putting the plastic bags on the ground while we stood in place. Every ten minutes we took a step forward and I gathered them up again. As soon as I put the bags back on the ground, ants swarmed them.

"Tama has changed, man—it's a big shit show these days," Gary said. "I had to sell my share of the restaurant." I had no idea what he was talking about but nodded my head in agreement.

"I hear ya, Gary. Well, I'm psyched to get back to Tamarindo and settle in. It's going to be fun to finally live down here."

"Fucking shit show, man. You'll see."

"Okay, sure. So what's going on with Pistol, anyway? His family didn't seem to know much before I left."

"They're pinning him to the wall because he's a gringo," he said, eyes twitching.

We stepped forward into the shade, where it felt ten degrees cooler. I touched my passport in the pocket of my shorts to make sure it was still there. We were getting close.

"When he got arrested no one knew what the hell was going on," Gary said. "His neighbors called me and I went right over but they'd already taken him away. The place was trashed—those bastards went through all of his stuff."

"This is Lena's house you're talking about, the one he was renting?" I asked.

"Yeah. That bitch called the cops on him and now he's fucked."

"So it was her?"

"Well, who knows? Theresa was acting crazy when she and Pistol broke up, so some people thought it was her. I saw her walking on the street one time after that and I went off on her. Then I heard she left town."

"Damn, I can't even imagine."

"So anyways, when I found out he got arrested I went to the house and took the air out of his tires so no one could steal his Blazer. Then I trashed Lena's office, even pissed all over her files."

"You did *what*?! You pissed on her files?!" I couldn't help but laugh, but then stopped myself and looked down at the ground. "So, do you think he's safe in here? I mean…is anyone fucking with him?" Thoughts like those had been keeping me up at night.

"Hey, come on—we're next." The line moved again and we were at the front. A round-faced Tico sat behind a barred window, looking out at us with sleepy eyes. Gary told him we were there to visit Joseph Francesco. The guard thumbed through his list of prisoners, tracing down each name with his finger. Gary tapped his fist on the counter.

"Joseph—you know, the gringo. *El gringo!*" he barked. The man understood and wrote in his log book and then collected our passports, stamped them, and handed us receipts. We circled around toward the front gate and fell in behind the mothers and daughters who pushed for position. A guard with mirrored sunglasses and a shiny black nightstick stood on the inside of the steel-bar door. Every few minutes he opened it and let a few people in. When he reached for his keys, the mothers yelled and shoved each other, desperate to get out of the sun and into the jail. Gary was pushing right there with 'em as I tried to keep up.

"Oops, I'm sorry. *Discuple*. Sorry." I apologized to the mother for stepping on her toes, apologized to the daughter I'd hit with my sweaty towel, and apologized when one of my bags ripped, spilling apples, and I bumped three of them with my butt when I bent down to pick them up.

"Norm, come on, man. We're in." Gary pulled me by my arm through the crowd. The man at the door let us in and locked it behind us. We were in a narrow hallway, one wall covered with bars and the jungle outside, the other side a high concrete counter. Flies and guards were everywhere and the air didn't move. The visitors put their bags on the counter and the guards went through them, looking for contraband. They ripped open bags of rice and cut avocados in half and fished around plastic containers of beans. We put our bags on the counter and waited. The guards helped everyone but us.

"Hey! Perdón, señor! I know we're gringos but come on—we were waiting, too!" Gary yelled at them. "Rapido, rapido, come on, let us through!"

I shied away to show I wasn't with him, just in case they decided to beat us with their nightsticks. A female guard helped two more visitors and then got to us. She took everything out of the bags and lined it all up on the counter:

5 packages of Ramen noodles
2 packages of deli ham
2 rolls of Pringles: one jalapeño and one regular flavor
2 packs of strawberry vitamin C lozenges
2 packs of Oreo cookies
12 apples, half of them bruised and covered with dirt
1 plastic jar of peanut butter
1 plastic jar of honey
1 loaf of bread
2 boxes of granola bars
12 small bags of assorted potato chips
18 juice boxes
1 roll of strong rope
1 towel
2 Whoppers from the Burger King in the nearby city of Liberia
1 Old Spice deodorant
2 books: a sturdy biography of Bill Clinton and a soft-cover on politics
4 magazines: *Time, Sports Illustrated, Newsweek*, and *The Economist*
3 newspapers: *The Sunday New York Times* and two hometown rags from Rochester.

It was all there, checked off the list that Pistol's mom had emailed me before I left the States. The lady guard unwrapped each item and lined them up. She opened the Pringles cans, and Gary held out one of the plastic bags and she poured them in there. She did the same thing with the Oreos and took the plastic wrap off the juice boxes, Ramen noodles, and even the Whoppers, so they were all mixed up loose in plastic bags.

"What's she doing?" I asked.

"They check everything because they're not allowed to have certain stuff. It's like this every week so try and remember what you can't bring."

"Why are they taking off the wrappers?"

"The inmates roll up the plastic and smoke them to get high off the chemicals." Damn, I'd seen some funny shit, but never heard of someone so desperate that they'd smoke a Whopper wrapper. "The Pringles cans are made of metal and can be shaped into a weapon. No metal and, of course, no glass." The guard put six apples in a bag and then threw the rest of them into a 50-gallon trash barrel.

"Oh yeah, you can only bring in six pieces of fruit. If you bring in more they think the prisoners are going to keep them until they're rotten and fermented to make alcohol," Gary said.

She opened the peanut butter and stuck a knife inside. She turned the books upside down and shook them out and checked the bindings to see if they'd been re-glued. Satisfied, she tossed it all back into the bags, including the rope.

"So they're allowed to have rope but they can't have apples?" I asked. "What's that for, anyways?"

"Right? I don't really know, their rules are crazy. A few weeks ago, when his new girlfriend, Veronica, came to visit, they made her take out her tampon and searched up there."

"Damn, you're serious?"

"Yeah, but she got a ride up here with a guy who was smoking weed so maybe they smelled it on her. I'm telling you—it's a giant shit show, man. I'm glad you're here to visit him from now on." He slapped me on the back. I felt little solace that the cavalry had finally arrived—and it was just me. I helped Gary collect the plastic bags and we were ushered forward by an old woman who needed the counter for her pot of *sopa de pollo*, chicken soup, and a clip-on fan.

We walked to the end of the hallway, where a fat guard with a thick mustache said, "Hello." He had an inkpad and a stamp. Gary held out his forearm and the man stamped it, like he was leaving a nightclub. Then it was my turn. I held out both arms and he took my left one.

"*Is first time?*" he said in broken English.

"Yes. Si, señor. First time visiting my friend here."

"*El gringo?*"

"Yeah, the gringo, Joey Francesco."

He shook his head.

"What's the stamp for?" I asked.

"*It is get in get out of cell. No sweat off or no get out.*"

I looked at his face to see if he was kidding, but I didn't think he was, which made me sweat even more. He looked at the shiny, white skin of my arm and stamped me six times right below the shoulder instead.

"*Suertes*," he said—good luck. I read the stamps on my shoulder, already fading; "D2B." We walked around the corner into an area the size of a closet and three guards frisked us, looking in our shoes and finally telling us to go on. We stepped out of the back of the registration building into the sunlight. We were in the prison.

Everything was open and outdoors—not like the jails in the States or that I'd seen on "Locked Up Abroad" on TV. Gary hurried down a concrete sidewalk.

"Whooo, that was brutal. Is it always that bad?" I asked.

"Man, that was nothing," he said. "A super easy day."

We wound past the cafeteria where a few guys wearing dirty aprons but no shirts stood outside and waved. I waved back.

"So, is he okay in here?" I asked again, swallowing hard.

"So far he's been cool. My Columbian friends made some calls and put the Columbian Umbrella over him so they're watching out for him in here. But I told his mom I need more money to visit. They still owe me $80. I told them I'd visit because he's got no one else, but I'm not taking the chicken bus to the prison. No way I'm taking the chicken bus, man. That would take all day."

The Columbian Umbrella? I didn't know what that was, but it sure sounded cool. I just had an umbrella from TJ Maxx, made in China, but I was glad Pistol had the Columbian kind.

"What are his lawyers saying?" I asked, trying to seem casual but dying for information. It had been three months since he'd been arrested and from my vantage point in the States I still knew very little, even after emailing with his mom daily. I knew his ex-girlfriend, Theresa, from my previous visit to Tamarindo but hadn't heard from her. And Lena, the local attorney who was renting the house to him where he got busted, well...I knew her all too well.

We walked past the good-behavior cells. Their doors were open and they had yards with grass. The inmates hand-washed and hung their clothes out back or lifted concrete weights on makeshift wooden benches. There's no way that rickety thing would support my weight, I thought. Prisoners huddled around a small television set, watching a soccer match, but there were no guards in sight.

The sidewalk wound between concrete block buildings, each with a single window. Brown-skinned skeletons pressed between the bars like broken piano keys, shirtless or in white wife-beaters, arms and legs and shocks of dirty black hair akimbo. They yelled and whistled at us visitors as we passed—anything to get our attention, especially the women. When Gary and I walked by they went crazy, grabbing the bars, yelling and cajoling to get a reaction from us gringos, an unheard of phenomenon in the prison…until recently.

"Hey, gringo! What's up?! Hola, amigo! Hey! Give me some Colones—throw me a coin, man! Hey, GRINGO!!!"

Gary ignored them and walked right by. I tried to do the same but the yelling freaked me out, my heart racing. I lowered the big white sunglasses that still rested on my head but I felt ridiculous in those shades, embarrassed by my own existence. I could see myself through their eyes: soft and pale like a whale's belly, even my simple cargo shorts, Nikes, and sweat-soaked t-shirt appearing opulent in that place. The guys were all so skinny and desperate, reaching out for us even though we were ten yards away like through sheer wild determination they'd be able to stretch and grab hold of us, and then…

"Throw me one coin NOW! 500 Colones! Gringo! Hey, PUTA GRINGO!" They had nothing but time and could talk as big as they wanted stuck behind those bars. I felt dizzy from the heat and the yelling. I couldn't ignore the question that had been haunting me for three months—what if it was *me* locked in there with them? How long would *I* last?

"It's just up ahead…" Gary was talking to me. "Hey, are you alright?"

"Yeah, yeah, I'm fine." I stood up straight and tried to put some cool in my voice.

"Man, don't worry about them. They just want you to throw a coin. They'll take all night fishing it in from the grass with a string and a hook. They got nothing better to do."

"Gotcha. So next time bring a coin to throw to them." I added that to my mental checklist—I was learning fast.

"No! Don't throw *anything* to them. You can get in big trouble if the guards see you."

I crossed that item off my mental checklist. Once we got past those cells, I exhaled. The path wound through the jungle and onto a bridge over a creek. It was so quiet again that I could hear the water.

We passed an old man in a baseball cap sitting in a wheelchair along the path. He held a beat-up plastic cup filled with coins but he didn't ask us for money.

"*Buenas tardes*," he said—good afternoon. His eyes were good and he had a kind face. *"Mi amigo, are you on the right path?"* he asked.

"What's that? Yeah, I think so—this way, right, Gary?" But he was up ahead. I wished the man good afternoon and walked on. Was he a prisoner? He seemed out of place.

Finally we arrived at Pistol's cellblock, D2B, the last building in the prison compound. Back in the States I'd envisioned that place for three months but in real life it all felt worse; I realized there was no heat in my nightmares.

The guards looked at the stamps on our arms and brought us through a heavy gate. The sunlight didn't reach inside and there were no light bulbs.

I was locked in a cage waiting for the next door to be opened into the unit. I went to wipe myself with the towel but I wasn't holding it anymore. Between the bars I could see a buzz of humanity: teenagers and men and guards crossing my field of vision like someone had kicked up a beehive of bodies. Our presence caused a commotion and there were yells for Joey. It was loud, but I couldn't understand anything that was being said. And then, through the bars, I saw his face.

He definitely looked thinner than when I'd seen him six months earlier, but he wasn't wasting away like it seemed in the U.S. Embassy's reports. He'd lost some of his drinker's belly but the rest of him looked the same—classic Italian good looks, a slightly pug nose, short-cropped black hair. He still had the gait of an athlete even though he hadn't played sports in fifteen years. I noticed he was wearing his familiar Birkenstocks and a golf shirt with the University of Rochester crest on it; he'd dressed up for the big day.

His mouth turned up into a slight smile as the guard unlocked the final door and let us in.

"Normando, what's up, bro?!" he said with small laughter in his voice, like we were just meeting up to watch a Yankees game at our neighborhood bar.

"Hey, Pistol! How are ya?" I didn't know if we were going to hug or shake hands or what, considering the circumstances. I was anticipating bulletproof glass with two phone receivers like in the movies. He gave me a homie hug and I slapped his back.

"So, what's going on? When did you get in?" he asked.

"You know, nothing much. I got into Liberia last night." I was relieved to finally see him and see that he was the same person. I'm not sure what I'd expected. "So, how are you?"

He shrugged and nodded to his surroundings. "Could be better, Normando. It could be better." The door slammed and locked behind us.

"I hear ya, man. So how are you?" I realized I was repeating myself but I didn't know what else to say.

"Here, let me help you with those bags. Come on in, let's go over here." He led us into the unit, a 50-foot-by-30-foot enclosure with a smooth concrete floor and plain concrete walls. A single phone booth looked out of place in the middle of all that concrete. The only view of the sky was through a chain-link-fenced roof. There was no visiting area—they just locked us in with all of the prisoners.

The courtyard was jammed with visitors and families, sitting together or lying on filthy foam pads along the ground. Young punks with bandanas swaggered around trying to look cool, showing off their muscles.

"Ellos siguen jodiendo conmigo! JODIENDO conmigo!" an older man yelled to himself, walking in circles.

Pistol led us over to a concrete ledge that served as the only seats. Two young Ticos sat there but got up and spread out a blanket for us when we approached. I sat down facing Pistol but Gary remained standing behind us, fidgeting.

"So, what's new, Normando?" He looked at me. I mean really *looked* at me—straight into my eyes, unblinking, like he could read my thoughts, the way he always did. I met his gaze but then looked away.

"Oh, you know, nothing much. Just psyched to be here and see you. So, how ya holding up?"

"Ahhh, I'm alright, though I'll be damn excited to get out of here soon. You finally made the move, huh? I didn't think you were going to do it—everyone talks about relocating to Costa Rica but no one ever does. So, how was it leaving Cali?"

"It was good, it just took a while to wrap everything up. I was lucky and sold the Land Rover on eBay Motors my very last day. And the house is up for sale, but I won't make any money on it. But it's good to be down here." I was talking too much. "Here—I brought you two Whoppers, but they made me take them out of the wrappers. And I got you all of the other stuff that your mom asked. Here are some magazines."

"Did you bring the money?"

"The money—yeah, I did. I have 30,000 *Colones*—$60." I touched the folded bills in my pocket. "Do you want me to take it out right here, or...?"

"Do it on the sly and slip it to me," Pistol said.

I gazed around, trying to look as inconspicuous as a gringo visiting a Third World jail could possibly look. I palmed the money and slid it over to Pistol, sort of bungled the exchange, and then drew my hand back when he had it.

"Bring more next time," he said, sliding it into his pocket without looking at it.

"Your mom said they only allow 30,000 in at a time."

"It's okay—bring more next time."

"Really? What do you need it for?" I assumed the one and only benefit of being incarcerated was that you had free room and board.

"Everything costs money in here. I have to pay to get my laundry done. I have to buy phone cards to make international calls. It costs to get better food. I pay for laundry—a lot of things."

"Damn, I'll ask your mom for more, but I think they're hurting for money like everyone else." In the sunlight I could see him better, and, for the first time, his jet-black hair had hints of white.

"Thanks for the food, man. Try to bring some healthy stuff if you can. They don't feed us much in here and I've been eating too much junk."

"Sure thing. Just tell your mom what you want and she'll email me a list. What do they feed you?"

"At 6:30 they wake us up and give us two hotdog buns. At noon we get rice and beans, then at 4:30 p.m. we get leftover rice and beans and one more hotdog bun. 800 calories a day, that's it."

"Wow, bro, I'll definitely bring better food."

Two guys argued over the phone and then walked to opposite ends of the courtyard, but their tension echoed off the walls with no place to escape. One of them walked toward Pistol and gave him a nod. He was short like a bulldog, roped with muscle though I guessed he'd never been inside a gym, his arms and one side of his face crossed with knife scars.

We chatted a little more and Pistol ate a burger while I sweated. We talked about baseball and I told him the Phillies were in first place and looking good. I told him our mutual friend, Reilly, said "hi" and sent his encouragement. He asked me about politics and the economy and the upcoming elections, but I had no idea. After all of that time, months of stress and speculation, I wanted to ask him so much now that we were finally face to face. What was going to happen to him? Were they messing with him? Beating him up? Or worse? I was relieved to see there weren't any bruises and he seemed at ease with the other prisoners. I didn't know if it was okay to just come out and talk about it, but I was dying to scream the most pressing questions of all: "What the fuck were you *thinking*? And how the hell did you get *caught*?"

"So, how many plants did they get you with, Pistol?"

"Like 120," he sighed. "But most of them were small and still growing indoors. The police didn't even read my fucking rights or give me a translator, just cuffed me and took me away. They made me stand for hours with a machine gun pointed at me and wouldn't even give me water. I had to wait two days before they let me call the U.S. Embassy. It's bullshit because I'm in here with murderers and rapists and coke traffickers and they're worried about me and a little weed, just because I'm a gringo."

I nodded my head, not wanting to interrupt now that he was finally talking about it.

"They're all so corrupt. Right after the police came, Lena showed up at the house with the prosecutor. She's in thick with the judges and the police because she's an attorney and her dad is chief of police in the province. She even used to date the prosecutor. They went through all of my stuff and someone stole my iPhone and my hard drive. It was a brand new fucking phone. Someone used my ATM card that same night to take out $300. I'm going to file criminal charges and get all of those scumbags thrown in jail."

He sounded like the old Pistol I knew—fired up and throwing punches with little consideration for where they landed, the guy I'd met in Colorado fifteen years earlier, the best spring break road dog you could hope for, the guy I'd visited for vacation right there in Costa Rica six months earlier, before I made up my mind to move down.

"So, what's going to happen now?" I asked.

He scanned the prison courtyard but didn't answer. A guard yelled that visiting hours were over and rapped his nightstick against the bars. People stirred from their seats and said their goodbyes.

"Hey, do me a favor and take this out with you." He handed me a stack of notebook pages filled with handwriting in pencil. "Hide them on the way out so no one gets their hands on them. Transcribe the pages and send an email to my attorney and the U.S. Embassy and my mom."

"Okay, you got it." I took the pages and folded them up and put them in my pocket. "I'll come visit you next weekend. Good to see you, bro."

"Try to bring more money," he said. We got up and hugged again. "And thanks for the Whoppers." He said goodbye to Gary and we filed toward the door along with the other visitors. I was relieved that it was almost over with, but it was weird that he couldn't just walk out with me, that we couldn't just jump in his Blazer and go drink rum and talk to pretty girls by the pool, like old times. I turned back.

"Hey, Pistol, I forgot to ask...what's the rope for?"

He measured me with his dark eyes and took too long to answer.

"It's for my clothes—to make a line so I can hang them out to dry."

"Oh, okay. See you soon, bro." I walked out, but jumped when the iron door slammed behind me.

Bienvenido al primer día de mi nueva vida en Costa Rica. Welcome to the first day of my new life in Costa Rica.

CHAPTER 2

WELCOME TO THE SHIT SHOW

Gary and I sped along Highway 21 toward Tamarindo. I was relieved to be headed away from the prison because I'd been dreading that first visit ever since an otherwise quiet morning in May when I got word that Pistol had been arrested. Three months later, it felt weird that I'd finally laid eyes on him. Hell, everything felt surreal since I'd decided to uproot my life and move down to Costa Rica.

We passed lush fields flecked with groves of Guanacaste trees and grazing cows. They were fenced in and each fence had different colored posts. I watched them blur by—blue and white, red and white, blue and yellow.

"Everything in those blue and white posts is land owned by the Estrella Hotel in Tama," Gary said. We passed a row of shacks where they sold bottles of Coca Cola, hammocks, and inflatable dolphins for the pool. I saw a lot of one-room houses with people sweeping their front yards, but no pools. It all looked familiar.

"Hey, Norm, look through the glove box to see if there's anything to smoke out of."

"Really? Are you sure this is the best time to smoke?" But I rummaged through the glove box and pulled out maps, a flashlight that somehow was still on, an empty Imperial beer can, aviator sunglasses, and a six-inch hunting knife.

"What the hell? He's carrying around a knife?"

"I'm not surprised—you need one down here. You need something. Some fucking Critters just jumped me outside Aqua and smashed a bottle over my head." He showed me a scar on his scalp. "Keep looking—I want to smoke."

I looked through the glove box and then the center console and checked behind the visors. I found a wooden one-hitter, a glass bowl stained with marijuana resin, a baggie with the shake remnants of weed, five lighters, and a half pack of condoms from 2004.

"Jesus, Gary—you didn't check the truck before we went to the jail? The last thing I need is to end up in there with him."

"Don't worry about it, man."

"Don't worry? This car needs to be clean if I'm going to drive it around." Gary had been using Pistol's truck since the arrest, but Pistol's mom had serious doubts about his reliability. Several times he was supposed to visit the jail but flaked, and she complained that his math was getting fuzzy when it came to the money she was sending down. Even though I'd never met her, she was pleased that I was moving down and could help with the situation. Other than visiting Pistol she also asked me to hold onto his truck and help out with a few other small things. It was the least I could do. She was so desperate, so worried about her son, and the whole family was counting on me.

"Hey, Gary—what's this stuff in the back seat?" I asked, taking the lid off two cardboard boxes filled with children's toys, art supplies, and games.

"I think he was planning to donate those to the elementary school in Haucas or something. But I guess he never got the chance."

I smiled. Pistol was always doing stuff like that, a real humanitarian at heart.

"Do you want to stop and see the new restaurant I'm opening?" Gary asked.

"No, it's cool. I sort of want to get to my new apartment and get settled." I had the entire contents of my new life, two overstuffed duffel bags and a backpack, in the back of the truck and felt weirdly vulnerable that someone could just break the window and walk away with everything I owned in the world.

"I'm supposed to meet Tania at the apartment at four but I don't even have an address—you sure you know where Villa Verde is?" I asked.

"Yeah, I think I can find it." He balanced the knife in his hand as he drove. "How do you know her, anyway?"

I'd actually never met Tania, who was going to be my new roommate. We had a bunch of mutual friends from my time vacationing in Tamarindo, and somehow we'd found each other on Facebook. Over the months of online conversations a friendship ensued. She spoke perfect English and had a great job at Premier Realty. I had a hundred questions about moving down to Costa Rica, and she had the patience and the English to answer all of them. When Pistol was arrested she helped translate some important documents, arranged phone calls, and contacted the Costa Rican public defender for us. That was really cool of her. She looked cute on her profile picture and we flirted a little bit, but the last thing I needed was another tangled relationship so I left it alone. I was way smarter than to "go there" with my only remaining friend in town.

As it got closer to my July 13 departure date I started looking around for an apartment and Tania was helpful, as usual. She emailed me pictures of houses and apartments for rent. They all looked okay to me, but I had no idea if the prices were fair or about the locations (there are no accurate maps, street names, or even mailing addresses in Tamarindo). The only nice hotel I knew in town was the Estrella, which would cost me about $120 a night, so if it took me a week to find a place once I got there I would have spent more than one month's rent. Considering everything I had going on with my life-changing move and Pistol's situation, I wanted a nice, safe home base arranged before I got down there so I wouldn't feel so out of control.

When I first told Pistol that I was thinking of moving to Costa Rica he proposed that we rent a house together. But even then, before he got in trouble, there was no way I was going to live with his crazy ass; he ran way too hot for me. Drinking by the pool and smoking weed all day was fantastic for a vacation, the perfect remedy to my cold museum life in the States, but I'd be a hot mess if I tried to keep up with him over the long haul. Plus I had big things I wanted to tackle. My fortieth birthday was in February, only eight months away, and I'd set three epic goals to achieve by then, the *real* reasons I'd moved down.

Besides, Pistol and Theresa, his long-time Costa Rican girlfriend, fought like rabid wolverines. Day and night I had to listen to them arguing, berating each other, threatening to move out, and throwing each other's clothes on the front lawn—and that's when things were good. The more Pistol partied, the more trouble he'd get in when he came home, so he'd just get drunker and stay out longer to deal with it. Then she'd come looking for him, ready to drag him out of the bars and castrate him with a rusty spoon in the middle of the street. Hell hath no fury like a *Latina* woman scorned, or even just mildly cranky.

When the heat was on he avoided most of our usual watering holes and instead drove out to Tuanis Bar in the middle of the jungle to drink rum and smoke in solitude. There would be hell to pay when he showed up in town again, so why rush? But they always got back together before long. They'd be on the couch eating Chinese food and making plans for Valentine's Day, and we'd all enjoy a couple of nights of domestic tranquility before the whole circus started again. Unfortunately, I was guilty by association, so no matter how nice I was to Theresa I got the evil eye when Pistol was on a bender. It got to be damn uncomfortable and borderline nasty by the time I left.

Tania proposed an idea that could help me with my housing dilemma. She had to move out of her apartment soon and was looking for a place as well. She had a hookup with the owners of a nice unit in the Villa Verde apartments, where a three-bedroom place only five minutes from the beach would cost us $800 a month. We'd split the rent and utilities right down the middle and have a fun, chill place to live. It sounded fine to me, and she assured me that the place looked great. She could move in before I got there and make sure the little things were ready: Internet, cable, towels and sheets, and food in the fridge.

My only concern was letting her know that I didn't want anything romantic—we were *just* going to be friends and roommates with no funny business. She understood. I said it again because we'd been flirtatious and I didn't want to mess up a good living arrangement. She said she got it. Cool—crystal clear and there would be no problems there. We signed the lease but at the last minute she needed me to float her half of the rent for a week until she got paid. I wired down the money through Western Union, reluctantly but with her full assurances. She'd been great so far helping with Pistol, so I knew I could trust her.

"Actually, I don't know her that well, just through Facebook and mutual friends," I answered Gary. "But she seems cool and has been really helpful so far."

"Good luck with all that. Costa Rican broads are fucking crazy, man."

"Nah, not her. She's alright."

"Okay, whatever you say. But I'm telling you." He pulled a sharp turn by a bus stop, sending a dozen Ticos scrambling out of the way. "Here we go—only half an hour to Tama."

I'd driven that route dozens of times before but somehow it all looked different—dirty, more desperate. I remembered clear sunny days and a big party, but now the sky was gray with insufferable humidity. The cows looked skinnier and the mosquitos fatter. Was this the same place? Damn, had I been *that* buzzed the whole vacation?

We followed the one paved road in along the beach, with a view of the Pacific foaming to the west, past Joe's Beachside Bar and Witch's Rock surf camp, past Kelly's Surf Shop, and past the smooth, white, ivy-covered walls of the Estrella Hotel, then onto dirt roads. We took a few turns and then pulled up at the gate of a red stucco condo complex. I was home.

My face was flush and I couldn't stop sweating. I'd been anxious about moving there and visiting Pistol for months, and now that it was all happening, I felt like I was moving way too fast.

You think about making life changes—maybe you get a new job or move into a different house or go back to school and that in itself is a huge event. But within a few short months I'd completely turned my life upside down; I'd said goodbye to all of the friends I'd made over my eight years in Sacramento, walked away from a great job with a law firm, left behind a nice girl I'd started seeing right before I left, sold my house, my cars, donated all of my possessions, and hit the road to live in a Third World country, where I didn't speak the language and my only friend was in prison. I'd rattled my own cage so hard I didn't even know which way was up. It all felt like a magic trick where I'd been sawed in half, but now the audience had gone home and there was no one to put me together again.

The previous day I'd woken up at 3:00 a.m. to drive into New York for a 7:00 a.m. flight. After landing in Costa Rica, I managed a few hours of sleep at the airport Hilton and then met Gary and headed to the jail first thing that morning. A big part of me felt like taking the next plane back to the States with my tail between my legs so I could sit on the couch in the AC with a cold beer and watch SportsCenter, but that wasn't an option anymore. Now it was time to complete the journey by meeting my new roommate for the first time—who, by cruel default, was the only person I had in my new world.

We pulled up and climbed out of the truck. A ridiculous thought occurred to me—how would she know it was me? Maybe because there weren't that many other pale, jet-lagged gringos sweating like hostages unloading everything they owned at Villa Verde at four in the afternoon? We walked through the gates into a courtyard with a pool and a waterfall, palm trees, and tropical flowers. I saw Tania standing by the door of an apartment with a beer in her hand, wearing some sort of lacey number. I was a little confused why she was outside in her underwear.

"Nnnnnnnnn! You're finally here!"

I walked over and said "hi" and we hugged. I apologized for sweating all over her but she didn't care. She was happy to see me and welcomed me to my new home with the hospitality of a Hawaiian girl handing me a lei. I just stood there beaming and sweating like an idiot because I didn't know what else to do or say.

"Here, have a beer," she said, and handed me her half-finished can, cracking a new one for herself.

"Ummm, thanks."

"So, how was your flight? Do you feel like partying?" she asked. I wasn't sure if that meant more warm beer, a plate of cocaine and shooting off *pistolas* in the air, or a lingerie pillow fight. What I really wanted was a cold shower and a nap. Damn I was getting old.

"I can't believe you're finally here!" she said. *"We're going to have soooo much fun!"* Her voice was surprisingly gruff, like something you'd hear in an anti-smoking public service announcement. She wasn't un-attractive, but definitely didn't look like the sun-kissed starlet in her Facebook picture. She was only 24 years old but had a perfectly round beer belly, appearing to be about 35. Then again, in the picture I'd seen she was wearing a sunhat and big shades and leaning over with her boobs hanging out. The boobs I recognized. I was relieved that we'd had "the talk" about just being friends.

"Hey, Gary, could you help me get these bags inside...?" But he was already waving goodbye and then driving off in a cloud of dust.

"Soooo...what do you think?" Tania asked as she led me inside. The apartment was small but nice. There was a foam couch in the living room and one plastic chair, but that was about it for furniture.

"Yeah, it's great. Thanks so much for getting it for us. It's really helpful to have a place to come to on my first day. Especially after the jail."

"Oh, no problem—I'm sooooooo glad you love it! Here, let me show you your room." She took my backpack and led me up two flights of stairs. The whole third floor was mine, a big bedroom with tile floors and French doors opening up to a balcony with a great view of the courtyard and the pool. I liked it and was relieved to see a wall AC unit. There was a bed but nothing else. One more trip heaving my second bag up the stairs and I began to feel at ease. I had her show me how to crank the AC up to arctic blizzard level and laid on the bed as she went down to get more beer.

It felt great to finally be there, and I could slow down and breathe for the first time all day. I took a cold shower and changed out of my travelling clothes and went downstairs to say "hi."

I was hungry so Tania and I walked down to Caracolla's by the beach for fish tacos. A few of her friends joined us, so I got to meet curly-haired Yazmin and Sofia, and a few others. I sat on the end of the bar and sweated and drank way too fast while they examined me like the newest exhibit in the zoo, comparing notes in Spanish. Eventually I loosened up a little and we all laughed. The fish tacos tasted incredible and I paid our bill and we stepped out into the tropical night. We were right next to the beach so I could smell the salt air and hear the ocean roar somewhere in the blackness. *That's* what I signed up for!

We walked home and I stumbled up the three flights of stairs and lay in my cold room, my bags at the foot of the bed. I was spinning from the beer and 48 hours with little sleep. Tania came up with two more beers and knocked on the door.

"Are you asleep yet?"

"Huh? No, I'm just chilling. Thanks again for everything."

"Yeah, no problem! It's fun to have you here!" she said. *"Do you mind if I hang out and talk a little while?"*

"Sure…of course."

"Okay, but first let me change into something more comfortable." Thank God. Maybe she would put on some more modest clothes.

She came back wearing the identical lingerie bikini thing, but in black instead of red.

"That's much better," she said.

"Are you going for a swim this late?"

"Of course not, why? Can I sit on the bed since you don't have any chairs?" Yeah, what happened to that? My bed was big but she sat right next to me.

"Do you want a beer?" she asked.

"That's the last thing I need." We talked a little while, or, more accurately, she talked and I tried not to fall asleep. She inched closer. Don't go there Norm. Friends. She smelled like perfume. Roommates only, dammit! Don't mess up the whole dynamic. I tried to pretend like I was asleep but felt her lie down next to me. No way. I was smarter than that. In my 39 years, if there was one thing I'd learned, it was not to spit in my own rice bowl, as the Chinese say. She started rubbing my back. Absolutely not. DO NOT sleep with your semi-attractive beer-bellied roommate on your first night. I pretended to snore. She reached over and started rubbing my leg. Be good. Be strong. Do the right thing. Her hand moved up.

Three and a half minutes later, I rolled off her, sweating and breathing hard. God dammit. She giggled and opened the balcony door and lit a cigarette.

"Soooo…all in all, how was your first day in Costa Rica, N?" But I was already drifting off.

"It was a grade-A shit show," I mumbled.

"Huh? What's that?"

"Just perfect…" I lied, and everything faded to black.

CHAPTER 3

RAIN, WRITING, AND A BLIND DOG NAMED DISCO

My first morning in Tamarindo I woke to the rain against my window. For an instant I had no idea where I was, a long-dormant sense of traveler's vertigo, but after looking around I realized I was in my new apartment. However, there was no going back to sleep for me. I was charged with the excitement of my new life—finally a resident of Costa Rica.

There was a lot I wanted to accomplish on my first day: unpack, get the Internet hooked up, get a local cellphone, join the gym, and buy a desk so I could start writing. I got dressed and walked out of my room into the unlit stairwell, but tripped over something that sent me sprawling to the tile. Whatever I'd tripped over let out a grunt. A black lab snoozed on the floor, a nice-looking dog with a shock of white hair on her chest and front paws. She seemed confused by my presence but didn't look straight in my direction. We had a dog? Cool! I got down on the floor to rub her head and let her smell my hand. When I got up and walked down the stairs she followed me but Bam! she walked right into the wall, and Crash! she tripped down the last three steps and face-planted into the couch. I touched her head and she looked up; her eyes were clouds of grey, without pupils.

"I see you met my dog, Disco—she's blind," Tania said. She stood by the front door looking out at the rain, smoking a cigarette and wearing an even skimpier poolside/lingerie outfit. Even in the morning?

"Disco?! Seriously? She's blind?"

"Well, about 80% blind. She can see some light. When she was a puppy she had a bad fever and almost died, and came out of it with a loss of sight. But she's a great dog."

I ran my hand through Disco's field of vision three feet away, but she just panted. I brought my hand closer until it was only a few inches from her face and then she got excited and wagged. Wow, a blind dog. That must be challenging, especially in Costa Rica in the jungle. I petted Disco's head and she closed her eyes blissfully.

I walked out front and watched the rain, too, wetting palm fronds and red flowers, circles forming when drops hit the pool.

"Damn, it's really coming down. I don't think I saw rain once when I visited last December," I said. Hopefully it would clear up by afternoon because I wanted to hit the beach and work on my tan. "When do you think it's going to stop?"

"Probably around November," Tania said.

"I'm sorry, I thought you just said 'probably around November.'" Maybe her English wasn't as good as I thought, because it was the middle of July.

"Yes, this is the start of the rainy season, so it should be on and off until October. That's when it REALLY rains, every day. And then in late November it should start getting nice."

"Huh. Interesting. Maybe this wasn't exactly the best time of year to move down here," I said, half joking. Tania shrugged and went to the fridge, Disco following her every footstep, and then sat down on the couch. She cracked a beer and guzzled half of it. That struck me as odd behavior for 8:00 a.m. on a Thursday morning.

"What time do you have to be to work today? Gary's supposed to drop off the truck, so I can give you a ride if you want." It would be nice to have the house alone for a few hours to settle in.

"Oh, I'm not going to work." She took a long sip of beer and put her high heels up on the couch.

"Why not? Do you have the day off?"

"No, I don't work there anymore."

"What?! At the real estate office? That seemed like a great job. What happened?"

"I got fired."

"Oh shit. I'm sorry—that sucks." My mind turned to the issue of paying rent and the money I'd already fronted her. "So...what are you going to do for work?"

"I'm going to sue Chris, the owner. He's a gringo but he never had the proper paperwork as an employer here in Costa Rica so he can get in big trouble. I'm suing him for all of my back health insurance money—it should be like 4,000

dollars. When that comes in, I'll be fine." Well, damn, that might complicate things, but she didn't seem too concerned, and four large was a lot of money.

"So, what are you going to do today? Look for another job?"

"No, I think I will take a vacation. Just do nothing." And nothing is what she meant, because she seemed content to sit there and drink beer and chain smoke all morning, both her and Disco staring blankly out the front door.

I went to the kitchen and poured myself some coffee.

"So did you sleep good your first night?" Tania chuckled, breaking the silence of my thoughts. It all came back to me—that I'd violated my cardinal rule and fooled around with her the night before. Mama mia, that made it awkward. I didn't know what to say.

"Umm, look, Tania, I hope last night doesn't make it weird for us or anything." She looked back at me like she had no idea what I was talking about. "Well, it was great and everything, don't get me wrong, at least *I* enjoyed it—and I hope you did, too. It sure *seemed* like you enjoyed it, though I'm sure you wished you could have enjoyed it a little *longer*, but it's been a while for me, and you know how that goes...but dammit, that's not the point." Reel it in and wrap it up, Normando. "The *point* is that I don't want to ruin our friendship. We're roommates and I just want to make sure we keep it only that..."

"Stop worrying! It was fun but it didn't mean anything," she said and tossed her cigarette butt out the front door.

"Okay. You mean it—you're okay? With us just being friends?"

"Of course. Just friends. Nothing more."

"Cool." I smiled, relieved. No complications, no expectations, no heavy relationship bullshit that I didn't need. No one else would have to know—just a drunken mistake among friends.

I stepped outside to look around, sipping my coffee. People were out front of the other units, too. No one else had jobs they needed to go to? Not even something part time? Apparently not. But they all sure seemed friendly. One by one they waved and yelled over to me.

"Tudo bem, amigo! My name is Avellino. You are the new boyfriend of Tania, I hear?!" said the Brazilian musician next door.

"Ahhh you must be Tania' fiancé! I hear you two much in love last night. Que romantico!" said the little old lady in 12B, holding her Bible.

Even the maintenance man, a pleasant young Nicaraguan named Antonio, took time to put down his broom and greet me. *"Hello and welcome, friend. You help me practice English, yes? Tania tell Tamarindo she girlfriend you."*

Yes, apparently Tania *did* tell all of friggin' Tamarindo that she girlfriend me. How the hell could she just ignore everything we'd talked about? I waved back, trying to explain the whole situation by yelling across the courtyard through the rain: "Oh no, you must be mistaken. We're just friends! Amigos! Believe me, solemente amigos - we had THE talk. Yoohoo, over here!" but they couldn't make out what I was saying and thought I was either drunk or very passionate about greeting my neighbors or probably both.

I'd moved from the States to *simplify* my life and get away from all of the negative crap, and here I was falling right back into it between Tania and Pistol. It sounded so awesome on paper—give up everything and start over in Costa Rica, where I could live in a little surf town two blocks from the beach and finally chase my dream of writing a book—but somehow it wasn't panning out to be that easy.

I walked back inside but conveniently Tania wasn't sitting there anymore. So I went up to my room, stepping over Disco, and shut the door. I opened it back up, let Disco inside, then shut it again.

I stared at my bags for a moment piled at the foot of my bed. I took a deep breath and unzipped my backpack, taking out a small wall calendar and a red pen I'd bought at the airport gift shop in New York. I flipped through to February and put a red circle over the ninth day, my birthday.

To be honest with you, part of the reason for my move to Costa Rica was the inevitable reassessment of your life that happens as you approach a milestone birthday. 40. What did that mean? I didn't feel that old; I still felt like a confused kid trying to figure it all out. I'd tried to do what I was *supposed* to, what everyone told me to: settle down, put all of your energy into a career, and accumulate as many shiny material things as possible along the way, but each day I'd wandered further from who I really wanted to be.

I hadn't thought about that in a long time, asking myself the supreme question: If I could do *anything* in life, with no limits or conditions, what would it be? It took me a while to answer, but once I did, my path was clear.

When I left California a lot of people thought I was crazy; there were whispers. Hell, I don't blame them—I thought the exact same thing most days. But all I knew was that I couldn't NOT try. I might be crazy, but at least I'd be crazy chasing my biggest dream, on the biggest stage I could think of: the whole wide world.

I had a heart-to-heart talk with one of my oldest friends, Adam, who lived in the foothills past Sacramento. We walked his property one evening with fishing poles in hand, watching the sunset and listening to his two sons play inside.

"Are you having a midlife crisis or something, buddy?" he asked me.

I thought for a moment.

"Not at all, Adam. *My* midlife crisis was settling down and chasing money. This is me getting back to my *real* life."

Four decades on the planet. My God, where had it all gone? The scariest part was that it was going by faster and faster. No matter how I looked at it, I wouldn't be around forever. Whether I died of a heart attack or a broken heart, had one hundred years to live or went the next morning, there were a few goals I wanted to achieve, no—*needed* to achieve.

I packed light, getting rid of everything in my life that didn't aid my pursuit of those goals. I needed as much space and simplicity as possible. From there, I knew that everything else would fall into place. And hopefully, by the time I reached that red circle on the calendar, I would:

Be in the best shape of my life. I would honor the physical form I was given.

Be happy. When people asked me if I was happy, I didn't know exactly what to say.

Write a book. It's always been my dream to write a book, but not just frivolous fiction, and definitely not to make money. It's because I had this tiny acorn of an idea that had grown into a full sense of social responsibility, and my dream was to spread that message.

Those were my three grand endeavors. I wanted the energy of those accomplishments to reach somewhere far off, to help someone, or, hopefully, a lot of someones. That was the legacy I wanted to leave.

But I had a long way to go. In fact, I didn't even know where to begin. All I understood was I needed to throw a dart at the map of my life and get started, no matter where it landed.

I did exactly that, and somehow ended up in the tropics in Costa Rica, visiting my buddy in prison and with a new roommate who had a blind dog and a proclivity for leisure. Life sure had a hell of a sense of humor.

I hauled my duffel bags up onto the bed. I hadn't just packed for a vacation; my entire world had to fit into those bags because I was moving down to Costa Rica to live for an indeterminable amount of time (I called it semi-permanent when people asked).

For instance, my brand new printer was too big, so I traded it to my sister for a ride to the airport. Two Bose speakers earned a place in my luggage, but towels and sheets took up too much space so they were left behind. Priorities.

I unzipped my bags and started taking things out, sorting them into piles on the bed.

I pulled out the one book I'd carried with me and turned it over in my hands, *Walden* by Henry David Thoreau. "*Most people live a life of quiet des-*

peration," I said out loud. Disco groaned and rolled over. I tossed the book on the bed and it fell open to my favorite passage, heavily creased and underlined:

> *"... I wished to live deliberately...and not, when I came to die, discover that I had not lived. I did not wish to live what was not life... I wanted to live deep and suck out all the marrow of life."*

Damn, that hit home. "*I did not wish to live what was NOT life....and when I came to die, discover that I HAD NOT LIVED*." Preach on, my brother. Months earlier I'd asked myself if I was living some lesser version of my own life, and the answer hadn't pleased me.

I took out a beat-up pair of running sneakers, a nicer pair of Nikes, and three pairs of flip-flops.

This seemed like a lot of stuff but only a few months earlier in Sacramento I'd owned a big house, fancy cars, five televisions (including one in the bathroom), three stereo systems, a hot tub, two wet bars, four fridges, two storage sheds filled with random crap, and plenty of beautiful furniture. To everyone else it looked like I'd "made it." But now it was all gone. I'd sold what I could in the biggest karmic garage sale in history and donated the rest to charity. I only kept my books and my artwork. In some way, all of those possessions were possessing me, but now I was liberated.

> *Twelve t-shirts, most of them with brightly-colored surf themes from my local land-locked Old Navy.*

I hadn't anticipated this happening in my life. I'd worked so hard and finally achieved a plateau of comfort, but the realization that I wasn't on the right path crept into my thoughts late at night when I couldn't sleep. I wasn't leading a life of meaning, my true life. I couldn't escape the fantasy of letting it all go, humbling myself to nothing so I could instead pursue my long-forgotten dream.

> *Five pairs of shorts, six pairs of workout shorts.*

I wanted to write. Ever since I was a kid, I'd been vexed by literature, the delicious voodoo of the written word. I loved books, the smell of them, the feel of the pages, the worlds they opened up to me. Salinger, Fitzgerald, Hemingway. By putting their pen to the page, these writers became immortal. Vonnegut, Orwell, Lee. There was great magic in showing us their most intimate, unique humanity. When they took off their masks, they somehow awarded us gentle permission to do the same. Hesse, Kerouac, Bukoswki. They laughed at death and danced at the latest hour, just when the rest of us were worried the lights might go out. I, too, wanted to add one line to the eternal conversation, and if I was lucky to have one more dance. Schriever.

Four swim suits.

My mission on earth is to help people. There's so much that divides us as human beings, so much unnecessary suffering that's caused by our fear, our hatred. So many people are just barely hanging on, struggling every day with their time on this planet, dangerously close to giving up. I have the chance to reach out and place the mantra in their souls: "It's not you who's crazy, it's the world. Hold on. Keep hope." I believed I could do that with my writing, the chance to change the world, even just a little bit. That was a great responsibility but one that I would gladly accept, even if it meant living a life of poverty and hardship for myself. Bring it.

A MacBook computer and a set of oversized headphones.

But where should I begin? That was a daunting undertaking. Who the hell was I? I didn't even trust my own voice. And to ascend the peak of writing a book? Well...it was too big to dream. It was easier just to forget, and do what society told me should make me happy...

A $10 white, plastic watch.

So instead I dedicated all of my days to grinding on that hamster wheel of work and paying bills. Little by little my life became consumed with the struggle of this frenetic pace until one day it became who I was. Piece by piece, I'd sold my happiness. That scared the hell out of me. The fishbowl of my life grew smaller and smaller until I found myself swimming in circles but going nowhere. Every day I stressed more and smiled less.

A set of hair clippers so I wouldn't have to pay the village barber every week.

One day I looked at myself and realized I had no hope for my future, I'd given up. I was turning to stone, and soon all that would be left of me was a cold statue.

Eight workout tank tops and sleeveless t-shirts.

There had to be something more. A bigger purpose to life. I refused to die like this. I refused NOT TO LIVE like this.

Two pushup bars, my boxing gloves, and a jump rope.

So I gave up everything that was comfortable and 'normal' and moved down to Costa Rica to give my dream of being a writer one last chance. Undistracted, completely free, one final hurrah to save my own life.

A toilet bag with travel-sized shampoo, soap, toothpaste, and deodorant to get me through my first week. A pack of fifty condoms, which I thought would only last me a few weeks (though I still have almost all of them to this day).

It felt so good to take apart my life and then put it back together again exactly how I wanted it to look, to be the conscious architect of my own existence. It was like finding the loose end of a thread one day and tugging it a little bit, just out of curiosity, and right before my eyes the fabric of my reality unraveled like an old sweater. It was intoxicating, so I pulled more...

A bunch of black Nike ankle socks, ten wife beaters, grey and black, ten pairs of boxer briefs.

I felt space and time opening up like I hadn't experienced in a decade. My choking anxiety eased a little, and I could actually sit there and have a conversation with a friend or loved one and be 100% present. I was starting to smile again.

One floppy beach hat, one Phillies baseball hat, and, of course, a well-worn book, Walden *by Henry David Thoreau.*

That was everything in my new life, the only artifacts of my past existence.

I threw the empty bags under my bed and went over to the window. It looked like the rain had finally stopped.

CHAPTER 4

BLACK MOLD AND THE HOUR OF CHAOS

"How much weight do you think I need to lose to be ready for the beach in Costa Rica?" I asked Glen Fu, rolling myself over and struggling to get up from the wet gym floor in my hometown. I thought he'd say, "Ten pounds, or maybe fifteen at the most."

"You're between 30 and 40 pounds overweight," he said. Whoa! My initial reaction was to tell him to kiss my big ol' ass. Who the hell did he think he was, anyway? But two things about that:

1) He was a nationally renowned athletic trainer, responsible for the fitness and performance of high school, college, and even NFL athletes.

2) Glen could kick my ass with his little pinky. Even though he was only 5'3" and lean, he was a black belt in karate and held several Connecticut power lifting records.

"What?! 30 or 40? You're crazy, Glen Fu. Are you just pulling that number out of your ass or what?" Maybe 10 pounds, I thought. I'm almost there. I'm just muscular. I'm big boned. I don't want to be too skinny. He's probably judging me against pro athletes. The excuses kept coming.

Actually, he'd just put me through an hour-long dynamic workout at the gym by my sister's house in Connecticut, so he knew me well. I was moving down to Tamarindo in a week, so I wanted to step up my workouts and get his professional guidance.

"Yeah, about 40," he shrugged after looking me over again like I was a float at the Thanksgiving Day Parade. Damn him—the definition of a straight shooter—but that was hard news to swallow.

We talked about what workouts I could do with limited equipment in the tropics and he gave me several diet and training techniques, and then we hugged it out and said goodbye.

"Drop me an email if you have questions and keep me updated," he said and got in his car and drove off. I went about my day, but there it was, floating around in my head no matter how much I tried to ignore it. 30 or 40 pounds overweight? How the hell did I get *that* bad?

I left Sacramento the unhealthiest I've ever been in my life. I felt like a bloated pumpkin weeks after Halloween, rotting from the inside out. I seriously didn't know how long it could go on, or how it would end, but I wasn't optimistic.

My whole life I'd yo-yo'd between being in great shape and then letting myself slip into dormancy—from Fabio to Flabio, and back again. I look back now and say there was a huge emotional component that caused me to self-sabotage my health. But when I was in my twenties and early thirties getting in shape was also easy. Three weeks—that's all it took me to get in fighting shape. I'd do pushups and sit-ups every day, maybe a few curls and pull-ups, and hit the heavy bag or take a few runs. I'd go on the salad and oatmeal diet and in only three weeks I was in great shape. Damn, I miss those days.

But as the birthdays rolled by, and my paychecks and commitment to work grew, I became way too comfortable and packed on the pounds. For the first time in my life I couldn't just flip a switch and get in shape—the three-week plan didn't work. I started suffering nagging injuries—straining and pulling just about everything from my cankles on up. The injuries weren't severe but enough to derail my workout momentum.

By my last year in Sacramento, I was as heavy as I've ever been—pushing 220 pounds. I was wearing size 38 shorts, which I told myself I needed because I had a big butt (I've got plenty of room in 34s now). I was wearing baggy XL or even XXL shirts, when only a few years earlier, when I was boxing, I wore some larges. I tried to find loose button-up shirts like circus tents to hide my bulk. My body was so swollen and inflexible that I could barely lean down to tie my shoes. I groaned when I got up from the couch. Everything hurt in the morning. I walked down the stairs sideways, like an old man.

I couldn't breathe. The air quality in Sacramento is among the worst in the country to begin with, but every year my allergies got worse, until I had serious asthma and barely could take a deep breath. I developed a strange scratch in my throat that just wouldn't go away. It turned into a debilitating cough, especially when I was outdoors—or I was nervous. I'd cough and cough in the shower until I threw up. Is there mold in this house? I thought. But I think the black mold in my life was the bigger problem.

It was the stress, man, that shit will kill you. Where do I even begin?

I worked for a local law firm that helped people with their financial issues, particularly with credit card debt. All day long I hustled my ass off to help people, offering my time and expertise for free and consistently saying "no" to the easy money that my industry peers were raking in. I truly loved being of assistance, but carried the heavy load of negativity and stress from clients who couldn't handle where they were in life. No one wanted to take responsibility for their own choices, everyone wanted a bailout. I've never helped so many people in my life, yet felt so constantly under attack. On that sinking ship of a depressed economy people ranted, complained, and threw around lawsuits like they were paper airplanes, never mind if they had any foundation in truth or not—anything to capture the almighty dollar. I jumped when my doorbell rang, and soon stopped answering it all together.

But we did things the right way and our attorney was second to none. I worked 60-hour weeks for less and less money until pretty soon I was actually *losing* money every month, but I was proud to say our ethics never wavered. I had to hustle at 100 miles an hour every day just to pay bills and try to maintain what I had. It was like juggling chainsaws—I knew that sooner or later they'd start coming down.

Every morning I'd wake up with fear in my belly and rush through getting ready, brushing my teeth at a frantic pace as I thought about what I had to do—347 things on my to-do list. I'd scramble all day but at the end I'd have 348 things on my list. It ground me down, but there I was again the next morning, rushing through brushing my teeth because I didn't have the extra seconds to spare.

Friends and coworkers asked to borrow money, and for a while there I was in a financial position to help them out. I never got a cent back from most of them. These are the same folks who talked a lot about being such good Christians but who wouldn't return my phone calls, and then I'd see pictures of them in Vegas and Disney World on Facebook. If it wasn't loans, it was called an "investment," and they'd take your easy money and then go bankrupt. Where I'm from, if you do something like that you'll end up in the trunk of a car.

My relationships were shit and kicking my ass. The previous summer I'd met a girl who was cute and I thought pretty cool and we started dating. This one has potential, I thought and let my guard down a little, even making plans to bring her home to visit Connecticut and meet my momma. It turned out she was the town whore and everyone knew it—except me. Yeah, that didn't go so well.

I threw charity fundraisers but people acted like animals, spilling everywhere, treating my house like a trashcan, breaking towel racks and door knobs, my neighbors complaining about the noise and calling the cops by 8:00 p.m. Someone stole money out of the proceeds for the charity. My house was burglarized and I was cleaned out.

I couldn't take it. Things just kept getting worse, and the people who were supposed to be my friends, who I helped out the most, screwed me over again and again. The culture of depravity shocked me.

I felt like a beaten dog, jumping at every sudden movement. It became harder to work out and keep the weight off, and easier to eat away the stress in my life.

I couldn't sleep; I couldn't breathe. I didn't want to leave the house. I withdrew from the real friends who truly loved me and had my best interests in mind. I really did appreciate them and wanted to be closer, but I just had nothing more to give after all of the bullshit was over. I felt ashamed of my weakness. My anxiety became crippling. Surely everyone could see right through me, that I was about to fall apart.

But food was always there to fill the void; she never let me down. Nighttime was the worst, when I'd lie in bed and eat pizza or ice cream until I was sick to my stomach. I didn't want to answer the door or answer my phone or see anyone. I didn't want to leave my bed—I was safe in there. It's like when you're a kid and the floor is made of lava and if you step off the bed you'll burn up.

My health got worse, to the point where I couldn't even jog a mile at the park without a coughing attack. Rationally I understood that I should have just meditated, done yoga, and eaten a clean vegetarian diet to turn around my health, but I didn't have the mental discipline to do that consistently. I sank deeper in a hole until I couldn't even see daylight anymore. I'm big on momentum—when I'm into something, it's easy to keep cruising in that direction, but once I put on the weight and stopped working out, it was hard to get out of that negative spiral and jumpstart my energy in the right direction. I think I psyche myself out—it all has to be all or nothing, but sometimes moderation and balance are the most difficult milestones to reach.

I was holding on so tight, something had to give. My deepest fear was losing everything I'd achieved and worked so hard for, watching my castle crumble around me, but that's also why it became so liberating to purposefully engage it. When I decided to move down to Costa Rica I immediately felt better. It was like a horse had been standing on my chest for all those years, and now it stepped off and I could breathe again. But I still had a long way to go—my body and my psyche were ravaged from stress, and I was the heaviest I'd ever been at 39 years old.

I worked out consistently before I left but it barely made a difference—my mind was still holding me back. Then, suddenly, one day I was standing there in Costa Rica. I distinctly remember that first day, arriving at my apartment complex to Tania and her friends and jumping in the pool. I took my shirt off and felt horrible. I sucked in my gut and tried to flex my pecs without looking like I was flexing, but there was flesh everywhere.

There's no hiding in a beach town, there are no illusions—you're either in shape or you're not. It was always hot, and guys usually just wore board shorts and flip-flops—a tank top if they felt like getting overdressed and a t-shirt if they were really going for it. You're either at the beach, in the ocean, in the pool, or walking to and from those places, but you're always sweating. I was amazed to see what kind of shape everyone was in—impossibly lean, with six packs and surfers' bodies.

Most guys in Tamarindo looked like models for *Outside* magazine, but I looked more like a centerfold for *Inside*.

That's why I set one of my three big goals to be in the best shape of my life. It wasn't just about fitness or looking good, it was about healing, and valuing this chance at life I'd been given by respecting my health. Glen's advice was starting to sink in. I had a huge mountain to climb but I was on a mission to do it right, so I could be a new and improved person by my fortieth birthday.

CHAPTER 5

THE GIFT THAT KEEPS ON GIVING

"*Soooo, are you forgetting something, N?*" Tania asked. We were sitting in our apartment, waiting for the rain to clear.

"Huh? What?"

"*What about my presents*?" she asked. Oh, that. I ran upstairs, grabbed them, and came back down. There were two dildos, pink and purple, and three bottles of edible lube. Disco perked her head up.

"I swear, Disco, that's what she asked for." The blind dog titled her head at the sound of my voice. "Don't look at me like that!" She let out a disapproving grunt and put her head back down on the tile.

I handed everything to Tania. "*Thank you, N, I looove them!*" she said, hugging them like I'd given her a stuffed teddy bear. I'm sure glad she loved them because getting those little bastards into Costa Rica was no picnic.

Back in the States, just when I thought I had my luggage organized, things got weird. It's difficult or ridiculously expensive to buy a lot of everyday items in Costa Rica, so the best way to get them is to ask visitors to carry them down from the States. Mailing things doesn't work because even if they aren't stolen, there is a dollar for dollar import tax. But when someone comes down on vacation they can easily throw a couple of requested items into their bags and then leave them on Costa Rican soil. When someone comes down with luggage space, word gets out.

When I'd visited Pistol in December for vacation he'd asked me bring some strange cargo: bottles of organic fertilizer, parts for his truck, and an inflatable kayak. If that doesn't say "I'm building a homemade bomb" then

I don't know what does, but the customs officials in Costa Rica didn't even look twice.

Now that I was coming down again, Pistol's mom emailed me and asked if I could bring one or two things for him. Of course I said yes, I wanted to help him any way I could. She mailed me a letter she had written and a wrapped birthday present from his sister. Then a battery-powered radio showed up unannounced. I checked with Pistol's mom and she apologized for forgetting to ask me. No problem, I said, just keep in mind that I have very limited space in my bags. Special rechargeable batteries arrived. Magazines and a hardcover book. A fuel pump for a Chevy TrailBlazer. Whoa! My 50-pound baggage weight limit was in serious jeopardy.

The bags were repacked without an inch of extra space. I had to sit on them to get the zippers closed. Then Tania emailed and asked if I could bring down something small for her. What was it, I asked? A purse? Shoes? Some special brand of cosmetics? No, it was a vibrator, she said.

She was serious. For some bizarre reason, all forms of pornography are illegal in Costa Rica, so even sex toys are hard....err...difficult to get (though prostitution is perfectly legal—figure that one out!) She needed me to order it and then she'd pay me back once I got down there.

First off, I wasn't sure if people called them vibrators or if the correct term was dildos. I'm not sure I even wanted to know, but sheepishly I logged on to Drugstore.com and placed an order for the "Pipedreams Multi-Speed Deluxe Pearl Rabbit" while looking over my shoulder. In Pink. It cost $29.99 and would be delivered in three to five business days. Super.

I was staying at my mom's house in Connecticut for a month before heading down south, so I watched the mail intently and avoided eye contact with the postman. Then one day the package came. I whisked it into the basement before it could be discovered, like a grade school kid hiding a bad report card.

Now I had a real sticky situation on my hands....err...I had a dilemma: how to pack it? There was no way in hell I was going to put it in my carry-on bag and risk getting exposed with a pink dildo going through airport security. Should I leave it in the box and original packaging? The box took up a lot of space, so I decided to open it up and roll the little love missile into a t-shirt and conceal it deep in the recesses of my clothing. I tore up the box in fifty pieces and buried them deep in the garbage can beneath coffee grounds and orange peels and offered to take out the trash that Sunday night.

I reported back to Tania that "the eagle had landed." She emailed back that her best girl friend heard I was bringing a dildo and desperately wanted one, too. Could I find it in my heart to bring another one down? If it was a hardcover book for Pistol I'd have to put my foot down, but there was something dashing and risqué about being an international dildo smuggler, like a sexual secret agent. Bondage, James Bondage. I emailed Tania back and told her that would be fine because, like I always say, what's one more dildo among friends who you've never even met before?

I was becoming a connoisseur in ordering sex toys, so I logged on and ordered another Pearl Rabbit, but this time in a lovely lavender shade. My order of two dildos within a week must have triggered some Drugstore.com auto-preference because all of a sudden I was getting ads for all sorts of new freaky stuff, to go along with my own normal freaky stuff. Delete. Delete. Wait, what was that one? Oh, sorry...delete.

The purple dildo got delivered, taken out of the box, and rolled up in a pair of basketball shorts. I stuffed it into my luggage next to its partner in crime and sat on my bag in order to get the zipper closed again. Okay, Tania, I emailed, I got the second one and was all set to come down in a week. She emailed back that she *really* wanted personal lubricant. Jesus Christ—now it's lube? And does it come in any other kind but "personal?" How *impersonal* can you possibly be if you're breaking the lube out? Well, I guess having a dildo without lube is like going to the movies and not ordering popcorn. I didn't bother Googling the Costa Rican statutes on the legality of lubricants, but logged right back onto Drugstore.com. The size of the lube she wanted was ridiculous—I buy Ketchup at Costco in smaller sizes—so instead I ordered three small bottles of "Aqua Brand Warming-to-the-Touch Personal Lubricant" for $14.99, ending the whole sordid affair once and for all.

They got delivered by a suspicious postman who winked at me, and then the package was whisked into the basement, wrapped in individual plastic bags and duct taped shut, sealed in my toilet bag in case they opened, and stuffed in my luggage. I didn't confirm with Tania for fear that she might order fuzzy handcuffs or a blow-up doll.

I was itching to get out of the States, the anticipation killing me. Months of planning my great escape, worrying what I'd see when I visited Pistol, had taken its toll. I felt like a boxer about to go into the ring, amped with pre-fight adrenaline. I couldn't relax, I couldn't sleep. It was all unknown, there was no terra firma for me to stop and rest. My last week in Connecticut I paced the house, yelled at my mom for driving too slow, and re-weighed my bags five times to make sure they were under 50 pounds.

People told me that I was brave to give it all up and move to the tropics. I sure didn't feel brave; I felt like a coward. Everything scared me, even the mundane; standing in line at a store, answering the phone, or walking into a room full of people gave me anxiety. Time slowed down. I didn't know what to do, how to act. All of those eyes on me. Sometimes I cowered from its throat-lock, but most of the time I made myself forge ahead. I resolved that this would be one of those times, for I'd put myself in a position where there was no other option.

My sister drove me into New York at four in the morning. The airport was a madhouse and Continental kept changing check-in lines, so I had to sprint back and forth lugging my bags before finally getting checked in. My bags weighed in at 52.8 and 54.1 pounds, further confirming my theory that airlines rig their scales in order to set people up for bullshit fees. But a little small talk distracted the airline worker and I didn't get charged. I sat down in my window seat, put on my headphones, and started to doze as the plane lifted off for a four-and-a-half-hour flight to Liberia Airport in Costa Rica.

Somewhere over Mexico I was jarred from my pleasant snooze by a horrific thought. I'd made it through security in New York but on international flights you had to go through customs once you landed. The last time I visited Costa Rica the customs agents went through my luggage with a fine-toothed comb, making me take every single thing out and placing it on a metal table for examination—my risqué contraband would be found!

Since pornography was illegal in Costa Rica, I was technically breaking the law by bringing those dildos into the country. The customs agents would go through my luggage and I'd be exposed as a sexual deviant who incorporates Chevy fuel pumps and dildos the color of Paas Easter eggs into his love-making repertoire. That's some Japanese-level kink. Oh the shame, the embarrassment. I envisioned lube-sniffing K9s barking ferociously and the customs officers ripping through my bags and waving pink and purple dildos overhead while yelling for security. Everyone in the airport would see me taken away in handcuffs and my puzzled, excruciated face would be all over the evening news. I was mortified by the thought, sweating in my seat even in the cold artificial air at 30,000 feet.

I looked around for an escape. Maybe I could find a nice drug trafficker on the plane and switch contraband with him before we hit customs? I'd rather take the fall for ten kilos of coke and do twenty years in jail than have a whole airport full of people see I'm one of those double-dildo-edible-lube-fuel-pump freaks. But much to my chagrin, no one around my seat looked remotely like a drug trafficker, though that nun in first class looked a little suspect.

Even Pistol would pretend he didn't know me if I got thrown in jail right alongside of him. What are you in for? *Stabbed a man.* What are you in for? *Stole a car.* What are you in for? Smuggling two dildos and a quart of personal lube into Costa Rica. Dammmmmm...you a *baaaaddddd* mo fo!

All of the tourists on the plane were excited to land, ruffling their hideous flowered shirts and passing guide books back and forth, but I beeped the flight attendant and asked if we could take a few more laps over Costa Rica to enjoy the view, delaying the landing for an hour or so. "Sir, please put your seat back up and your tray table in the upright, locked position," she replied.

We landed and walked down a metal staircase and across the tarmac to the open-air terminal. The other tourists talked about how good the breeze felt, squealing with the excitement of being in the tropics, but I didn't share their enthusiasm. I got my bags and took my place in the customs queue. The stern-faced agents were checking approximately every other bag, even looking in toilet bags and turning shoes upside down. I tried to time my approach to coordinate being the next one *not* to be checked. I urged a family from Sioux Falls to go ahead of me and then cut in front of a guy in a wheelchair, but it was still going to be a crapshoot at best.

Finally, it was my turn. My shirt stuck to my chest. My hair was soaked. The customs agent asked me to put my bags on the metal table and open them. I tried not to make eye contact with him but didn't want to fully avoid his gaze either, so I looked directly at the top button of his blue shirt like it was the most interesting thing on earth. He stared at me for what seemed like an hour. He must have known. This was it—the end, the pressure was too much. I was seconds from blurting out my confession and begging them to take me away in handcuffs just to get it over with.

He handed my passport back and smiled. *"Pura vida. Welcome to Costa Rica."*

I uncrossed my eyes and smiled back and walked out of the airport into a taxi-stand wall of humidity, a free man ready to start my new life.

I was officially an expat.

CHAPTER 6

WET TOWELS

It rained my first day in Tamarindo, and my first week, and the whole month of July. I spent a lot of those first days in my room, reading books and talking to Disco, who was always great company.

It was so humid the walls seemed to sweat. Water dripped from the ceiling of my bathroom. My towels never dried. I'd hang them up in the bathroom or on the railing of my balcony, but when I picked them up several hours later they seemed to be even *more* wet. Everything I wore was splattered in mud, especially in back where it kicked up as I walked. It was the same with everyone in town—we all looked like we needed adult diapers.

Every morning I made coffee and poured a second cup to bring to Antonio. I enjoyed talking to him. He looked me in the eye and said thank you, and when he was done with the coffee he washed out his cup. Antonio was from Nicaragua, a poor country to the north, and had migrated to Tamarindo for better work opportunities. He worked seven days a week and lived in a one-room apartment with no AC along with a bunch of other guys. He didn't drink or smoke and sent every dollar he could home to his mother. On Saturday nights he went to church for entertainment, and invited me along if I ever wanted to come. Antonio practiced his English as we drank our coffee and I used what little Spanish I knew. We both liked baseball and boxing. It was a shame that Antonio was destined for a life of hard work and poverty—he was one of the good ones.

Antonio told me that everyone was waiting for *Veranita*—the "Little Summer"—a spell of sunshine in September before the *real* rainy season came in October. I couldn't wait until then to explore the town, so I ventured out.

I wanted to bring Disco with me to the beach so I asked Tania one morning. She couldn't go with us because she had a meeting with Chris, her former boss, and his attorney in an hour and was busy picking out which lingerie outfit looked most professional.

"Sure, you can take her with you, but I'm telling you, she won't," Tania said. *"She only comes with me."*

I petted her head and rubbed her belly and offered to give her a treat if she was good. Then I did the same to Disco.

I opened the door and tapped my leg and called Disco's name. She got up and scooted across the floor, sheepishly looking back to make sure she wasn't in trouble for leaving, and out the door toward the light.

"Wow, I've never seen her go with someone else," Tania said. *"She must really trust you. Okay then. Just be careful with her."*

"Dogs and mothers love me. It's just everyone else I have a problem with."

"*Que tonto—you're silly*," she laughed. *"And please pick up some dog food on the way back because we're out."*

I waved and shut the door. The dog food was out two days earlier, but I'd already replaced it with a big bag of the good stuff.

From Villa Verde I walked down our mud bath road and turned onto a wider, flat road that led through town. It was only paved on one side. Every year the municipality went to the business owners on that stretch and collected money to get the whole road paved. Every year they paid and every year the money disappeared and nothing got done, so the road remained half paved. Cars, delivery trucks, stray dogs, motorcycles, barefoot surfers carrying boards on their heads, bicycles, and Ticos going to work all competed for space on that one paved side.

Disco often tripped me up, sending me stumbling and laughing. She liked to feel she was right beside me because there were a lot of things that could hurt her out there in the big, scary world. There were already too many three-legged mutts limping around Tamarindo who'd been hit by motorists.

I sang her name so she would know that I was right there to keep her safe: '*Disco, Disco, Discito*." When a car came near, I held the tip of her ear so she'd know not to wander, our version of a leash. She stopped and panted happily until the car passed. "Good girl, *Disco, Disco, Discito*."

But when we got close to the beach there was no containing her. She heard the crash of the waves and smelled the water and couldn't help but run toward it, looking back in my direction to sense if I was keeping up. Out on the beach, there was nothing that she could run into that would hurt her. She rolled in the soft, pillowy sand. She bounded bravely into the water and tried to bite the waves when they splashed up at her. She ran in circles around me and barked. We didn't have a tennis ball, so I threw coconuts for her. She knew which direction they were headed and could run and sniff them out and bring them back to me. No piece of wood or coconut was too big, and at one point she dragged half a dried-up tree back to me.

Playa Tamarindo is a three-fourths mile stretch of gently curving sand only interrupted by the occasional tidal pool or beach-rooted Guanacaste tree. It runs from the rocky point of Playa Langosta to the south all the way north to the estuary mouth. On the other side of that estuary was Playa Grande, wild and deserted except for surfers and a few locals. Crossing that estuary meant hiring a fishing boat to shuttle you to the other side for 500 *Colones*—$1.00. You could wade and swim across if the tide was low, but you had to be careful because it was plagued by crocodiles. I'd been warned not to swim in the estuary during the rainy season because that's when the crocodiles ventured farther out onto the shores, or even into the ocean. They snapped up dogs that got too close and dragged them under, the only thing left to find the chewed-up remnants of their ears. A British journalist went missing a few years earlier and the consensus in town was that either the crocodiles or the coke dealers got him. My money was on the coke dealers, but still I didn't swim in the estuary when it rained.

Looking out at Playa Tama you saw nothing but big bay, rows of fishing boats, and a few sailing vessels. It was stunningly gorgeous, even in the rain, an instant reminder why I'd moved down there. Tama was a surfer's paradise, boasting some of the most consistent waves in the entire world. Every day I walked from rocky end to estuary shore, bringing Disco whenever I could, even when it rained or there was lightning, *el relámpago*, streaking across the sky, sending surfers paddling furiously for the shore. I'd arrive back home wet, muddy, and always feeling a little better about my move to Tamarindo. I'd hang up my wet towel even though I knew it wouldn't dry.

My first weeks in town I ate almost every meal at Kahiki's restaurant at the bottom of the hill going up to my apartment. The people were nice in there and the Tica waitresses were pretty. I'd chat with Snooky, the Filipina bartender, or George, a salt-and-pepper expat from Arizona who owned the place. I sat and drank fresh coffee and used their Internet. But soon Tania would walk by and spot me and come in and order food and ask me if I could pay just until her money from suing Chris came in. I tried to leave a seat between us so the waitresses wouldn't think that she was my girlfriend, but she would scoot right over to the next seat. I would go to the bathroom and sit back down two chairs over but she'd follow me again. Pretty soon we were sitting at the end of the bar by the wall and I had nowhere else to go. The bill came and I paid. Of course she would pay me back, no problem, she said. I did it reluctantly, but she was helping me out a lot with Pistol and getting settled, so I didn't protest too vehemently.

We didn't have Internet hooked up at our place, so I was able to check my email at Kahiki's, an exciting ritual because it was my only connection to my old existence in the U.S. I got a barrage of emails from Pistol's mom, his sister, and his younger brother. Gary had already dropped off the Chevy TrailBlazer to me upon their request. I really didn't want it, but they asked me to keep it safe and use it to visit him on the weekends. They sent me emails asking me to fill the truck with gas, get the oil changed, get a tune up, get the new fuel pump installed, get the window fixed, and to have it reregistered. His possessions were with his Canadian friends, Carla and Craig, and the family wanted me to go through it all and make an itemized list, and also look for his school diploma, business certificate, and find the shaving razor he liked. Oh, and I still needed to transcribe the notebook pages he'd given me.

They also forgot to mention I was expected to drive three of the students in Pistol's study abroad program to and from school every day. The Oyer sisters were three sistas from the States, pre-med college track stars, each one more beautiful and intelligent than the next. All of their names started with M, and for the life of me I couldn't get them right. They weren't supposed to know that Pistol was in jail, so I had to play it off like nothing was wrong as I got us lost on unfamiliar roads and sweated profusely. But they must have known something was wrong by the frequent emission of bad jokes emanating from the driver's seat. I figured that if I didn't give them a chance to talk about anything serious, then they couldn't ask me about Pistol and I wouldn't have to lie.

"Where is Joey? Are we ever going to meet him?" they'd ask.

"Look, girls—another rooster! Anyone hungry for chicken wings?... hahahaha. Okay, we're here. I'll pick you up this afternoon. Hey, Michelle, you forgot your backpack."

"That's Monique's backpack."

"Oh, okay. Here you go, Monique."

"I'm Melissa."

"Look girls, a goat!" And I'd hit the gas and drive away before they could ask any more questions. To this day I have more un-funny goat and rooster material than any person on the planet.

It sounded great to have the use of a truck, but it was turning out to be a pain in the ass. I drove it down to the roundabout in town one evening to get dinner but I almost couldn't make it back when a tropical squall blew in. I was stuck in the restaurant, looking out for the rain to slow, but it just kept raining harder. Where the hell was all of that water coming from? It seemed impossible.

The Rasta man was even there with us, washed out from his regular perch under the coconut trees in the center of the roundabout, twirling his locks and looking up at the sky.

"Dis that Woman Rain," he told us. *"Dem call it en el Caribe 'cause when it rain so hard, every woman deserve ta be made love ta, seen?"*

We listened to the rain playing music on the zinc roofs for a while and watched a garbage can float down the street. The lights flickered. Finally, I realized if I didn't want to be stuck all night I had to get moving. So I made a break for it but got soaked to the bone within seconds before I could hop in the truck. I started driving home, but I couldn't find the streets; they'd disappeared in a river. The rain overran the storm drains and flooded the town, water five feet high in places.

The tops of the street signs peeking out of the water were the only familiar landmarks, so I didn't know where to drive—to the left there was a deep ditch, to the right a submerged cement wall. A few cars had already gone off the road, their tail ends sticking straight up in the air, the front half submerged. I plodded on at five miles an hour, rain leaking into the roof of his car and the window seals. I couldn't see a damn thing. There was no one else on the street. Should I just leave it? No way—it would flood and the engine would be ruined.

The water was a little shallower uphill toward my apartment. I put it in gear and managed to slip and slide up the incline, but then I stopped at the top. Right by Villa Verde, where two dirt roads used to converge, there were now two rivers rushing together, runoff from the surrounding hills. Where those rapids collided, they launched water straight up into the air, like a reverse waterfall. I've never seen anything like it. There's no way I'm going to make it through that, I thought. I managed to park the truck on high ground on the crest of the hill (I hoped it was ground and not the roof of someone's house) and got out and trudged the rest of the way into my apartment, covered in mud. The truck was there the next day, but the electrical system was all screwed up and the roads were swamps for a week. Forget it, I'd just walk from then on. They told me that only locals and crazy people stick it out during the rainy season, and I'll add writers to that list.

That week, safely back at Kahiki's, I was relieved to get emails from my mom, my sister, and friends in Sacramento. They all asked how I was doing.

I typed an email telling them that I was stressed about Pistol, frustrated, homesick, and felt lonely because I had no friends. There was nothing to do and it rained every day, and everything looked different and *felt* different than my last time in Tamarindo. I told them I thought I'd made a mistake giving up everything in my old life and moving down here, and that writing a book was a crazy idea anyways and that I just wanted to come home and go back to my safe, comfortable life and pretend it all never happened. I read it again, and then erased it. I wrote a new email that said I was doing great and sent it.

I ordered another cup of café from Snooky and had her put a shot of Baileys in it; there was more work to be done. I took out the notebook pages that Pistol had given me. It was a detailed account of his arrest and the aftermath, including names and times and dates. I read on, enthralled, because for the first time I could put the pieces together and hear what really happened.

Pistol had been renting a nice house from Lena outside of town. He was growing marijuana there, about 120 plants. The young plants were cultivated indoors with hydroponics and grow lights. When they grew bigger, he put them in pots outside.

As would be expected, she got word that he was growing marijuana at her rental property. The house had a gardener and a maintenance man who were there all the time, so I have no idea how he expected NOT to get caught. The electric bill was also inordinately high due to the heavy usage of the lights. Lena sent him an email saying that she wanted him to pay the bill and then move out.

Pistol sent an email back ripping into her. He'd cc'd me and Reilly on it, as if bragging. He told her that she was a thief and the bill was too high and she was blackmailing him. He knew his rights as a tenant and she couldn't just evict him like that. If she wasn't careful he'd end up living there rent-free for years until she could legally get him out. Everyone in Tamarindo knew she was a crook and stole from gringos. He wasn't going to stand for it. He had friends in high places; he knew attorneys in the U.S. State Department personally and was a big hitter involved with the Clinton Trust that donated tens of millions to Costa Rica. He'd done so much to help the people of Costa Rica in his six years living there. He wouldn't pay.

The tone of that email shocked me. He cursed and threatened and accused. When I first saw the email, before he'd been arrested, I remember hoping he knew what the hell he was doing. Pistol wasn't a bad guy at all. In fact we'd had many conversations and his politics always focused on human rights and social responsibility, but he was definitely a madman when it came to partying. But I had no idea what he was thinking taking Lena on like that.

According to the police, an anonymous informant called the cops and told them he had a grow operation. On the morning of April 29, the OIJ (the narcotics taskforce in Costa Rica) smashed down the front door of his rental house, threw him on the ground, and arrested him.

He was kept cuffed for hours while a team of police, OIJ officers, and the local prosecuting attorney went through his house and possessions with a fine-toothed comb.

Shortly after the police entered, Lena showed up at the scene and had a long conversation with the prosecutor and the police. Pistol was put in the back of a car and transferred to the jail in Santa Cruz for arraignment. He was held overnight and not given food or water or phone calls.

He was arraigned and charged with drug trafficking and moved to the prison outside of Liberia, where I'd first visited him. His family eventually found out through Gary, who also knew Reilly, and that's how I got a call on a pleasant morning in early May while I was eating my breakfast at Denny's. Reilly didn't know much yet—just that Pistol had been pinched with marijuana. I didn't know what to make of it but didn't think it would be a big deal; I assumed he'd been caught just with his bong or a small amount, so I went back to eating my breakfast.

A few days after he was arrested, the family arranged for Pistol's new friends, the Canadians Carla and Craig, to come get all of his possessions at the rental house and hold them in a safe place. They turned out to be his guardian angels in the first couple of months, visiting him in jail, taking care of his possessions, and communicating with the family, even though they'd only known him a few weeks.

The family went through Pistol's records and saw that someone was still using his iPhone and had withdrawn $300 from his bank account only hours after he'd been arrested. Someone had stolen his phone and debit card.

No one knew yet what would happen, but the public defender told them the normal sentence for cultivating and selling such large amounts of marijuana was eight to fifteen years.

He'd pushed so hard with the pencil that the pages were almost worn through in places. Almost every line ended with multiple exclamation points and most of it was in capital letters. His letter talked about how his rights had been trampled and how the prosecutors had no concrete evidence and it was a travesty of justice in a country that was supposed to be known for human rights. It was all a grand conspiracy against him, but he'd get to the bottom of it and not only be released but also bring those who had plotted against him to justice. He'd been framed by very important people in Tamarindo and if they didn't let him out immediately he was going to expose them all.

I felt sick to my stomach as I read it. No evidence? They caught you red-handed with 120 plants, Pistol. It sounded like a manifesto, the ranting of someone who was highly intelligent but not entirely lucid. Was he really that far out there? He'd seemed fun-crazy, but not crazy-crazy, during my month-long vacation, but then again we drank day and night and he was high all the time. It dawned on me that maybe it hadn't been a superman effort to party just because I was in town, but that was what his normal life in Tamarindo looked like for the last six years.

God dammit, Joey, what have you done to yourself?

I transcribed the letter then emailed it to his mother and his attorney. I asked the pretty waitress for my bill and packed up to leave, but before I closed my laptop, a Skype message popped up.

"*Hola, Norm. Are you in Tamarindo?*" It was Lena.

I froze. I didn't know what to do

"Hello, amigo. Are you there?" she messaged again. I realized she could see that I was online. My brain sped through it. There was no avoiding her. It was a very small town, so eventually I'd have to talk to her.

"Yes, hello, Lena. I'm in Tamarindo," I messaged back. I waited for what seemed like a long time.

"I need to see you and talk," she said, the attorney who got my friend arrested and ruined his life, the woman who I'd slept with the last few nights of my vacation six months earlier. Blood rushed to my ears.

"Okay, Lena. Tell me when and where."

CHAPTER 7

A SERPENT IN THE GARDEN

Lena showed up twenty minutes late and parked her black Mercedes SUV in front of the restaurant, blocking everyone's view of the garden out front. She got out in mid-conversation on her cellphone, speaking in near-perfect English. She wore lipstick and high heels, almost unheard of in Tamarindo, and made a big show of tiptoeing across the ten feet of dirt.

"Yeah, yeah, I know…I KNOW, girl…hahahaha. No I won't do THAT. Oh, you are BAD! …Okay, I'll drop my kids off and we'll go… Oh, you know ME! …Okay, ciao ciao y hasta pronto." She hung up and looked around the room, then smiled and blushed when she saw me.

I'd arrived at Baula's Pizza fifteen minutes early and chosen a seat near the back of the restaurant. She'd suggested we meet there on Thursday night, a couple days after our conversation on Skype. I asked her if we could meet at the more crowded and visible Voodoo Lounge, but she'd insisted on Baula's. I already knew where the exit was, through the kitchen.

She greeted several people on the way in, Ticos from the city that had lighter skin and wore golf shirts. Then Lena walked up to my table.

"Ughhhh, it's raining so much. What a mess. Hello there!"

"Hi, Lena," I said. "Long time no see." I hugged her and gave her an air kiss on the cheek. She slid into the booth across from me and placed her big purse next to her.

When the waiter saw that Lena was with me, he looked surprised and rushed over and wiped down the table again, even though it was clean. She asked about his parents in Spanish and ordered a water. I ordered another beer.

"So, how have you been?" I asked. She smiled broadly, but it was all cheek. Her eyes didn't move.

"I am soooooo busy, too much work for me. Costa Ricans just don't know how to do business."

The waiter brought our drinks and asked if we were ready to order.

"What would you like?" I asked, scanning the menu of pizzas.

"Nothing too bad. I am eating healthy." I wondered why she suggested meeting at a pizza place.

"How about the veggie pizza?" I asked. She ordered it in Spanish and made several changes.

I looked out to the road for blue lights, but so far the coast was clear.

"You look good," I said. I figured it couldn't hurt.

"Oh yes, I know. I do Pilates and yoga and run on the beach every day. I have to stay sexy now that I'm almost thirty!" When we hung out in December, she'd revealed that she was 37.

It's not that Lena was unattractive, in fact the first night Pistol and I met her she looked pretty damn good. We ran into her at an Italian restaurant that was tucked into the jungle, along with her inseparable best friend, Pepito. He was a *mariposa*—a butterfly, the Spanish term for a gay person. Like so many other Spanish speakers, he couldn't easily pronounce "Norm," so he called me by my old traveling nickname, "Noel."

But for some strange reason, Pepito insisted on calling me *Papa* Noel, which means Santa Claus. They joined our table and we all drank way too much wine and did so many shots I had to start chucking them back into the bushes. Pistol and I were both jockeying to sit next to her—she was all sex appeal and curves in the right places, and frankly, the other option was to be paired with Pepito. We all went dancing afterwards. Pistol danced like an arthritic hippy, while I could break out a few phony salsa moves before faking an injury to quit while I was ahead, so Lena and I hung out that night. And the next night, too.

I don't remember how we first became romantic, other than going home with her was a great excuse to stop drinking and get a good night sleep. The sex seemed great…for her…. I just laid there and watched a lizard crawl across the ceiling. Her skin didn't feel warm. She'd gone under the knife so many times that she was stitched together like a patchwork doll—perfectly shaped but not *real*.

After that night every time I saw Pepito in town he'd yell after me, his teasing, shrill voice loud enough for everyone on that side of town to here: "*Papa Noel es un chico mallloooooo!!*"—Santa Claus is a baaaddddd boy! Whenever I was trying to lay low or talk to another girl he'd magically appear, pedaling his pink bicycle with Lena's poodle sitting in the basket, waving his finger disapprovingly like the Wicked Witch of the South.

When my vacation was over and it was time to head back to the States, Lena gave me a ride to the airport. It was a merciful exit—I'd abused my body so hard trying to keep up with Pistol that I couldn't sleep more than three hours at a clip, soaking the bed with alcohol sweats. My left elbow wouldn't stop twitching, and then it started moving up to my eye. I hugged Lena goodbye but she wanted a kiss, so instead I handed her $50 to donate to the church in Tamarindo and ran for the plane.

"So, how do you like living here?" she asked as we waited for our food.

"Yeah, I like it. But I love the beach."

"And how long are you here for? What are you doing for work?"

"I'm not sure how long, but at least a year I think. I'm finishing up some things for the law firm in Sacramento, but I want to write a book."

"You are writing a book. Really? A writer? Wow, I'm having dinner with a writer?"

"Well, I haven't written anything yet. It's a ton of work, so we'll see. But it will keep me out of trouble."

"Oh sure! I know you, Norm. Bad boy—chico malo!" She winked. *"I'm sure you meet lots of nice Tica women here. I heard you have a girlfriend."*

"What? Who said that? Oh, I bet I know. No, no."

I decided it was time to shift the conversation to Pistol. Let's get this over with.

"No girlfriend for me—I'm way too busy helping Joey out."

"Oh, yes." She nodded, like his name was just another in her file cabinet, hardly recognizable. The waiter brought the pizza over.

"It's too bad what happened to him," she said.

The days that led up to my meeting with Lena had been intense. When I told Pistol's family that Lena wanted to meet, strategy planning ensued like we were going to war. Emails flew back and forth and everyone had an opinion. In the end I was instructed to get as much information out of her as possible, but also to cut to the chase and ask her what it would take to make the whole thing go away. Pistol insisted that he'd been set up by Lena from the beginning. She knew the prosecutor and the judge and her dad was high up in the police force, so he was sure that she was sitting around, thinking of ways to screw him over. I wasn't so sure. It seemed to me that he'd forced her hand by sending that nasty email and refusing to leave her house. I didn't want to be the one to remind him that the definition of "framed" was something you're *not* guilty of, but by sheer force of personality Pistol had his family convinced that Lena could just wave her evil witch's wand and make it all go away.

I wasn't too keen on being the only Christian thrown to the lions. Lena said that she *needed* to talk, but what could possibly be the reason for that, other than she thought I had something to do with Pistol's illegal activities? She'd met us together, knew we partied together, knew we were old friends, and he'd told her that we were going to live together once I got down there, even though that wasn't my intention. She must have thought I was in on it.

I was guilty of smoking *motta,* marijuana, almost every day on my previous vacation in Tamarindo. There would be records of phone calls and emails between us, and plenty of pictures together. I'd brought him biofertilizer in my luggage. Now I was driving his truck and visiting him every weekend in jail. None of that was illegal, but it could be pieced together as evidence of corroboration *if* someone was powerful and had an agenda.

"So, Lena, you wanted to meet with me tonight. But there is something I wanted to ask you, too. I need your help."

"*Yes? What do you need*?"

"I want to hire you as an attorney."

She put down her pizza and sat up straight. I had her attention.

The days before my meeting with Lena, I'd grown increasingly anxious because there was a good chance she was setting me up. I'd show up and the police would come in and haul me off to jail, too. If she thought I was involved it would be nothing for her to call her friends in the police department and have me arrested. Sure, I'd probably be found not guilty...eventually, but it could take years and tens of thousands of dollars for "justice" to be served.

I'd been to jail before and had no intention of going back in this lifetime. Right after college I was living in Colorado. One night the cops came to my apartment on a noise complaint and saw some weed sitting out. They woke up the judge and got a search warrant and found eighteen plants and a pound of mushrooms that all belonged to my roommate. I took the fall right along with him and had to do a couple of weeks in jail, narrowly avoiding a four-year Federal sentence. I got the hell out of town as soon as I could. Waking up in a jail cell is the worst feeling in the world, and being locked up in a Third World prison? Well, to be honest, I'm not sure I could endure it.

This was all beginning to feel horrifically *real.* I knew I might end up in jail that night.

I'd planned accordingly; I had a photocopy of my passport and some cash on me, but left my watch, wallet, and passport hidden in a cereal box. I sent an email to my family telling them I loved them without trying to be too obvious that something heavy was going down, and another one to Reilly telling him where I was and whom to contact in case I disappeared.

I wore sneakers and socks instead of flip-flops, just in case I had to run… or spend the night on a cold, dirty concrete floor. Before I left my apartment, I picked up a long kitchen knife and put it in my pocket, but then I thought about it and put it back down. I left my keys on the table and locked the door behind me—the cleaning ladies could let me in if I made it back. I walked past the restaurant one time to see if there were any police around or if anything looked wrong. Then I went in and got a table in back, by the kitchen where it was dark. I ordered a beer and reminded myself to breathe. I was ready.

"I want to hire you to help me get Joey out of jail," I said.

She went back to eating her pizza. *"Oh yeah? He's in some big trouble I hear."*

"Well, that's why I need your help. I mean, you're the best attorney in Tamarindo, and you know everyone in Guanacaste. You have a lot of contacts that could help him."

"*Well, this is true. It could be expensive. But I am listening.*"

My tactic was this—I'd ask for her professional help to get Pistol out of jail. It sounded crazy, but if it worked it was a perfect front. Pistol had instructed me to find out exactly how much money it would take to make it all go away. He thought that at a certain number she would call off the dogs and he'd be able to walk out of there. I didn't see how it could be that easy once he was in the system, even if it was Costa Rica. So what I was offering to her was a bribe, of course, and pretending it was an offer to hire her.

I had to be subtle, to play the game correctly, especially if she had the agenda to throw me in a cell right there with him. I didn't want to give her any more rope to hang me with. I wasn't sure how it worked in Costa Rica, but if I were her client then it would be a conflict of interest for her to inflict any legal harm upon me—or even testify against me. Who better to help Pistol out? If she truly was the one who made it all happen and she had plenty of financial motivation then it would be easiest for her to undo it.

It was a long shot, but I had nothing to lose.

"I want to hire you but I don't have much money. I'd have to cash out my life savings and get help from Joey's parents." In reality it was the opposite—when Pistol was first arrested, I heard through Gary they were trying to scrape together enough bail money to get him out. Pistol's mother, Betty, was in her seventies, and his father was eighty and had health problems. They didn't have any money. Betty was worried they might never see him again. I had bad dreams about what they might be doing to him in a Third World jail, so I told her that I could chip in $10,000, a large part of my life savings, if it meant we could bail him out immediately. Pistol's attorney, Carlos Montero, was optimistic, so they wired him a $5,000 payment via Western Union. And then, the day before the bail hearing, Carlos went to the jail and demanded that Pistol get him another $5,000 and the title to his SUV or else he wouldn't show up at the hearing the next day. Fucking crook. Of course they didn't send the money over, and we all scrambled to find a legitimate attorney to help him. Eventually I found a Tico defender who worked alongside a well-respected gringo attorney in San Jose. They wired a retainer to him and waited for the bail to be set.

The day of the hearing, Pistol had a handful of character witnesses show up for him, Ticos he knew from Tamarindo. Lena was there, and she took each of them in a side chamber for a few minutes. When they came out, one by one, his witnesses walked right out of the courtroom and never testified, avoiding eye contact with Pistol. The judge set the bail at $100,000, but unlike in the U.S. where you could post a bond for 10% of that and walk, he had to come up with the whole $100,000. So they put him in shackles and took him back to the prison.

Strangely, they didn't seize his passport. Gary had a plan: the moment Pistol was released on bail they'd sneak him over the northern border into Nicaragua under cover of night and then transport him to Managua, where he could get on the first plane back to the States. It sounded like a shit show to me, where everyone would end up in jail.

"Do you think you could get him out?" I asked Lena. "Probation, house arrest, get him deported—anything?"

"I don't know. I would have to see how much money I have to work with."

"I'm not sure. Times are tough. How much would you need?"

"I will think about it, but for something like this, it could be up to 100,000 dollars."

I laughed and took a gulp of beer.

"Lena, no one's got 100 grand. It would be impossible to even come up with half of that. But think about it a little and give us a number. I could really use your help on this—as a friend."

"Okay, I will think about it more and let you know," she said. At least it was out there.

When I visited Pistol in December, he was growing marijuana, but only a few plants so he didn't have to keep buying it from other sources. His first five years living in Tamarindo he had to endure buying weed from the surfers and dealers on the beach at ridiculous prices. There was always bullshit, bags that didn't weigh out, and bad quality. Then, a year ago, they started manufacturing grow lights in China that were small enough to transport in his luggage and perfectly legal to bring into the country. He brought two down to Costa Rica and began growing a couple of plants, just for personal consumption. And he did smoke A LOT of weed himself.

One time when Pistol and Theresa got in a particularly nasty brawl, he wanted to lay low for a couple of days, so we moved all of his stuff, including his little homemade grow operation, out of his apartment to a friend's place that was vacant. We'd loaded up his Blazer with plants in Dixie cups and pots and hauled it all over to the new place. I hung out and watered the plants while Pistol set up the lights and the humidity control, and we were out of there within an hour.

I've been around marijuana my whole adult life, and it was a small amount, so it didn't seem like a big deal. After all, Costa Rica was a tropical surfer's paradise where you could buy coke and hookers on every corner. He'd been down there for five years partying his ass off and never got in trouble before, so surely he knew what he was doing?

"Let's go dancing Tuesday night at Voodoo. I will teach you salsa again," Lena said.

"I'd love to, but I'm not going out much these days."

"Okay, then I can make you dinner at my house."

"Thank you, Lena. Yeah, let's do that some time."

"What time? Tell me when."

"Umm, let me look at my schedule and get back to you."

"You don't want to be with me again—is that it?" she snapped.

I squirmed. There was no way in hell I was going to hang out with her socially again, with or without the Pistol situation, but I also had to be careful not to straight-out reject her.

"Well, Lena, it's not like that but…"

"Las mujeres somos como la gitarra, si no la tocas no suena," she hissed.

I laughed nervously. "I don't understand. What does that mean?"

"They say in Costa Rica that we women are like guitars. If you don't touch us enough then we don't sound good."

So *that's* what this was all about? That's why she wanted to meet with me? She wanted a *date*? She had to be the most vain woman in the world—the audacity to get someone thrown in jail and then try to hit on his friend. Can you even imagine sending someone to a Third World prison for fifteen years for growing *plants*? She had to know that as a gringo in a Costa Rican prison he could be beaten, tortured, and raped—every day would be a living hell, and that's *if* he survived. It was pure Schadenfreude, a level of cruelty I couldn't comprehend.

I wanted to tell her what I really thought of her and then get the hell out, but I remembered where I was—a gringo in someone else's country. The last thing I was going to do was piss off a powerful, spiteful…and pathologically vain attorney. Who knew what she was capable of? And if she couldn't get to me, then maybe she could turn the screws tighter on Pistol.

"Listen, Lena, you're a beautiful woman, but…"

"*And you are a nice man. I have many men who want to be with me. I am very pretty and look at this body.*" She ran her hands down her torso.

"Yes, you are. Of course. I'll tell you what, let's get our business taken care of first and then we can talk about going out on a date."

A flash of anger crossed her face.

"*Why do you care so much? About Joey?*"

"Well, he's my friend and I just want—"

"*You know what I think? I think you have something to do with this. No one would do this much to help if they weren't involved.*"

I tried to stay calm, but my eyes squinted and my mouth tightened. The East Coast kid was rising in me and I couldn't keep him quiet forever.

"*I see your face and I don't think you are telling me the truth,*" she said. "*I think you are—what is the word in English? Dishonest, with me.*"

I leaned forward and looked her in the eye, talking slowly, just above a whisper.

"Hey, Lena, I'll tell you what—you can think whatever the hell you want, but it's not true. I'm just trying to help him. So just come up with a number, or don't, but it doesn't matter to me."

"*I don't know, Norman, you are handsome, but I think you are a chico malo,*" she said in a teasing tone. "*But maybe we can be friends. Let me know about salsa dancing.*"

I sat back and gave a big fake smile.

"I will. And you think about the thing with Joey and let me know."

We finished our drinks and managed to talk about the weather, the freshly painted pews in the church, and how her son was always getting in trouble. We ate our pizza like any normal guy and girl out on a Thursday night, not two people bargaining over someone's life.

When we were done the waiter brought the check and put it down in front of her with shaky hands. She slid it across the table to me. I paid, we said goodbye and kissed on the cheek, and she whisked off in her black SUV.

As I walked home it started raining again. I slowed down and let it soak me to the skin. It felt good. When I got home the night watchman let me in, and then I got good and drunk.

CHAPTER 8

THE ELECTRIC CUP-O-SOUP SPECIAL

Grab a bicycle and pedal fifteen minutes out of Tamarindo toward the village of Villareal and you'll find the Automercado, a grocery store in an otherwise empty upscale shopping center. Everyone called it the Gringo Supermarket. I loved it in there—the AC washed over me as I walked through the automatic doors, instantly twenty degrees colder than outside. They had clean produce and a butcher's counter without flies and a whole section for breads and pastries. Booze had its own glorious row. I took my time wandering up and down the spotless, organized aisles where there seemed to be two employees for every shopper, though they all looked a little confused about what the hell they should be doing.

You could find American products in the Gringo Supermarket: Budweiser, Ragu spaghetti sauce, Oscar Meyer hotdogs, Baileys for my morning coffee, Smucker's jelly, and my favorite, Peanut Butter Cap'n Crunch. Whether I bought them or not, it was comforting just to know that they were there. But a visit to the Gringo Supermarket was dangerous to the budget because I'd buy basic food for the week, which might cost $80 in the U.S., and the bill would come to $150. I learned to feed myself mostly with eggs, spoonfuls of peanut butter and honey, and spaghetti for dinner. Most everything else was too expensive (okay, Captain Crunch and Baileys stayed in the cart). It was much better than the little market in Tamarindo, owned by Luigi and his Italian cousin. It was right in the center of town so it was convenient to buy toilet paper or a bottle of water there, but their produce was wilted and they charged even higher, tourist prices.

Most of the time I didn't go to the Gringo Supermarket for myself, but to shop for Pistol. Every week his mom emailed me a list of groceries and sundries he'd requested and I'd go get them. Providing him some good food and a few comforts from home was important since they barely fed him in prison.

My first few months in Tamarindo I visited Pistol in jail almost every weekend, four out of five at one point. He had no one else. His family had little money, and although he had four brothers and sisters, his mom didn't want to burden them because they all had problems of their own. He had no real friends in Tamarindo; they were all smoking and drinking buddies who'd scattered like roaches once he was arrested. Veronica, his new twenty-year-old sexpot girlfriend, couldn't handle the situation and stopped answering calls and emails by the time I got there. Gary went back to the States to work construction, abandoning his bright future in the restaurant business, so only I remained, the lone lifeguard on duty on a beach where people were drowning left and right.

Visiting him was a big production that took most of the day. I had to wake up early, make sure to remember my passport, drive to the bank and withdraw money for him, go to the grocery store and buy everything on his list, stop to get gas, and then start the one-and-a-half-hour drive to Liberia. It seems like everything takes three times as long in a Third World country, hence the name. He also wanted me to stop at Burger King in Liberia and pick up Whoppers and fries on the way. The jail was a twenty-minute ride from the city center on the bumpiest of dirt roads into the jungle, or forty minutes if it was raining hard. Visiting days alternated—it was on Saturday and the next weekend it was on Sunday, so my whole schedule revolved around his visits.

Before I left in the mornings Antonio would be the only one awake. He whistled as he cleaned the pool filter and swept the sidewalks while everyone else slept blissfully after a night of partying. I apologized for not being able to bring him coffee those mornings and told him why. "*No problem*," he said, "*suertes para ustedes*,"—good luck to both of you. He said that I looked sad on visiting days. His English wasn't good, so maybe he meant I looked tired or serious or preoccupied, but probably he meant sad.

The first time I had to visit the jail by myself my stomach was too nervous to eat breakfast. Pistol's sister emailed me directions that she'd received in an email from Veronica.

> hi the name of jail it's carcel de Liberia calle real. little town has the same name "calle real" I always go in taxi they know where is it ... I don't know how to explain the address but you can ask

> Gary maybe he knows how to explain better than me jejejeje ..when you're in the middle of liberia where traffic lights are... turn right and go in that direcion as 2 km and then turn left where it is a company it's called "Dos Pinos" in that corner from there are about 2 km you have to see a cruise must turn to the left you have to go straight is a dead end where it is located. well the taxi driver knows where is it!! jejeje

Not a lot to go on, but somehow after asking a few passing Ticos I found the turnoff from the paved road by the *Dos Pinos* billboard. They were confused why a gringo would want to know where the jail was and asked me twice to make sure I knew what that word meant, and if I really intended to go there. I got lost on the little dirt roads in Calle Real but eventually found my way using landmarks: forking left at the chicken stand and turning onto the jail road where the massive Ceiba tree lay fallen.

The check-in process took anywhere from one to two hours, and then the visit itself was about the same time. On the way out it didn't feel so bad because I was free, so I'd roll the windows down and enjoy the feel of the wind and thank God I had six more days until I needed to do it again. I reminded myself that I had nothing to worry about as a visitor—I was innocent, but it was bullshit because just being in that place was a sentence.

I'd finally get home around 4:00 p.m., my sweat-soaked shirt smelling of adrenaline. I'd feel wiped out, confused, and a little...well, like Antonio said, *sad*. I'd want nothing more than to jump in the ocean at sunset and wash the jail off me, and then be by myself to eat a good meal and watch a movie at night.

I never got used to visiting the jail. Every week I thought it would somehow get easier, but it never did. Sometimes the Liberia River flooded, washing out the bridge over that canyon, a vantage point where you could see all the way up to the smoky volcano, Rincón de la Vieja, on a clear day. I'd have to turn around and take the long way around to the jail, which added another 45 minutes. The truck would break down if I even looked at it funny, so it seemed like each week I'd find myself stranded by the side of the road. I'd have to wait an hour to flag down a taxi or beg to use someone's phone so I could call a repairman to come out to me, who was just someone's cousin who would get under the truck and rig the transmission with plastic twist ties and duct tape because the only tow trucks in all of Guanacaste Province were two hours away in Santa Cruz. I was able to roll home at 25 miles an hour that way, but it added mid-week trips to the local mechanic, a chain-smoking and drunk German working with homemade tools from his house deep in the jungle. The bank machines would be inoperable or Pistol's account would be out of funds, so I'd have to find another bank and take money out of my own account for him. The prison would be busier than usual because yet another person got caught smuggling in drugs, so the guards wouldn't let me bring in the exact same items I'd brought in the week before.

Sometimes Tania came with me—I thought it was really nice of her to help out. Not surprisingly, she knew a bunch of guys from Tamarindo who were in the jail, but the guards almost always refused her entry because her skirt was too short or her heels too tall. The female guards especially disdained her, and each time she was turned away she had to wait in the car. I encouraged her to wear less revealing clothing, but her most conservative skirt barely covered her whoo-haw. I kept it all together but I was beginning to feel defeated, a ragdoll shuffling from one place to another, ready for the next thing to go wrong, my time and my *life* not my own. I always came away from the jail with a first-hand lesson in the paucity of human existence, including mine, for it was nothing but cheap flesh, concrete, and mid-day blackness in there.

Remember that I didn't visit him in a nice cushy visiting room or even have guards watching out for me; I was locked right in there *with* the prisoners—a prisoner myself, effectively, for those hours. If someone felt I was "big timing" them or just didn't like the look of my face, they could get to me easily. There were riots, stabbings, fights, hits, and gang violence going on all the time. Then, on the outside, there were plenty of friends, brothers, cousins, and gang members who could take care of the lone gringo walking to and from the parking lot in a nearby field every weekend.

Each week I dreaded that long, solo walk through the permanent housing cells. I tried to ignore the prisoners as they yelled from their windows but I just couldn't. So I said "wassup" and tried to bullshit long enough to get past. The others in the next cell heard me coming and started yelling even more vociferously for my attention. I give them a thumbs up and told them "Disculpe, amigos—yo no tengo dinero, pero proxima fin de semana!"—Sorry, friends, I don't have any money, but next weekend.

I reminded myself to bring a few 500 *Colones* coins for my next visit to toss at the windows. I even started a little collection in a glass on my nightstand. But if I threw coins could I get in trouble? Other visitors told me to do it when the guards weren't looking, but I couldn't bring myself to it.

Sometimes I'd get lucky and women would walk by at the same time. They were far more interested in eye fucking and hooting and hollering at Ticas, so I could slip by almost unnoticed. I began timing my walks to coincide with groups of mothers and girlfriends, using them as camouflage.

I didn't *want* to get comfortable. If I had to be there I wanted to remember it always like I truly felt—scared shitless for my friend behind those walls and unsure of my own safety, even though I wasn't involved. I never *wanted* to grow used to it. Maybe I was being paranoid, but paranoia served you well there. I wished Pistol had exercised even a hint of that caution and he wouldn't be behind bars to begin with.

That morning of my first solo visit I'd arrived a little late but got in quickly. The buses couldn't get through because of heavy rains, so there were less people. On my way to his cell I passed the old man in the wheelchair and said, "Buenos dias—good day." He gave me a warm smile, the only comforting thing about my trips inside, and then asked me again:

"Are you sure you're on the right path, mi niño?"

I knew where D2B was so I thanked him and went on. I passed a checkpoint where two stony-faced guards sat. A baby deer walked right up to the fence behind them. I was so amazed to see a deer that close that I grabbed one of the guards by his shoulder and pointed it out to him—"*Mira, mira, un venadito,*"—look, look, a baby deer!, my voice rising three octaves in childlike wonderment. The guard looked at me with disbelief that:

A) I had touched him, and

B) I could quite possibly be the biggest bitch alive by pointing out a baby deer in a Third World jail.

I sort of saw his point. What was next for me, skipping down the sidewalk as I caught butterflies, blowing them over to the inmates? Jesus Christ, Norm, toughen up a little. But on that particular day, he decided to show mercy and didn't crack me in half with his nightstick.

When I got into D2B a sketchy Tico trustee offered to help me with the bags I was holding, to get the food over to the cafeteria. I declined. Pistol had warned me that they'd take the bags and steal everything and he'd never see it again; it happened a couple of times when Gary brought stuff in. People got pretty fucking sneaky on 800 calories a day.

Pistol said "hi" and we hugged it out.

"Here, I brought you some more food and three Whoppers."

He took the bags without looking inside. "Did you bring the money? Okay, good—slip it to me."

I did so, sliding it in his palm as we pretended to shake hands.

"Cool, you brought a new pillow. Damn, I need one. Let's go throw this stuff in my cell."

We walked into his cell. Each unit contained a dozen individual cells, just concrete rooms with a big iron door. There was one barred window to the grounds outside and I could see where the inmates saw us visitors walk by. Other prisoners lounged around on flimsy wooden bunk beds, walking in and out into the main courtyard as they pleased during the day. There were no medium security cells for small-time criminals or segregation cells for violent offenders or the mentally ill; everyone was together—lifers and those serving two months. Laundry hung from every bed and bar. The air was mossy, like in a cave, lifeless other than a few small clip-on fans blowing. A knife-sharp feeling of claustrophobia sliced through me.

"These were built to hold 24 prisoners but there's usually 50 in each cell," Pistol explained. He led us to a corner of the room where flimsy foam pads laid on the ground and unrolled one.

"This is me."

"What do you mean? You don't even have a bed?"

"Not yet—I've been sleeping on the floor for three months because they're so overcrowded. I'm next in line, so I should be getting one soon."

"I'm sure it will get a little bit better once you get to the permanent cells," I said.

"Actually it's even more crowded over there—about 70 to a cell made for 24."

From what I'd heard, this was the second-best jail in all of Costa Rica. I couldn't even imagine what they looked like in San Jose or Limon—that would be a death sentence for a gringo. Pistol hid most of the bags beneath his bed roll and signaled to a guy nearby to watch over his stuff.

We went back outside and into the cafeteria because it was raining out, just another airless box with concrete tables and benches. We pressed in rump to rump with families bringing soup and chicken to their sons, their wet clothes steaming. There were no free seats but a guy moved over to let us in. We sat facing each other.

"So, what's going on, Normando?"

"Oh, all good—just keeping it simple. Been writing a lot and working out every day," I said, wiping sweat from my face with the arm *without* stamps.

"Yeah, you look thinner. How's Tamarindo looking? A lot of people in town?"

"Not really—it's pretty slow," I answered. He looked tired. "How ya holding up?"

"Yeah? You've been hooking up with any nice *esperanzas*?" he said.

"Nah, not much time for that."

He watched everything in the room, including what was behind him. There was a wild desperation, almost a panic, in his eyes that wasn't there before. I wanted to stop talking about superficial things and reach the place where that was coming from.

"Okay, so tell me about it in here, Joey," I said.

He laughed. "It sucks, Normando, what do you want me to tell you? I can't wait to get the fuck out."

"Well, like what does your typical day look like?"

"Not much going on—I keep to myself and sleep as much as possible. Other than that, it's always the same."

A teenage prisoner wearing nice Air Jordans sat down next to Pistol.

"Hey man, you live Tamarindo? My cousin live! Tell Armando he cousin Raul say pura vida! You speaks Spanish?" he said. I promised to ask around for Armando. The kid hung around for a while, excited that I knew a few words of Spanish slang and lived in Tamarindo. Pistol gave him a glance and a head nod and the guy said, *"Hasta luego, hermano—see you later, bro,"* and scooted off.

"He's not a bad guy," Pistol said.

"Yeah? You have a few friends in here?"

"There's no such thing as friends in here, but most of them are okay. A group of us look out for each other." A squat monster of a Tico walked by, only about 5'8" but twice as thick as most of the other guys. He wore a dirty t-shirt over jailhouse tattoos. He nodded to Pistol and they slapped hands on the way by.

"That's Mike Tyson. That's what we call him," he laughed. "He's a good guy to have on your side."

"Yeah, I bet. What are all these guys in for?" I asked.

"All sorts of things, but mostly drug trafficking. Stealing cars, murder, you know. Assaults and rape, stuff like that usually get in and out faster. See that guy over there?" He pointed to a regular looking young man with glasses on and a book in his lap. "When he was sixteen he worked at the Marriot. On his day off he got drunk and got in a fight with his girlfriend because he thought she was cheating, and he stabbed her 42 times. The next morning he got up and went to work like nothing happened. They went to question him and he had the body in the trunk of his car. The flies gave it away."

"Damn, that's all bad."

"Yeah. He got 30 years. He went to one year of law school on the outside, so he's the jailhouse lawyer."

"It makes you wonder where he'd be if he didn't do it."

"He says I can get off on a technicality. The prosecutor in Santa Cruz wrote down the sentence as six years, but that's the old criminal code. The new one is longer. Based on that error, I might walk, as soon as next week."

"Seriously? That's great news!" I wanted to believe him, but I was skeptical. I'd heard too much bullshit in Costa Rica. "Let's keep our fingers crossed—even if that doesn't work out." I could tell that Pistol was getting uncomfortable talking about his case.

"Yeah, but I have to pay him to help with my case, so I need more money. Tell my mom and bring in 60,000 next week."

A prisoner interrupted us by putting a clipboard in front of me with a row of numbers on it.

"What's this? Que es ese?" I asked.

"*La lotteria*," he encouraged. I looked at Pistol, but he just shrugged. I shook my head no and Pistol shooed him away.

"Everyone's got their thing in here. He's the jailhouse lawyer, other guys sneak dope in, some guys sell it, some guys are the muscle. Some guys cook, you get it."

"I get it. So what can you do in here?"

"Teach English. We play a game like Scrabble every day and when I use a Spanish word I get double the points and when they use an English word the same thing."

"That's great, Pistol," I said. I finally found something positive for him and wanted to encourage it. "Since you were in education on the outside, maybe they'll let you do formal classes and get credit toward your time."

"And I teach them how to grow weed."

We all smoked weed when we were younger. When I was in college, I was a first-class high-ass—bong hits before class, or when I skipped class I'd smoke and listen to Counting Crows and write horrible poetry. Hey, don't make that face—it was a weird time in my life. After (barely) graduating college, I moved out to Colorado and found out that those cats took their weed seriously. Already by then the kind bud was too strong for me, spinning me out and fraying my nerves. I was the conservative guy in town at the ripe old age of 24, the only one of our friends who had a real job, didn't smoke often, and ate three servings of vegetables a day.

Good thing I met my buddy Reilly, a mongo redneck from Illinois who owned plenty of guns and drove Harleys. He knew everyone in town and was deep in the marijuana scene, but treated it like a business. Together we were the anti-hippies, and had more fun than you can imagine tormenting them. Those poor Patchouli-wearing, falafel-eating burn-outs didn't know what to make of us. When we went to concerts at Red Rocks amphitheater—Phish, Dave Matthews, and Rusted Root—we strolled around the parking lot and the hipsters automatically assumed that we were undercover cops. They'd get wide-eyed and run away like we were Frankenstein and they were villagers, our presence alone giving more than one hipster a bad acid trip. Reilly and I joked that we should start rolling up on people like we were 5-0 and confiscate their drugs.

Pistol was Reilly's roommate. We got along great because he was from the east coast, too, and hot damn, he was fun to hang out with. Weed was everywhere because, after all, it was Colorado, but we were considered the clean-cut guys because we weren't dirty tree huggers and liked to booze and didn't mess with coke or heroin. I don't remember Pistol smoking any more than everyone else, which is to say all the time.

"These guys all want to learn how to grow weed from me. They read about my case in the paper and it was on national TV. No one in this country knows anything about weed, so I teach them how to grow a little at a time if they're cool with me. Of course I make it seem more complicated than it is."

"That's crazy. So do...do they still smoke sometimes in here?" I meant *him*, of course.

"What do you think?" he said sarcastically. "That's all there is to do in here—smoke and read and sleep."

"Well, you could work out—even if it was pushups and simple stuff. Or write a book. I'll bring you notebooks and you should definitely write a book." He dismissed those activities with a wave of his hand. I realized that he wasn't looking for a lecture on constructive activities like I was his summer camp counselor:

"Welcome to Camp Tico Hell! Archery is at 10:00 a.m., then we'll make bird feeders out of acorns, and after lunch we'll learn how to properly file down your toothbrush so you can earn your Shanking Badge! Yippeeee!

"They just busted someone bringing a lot of coke in so they've locked down the whole place and tossed our cells. The whole jail's been dry for four days, no weed at all. I've been smoking every day for twenty years and this is driving me nuts."

"What's the longest you've gone without smoking in your whole life?" I asked.

"Including now, in jail?" he asked.

"Yeah."

"Four days."

I was pretty shocked that he was still smoking weed in jail. That's what he got *caught* for, and I just assumed that the experience had scared him straight, at least until he got out. No wonder he needed so much money in there.

"Pistol, you might want to think about leaving it alone," I said.

His face twisted up into a scowl. He wanted to say something but stopped himself, and then eased into a smile again. "Yeah, it's not that easy, Norm."

I left it be.

More people came and went as we talked. A nice family offered us chicken and rice. He told me more:

He was getting a prison education every day. The other prisoners gave him a lot of cred as the weed expert, and that had kept him safe so far. Most of the guys were low-level coke mules who transported stuff from point A to point B for the bigger traffickers. Every day they got busted with eighteen wheelers, boats, and warehouses full of coke—thousands of kilos. They only got a few dollars for moving a huge amount of product, something like $1,500 per kilo. There wasn't much fat on the bone for the deliveryman. There were a few big hitters in the jail—Columbians and cartel and MS13 from Guatemala or Honduras, but they usually were smart enough to have someone else do their dirty work, or could violently intimidate witnesses and judges and throw so much money around that they were above the law. For the rest of those poor schleps it was toss-up between feeding their families or doing ten years; they'd rolled the dice and lost.

Pistol went into one of the bags I'd brought and pulled out a soggy Whopper and loose fries. He ate as we talked. It was almost one o'clock and I hadn't had anything all day but coffee and a spoonful of peanut butter. I looked at his Whopper as he ate it. Mike Tyson walked by and he gave one of the extras to him, who took it with much thanks and walked away. There was still one left. My stomach growled. I thought about asking him for the extra Whopper, but I stopped myself. What the hell was I thinking? What kind of asshole brings his poor friend food in jail and then wants to eat it? My life was all blissful luxury compared to his. He saw me looking.

"Want some fries, bro?" he offered.

"Nah, I'm cool," I said. "I'll eat on the way back to Tama."

"You're not hungry? I can fix you up a Cup-o-Soup quickly if you want?"

"No, no thanks, Pistol. But how do you make all this stuff I bring, anyways? I never thought about it."

"They have microwaves in the cafeteria, but only trustees can use them. But we cook all kinds of things. You can make Cup-o-Soups and Ramen by taking apart the outlets, and putting both contact wires in the water at the same time. It heats up quickly and actually works great. You sure you don't want some?"

I felt subhuman for wanting that Whopper, like a bastard for judging him. So what if he was still smoking weed? Of course he would do whatever he could in that hellhole to help the time pass. Anything. Wouldn't I do the same? But I couldn't help it—what the fuck had he been thinking? He'd broken his mother's heart and she was eating leftovers out of the freezer because they didn't have enough money. And now everyone was bending over backwards to visit him and do his errands and bring him money in jail. The whole circus revolved around him, and he was draining his parent's retirement funds so he could stay high in jail. Clinical words like "enabling" came to mind, but they didn't seem to have any meaning in here. Of course I would smoke weed, too, if it made the time easier, but that didn't make it right.

"I'm okay, thanks." I let him eat his Whopper in peace and told him more about the shit show that was my living arrangement with Tania in Tamarindo, my plans to write a book, and how the Phillies were in first place and had just traded for Hunter Pence. He loved all of it, starved for information from the outside. It was one o'clock, so the guards yelled for everyone to leave.

"Hang in there. Take it slow and I'll see you in the next week or two," I told him as I got up.

"Try and come next week—the money," he said. I nodded that I would and started to walk out. "And thanks, Normando," he called out. "I appreciate it, bro."

"I know you do." I smiled.

I skipped Burger King on the way home and raced right for the ocean.

CHAPTER 9

THE ANGRY, UNWASHED MOB

I walked down to the local Internet office in town, Claro, but they weren't open because it was lunchtime. I came back later but they still weren't open because it was siesta time. Then the next day was a national holiday so they were closed, though no one could figure out which holiday it actually was. Tania was supposed to set up the Internet by the time I got down there, but she'd been too busy. I completely understood—it takes a lot of time out of your day to drink beer in lingerie and sue someone. An Internet connection was crucial to me because it was my only way to stay in touch with my family and friends back in the States, easing my homesickness. I also needed to get emails and use Skype to tie up loose ends with my former job, and download eBooks and movies to keep me company at night when there was nothing else to do. Disco liked romantic comedies.

After eight more trips to Claro, where two clueless local gals bore the brunt of my mounting frustration, I still had no working Internet connection. Finally they said they'd send out a work crew *ahorita*—right now—to hook it up. Two days later, they showed up. "*Big problems*," the guy told me as he wiped sweat from his face and shook his head, "*muchas problemas*." For some reason, my apartment had been built without the necessary cables running underground from the junction box, so another crew had to come out to run the cables. They'd be there *ahorita*. They arrived the following Monday and uncovered a junction box buried in the front lawn to reveal a spaghetti of electric wires and cables, none of them insulated, wrapped in PVC, or labeled.

They couldn't figure it out so they left the box open, but it rained like the dickens that afternoon. The box filled up with dirty water until the cables were submerged. I couldn't believe they would have un-insulated electric currents floating around in water, but they said the box filled up like that every time it rained and it was no big deal. No wonder the lights flickered. Eventually, after hacking through the walls of my apartment with handsaws and sledgehammers, the lines were installed and they equipped me with a modem and promised that everything worked fine. It didn't. I marched down to the office and when they saw me coming they tried to put a *Cerrado*—Closed—sign in the window, but I squeezed in. It turns out that the modem needed to be configured but no one at the office knew the correct code, so we had to wait for a supervisor from Santa Cruz to come into town. But they would get it for me…I know, I know, *ahorita*.

After a three-week odyssey the Internet finally worked. It was such a relief to be able to check on my mom and Facebook my friends without trekking out of the house to a restaurant. But the challenges didn't stop there. Any given day the Internet might be out, or the electricity, or even the water. Usually it had been shut off because of nonpayment.

"So, where are the statements for the bills?" I asked Tania. "What day of the month do they get mailed to us?"

"They don't."

"They don't what?"

"They don't mail us the bills."

"The cable, electric, Internet, and water bills aren't mailed to us?" I asked, "Oh, so we can see them online?" Costa Rica must have a paperless billing system that was environmentally friendly—how cool!

"No, I mean we never get a bill," Tania answered.

"If we don't get the bill then how do we know how much we have to pay, or when?"

"Ummm…" She thought about it, as if for the first time. *"We sort of don't know. We just have to go down to the grocery store and check."*

"What's at the grocery store?"

"That's where everyone goes to pay their bills."

Actually, that seemed pretty convenient.

"But how do you know *when* to go pay it?"

"Because it will get shut off, I guess," she shrugged.

"So let me get this straight—they don't mail us the bills and we don't know how much they are or when they're due but we just have to head down to the grocery store every month to pay once they get shut off?"

"Yeah," she said.

"Sounds about right."

We never knew when a work crew in a white pickup truck might drive up and shut everything off. Usually it happened on the hottest days or before a long weekend. I'd light candles and wash the sand off Disco or do dishes with the hose in the grassy common area. Instead of taking a shower I'd jump in the pool or the ocean. I'd buy bottled water to brush my teeth and fill a five-gallon bucket from the hose and lug it up three flights of stairs to flush the toilet.

Actually it was pretty fun, not knowing what curve ball would be thrown at you next and having to adapt, except when the Internet went out.

When we were shut down Tania and I would run down to the grocery store and wait in line to check our account. They'd look up on their computer how much we owed and we hoped that we had enough money on us to pay. Actually, I should say we hoped that *I* had that much money because, of course, Tania was always coming up short. I had to run to the bank and wait in line and then back to store to pay the bill.

We'd spend the rest of the day looking around town for the work crew because they were the only ones who could manually turn our water or electric back on. The rest of the people in town did the same. No one wanted to pay their bill, nor did so regularly, but when their services got cut off there were flocks of angry and unwashed people running to the grocery store. They waited in long lines to pay, got their receipts, and sprinted around looking for the two guys in the truck. Whole mobs of people cursed and sweated profusely as it got closer to midday, chasing the whereabouts of the servicemen.

"Hey, compadre, I saw the truck going toward Casa Sueno apartments an hour ago," their neighbor would yell, and the gang of Ticos with bed head would chase after them.

"Oh yeah, they were up by my brother's house around lunchtime," said the security guard outside the car rental place, and the whole mob would flip directions and start running again.

Most of the time the servicemen were hiding out, taking siestas in the shade near the beach. But when they showed their faces in town they'd have a crowd of irritated Ticos yelling, begging, and bribing them to come to their home first to turn on their utilities, like a bunch of little kids sprinting to catch up to the ice cream truck. The whole thing looked like an old Monkees music video in fast motion with frantic people running around in every direction bumping into each other.

I could only imagine the wasted time, money, and manpower in using this system—or lack of system—but in Costa Rica, and especially out there in the provinces, things didn't operate based on logic. As long as there was ocean and sun nothing else needed fixing, and that was fine by me…as long as the Internet worked.

CHAPTER 10

GET LOCAL

The biggest badge of honor you could earn in Tamarindo was to be considered a local. It meant everything. It was an elusive designation because there wasn't exactly a checklist of requirements you could follow. Instead, the native sons voted their consensus in the scorching streets, on a whisper when you walked by, or on the dance floor at Pacifico's on reggae night where people were going just about mad with sex.

I'm not talking about gaining citizenship of the country but being considered worthy of "local" status. For those gringos and international visitors who stayed long enough, and went through the same sufferings and joys as every other real Tamarindian, they might just earn their place by the fire.

I did not resemble a local in any way—I was chubby, where most of the Tama guys were lean like Greek statues from paddling in the waves all day with the caloric intake of approximately three-fourths of an apple. My hair was cropped short; I didn't have sun-kissed dreadlocks or a surf fro. I had a farmer's tan. I took regular showers. I didn't ingest a large amount of drugs or drink every night, staying out until 4:00 a.m. To the contrary, I woke up so early that most others were just coming home. I sweated and sweated and sweated more. Mosquitos loved me. I used my air conditioner every chance I got. I definitely was not "local."

The favorite sport in Tamarindo was surfing. Number two was surfing, followed by surfing coming in third, then maybe beer pong. The surefire way to earn your local wings was to be a good surfer, so if you could shred some waves you'd be accepted into the Tama hierarchy immediately. For the rest of us, there was a complex structure of indoctrination that made winning "Most Popular" in an all girl's junior high school look easy.

I didn't surf so I had my work cut out for me. I loved the ocean, free swimming in huge waves for hours that would have drowned a lot of surfers, but I never pretended to be a surfer, so I'd have to earn my local status some other way. At first I tried to take my clues from others like me.

There were a good number of Americans down there. The Costa Ricans called us "gringos," a racist, derogatory term meant as a scalding insult. After a while, we called ourselves "gringos," too.

There was Sarah Long, a cute surfer chick from SoCal who worked for Robert August; Big Chuck the Chef; Gringo Grant, a tall cup of water from Fresno who eventually bought Bar One; Sarita from Rhode Island, who owned a great little café, and her chef boyfriend, Jason; a retired Lt. Colonel named Trapp, who puffed reefer and fished every day; Mack White, the friendly beer hound; Ben, who had a mohawk and ran Sharkey's Bar; Cornejo, who had a mohawk and bartended at Kahiki's; "The Buzz," a petite blonde girl who spoke Spanish with a thick Southern accent and had a penchant for drinking Ticos under the table; Jamie Peligro, the old school rock n' roller who ran the little bookstore in town; Chris, who ran the real estate office and was getting sued; my sweet neighbor, Sarah; and cantankerous, rotund Doug, with his dog, Pinta.

None of us could hack it back in the States. We were all running from something—criminal records, tax collectors, exes who'd smeared our hearts through hometown streets, the reoccurring nightmare of working nine to five for the next 40 years and slowly dying of boredom, sky-high recreational drug prices, the scorn of being functional alcoholics, the inability to get laid, or deep emotional problems. Or, in my case, all of the above. But in Tama it was okay to be different—everyone was; it was our land of misfit toys. We'd all decided to park our short buses there, and it made for a hell of an entertaining tailgating party. With our same mental states we were considered sub-normal back in the States, but since we lived in Costa Rica, it made us sort of…cool.

Even though our intentions were to settle in and enjoy Costa Rica as long as humanly possible, we were only granted 90-day tourist visas. Officially, we were just vacationers on a loooong holiday. Every three months we had to leave Costa Rica to get an exit stamp on our passports and then return on another 90-day tourist visa. This was called the "Border Shuffle." It didn't matter where we went as long as we left the country, but the closest border was with Nicaragua, a two-hour trip to the north, at *Peñas Blancas*.

There were plenty of gringos who came to Tama and couldn't cut it—the majority, in fact. Only a rare few stuck it out and became local. The average pale-faced couple showed up for vacation and bought into the dream of living the easy-breezy life in paradise. They moved back to Tamarindo and bought a ridiculously overpriced condo with a nice pool and had the wonderful idea of opening a surf shop, bikini shop, or restaurant. Conveniently, there were dozens of those same establishments going out of business nearby, so it was easy to scoop one up and pour their life savings into it and reopen the doors three months behind schedule. Costa Rica made it damn near impossible to start a business as a gringo, so they got a very honest and trustworthy Tico to be on the paperwork with them. Ahhh, paradise.

Fast forward six months and the shop was hemorrhaging money and going out of business, the Tico ripped them off, their condo was falling apart and had frogs in the pool, their marriage was failing because of infidelity, and they both had vicious coke problems. They headed back to the States soon after that, wiped out and ready for the good life back in civilization. Ahhh, civilization.

For those who did stick around job opportunities were limited. The only time you could make good money was during the high tourist seasons: Christmas, New Years, spring break, and Semana Santa—Easter. Most of the gringos in Tamarindo were personal chefs. From what I could see, "PERSONAL CHEF" was some arcane code for "unemployed and not really looking; doing a lot of drugs and sitting around with skin the color of an asthmatic fat kid in Minnesota even though living in the tropics." I conducted an official poll and determined that 89.4% of the residents of Tamarindo were either personal chefs, masseuses, or an instructor of some sort (yoga if you were a girl, surf if a boy, Spanish non-sex specific). 21.7% of the gringo population was some sort of combination of chef-masseuse, masseuse-surf instructor, yoga-chef, etc. 6% were all of the above. A few gringos did manage to get steady jobs, like teaching at the school in Villareal, where they earned $700 a month.

You could acquire things to speed up the process of being accepted as a local. Getting a bicycle helped, getting a motorcycle or ATV really moved you along, and owning a car meant you were stuck there forever. You could get a post office box in Villareal. A Costa Rican driver's license was a great thing to have, but mostly just for bragging rights when you were in the States because it had no practical use in the country itself. If you got pulled over the cops were only interested in a 20,000 *Colones* bribe (each), not if you were qualified and licensed to actually operate the vehicle.

To be considered a local it was recommended you get a girlfriend, then another. Girls doubled this quota with their boyfriends. Having a dog definitely helped, so you could play with him on the beach at sunset in sight of the real locals, who would remember the dog's name but never notice the owner alone. A nasty coke habit came in handy to be seen as local, as did puffing ganja every day. If you caught dengue, like the Danish girl in apartment #17, you got special local consideration, as you did if you got stung by a scorpion or had a run in with a crocodile.

Yup, I had a long way to go.

It took me a long time to get my local card, but in those first weeks I found a wonderful way to jumpstart the process: Tourist Abuse. The best way to distance myself from the bottom of the totem pole was to mercilessly tease the flocks of tourists in town, who were, by definition, *anti*-locals.

Tamarindo was already a hot-spot for international tourism but thanks to the expansion of the Liberia airport, more Americans were heading there daily. They were surfers but also folks getting married, their wedding parties, honeymooners, divorcees, church groups, college kids on spring break, nature enthusiasts, retirees, brothas who spilled over from Brazil since it became too expensive, and office slaves using their precious vacay wisely.

They wanted to get as tan as Somalians and as drunk as college freshman, drowning out any haunting recollection of their drab work-a-day lives. The tourists would make some questionable decision, behavior they would never exhibit in a million years back in the States. Of course that was entertaining, but sometimes their behavior was downright deplorable. That's when it got *really* fun.

Tamarindo had statues all over town, three-foot-high cement renditions of indigenous deities, similar to what you might see in Mexico. These anatomically-correct figures were good omens to fertility, abundance, and a good harvest. They stood along the sidewalk in front of the Estrella Hotel and beside their beautiful pool. Well, one time a tour group of middle-aged women from the U.S. began buggering the poor statues. These gringas got so blotto on strawberry daiquiris that they started simulating fellatio on the statues with Kool-Aid red tongues. They snapped photos while they pretended to ride them reverse cowgirl style, yelling with the uninhibited glee of menopausal crazy cat ladies in a private screening of Magic Mike. The blushing Tico workers thought it was funny at first, but recoiled in horror when a legal secretary from Stockton started shooting strawberry daiquiri out of one of the statue's members, the emissions landing in the shallow end of the pool and turning the water pink. When she was done she lit up a cigarette and jammed it in the crack of his mouth. Hotel security arrived in time to find a plus-sized lady hanging in midair off a statue's sizable *pinga* by the swim-up bar. They tried to pull her off but she fought to hold on with both hands, yelling that she hadn't had one that big in decades and there was no way she was letting go.

Reports of the incident so offended Viktor, the German owner of the Estrella, that the next morning he ordered his staff to cut the *pinga* off every statue in town. A team of maintenance men, scratching their heads at the request, drove around town with a Sawzall and publically dismembered every one of those poor male statues. They had to use a chainsaw for the big one by the fountain. To this day you'll see neatly cut stubs on the statues all over Tamarindo, their severed *pingas* stored in a cardboard box on the top shelf in the maintenance shack. They didn't have the heart to throw them out, secretly hoping that one day the work order would come down to Super Glue them back on.

The tourists stayed for a week and then disappeared, and I was just another character on their fantasy island. Our whole relationship was condensed to six nights and seven days and then the next plane-load came in. For a tourist provocateur like myself it was like having Christmas every week, with brand new toys to play with.

I acted aloof toward the tourists, taking so long to answer their questions that it became socially awkward, like I was on some tropical time clock and couldn't be bothered. "Shhhh...don't speak to me right now—I'm checking the position of the sun and calculating high tide." I avoided them as if they had horrible contagious diseases (which they probably would upon departure) and perpetuated this whole mellow-surfer-beachy-weed-smoking-bald-spot-Rasta-genius-writer-dude persona, though everyone in town knew I was none of those things (except balding). I'd only lived there six weeks, but as far as they knew, I'd been stuck to Tamarindo like a barnacle for ages.

I could see them coming all the way across town, with their off-the-rack fedoras and floral print shirts like massacred shower curtains. They'd stop me for information because I *looked* like them but walked through town slowly, yapping with the locals.

"Excuse me, yes, um, which way is the beach?" they asked.

"Que? La playa?" I'd say.

"Oh, I'm sorry—do you speak English?"

"Just a little bit."

"Well, we're looking for the *BEACH*."

"Okay, just turn left and walk until you hit water and the look up and down for 500 miles—you can't miss it."

"Oh, thank you!"

"*Pura vida*."

"Oh, Arthur, he said that 'puta vida' thing we read about in the guidebook! Wow, everyone here is so friendly! Arthur, aren't they SO FRIEDNLY?!"

The tourists always *wanted* something: jet skis, horseback riding, yoga, a tramp stamp with "pura vida" spelled out, hand-woven friendship bracelets, deep sea fishing, trips to the jungle, trips to the volcanoes, trips to the mud baths, surfing, paddle boarding, booze cruises, zip lining—Jesus, it never stopped. They wanted to cram a lifetime of the tropics into one week. Everything was a photo op. To miss a photo of something would send them to the mental asylum, a moaning sack of regrets.

"Oh, look honey, a parrot! Just lovely! Is it real? Wow it is! It's a real Costa Rican parrot! Quick, grab the camera. No, it's in the bag. The OTHER bag! Look, it flaps its wings! Hello, Mister Parrot! Can you say something? No not YOU, Arthur! Well, take the picture then! Wait—does my hair look okay? The battery? I put it in there, too. No, YOU forgot to charge that one. Quick! Arthur, grab the God damn camera! TAKE IT already—it's flying AWAY! OH MY GOD, YOU MISSED THE PICTURE OF THE REAL COSTA RICAN PARROT!!! YOU FUCKING BASTARD, ARTHUR, I HATE YOU!!!"

I assumed they would file for divorce immediately upon returning to the States; how could they *not* after displaying that kind of behavior in public?

Poor Arthur. He looked so tired. Walking up and down carrying shopping bags filled with $40 ashtrays (which were really just overturned seashells) and t-shirts that would shrink to nothing the first time they went through the dryer. The poor man just wanted to drink rum and lie in the sun and take a nap in peace for the first time since the day he got married, but he was doomed to spend his vacation trying to snap the perfect photo of his wife jumping in the air at sunset and paying off Mariachis in white pants to leave him alone during dinner. I felt for him.

Whenever possible I tried to set the tourists up for good-natured joshing, and possibly infectious diseases, with my Monkey Champagne trick. The tourists certainly made it easy. I get it—monkeys are really cool.

"Excuse me, sir? Hello? Yes, do you speak *English*?"

"Dude, I just talked to you like two hours ago."

"Oh, yes, you are the friendly one who pointed us to the..."

"The *BEACH*, yeah. Did ya find it?"

"Arthur, just ASK HIM! It's too hot out here! It didn't say it was going to be this hot in the brochure! Get it over with!"

"Okay, okay…I was *getting* to it. Jesus, woman. Okay, kind sir, do you know where we might be able to see…*MONKEYS*?"

They said *m-o-n-k-e-y-s* like they were some little mythical Leprechauns who would give them a pot of gold and a hand job if discovered. I'd tell them where a family of Howler monkeys always hung out—in the grove of trees near the shack where fishermen unloaded their catch. But I made sure they knew that approaching monkeys was *very* tricky—if they wanted a photo then it was important that they stand directly under them and tilt their heads back and make little "Oh" sounds. No, not like that, with your mouth wider—like "OHHHH." Good. This was CRUCIAL, or else the monkeys might scamper away. Wifey was already running after them, shrieking in ecstasy at the thought of a real photo of monkeys on her screensaver at work, Hubby following in tow with all of those shopping bags bouncing. Sure enough, they found the family of monkeys high up in those trees just like I told them. They stood directly under them and made "OHHHHH" sounds with their mouths wide open and…like clockwork, the monkeys peed on them.

Monkey Champagne.

If shenanigans like that didn't endear me to the locals then nothing would.

If a Spanish speaker didn't understand what they were saying, they'd talk s-l-o-w-e-r and LOUDER to try and make others magically understand. Apparently they didn't know the difference between someone who spoke another language and someone who was deaf. I pretended to not understand, as well, just to torment them.

"Hello there! Hellllllllooooooo! Excuse me, sir. Yes, do you speak *AMERICAN*?"

I looked at them blankly.

"We need to find some sunscreen. Do you know where they sell that?"

I shrugged like I didn't understand.

"Suuuuunnnnnnn scrreeeeeeeen. My husband-O is SUNBURNT-O."

Arthur did look like he had a fourth degree burn everywhere but his testicles. I grunted and pointed to my ears.

"*Suuuunnnnnn Screeeeeeeennnnnn-O*! Do *YOUR* people use *SUNNNNNNNNNN SCREEEEEEEEEEEENNNNNNNN-O?!!!!*" She started an elaborate reenactment of the history of sunscreen and all its uses like a Mayan war dance, pointing to the sun and trickling her fingers downwards to illustrate the harmful rays and then grabbing Arthur's face and showing how one would apply the crème. It was quite impressive theater, actually.

"JESUS CHRIST, ARTHUR, you said he looked like he spoke American. Where can we get any HELP around here?! No BUENGO!!!!" She was really losing it now, speaking in tongues. "He doesn't even know what SUNNNNNNNN SCREEEEEEEEEENNNNNN-O is!!!!"

"Lady, please, I'm from Connecticut," I said and walked away, leaving them in stunned silence. The quiet was nice.

At that rate, I could just *feel* myself becoming more local. However, if I saw a tourist *really* disrespecting my new homeland, *insisting* on being the ugly American, then I'd resort to the cruelest abuse of all to defend my turf:

"Excuse me, is it okay to drink the local tap water?"

"Why, yes. I highly encourage it."

CHAPTER 11

THE CRITTERS

On the dusty road rising from the center of Tamarindo sat a row of hostels. I passed them when I walked to the gym. They got progressively cheaper and rattier the farther up I went. La Botella de Leche was owned by Argentines, simple and clean, the only one with a swimming pool. Next was Chocolate, two stories high with peeling paint balconies and signs of a landscaper who was drunk, but at least on duty. Then there was Pura Vida, with its cool name and surfboards hanging from the trees but bedbugs. The hostels kept going until I reached the last one on the crest of the hill, before the road wound out the backside of town, past the cemetery, and into the jungle, nothing more than a cluster of shacks called Las Brujas—the Witches.

I never saw any sign of life at Las Brujas except one moonless night when jugglers and fire dancers emerged, spinning their arcane arts against the pitch black. The hostel grounds were filled with gypsy teenagers who travelled on karma alone and couldn't even afford proper drugs. The girls asked for money because they hadn't eaten in two days while their boyfriends played guitar and wore layers of hand-spun clothes and knit caps despite the heat.

That row of hostels intrigued me. It was like life; you started out somewhere and maybe you'd move up or down and end up somewhere else, but you were always better off than someone else. Then there were those of us who hit the end of the line and had nowhere else to go: Las Brujas.

Tamarindo was like that row of hostels, an ecosystem where everyone fit in somewhere; even the Critters had a place. The "Critters" was a not-so-complimentary name for all of the street hustlers: the part-time surfers, full-time partiers, touts, hawks, and petty dealers who infested the town.

At first I found it a tad offensive, but as everyone used it, just like the term "gringos," it became apparent that political correctness had no place in Tama. The Critters were everywhere, popping up out of nowhere at exactly the most inopportune times. They made a living by chatting up the tourists and selling them on hostels, surf lessons, taxi rides to the airport, zip lining, etc. then getting a kickback from the business owners.

Under cover of darkness, the tourists' appetites grew more primal. The Critters were on cruise control all day, lazing on the beach and hustling around town between siestas, but at night they punched the clock and their work shift really began.

Vacationers wanted marijuana, so they sold them bags that were horribly underweight and overpriced. They wanted hookers, so the Critters whistled over to China and her sisters, or the Columbian crew if they had deeper pockets and wanted lookers. Businessmen looking to show off wanted bottles of rum, Cuban cigars, and a VIP booth at the Disco Aqua. Every night they filled the demand for uppers, downers, crack, GHP, roofies, Viagra, Ketamin, and Chiclets, but most of all they wanted cocaine.

Always cocaine, lots of cocaine, a blizzard in the tropics. They were looking for that "Ohhhhh good God DAMNNNNNNN" rocket ship blast-off. The Critters would get the real stuff on consignment and cut it with so much baking soda that you were better off making a lemon Bundt cake than snorting it. Bathroom stalls were their corner offices. Cocaine fueled the night in Tamarindo, and on weekends the sun wouldn't rise without it.

I found most of the Critters to be hilarious, used-car salesmen without the cars, able to offend a tourist in five languages. They weren't dangerous at all...unless they were drinking Guaro, or they were jaw-grinding whacked out on their own blow, or it was the rainy season, or they sobered up and realized they hadn't eaten in a day, or they were coming down from a bad one. Then they were hair-trigger irritable and capable of expressing their feelings physically. The Critters always had an angle. They were hyenas in the jungle, looking for a weak straggler from the herd.

In that tiny beach town in the tropics there was no hiding—you saw everyone every day. Most gringos just ignored the more unsavory elements in Tama, like the Critters. I couldn't blame them, but that wasn't me. To me, arrogance was the ultimate sin—it was their country and who the hell was I to come there and look down on anyone? There would come a time when you passed them on the road and it was just the two of you with no streetlights, and then you'd be accountable for your own karma.

So I devised a conscious strategy how to deal with everyone in town. I decided to kill 'em with kindness. I'd say "hello" to everyone, no matter who they were, even the Critters and dealers. I'd show respect to them at 2:00 p.m. and hope that they remembered me at 2:00 a.m. But sometimes the most dangerous word you could utter in Tamarindo was, "Hi."

A hustler named Fedor was my favorite—he both intrigued and scared me. Short, shirtless, with bad skin and scars, he was from Alajuela in San Jose, a tough neighborhood by the airport. He spoke great English, self-taught by watching U.S. television shows with subtitles. Fedor was a cool guy when he was sober—you might even call him sweet if you didn't know his potential—but when he was drunk or angry, a switch flipped inside of him. Then he made it very clear that he hated gringos and wasn't afraid to show it with his fists. Or a bottle. Or a screwdriver. But he was just as eager to do the job with his bare hands because it would take longer, and he had a lot of anger to burn through.

When I was there on vacation, he saw me dancing with Lena at Pacifico's. Lena introduced us and he squeezed my hand too hard. He was swaying drunk but locked in on me.

"Hey, gringo. Do you know this is my sister? You better not do bad to her, gringo. Hey, listen to me. She is my friend."

"Yeah, relax, Fedor. *Yo entiendo.*"

"No, no, look at me. You listen, gringo." He moved his face closer to mine. It was bathed red in the lights of the dance floor.

"I hear you, no problem Fedor. It's *todo bien*," I laughed nervously, and took a sip of my beer.

"You are big, but I see in your eyes you are scared. Don't you forget." Damn right I was scared—people who have nothing to lose are always the most dangerous. There's no hesitation; they aren't burdened by a thought process before they act. For months, his words, his locked-in stare, visited me. Damn, I was as soft as margarine in the sun.

Later on, when I moved there, I realized I had to figure the pieces on the chessboard before I started making moves. I fretted running into Fedor because I was sure there would be a confrontation. Who knows what Lena told him? Maybe I could avoid him? Not likely—I ran into him approximately 2.5 hours into my stay in town at the hardware store. He recognized me and came over. I grabbed the closest item off the shelves, ready to rap him on the head with it, but unfortunately it was a rubber toilet plunger. Not usually my weapon of choice.

"Hey, man, I remember you! How are you, bro? Good to see you in Tama again—welcome back!" he said with a genuine smile. *"Oh, is your toilet fucked up?"* That began a mercurial friendship—we were as cool as a polar bear's toenails most of the time, but I always knew his potential to snap at any moment. I could tell there was good in him, but the devil sure was battling hard to steal his soul.

Fedor ran with a guy called Repollito, a nickname that literally means "Little Cabbage." If you did ten tequila shots, it was really foggy out, and you were ten meters away, Repo (as I called him) looked like Matt Dillon in the Flamingo Kid. Get closer and you'd see past the fedora and realize that he had a broken tooth and dead eyes—he was only 20 but looked worn out, like a janitor at a rehab clinic.

"Hey, man, your sister is so beauuuuutiful!" Repo yelled at every tourist couple walking through town. *"Hey, man, I want to marry your sister! Mi amore, where are you going?!"*

He was as slippery as the day was long. He loved fat gringas, and when he smooth-talked one out of the bars, he would strut her through town like he was walking the red carpet with a Brazilian super model. He had a way of just *being there*—in your periphery but not really on your radar, laughing at your jokes and being pretty damn entertaining himself, then inviting himself in whatever general direction your day was going, and then before you knew it, BOOM! you'd just bought him lunch. I'd be minding my business and he'd appear out of the ether and ask the loaded question: "Where are you going?" It sounded innocent enough, but once I answered, it turned out Repo was coincidentally going in the same direction. He wanted to walk with me and chat and the next thing I knew he'd leeched on and I couldn't shake him.

But I couldn't help but like Fedor and Repo, the dynamic duo, because they could outsmart, out-hustle, and outwit any ten tourists you put together. The Critters had a few goals on their daily to-do list, which they took seriously. In order of priority, they were:

1. Attempt to have sex with a gringa.
2. Get fucked up.
3. Sell something, hustle something, or steal something.
4. Get more fucked up.
5. Sleep indoors.
6. Eat.

The cheapest hostel in Tama cost $14 a night, so if they had a good night selling blow, they got to sleep in a bed. Otherwise they crashed with friends or on someone's floor. A good number of nights were spent sprawled out on benches in the skateboarding park. But most of the time it was easier to keep partying until 7:00 a.m. and then snooze on the beach.

Some of the Critters were trouble—like the three bad brothers from Villareal with surf afros. They followed around rental cars and smashed the windows or jumped tourists. I saw it a few times—one brother got in the face of an unsuspecting U.S. college kid on spring break and start talking junk while the other two or three or five stood behind him. If the kid said anything, or even twitched wrong, they'd smash him in the back of the head with a bottle. Dudes got cut open with bottles all the time. Tania came home freaked out one night because a Tico got sliced at Aqua and his intestines were spilling out as he held them in with his hand and screamed for a taxi to take him to the hospital an hour away.

The Critters always asked me for money, just a buck or two—surely I could spare it? They had an inexhaustible catalog of circumstances that warranted a small, risk-free hand out, just for the day of course. Their other game was to hit me up for beers. On the street, I played the delicate game of saying "hi" but trying to avoid them following me into a restaurant or a bar.

"Hey, buddy. How are you, my friend? What are you doing? Hey, buy me a beer please? Just one beer? They are two for one at happy hour at Nibbana's, so we can split one and I have the extra. Come onnnnnnn, man?" How could you say no to a fedora-wearing rehab janitor Matt Dillon? Most of the time it was just easier to buy one so I didn't have to deal with the stress of dodging them.

When they asked me where I was going, I learned to craft my answer carefully. I was engaged in psychological warfare with guys who huffed paint thinner and didn't own underwear. If I lied I'd surely get caught—it was such a small town that I'd be spotted because they were always in ten places at once. I couldn't just walk away because I had to play in the same sandbox as them for a whole year. Telling the truth was definitely not an option because I'd end up with one of those scrubs tagging along the rest of the day, so I attempted to confuse them.

When they asked where I was going, I looked frustrated, waving my arms vigorously in four different directions while telling them that I had to "go to Huacas to feed the dogs at Carla's because the pharmacy was closed for my special weekend medicine and I have to pay my rent but she's not at the office." Huh? That probably wouldn't shake 'em, they'd just look at me quizatively for a second, calculating their prospects of getting a free beer out of the whole operation, then announce that they wanted to come along, so I'd resort to Plan B: I told them that I had to go work. *"Work?! Oh noooo."* That got 'em backpedaling.

That was effective with all of 'em except Kenny G. That *bandido* had more jobs than the rest of them put together. Of course that wasn't his real name, but he looked exactly like Kenny G circa 1988 on the cover of his Christmas album: thin and angular with long tight-curled locks in a ponytail. All he needed was a mock turtleneck and a brass flute and he was a shoe-in for his stunt double. Kenny G worked the door every night at the Disco Aqua, dragging people in off the street and giving them a hand stamp. You also might find him renting jet skis, helping out at the hardware store, or selling pre-paid cellphones. Needless to say, he could get a tourist coke or weed if they wanted it.

During the rainy season, Fedor scored a steady job as a bus boy at the bar Voodoo, a huge victory. But he'd steal a bottle of rum from behind the bar and guzzle it down and get too drunk and then beat someone up. He'd get fired and lay low for a couple of days and then go apologize with his head down and they'd take him back. One time he beat up the bouncer, a huge, crazy Neanderthal from Rotterdam with a shaved head and tattoos all over his neck. Fedor hit him in the head with a rock until the guy was whimpering for mercy. It further reinforced my desire not to get on his bad side.

One afternoon in early September, I got caught in a rainstorm. I was at the bank, and when I came out it started dumping. I considered making a break for it back to my apartment, but I had my iPad in my backpack, which couldn't get wet, so I had to wait it out. Someone tapped me on the back and it was Mauricio, a dance-crazy Critter who'd just hustled some leftover French fries from a tourist. We talked a while as he licked catsup from his fingers, looking out at the sky and waiting for the rain to ease up. But it only poured harder. We knew we were stuck for a while, so we counted to three and bolted across the mud bath road to Voodoo next door. If we were going to get stranded, it damn well was going to be in a bar.

It looked like a few others had the same idea—Repo was there, brushing the water off his fedora, and Fedor had just gotten his job back. Soon Kenny G saw us and ran over, too. We all sat down and ordered beers and watched the street get washed away. Just when we thought it might slow down, a blast of lighting hit nearby. We all yelled, "Ohhhhhhhhh" and jumped back at the same time, then laughed and ordered another round of beers.

Sitting on the same side of the table were Fedor, Mauricio, "Little Cabbage," and Kenny G. If someone took a picture, it would look like the Last Supper of Critters. We drank more, but their money quickly ran out and everyone asked everyone else to buy them a beer until they all looked at me at the same time. Fuck stick! How do I get in these messes? I took out my credit card and ordered the next round.

The rain kept up. We got drunker. Someone ordered shots of *Guaro*—straight devil juice. Repo wanted to borrow my iPad to Skype his newest girlfriend, a tourist from Sweden whom he'd met the week before. I handed it to him reluctantly and kept one eye in his direction.

"This one is muy grande," Fedor said, puffing out his cheeks. *"She is three time the size of Repollito."* Repo pretended he was going to hit him, then stopped midair and thought the best of it. Kenny G. laughed at them both and readjusted the rubber band on his ponytail.

I didn't have headphones, so Repo had to talk to her in full earshot of the peanut gallery once they connected on Skype.

"Baby, baby, beautiful love, I want to kiss you on your big belly!" he said.

"Miguel, is that you? Oh, Repellito, I thought it was Miguel for a second," she said.

"Huh? Who is Miguel, beautiful baby?"

"No...no one. I said Repellito. Of course Repellito. It must be the Internet connection."

"Oh, momma, I miss us. I love you. I not live without," he said. *"My beautiful sweet Nutella biscuit, I want make your baby!"*

Jesus, he was pouring it on thick. Pace yourself, good man.

"What time is it over there?" she yawned.

"Don't worry the time, baby," he said. *"We have time rest of our life together."*

"I'm hungry," she said.

"I know, momma, I could just eat you too." He was really losing it now. His eyes were half-closed and he was pretending to lick the iPad.

"Repellito!" Fedor yelled. *"Get your hand above the table where we can see it!"*

"Oh my God, are you with your friends?! Can they hear me?" she said.

"Hiiiiiii, Sweden! Repellito is fucked up and wants to make your belly baby!" the rest of them chimed in.

"I don't care, I want the world to know us love," he said.

"By the way, I think you gave me a rash," she said. It sounded like she was chewing celery.

"I'll give you everything you want, mama. I promise." He gave the iPad a big hug to his chest and rocked it back and forth, sobbing. *"Aye Dios Mio! I love you so much, baby, I not live without you,"* he wailed.

"What? What's that...hello? I can't hear you. Re...Repellito...are you there?"

"Oh yeah, sorry, baby—I was hugging you."

"Oh, okay," she chewed.

"Give me big kiss, mama," and he puckered up his mealy lips and headed in slow motion toward the screen, tongue flickering. I jumped up and slapped him across the head, knocking the iPad away milliseconds before he made contact.

"Fucking A, Repo—you kiss it with those horse-shit lips you buy it!" I said.

After twenty more minutes of his sappy antics, my iPad was mercifully out of batteries. I pried it out of his hands, holding it as far away as possible with the tips of my fingers, and put it safely in my backpack. I'd have to scrub it with hand sanitizer once I got back to my apartment in case there were any stray fluids on it.

It was getting dark, so they turned on the outside lights. The rain kept on and I was spinning and scared to see my bill. We ordered *un zarpe*, the last round of beers, and then *uno mas zarpe*, and another. The street was empty except for a lone skinny tourist with a LL Bean rain poncho strolling by. The Critters waved him over—wide-eyed, fresh meat.

"Hi, fellas! How's it going today?" he said. "Mind if I sit down?"

"Bienvenidos to Tamarindo, new friend!" they said. He struggled to get his poncho off, managing to get both arms stuck through the neck hole and Kenny G had to help him out. He shook rain from his strawberry red hair.

He sat down at the table with us so we were all facing him. Which apostle from the Last Supper would he be, I thought? I didn't know many of them. Abraham? No that was something else. I knew there were the Corinthians and they were always writing letters, so maybe I would be one of them. Repo would be Joseph because he got laid about as much as Mary put out. Which one was Jesus? Probably Kenny G with all of that hair. So who was Judas? I scanned the table. We had plenty of candidates.

"So, what are you fellas up to?" Strawberry Shortcake asked.

"Oh, man, just getting fucked up and talking to fat Sweden whales!" Fedor said. *"Come have a beer with us!"*

"Oh no, I don't drink," Strawberry said. "I'm a medical student at Memphis Bible College."

"And I'm Queen of England," Repo said.

"It's Costa Rican tradition to drink when it rains," Fedor lied. *"You HAVE to,"* and looked at him hard.

"Oh, uh okay...well maybe just a few sips of light beer," the kid said.

Repo called the waiter over and ordered *Guaro* shots. I stealthily caught the waiter's attention and scribbled in the air—the international sign for "check please," so the rest of the drinks would be on Strawberry Shortcake's tab.

The *Guaro* came and he smelled it and retched and said, "I can't do it," but Fedor said "*Oh yes you can*," so he did. Once he got the shot down, he coughed and the Critters slapped him on the back and said, "*Don't worry, the next one will be easier.*" The rain was letting up so, I got ready for my escape. I'd thrown a virgin into the volcano, a sacrifice to buy my freedom, for now.

"Okay, kid, I'm outta here. These guys are like my brothers. You can trust them completely," I said, managing to keep a straight face. They beamed at him, and not one of them had flossed that day.

"Oh, okay, swell!" he said. "Gee, you Costa Rican Ticos sure are friendly!"

The Critters licked their lips.

"Yeah, we take you to Aqua tonight, man. Big party and we all get fucked up! Do you like snow?"

"Well, I went sledding with my auntie in New Hampshire last Christmas," Strawberry Shortcake said. Damn, this wasn't going to end well for him.

"Take care and have fun," I said. "And no matter what they ask, just say yes."

"Golly, this is so great," he said.

I got up to leave, backing away slowly.

"By the way, kid, what's your name?" I wanted to know what to tell the police the next day when they put his face on a milk carton.

"It's Graham," he said. We all looked at each other in disbelief. This kid was hanging with a bunch of coke peddlers in a Costa Rican jungle and his name was GRAM?!

"Yeah and I'm Kilo!" Repo hollered, *"and this is my cousin Dime Bag!"* and they all busted up and pounded the table and ordered more *Guaro* and howled at the moon.

I slipped into the shadows and disappeared. I can only imagine if Strawberry Shortcake made it through the night, but I never saw him again, and the Critters never talked about it.

CHAPTER 12

WOODEN SUBMARINES

The whole town was itching, scratching and jumping. Everyone battled the mosquitos and tried to keep dry during the heart of the rainy season. Before I left my apartment I'd remember to spray on Costa Rican cologne—Deep Woods Off. The locals were lucky because mosquitos didn't bite them as much, but there were still bedbugs and sand fleas for all of us to deal with. The Danish girl in apartment #17 contracted dengue. She got it from a mosquito bite, starting with a rash on her leg, and then the whole thing swelled up and turned black. She got to the hospital in Santa Cruz in time before they had to amputate but it took a month for the swelling to go down. In October the rain and the lack of tourists made everyone testy. Everything was for sale and the mosquitos were the only ones eating well. I'd been in town for three months and I could see my ribs again.

Whenever I went out I brought a backpack with plastic bags in it so I could cover my shoes, my laptop, or my head in case I got caught in a downpour. An umbrella just blew apart when the rain came in sideways so it wasn't even worth it.

Thursday night was reggae night at Pacifico's so I started walking toward the roundabout. I passed China and her girls, wearing cocktail dresses and big rubber boots, and said "hi." I called them out on the boots and they laughed and held up the flip-flops they carried for when they got there. Prostitutes worked every night in Tama, rain or not, a work ethic I respected. I gave them my plastic bags to keep their hair dry and we walked the rest of the way together.

They were charging cover at the door but the girls walked right in without paying, and I walked in behind them. That time of year the bars needed us more than we needed them.

The scene was hot at Pacifico's. The Critters were going wild on the dance floor, melodic reggae pounding their problems into submission. I ordered a beer and scanned the black-lit room, taking inventory of who was working, who was angling, who was too drunk and had bad energy that night, and who still looked *tranquilo*.

A girl at the bar almost fell off her stool, a good target to get roofied if she hadn't been already. I made a note to tell her friends to watch out for her. Two English guys went back to the bathroom with a Critter. In the midst of it all, some Canadian college kids danced their hearts out, oblivious that they were being watched. They thought they were in paradise. I wish I could be oblivious, too, but I knew too much.

The Lion King stepped out of the shadows. Twice the size of most Ticos, he wore his usual red tank top and red visor, golden locks spilling out. He ran the coke game in the roundabout. "*Que paso, mae*?" He walked by and nodded. He knew I wasn't a buyer but still we were cool. There was something different in his eyes that night; he looked half-crazed with adrenaline, his pupils black pin-pricks. When he shook my hand he squeezed it too hard. Jesus, he was geeked-out on his own product. I stayed clear.

The Lion King was running the show for the moment, but "*los jefes*"—the bosses—never lasted long. When things got too crazy they grabbed a bus out of town, laying low in San Jose or heading south to Playa Jaco to carve out some market share down there. Six months later I was more likely to see him in jail with Pistol than in the bar, but there'd be another head honcho stepping in and running things, or two.

During the high season the bars were filled with a balance of hunters and prey—there's a natural order, and making money is easy no matter what your angle. But once the tourists went home to their school books and nine-to-fives Tama's ecosystem leaned dangerously off kilter. There were two Critters to every tourist and three guys to every girl. Those are precarious ratios in a bar in a Third World country where everyone is coked up and drunk and the security guard at the door weighs about 150 pounds soaking wet and it only takes $10 to pay him off when he pats you down if you want to sneak a knife inside.

It's all about supply and demand and sometimes there just ain't enough to go around. On the street every Critter you pass hits you up with an invitation for weed or coke about as subtle as a wrecking ball. Sit in a taxi and before you can get the door closed they're asking you if you need coke or chicas. Surf instructors, cigar salesman, the old-school hookers who live up at the Casa Crack Apartments, and even the parking lot attendants have their hand in the yay-yo game and can hook you up with one quick whistle to their friends. The police are lazy and the hustlers are creative. One time some friends of mine were walking near the beach in broad daylight and heard someone whistling at them. They looked around but couldn't see where it was coming from. It got louder, and when they looked up they saw a guy sitting in the tree above them.

"Hey, man. Pssst, up here. You wanna buy blow? I have the best. Good price for you."

"No…no thanks, but what the hell are you doing up there?"

"If the police drive by they can't see me up here. Pura vida!" he said. Where there's a will, and a profit to be made, there's a way.

But this is all just small time.

Bless their little hearts, the Costa Rican authorities try their best to regulate their borders, but in a country where the median income is $6,000 a year and the average policeman's salary is $350 a month, for ten grand not only will they look the other way but they might just name their firstborn child after you. The last few years there's been a huge increase in policemen, and they're building more prisons to deal with overcrowding, but still they only have 10,000 prisoners in the whole country (compared to three million in the States).

There's just no way to slow down the unfathomable supply of cocaine that enters their country by speedboat, fishing boat, charter plane, helicopter, in the stomachs of human drug mules, in the luggage of prostitutes, hidden inside dolls, furniture, diapers, hollowed-out bibles, and everywhere else you can imagine. It's stored in clandestine warehouses, gutted buildings, and factories where it gets "stepped on" and repackaged for distribution.

They even transport it in wooden submarines.

Wooden submarines were first detected by law enforcement around 1993. Technically they're not submarines but semi-submersibles because they don't actually dive, but cruise along just under the water's surface. The very top of the cockpit or exhaust pipes rise above the water to access breathable air. These "narco subs" are built in clandestine shipyards hidden in the jungle, each one taking two million dollars and a year to construct. They're nearly undetectable by radar, sonar, infrared systems, or patrolling aircrafts. Most of them are handmade with wood and fiberglass, reaching 60 feet long end to end. They move pretty slowly—about seven to eleven miles per hour, powered by underwater diesel outboard motors and manned by a crew of four. They have fancy GPS systems but no bathroom.

Whether on a speedboat or a wooden submarine, the cocaína is vacuum-sealed and dropped off in the open ocean floating in 50 gallon drums with electronic location transmitters, later to be scooped out of inlets, marshes, and estuaries by local runners in fishing boats. Believe it or not the worst occupational hazard for those pick-up men isn't cops or bullets, but crocodiles. Costa Rica has a huge croc population along its wild coast and drug runners jumping in and out of the water at night serve as a tasty snack.

Each wooden submarine can transport up to ten tons of cocaine at a time. The financial windfall is staggering, almost incomprehensible. Check this out—in Columbia you can get a gram of cocaine for $2.50, $1,750 for a kilo (2.2 lbs.), and it is almost 100% pure. In Costa Rica the same gram, now 70-90% pure after it's stepped on, (which means you increased your product by 10-30% with no additional cost) will cost you $20 on the street, and a kilo is closer to $5,000. They step on the coke with Baking Soda, baby powder, or diuretic. I remember a college professor in my marketing class telling me that Arm and Hammer makes a fortune selling Baking Soda in the hood, marked up 800%. Think about it—they certainly aren't still in business by selling little boxes for 99 cents that you put in your freezer for a year.

Ninety percent of the cocaine in the United States travels this route, up through Central America and into Mexico and across the border, where it jumps up in price. By the time it gets to our streets the same gram is now two or three grams, meaning the coke is only 20-40% pure and will go for $90 per gram or $23,000 per kilo. So someone made about 50-70 grand off that original kilo for $1,750.

Keep in mind that someone is actually *doing* all that coke; for every seller there is a buyer. Or ten. Traces of cocaine can be found on four out of every five U.S. dollar bills in circulation. 35 million U.S. citizens have tried it, though only one out of four ever use it again. I'd say we have a problem, all right—a problem with the prevailing appetites of the citizens within our own borders. If no one was doing it in the U.S., then no one would buy it and therefore no one would sell it, so keep that in mind before you cloak yourself in judgment. Only a small amount gets converted to crack cocaine and sold in the hood. Most of it ends up in corner offices and country clubs, in the ashtrays of Porsches where everyone's making six figures. But there are huge racial and economic imbalances to how we combat and penalize cocaine. Crack has the exact same pharmacological makeup as cocaine (just prepared differently so it's cheaper, and smoked, not snorted) but the criminal penalties are eighty percent higher compared to the same penalty for possessing cocaine. That same imbalanced scale of justice is used to define and persecute many other drug crimes. Think about it—if Rush Limbaugh was poor and/or brown, he'd be called a heroin addict and thrown in jail, but instead he has an "Oxycotin dependency issue" and continues to do his radio show. Go figure.

Standing in a little reggae bar in a fishing *pueblo* in Costa Rica felt like a million miles away, but I was a lot closer to the source of it all. You could almost feel the chemical energy of profit, armies of desperation pressing at the borders. I was only aware of these things because I lived there and had particular insight because of Pistol's situation, but for everyone who danced with the devil and missed a step there were thousands of tourists who had a great time with no problems at all.

Does the drug trade make it dangerous in Tamarindo? Not really, if you mind your own business and keep some common sense. It was perfectly safe during the day, but at night was a different story. If you're buying coke at 4:00 a.m., getting sloppy drunk, or walking around on the beach in the dark, then you got what you deserved. But most of the tourists, especially the older couples and families, were oblivious to the game behind the game. They saw Tamarindo as an eco-paradise with glassy-eyed brown people who always seemed happy.

Everything worked fine until there was an imbalance in supply and demand or someone got the *cojones* to try and move up the food chain. Some fisherman found a body down by the river. It turned out to be a local prostitute, her hands cut off and her belly slashed open and gutted, a clear sign that she was a dope mule for someone but tried to get cute with their junk in her stomach. They found her, took what was theirs, and cut off her hands to send a message not to steal from the wrong people.

A Canadian was seen wandering around at 6:00 a.m. with blood coming from his head and died shortly after. He was partying at the afterhours spot with the wrong people. Two tourists pissed off the wrong Critters and got beaten up and knifed outside Aqua. My friend, Four Finger Fausto, told me that half of his index finger was missing because some bad dudes had sliced it off with a machete years earlier, because he owed them money when a drug deal went bad. An American girl who owns a surf shop near Witch's Rock has been missing for a month.

The bigger danger to tourists was themselves. The average weekend warrior from abroad was used to coke cut down to almost nothing, while the right stuff in Tama was three times as strong. When a tourist OD'd on coke they didn't list the accurate cause of death on the coroner's report. Instead the official story was that they either had a heart attack or slipped and fell and hit their head. Yeah, right—slipped and fell into a pile of coke. Or sometimes people just disappeared; Tama had its secrets. They didn't even need an official story when a local dealer or runner got killed—usually the body would be dumped in the estuary for the crocodiles to take care of before the police or ambulance were called.

What else did I learn about the cocaine trade while living in Tamarindo? That the Columbians ran shit.

My friend Marcello lived in Villareal. I met him through Pistol, who took me to visit him once. We met for a beer at the little local bar across from the town park, a big overgrown field of weeds and broken bottles where they erected a wooden stadium and had bullfights during the holiday season. The establishment looked like the bar scene from Star Wars, but I liked it because there was nothing touristy about it. The place was filled with ranchers carrying machetes, a few American ex-pats with bad teeth and sweaty cutoff t-shirts, and Columbians sitting in the shadows smoking cigarettes.

Marcello was late, so we sat out front where we could talk over the radio's sad songs and wait for him. Pistol and I watched ourselves because the Columbians were no joke, especially when they were drinking. A lot of them were strapped. One wrong move, you look at the wrong girl, and all hell could break loose.

Marcello showed up and said "hi" and sat down, easing the tension and turning away the stares. The waitress brought our beers and then also shots of tequila with baby turtle eggs in them, which is supposed to be good luck for fertility. He said he liked drinking there because everyone knew him and respected his family and no one bothered him when he blew lines right on the bar.

We drank and talked. He apologized for being late, but work held him up. Marcello's aunt owned a little hair salon in town and sometimes he helped her out, but their real income had deeper roots.

His family had moved from Columbia as refugees of the civil war 25 years prior, some of the first immigrants in that part of Costa Rica. They were well connected, stalwarts of the Columbian immigrant community, and therefore entrenched in the narco trade by osmosis.

Marcello was a kind, mellow guy, flashing a big smile and an easy way. He showed no signs of opulence or dealings in the coke game except for being particularly amped up at Voodoo Lounge on Wednesday nights. So how was he involved, I wondered?

"We know when the boats are coming in," he told me. Being a curious SOB, I had questions—Do they sell? How much? Do they make a lot of money? Why are they still living in a humble house in Villareal? Is his whole family in the business?—but I kept cool. Marcello didn't seem to mind talking about it but also let me know with a look that there were certain things I didn't need to know. *"We know when the boats come in,"* he said again, more slowly, and left me to figure out the rest. I got it.

He knew when the shipments came in and everything else that happened in the Columbian community in Tamarindo. So when a guy was shot a few weeks earlier, he knew what went down before the smoke cleared. My gringo friend, Trapp, was there and told me about it. He was at the late-night party spot, El Pescador, around 5:00 a.m. Two Columbian guys were drunk and high and started arguing. One took out a gun and shot the other one right in the stomach like it was nothing, then walked off casually. Trapp couldn't believe it, and he was a career Army Ranger so he'd seen some shit. Everyone crowded around the guy, trying to help and stop the bleeding, until five minutes later the shooter walked back over and took out his gun and shot him again in the chest, pop pop! finishing the job before walking away again.

But Marcello doesn't get his hands dirty and doesn't hurt anyone. He's no more guilty than the poor farmers who grow coco plants in the dry soil of the Andes Mountains a continent south, trying to feed their families. He's no more innocent than the CEOs who build prisons for profit in the U.S. and have a vested interest in making sure that business stays good. There are a million bars with ten million locals selling coke every day all over the world, but I just happened to be in one of them.

That night at Pacifico's the Lion King got into it with another Tico. It happened fast. I saw him standing by the front door and suddenly he charged another youth, a slim kid casually smoking a cigarette. I don't know what he said, who he sold to, or which wrong girl he was hitting on, but the result was like a keg of dynamite. He hit him with a thunderclap of adrenaline, 180 beats per minute pure chemical fury. The Lion King slammed into him, sending him flying back into the wall like a folding newspaper and mercilessly rained down punches and kicks. It only lasted a few seconds until the other Tico could react, scrambling away, disoriented and bloodied. He grabbed an empty beer bottle and they started to swing and dance. When they connected glass shards flew everywhere. People in the crowd screamed and started ducking and running. Fights with beer bottles were like drive-by shootings in the U.S.—the wrong people always got hit. I did what any macho real man would do: I hid behind a 90 pound Chinese tourist chick from New

Jersey. When it was over I got the hell out, but adrenaline was still in the air like an upturned wasps' nest.

I walked outside, watching a carload of Columbians flash signs and yell at the Lion King before driving off. They'd be back, but I wasn't going to wait around. I grabbed a shish-kabob from the vendor grilling outdoors and start walking back toward my apartment. The street was empty, lit only by the moon. A basehead slithered past me, wearing only one flip-flop, eyes zoned out. I crossed the street.

Farther up I ran into Marcello walking toward Pacifico's. He said, "What's up?" and we talked for a while. It was always good to see him. He asked how Pistol was doing and I asked about his mom and his family. I could tell that he was boogying because he looked pale and was clenching his teeth, but he was in a great mood and heading to the bar to meet his girlfriend and some friends.

"*Hey, Norm, can you do me a favor, hermano?*" he asked.

"Sure, what is it?"

"*Man, I'm short on cash—can you lend me $3 for a beer?*" Marcello was no Critter and I didn't mind him asking. He was practically royalty in Tamarindo and had been good to me.

"Yeah, of course, no problem." I took out my wallet and handed him the money.

"*Just until tomorrow—I'll pay you back.*"

"Don't even worry about it. It's all good, Marcello." He slapped my hand like homies do but slipped something into my palm.

"What's this?" I asked. I looked down at a baggie of bleach-white coke, tied off at the top. It would probably go for $100 in the States and looked ice-pure.

"Hey, hey, no—Marcello, no, it's cool, *hermano*—I don't want anything."

"*It's okay—just take it. I know you party. Just take it for the $3.*"

I laughed that he thought I used coke.

"Nah, I'm all set, man, I'm good for tonight." I grabbed his hand and put the baggie back in it, suddenly realizing that I was standing in the middle of the street with a well-known Columbian coke family member, passing money and a bag of coke back and forth. Someone in Tamarindo was always watching. "But thanks, man. The beer is on me." He nodded his appreciation. "And thanks for helping with Pistol, too," I said. "You know, the umbrella."

He smiled and patted me on the back. "*I do what I can for him. And you—you tell me if you ever need anything.*" I said goodbye and went back to my shish-kabob. He walked on toward the bar, red-light music pulsing into the street like blood yet to be spilled.

Just another night in the jungle, and the big cat's gotta eat.

CHAPTER 13

LOOKING FOR ANTONIO

One morning I brought coffee out to Antonio but he wasn't there. I didn't see him the next day either, but there was a new guy raking up, wearing his blue maintenance man shirt. I feared the worst; maybe he'd been fired? Or deported back to Nicaragua? How would he survive? Life was hard enough for him as it was.

But later that week Antonio was out by the pool, lying on a lounge chair in the sun with a drink in his hand. I almost didn't recognize him.

He waved me over and said "hi." I had to laugh because he looked like a tourist with his aviator sunglasses and flowery swim suit. Sitting next to him was an attractive gringa with brown hair who looked to be in her thirties. He introduced her as Shannon and she said "hi." She was an attorney from California down there visiting with her mom, Lori, who owned one of the condos. Antonio told me that she was a good friend so he'd taken two weeks vacation to hang out with them. Shannon and Lori were really nice and even invited me to dinner.

As the week went on it was clear that "friends" meant something more. They went running together every morning and hung out by the pool during the day. At night Antonio slept in their condo.

When their vacation was over Shannon went back north, but Antonio never went back to work. They were in love, he told me, and she was coming back for him soon. They were going to get married and move to California.

The new maintenance guy didn't do a good job. There were always leaves in the pool and the sidewalk went unswept. I didn't bring him coffee in the mornings—that was only for my friend Antonio. But I didn't mind—whenever I saw those leaves I thought: "How about that? Good for him."

CHAPTER 14

NEGOTIATIONS AND LOVE SONGS

I'd moved down to Costa Rica with visions of a free-loving paradise dancing in my head, soaking up the simple life where the locals trade shiny beads for beachfront property and the exotic, eligible women line up outside my door for one-night marriage tryouts. After all, I was a gringo. I must be a prize, right?

Not even a little bit.

Hitting the Tamarindo social scene was a real wakeup call because I was cold product. I wasn't in shape (though I was working hard to get there), I didn't surf, and as far as anyone could tell, I didn't have any money to throw around. Everyone else had cool hair—thick black curls or golden dreadlocks or mohawks—while I had a buzz cut with a bald spot. Furthermore, I didn't go out and get wasted every night, the only real chance for a social life in Tama. Some of the locals, like Tania and Yazmin, just couldn't understand this—they thought something was wrong with me.

Girls were into surfers and skinny dudes that had fun. And Frenchmen for some reason. Well *oui oui* all over you. Do you know how emasculating it is to lose a girl to a Frenchman, who carries a European handbag and can't bench press a baguette? That shit hurts, man—there's no bouncing back from that.

I realized early on that I didn't fit in. It looked to me like everyone had loose, devil-may-care attitudes while I'm sure I appeared too serious. Of course they didn't realize that I had some big things on my mind, like keeping my friend alive in jail, paying bills with no job, staying safe, and writing a book without knowing what the hell I was doing.

Most people in Tamarindo came and went, some in a week, some just long enough wait out the cold winters back home, so "long term" relationships were shorter than Hollywood marriages. The average age in town was around 22, so I was ancient, closer to everyone's parents' ages. When people asked and I told them, "*Yo tengo cuaranta años,*" soon, they assumed I had my Spanish numbers messed up and drew back in horror when they realized it was correct, checking me over for signs of a stroke and offering me a chair. Forty on my next birthday? Why the hell wasn't I married with 2.3 kids and a minivan like the rest of the gringos my age?

Good question—I got that a lot in the States, too. When I was in my twenties and all of my friends were getting married, I was the outcast, the bachelor pariah. But then the wave of divorces hit in our thirties and suddenly I looked like a genius; I wasn't stuck paying alimony and child support for the rest of my life. I had some friends who got married then divorced just in the year I was in Tamarindo. At a certain point you say, "Why even bother?"

In my twenties I was immature, so wild and emotionally turmoiled that I couldn't commit to regularly watering a houseplant, let alone a relationship. I'm sure I've left a wake of broken hearts and hurt feelings in my past. Now, years later, my life choices had ripped me half a world away from the comfort of the normal dating life I'd know in California. The irony was not lost on me.

Deep down I'm still a romantic. People assume I want to be single because of my transitory lifestyle but I actually love being in a good committed relationship. Unfortunately, the ones I've had just didn't work out for different reasons, and I've also dodged a few bullets that would have turned into a "future ex-wife" situations.

I still consider it a 50/50 shot that I might get married in my life; it would be great if it happened, but if not, well, that's okay too. But I wouldn't settle for the wrong person or do it for the wrong reasons—I'd rather be single and happy than married and miserable, and unfortunately, with 60% divorce rates in the United States, that seems to be becoming the rule more than the exception. If I do get married I'd guess it's to a woman from another country, or at least an immigrant who shares my more traditional values and idea of "family." The same thing goes for children, and if I don't end up having kids of my own then I feel deeply that my life calling will be to adopt a child who could really use the love, even if I'm a single dad.

Not that marriage is easy in *any* country; the Spanish word for "married" is "*casado*" and the word for "tired" is "*cansado.*" See the similarity? That's because, obviously, you are very, very tired if you're married. Don't confuse those with the word "*casada,*" a typical Costa Rican dish. I often got it jumbled and ordered a plate of fish only to have the waitress think I just proposed to her and then tell me to go take a nap.

Then again, if I went out and had fun more, I'd be able to connect with more girls and date. But the only options were travelers or Bar Stars, as I called them, the same Tica party girls who were out every night. Most guys tried to shack up with the steady stream of girls there on vacation, but the twenty-year-old blonde spring break crowd wasn't exactly my sweet spot. No way I could have a conversation with someone that young, and anyways they were always partying. I couldn't even pronounce the drugs those kids were on, which all seem to be named after breakfast cereals like "Special K," or a nondescript list of initials, like "GHP" or "MDMA" or some bullshit. Are we playing Scrabble or are we partying?! Whatever happened to good old-fashioned drugs like "weed" and "glue?"

Every blue moon there would be a single gringa closer to my age sitting at the bar, but even if she was attractive I avoided making eye contact with her—too much of a backstory. But at some point she'd end up moving over and sitting near me and, sure enough, I'd have to listen to her drone on about her messy divorce back in North Carolina and her career aspirations to become something that started with "assistant." She was there on vacation by herself and I did feel for her, so I donated 3.7% of my attention to her cause.

"...and then, after I'm a Junior Medical Assistant, I'm going to go back to school to be an orthopedist!" she said.

"Oh that's great—I just LOVE old people."

She looked confused, but just took a sip of her fishbowl-sized neon blue drink and smacked her gum.

"I really like you. I mean...you're so nice. You're such a good listener," she said.

"I'm sorry, what was that?"

"I *said* that you're a *good listener*!"

Or, if I met an attractive tourist woman on the street and stopped to chat, Pepito would pedal by on his bike and cackle at me, wagging his finger like he was Dikembe Mutombo and just blocked my shot, *"Papa Noelllll es un chico mallllooooo!"*

"Did that gay guy with the poodle in his basket just call you a bad-boy *Santa Claus*?" she'd ask, and then politely excuse herself.

So instead I'd sit down with Pepito on the bench in front of the t-shirt shop where he worked, enjoying the sun and practicing my Spanish. He told me how he was trying to save enough money to move to San Jose and enroll in university, and that his ultimate dream was to make it to the United States one day. Until then he was stuck living with Lena and working in the t-shirt shop seven days a week, though he confessed that he was doing quite well with the gringo tourists at the bar. At least *someone* was getting lucky.

It was difficult to date for other reasons, as well. The good girls left Tama for Villareal once their shifts at the banks or the stores were over in the evening. Out of the remains there were surprisingly few good-looking women there. I'm not just being a hater, if you drove through any other small town in the countryside in Costa Rica you saw more beautiful girls than there were in Tamarindo. There were probably two guys to every girl when you went out at night, and if you factored the healthy population of hookers into the equation, it was more like three to one. That's a whole lot of sausage for a veggie omelet.

Once the sun went down it was hardest to battle my solitude. I didn't want to party so all I could do was go to the gym and then watch a movie by myself. I went out to eat to the same place every night, sitting alone and reading. I woke up before dawn and exhausted myself during the day so I could go to sleep early.

I was lonely, but for the first time in my life it didn't matter. In some way I thought that it was the price I had to pay for my new evolved life. Screw it, I thought, if this is the sacrifice then I'll make it. I became more steadfast in my quest to write the book. For the first time in my life I had a higher purpose and each step brought me closer to that, no matter how painful. It was my legacy. As long as I got it out into the world I could be at peace, no matter what happened.

Don't get me wrong, I did have suitors, like Tania, who kept trying to sneak into my room at night, though I wasn't sure if her motives were to try and get in my wallet or strictly for free beer. I started locking my bedroom door at night. Lena still messaged me, always saying that she needed to meet. I made excuses to postpone or tried to let her down easy because I was concerned what she might do if I flat out said no.

She wanted me to come by her office and insinuated that we could "dance" right there on her desk. One thousand pardons, I typed back, but I've contacted Legionnaires Disease on my cheeky biscuits and the doctor says it's contagious. But maybe in eighteen to twenty-two months, when I'm fully healed? That's okay, she wrote back, she would nurse me back to health. What? What's that? I can't hear you…my Internet. Lena? Can't. Wait, Lena? Going through a tunnel…I can't hear…and I'd shut my computer and not turn it on for an hour.

My God, did these women have no shame? There's no force more powerful on the planet than a Latin women's horniness; that's why they name hurricanes after them (that's a medical fact). If they hooked up generators to their little Latina vajayjays, they could power whole cities and solve the energy crisis. But instead they just recruit them to dance in bikinis in bad music videos on Univision, grinding on a dude who looks like a 5'1" Edward James Omos with white sunglasses who's named after a breed of dog. I don't know about you, but I love the Earth, so I say let's solve the energy crisis, together.

So don't feel sorry for me—it's not like I was a social leper. I was just comparing my social life to my time in Sacramento. Word to Rodger Lodge Chuck Woolery, that little city with an inferiority complex is a dating goldmine. If you were a guy under 54½ years old with at least a part-time job, no visible STDs, and who went to the gym at least six times a year, you were considered a prize. When I grew up on the east coast, I was considered a crazy man, but on the west side I was some sort of prude nuevo-puritan. I couldn't believe the dating scene out there; people treated each other like barnyard animals (and not even the cute little fuzzy ones they kept in the front of the farm for the visitors to pet). Meeting female women of the opposite sex was easy: at charity events, at happy hour, and those six times a year I went to the gym.

There was even a steady stream of introductions through Facebook. It's easy to figure out if a girl is interested; if she "likes" one of your posts out of the blue, then it means she considers you a future reproductive partner, and if she's ever so bold as to "like" one of your photos...wow, she's basically already consented to unspeakable acts involving whipped cream on the first date. In Sacramento, people texted pictures of their body parts around like resumes at a job fair. But *of course* not me—I just wanted to watch *The Notebook* and cuddle.

Yeah, it was like that. I guess we can blame it on daddy issues? Right now I'd like to send a sincere "thank you" to all of the horrible fathers out there—keep on doing a bad job. Let me know if there's anything I can do to hurt.

But that wasn't Tamarindo, where I went dateless. I lowered my standards significantly but still got rejected. I was just too serious, too old, too boring. Hell, *I* wouldn't even date *myself* if I were one of those girls. One time I wanted to masturbate but even my *hand* gave me a thumbs down.

It didn't matter for me in the big picture, but I felt bad for some of the local guys who didn't stand a chance of getting a girlfriend there. Even if they could get a girl interested, where would they bring her? In most other countries young people still live with their families, three generations under one roof in cramped, humble conditions, so the beach was their go-to love motel. Any time of night a couple could sneak onto the beach and get it on. It sure sounds romantic—making passionate love under the moonlight on the beach in the tropics—but I imagine it wasn't as fun as it seems. First off, I'm not a doctor, but I do know that sand is not a lubricant. Ouch. And you never were really alone—there were plenty of troublemakers and robbers on the beach that would be happy to crash the party, so you had to be careful. At night the dividing line between the pavement and the sand was the exact line where all sorts of bad things happened.

The previous New Year's Eve I was hanging out with a Tica and we stepped out onto the beach to sit there and talk a little. Yes, I do mean talk. Normally we wouldn't do that, but because of the holiday the beach was packed with people partying around bonfires and lighting fireworks. We were at the end of the beach, where we thought it would be deserted, so we sat down and chatted. Our eyes began adjusting to the darkness and over the sound of the waves we heard noises. I looked around and in every direction there were people having sex, couples screwing right there in the sand only meters away. Right behind us a guy stood up against a palm tree with a girl on her knees in front of him, expressing her feelings orally. The more we looked the more we saw—it was "sexy time" on the playa.

Remember that I also had to overcome the language barrier. Let's say I saw an attractive Tica on the street. She's fine as wine, coco skin and brown eyes, in a yellow sundress. I really want to meet her. She could be the *one* and we're destined to make babies. Okay, here we go. My game would look approximately like this:

"Hola!" I wave to her. It sounds campy and extremely uncool, like Gilbert Gottfried reading *Fifty Shades of Grey*.

She doesn't see me, or assumes I'm a tourist looking for monkeys.

"Hola, amiga!" I step out in front of her. She's a little startled. "Como estas?" I ask—how are you?

"Bien," she says. She's good. It's going stellar so far, right?

"Ummm...Okay. Donde vives?" I ask, where does she live? I'm just trying to make conversation, here—I don't need an actual address or anything.

"Tamarindo." That makes perfect sense, since, after all, we are standing right there in Tamarindo. She notices me sweating like a hostage. Jesus, it's hot out. Why isn't anyone else sweating out here?

"Ummm...estas bien?" I ask, you are good? She shakes her head yes.

We've established that she's good. And that we're standing in the same town. Please move on, Norm. She remains silent, wondering why I stopped her. Now what? I want to ask her how the surf was that morning, or if she's going to reggae night at Pacifico's, or if she'd like to rent jet skis and power out to a remote beach, get naked, and rub lotion on each other's backs as we drink fruity rum concoctions out of coconuts, but that isn't even in my vocabulary. I don't even know the past tense. Or the future tense. And I bet that anything to do with riding jet skis has a tense of its own; yo jetski-o, tu jetski-es, usted…etc. In my mind I'm trying to conjugate verbs and desperately reaching for some useful phrases. The weather? Weak. Where is the bathroom? I know that one. She's just looking at me. I panic.

"Todo bien?" I ask, all good? Sweet Jesus we KNOW she is good! STOP ASKING IF SHE'S GOOD! She's never been fucking BETTER! By this point I'm thinking about sprinting into the jungle to get away.

"Cool!" I say, and let out a nervous laugh. Wow, I'm even creeping myself out.

She stands there with her hand on her hip, waiting for permission to walk away. Why the hell isn't she sweating?

"Okay, ciao, chica!" Good bye. I try to sound upbeat, saving one last thread of social grace by gathering up my trampled cool points and retreating. At least I didn't get maced or anything. It's going to bother me all day. Dammit, why couldn't I speak the f'ing language? Mierde! Hijo de Puta! Easy, big fella—you've still got your mojo, no need to jump off a cliff just yet. It's just the language barrier. If she spoke English then for sure you guys would be chatting and laughing like old friends by now. She'd be vexed by your suave to the point where she would run home and call her momma and tell her to put out one more plate for Thanksgiving. Or whatever Costa Rican holiday has the equivalent of pilgrims and turkey—you know what I mean. Instead I just bite my tongue and look down at the ground, give one last wave, and walk on. Sigh.

"Yeah, see ya later," she says, and walks away.

Well that couldn't have gone worse.

While we're on the subject, can I be honest with you? Are we in the Trust Tree? I was really worried about dating in Tama for another reason. When I finally did get the chance to meet a lovely nice young lady and we courted and went on seventeen dates and I met her family and got her father's permission and we got matching tattoos and Googled each other and were finally ready for a special, intimate night together, there was one possibility that could scare Little Norm right back into my drawers: Jungle Bush. You've heard of 70s Bush, right? Well Jungle Bush was (in my mind) the tropical equivalent of 70s Bush. I won't go into too much detail, but for my readers who weren't born until Puff Daddy started rapping, here's a snapshot: In the continental United States in the 1970s there was a whole generation of young people who were…how can I say this with the utmost sensitivity…they were all DIRTY. It was hip to wear filthy bellbottoms and man-blouses and everyone went barefoot and slept with each other because, of course, STDs weren't invented until the second term of the Reagan administration. They listened to horrible music with finger cymbals and three-hour sitar solos and did a lot of drugs. Somehow that was all supposed to stick it to THE MAN and bring the troops home from Vietnam. In my opinion, they should have made THE MAN listen to the music and they would have signed a peace treaty the next day. Anyway, a horrible byproduct of their lax hygienic life choices was that they didn't have time to focus on personal grooming south of their equators, if you know what I mean. So everyone walked around with 70s Bush, and when they took off their undergarments they all looked eerily similar to Kareem Abdul Jabbar's fro when he fought Bruce Lee in "Enter the Dragon." Somehow they found this attractive and kept copulating with reckless abandon—it must have been the drugs.

Yes, it was thirty-something years later, but I was in Costa Rica, a Third World country of rainforest where their main economic exports were bananas and sugarcane. Where were battery-powered personal shavers on that list, I wondered? It was called a *Brazilian Wax* and not a *Costa Rican Wax* for a reason. They couldn't even pave their own roads, for Christ's sake. Pornography wasn't legal and I had to smuggle in vibrators for the local women! I was terrified that when I finally got intimate with a nice Tica, she'd suffer from a case of Jungle Bush and I'd have to excuse myself from the festivities by faking a groin pull and climb out of the bathroom window naked and run away and possibly move out of town.

Yup, times were tough on the dating front. I flew solo and kept it semi-classy, but a lot of guys went the prostitute route. I could definitely imagine how that would be easier, and far less expensive, than trying to date a Tica party girl, who might be bleeding your wallet dry and dating three others at the same time. One guy described it to me as "taking *yourself* out for dinner and a movie and then just getting to the good part." This may sound cynical but that's just the way it was in Tamarindo. In fact in most other countries prostitution is just a normal part of life. Hell, it was even legal, and the prossies enjoyed a union with membership cards, medical care, and police protection. There was no judgment, at least on my part; they were just trying to make a buck and feed their families.

There were Ticas, the drop-dead beautiful Columbianas, and the voluptuous Dominicanas, who were looked down upon because of their darker skin and poorer country. There weren't as many Nicaraguan women—most of them had too much pride and would prefer to work. The prettiest ones wore cocktail dresses and worked out of the nice club, Aqua, and tried to get $200 a night. That was a joke because $100 was the standard price for tourists. Some guys might get a local discount, a rainy season discount, or a daytime discount as low as $50.

I said "hi" when I passed them on the street and treated them as equals, but when I saw them out on a "date," I wouldn't acknowledge them so their business with the tourist would remain undisturbed. They thanked me with their eyes.

But there were definitely mishaps as the tourists struggled to navigate the world of the *chicas malas*—those working girls.

I heard about a Canadian tourist who'd taken a prostitute home from Monkey Bar. Nothing remarkable there—that happened every night, but this guy paid for the hen and got the rooster, if you know what I mean. They started messing around and he discovered that *she* was actually a *he*. The tourist freaked out and refused to pay (exactly why they usually make you prepay), but shim said "*hell no he owed shim fair and square,*" so the tourist called the police. Big mistake.

The police came to the hotel in the middle of the night and there was a big commotion and the guests were out in the hall and the management was frantic trying to quell it all. The cops just laughed at the tourist and told him there was nothing they could do. What exact law did shim break? Having bits and pieces in a dress? False advertising? Wearing white after Labor Day? To add insult to injury, the police forced him to pay shim as previously negotiated (exactly why prostitution is legal in Costa Rica). He had to sit there in his hotel robe and count out 50,000 *Colones* and hand it to the tranny in the middle of the hallway with everyone looking. The next morning he disappeared out of town instead of walking the streets and dying of embarrassment. Yeah, he probably could have played that one a little better.

CHAPTER 15

'GOTTA LOVE THE LOONIES

The problem with Canadians is that they're all too nice. I dare you to try and find an asshole Canadian—I betcha can't. In fact, they're so pleasant that it makes the rest of us Americans look bad. I'd probably even consider moving up there if they had things like sun, women, and real sports.

They call Canadians "Loonies," a nickname for their currency, and a lot of them ended up in Tamarindo to wait out their gulag winters up north. My favorite Loonies were Carla and Craig, a couple who lived in Huacas with their three dogs, twenty minutes out of town. They'd moved down five years prior and bought a garden compound in the middle of the jungle, with high walls around an open *palopa*-roof house and hammocks on the porch by the pool.

Carla and Craig visited Pistol in jail several times when he was first arrested, even though they barely knew him. They brought him food and money, took care of his exchange students in town, and communicated with his mom in those nightmarish first weeks. They let Gary put all of Pistol's possessions in their storage room. Who the hell does something that nice? I was already cranky about doing so much to help him and I'd known him on and off for fifteen years.

Pistol's mom wanted me to go through all of his stuff, cataloguing each item, and then pack it neatly into his truck. The truck was breaking down again so it barely went over ten miles an hour, but later that week I needed to drive it to a condo complex nearby. Theresa knew the owner, so we could store it there.

I'd been meaning to visit the Loonies anyway because Craig was heading out of town for work soon. I messaged Carla and she answered with cheer, as always: "Come on over any time this week, Norm. We'd love to see you! And stay for dinner!"

It was always like that with the Loonies—they were so friendly that a simple visit turned into a three course meal, a dip in the pool, and enough rum to kill a baboon over a six hour stretch.

On the drive over I rehearsed my excuses to get off the hook from drinking:

"I really shouldn't drink because my stomach is messed up,"

"No thanks, it's that time of the month for me. I brought a note from my doctor, if you'd like to see it," or:

"None for me—I have to meet the President of Costa Rica later to discuss mango irrigation policies."

Of course none of those would work, and I could already hear their eloquent counter arguments:

"We don't give a shit, so drink, drink, and *definitely* drink!" Damn Loonies.

I pulled up the bumpy jungle road to their outside gate. Every time I came in I had to stop the car, get out, unlock the gate, swing it open, find a rock to hold it in place, get back in the truck, drive in, then get out, kick the rock away, close the gate, and lock it behind me. Columns of tropical cactus grew by the gate. They were tall and oblong green, with sharp three-inch spikes on the end of each appendage. Every time I bent down to pick up a rock to hold the gate open I stuck myself on the cactus, the spike going into my forehead like a rogue syringe.

But this time I was ready. I extended my leg and carefully pulled the rock toward me with my flip-flop, barely avoiding the cactus.

"Not this time, you nasty sons of bitches!" I said out loud. Pleased with myself, I got back in the truck and drove on.

Their hounds mobbed me when I stepped out of the truck, licking and jumping up with muddy paws. But that day only two of them greeted me. I spotted Reina, their black lab, chasing her tail in circles, trying to bite the air. Oh no, Reina—not again. I walked around to their back sun porch.

"Hey, Craig—don't tell me Reina licked *another* toad?"

"Yup, she's been tripping for 48 hours straight, now. We made her drink a gallon of milk and that's probably the only thing keeping her alive."

"Man, she just never learns. How about you, buddy? How have you been?" I asked.

"I guess I never learn, either, eh?" he said, raising his oversized plastic cup, filled with a mysterious brown liquid that gave off fumes reminiscent of paint thinner.

I loved their place—they actually had a lawn, a rare thing in Tamarindo, lined with purple orchids in the shade of palm trees. I was invited to use the pool anytime I wanted to stop by, and it was always peaceful there. Well, except when one of their dogs licked a poisonous toad and tripped like she'd dropped ten hits of acid. It was a big problem in the rainy season and many a dog had died after foaming at the mouth and howling at the washing machine for days. I can think of no worse demise than death by tripping balls. Milk was the only thing that counteracted the poison.

"Norm, it's so good to see you!" Carla said. I gave her a big hug and we all sat down at the table on the porch under the fan.

Carla had a bad eye. A decade earlier, she'd been in a horrific car accident that pulverized half her face. Twenty surgeries later they'd managed to reconstruct most of her orbital bones and reconnect most of the nerves so her face looked fine, but her eye still appeared less than fully alive, drooping where the tissue and bones were out of place.

I was uncomfortable looking, not because it was anything objectionable—to me she just looked like pretty Carla with a slightly beat-up eye, but I was uncomfortable because I *really* didn't want to make *her* feel uncomfortable, so I tried not to look straight at it, but then felt like it was obvious I was looking away, so I tried to half look, half look away, blurring my eyes to look at both of hers at the same time, until pretty soon I was the one with messed up eyes.

"Poor Norm—always cross-eyed and uncomfortable," she must have thought. Maybe Carla could tell I was being weird in my efforts not to look weird, maybe not, but she was great about it. She talked openly about her eye so I'd get used to it.

"I have to fly back next week for another operation. They need to graft another piece into my orbital bone because the last one didn't take and collapsed. You can feel it. Here, give me your finger," and she took my finger in her hand and ran it along the bridge under her eye where the top of her cheek used to be. I felt better after she did that, and she looked even prettier.

Craig and Carla were cute together because she was like the man in the relationship, and he the woman. When Craig got drunk he hugged everyone and cried because he loved them all so much and sat on her lap, nuzzling his head into her sizable bosom. She'd put her arm around him and smoke cigarettes and laugh.

Craig may have been emotional, but he was one tough goat. He worked on oil rigs off the coast of India, 30 days on and 30 days off. It was pure hell, he told me. The work was hard and dangerous, there was nothing to do, and it was such a cluster fuck that he didn't understand how the whole thing didn't explode or spill into the ocean on a regular basis. But they paid him well. I loved listening to his stories, he regaled me with tales from desolate ice rigs in the arctic north, or the time he got so mad at corrupt police at the Honduran border that he chased them with a baseball bat.

"Do you want a drink, Norm?" Craig asked. "We have rum, or I just picked up a 2-4 at the beer store if you want that, instead?" He took out a key and unlocked the padlock on their outdoor fridge. They kept it locked up so Merle, their maintenance man, wouldn't sneak in and drink too much on the job, then cut the hedges as straight as tsunami waves and pass out face down in the sun with the lawnmower still running beside him. Other than that he was perfectly trustworthy.

"Ummm, not right now, thanks," I said, then tried to change the subject as quickly as possible. "So, did I tell you about my book?"

"Yes, yes, tell us," Carla said. "It's so exciting! What's it about?"

"I think I'm going to write a book of short stories from my trip around the world back in 2000. I have four or five written already."

"That's great! Well, you know we'll buy a few copies. And if you ever need a quiet place to stay and write you're always welcome at the *cabaña* we have on the back of the property."

"I might just take you up on that! But actually I already moved out of my place and got my own apartment."

Carla gave me an I-told-you-so look without actually saying it. "Oh, so you're not living with Tania anymore?" she asked.

I shook my head no.

She nodded her head sympathetically. "That one's as pure as the driven slush, eh?"

I laughed and then told her about it; the only thing worse than going through a breakup is going through a breakup when you've never even had a relationship.

For some unknown reason Tania had put the word around town that I was her boyfriend. She even emailed Lena before I got down there and gave her the false news, just to rub it in. Since I'd discovered what she was all about, I did my own thing. When I was home, I hung out in my room with the door closed, but I had to stick it out to try and get my money back. According to what she said, her suing-Chris money was coming in any day.

I secretly planned my emancipation from the apartment. I was thrilled at the possibility of having my own place but also sad at the prospect of letting Disco go. She was my first true friend in Tamarindo, and I'd thoroughly enjoyed our deep talks—or, more accurately, me talking and her looking straight at the wall and wanting a treat. I stopped by a few rental offices, and my buddy, Mack White, stayed semi-sober long enough to show me a cute little two-bedroom place in Pueblo del Mar. It had French doors that opened up to a balcony overlooking palm trees and flowers around the pool.

I signed the lease within an hour.

Then came the hard part: telling Tania that I was moving out at the end of the week, September 1. That kind of confrontation makes me squirm, so I did what any mature, reasonable adult would do in that situation: I delayed it as long as I could. Finally, two days before our next rent check was due, we happened into the living room at the same time.

"Ummm, Tania, while you're here, there's something I think we should talk about..."

"Yes, good, because I wanted to talk to you, too. I don't think this is working, N. I don't think you need me anymore and we should probably move out. I think I'm going to move in with Yazmin. I know you'll be fine and I'm sorry things had to end this way."

"Oh. Okay. Cool."

"Really? That's it?! That's all you have to say?!"

"Well...I guess there's also: When are you going to pay me my money?"

She freaked out. *"I just can't do it! I can't do it anymore!"* she cried, pulling at her own hair with histrionics that even shocked Disco. *"I've tried and tried! I swear, I've tried to be good and make this work!"* she shrieked. *'There is only so much I can take in my life! Oh lord, I can't be good!"*

...and the Academy Award for "Best Dramatic Performance by a Free-Loading Bad Girl" goes to...the envelope please...TANIA!, for her performance alongside Hugh Jackman in *Les Make Gringos Misérables.*

"Exactly what planet are you living on?" I asked, but she ran out of the house sobbing, waving her arms over her head like a baboon. Wait a second, wasn't *I* supposed to be the one who was angry? But I couldn't help but feel a little sorry for her.

Still, I started locking my bedroom door just in case she decided to clean me out before I left. Under cover of night, when I knew she was out at the bars, I packed up Pistol's truck and brought everything to Pueblo del Mar. After three trips my things were in place. I went into my new apartment and closed and locked the front door, then took a deep breath. I decided it was probably a good idea never to leave again in case I bumped into her.

The next week I heard her business with Chris had concluded. He had no choice but write her a check for $4,000, it was either that or have the employment and tax people crawl up his ass. But I never saw one cent of the money she owed me. One day it was, *"Oh yeah just keep a tab and I know I owe you like $1,200 but you'll definitely get it,"* and then a few days later it was, *"I'm having trouble cashing the check,"* and then *"I need the money for rent this month so let me pay you soon,"* and then we'd moved out and she'd brushed off my inquiries all together.

What the hell could I do? Get mad? Scream at her? Sue her? I was a gringo in a foreign land, and I'd seen how quickly things could turn into a shit show if you took on the wrong locals. Of course I knew she was suspect from the get-go, but what pissed me off even more was Tania's attitude about the whole thing. She acted like I was inconveniencing her when I asked for the money she owed me. Apparently her shit didn't stink because she had a J-O-B. Oh, you mean like *everyone* else in the world, honey?

At least I had the money I'd paid for our security deposit coming back. Once the landlord returned that to me, I'd be close enough to indemnified it wasn't worth trying to get blood from a stone from Tania. But something as easy as that can be a nightmare in a foreign country.

No one knew who I needed to talk to about getting my security deposit back. The rental agency was run by a fat lesbian attorney named Marianella. That's just no way to go through life—well, except for the lesbian part, of course. The office was always closed, and when I did find someone there to talk to they told me the owner of the property had my money. They would contact him but they couldn't give out his information and he hadn't been returning their calls or emails. I waited and waited. I checked back weekly until finally I understood I was being scammed.

I managed to track down the owner's email address through the HOA, a New Yorker named Frankie Kiss, and shot him an email asking him for my money. He replied that he hadn't seen a dollar of rental money from that place in a year. It turns out that Marianella was collecting rents and deposits in Villa Verde and pocketing them. She knew that most of the owners were in the United States, and even if they did come down to confront her, she was an attorney and her father a powerful judge, which added up to a license to steal in Costa Rica.

I showed up at the next HOA meeting, clean-shaven and wearing a collared shirt. Marianella looked shocked to see me. The whole HOA meeting consisted of her and another lady, who took notes. I tried to explain in Spanish the best I could that she owed me money and what Frankie Kiss said. She apologized, but I wasn't allowed to be at the meeting without a notarized power of attorney from the condo owner. What? I hit her up about the security deposit and she said, *"No problem, just come by the office and I'll give it to you. And pura vida!"* Yeah, right, I knew she would just dodge me and bullshit forever.

Frankie Kiss came all the way down to Tamarindo just to fire her and try to get his money back. I met him one night outside the casino. He was a fake Goodfella who wore a Jets jersey and talked a big game about handling her "New York style," how he could put a hit on someone down there for $100. That part was true, though a good, quality hit cost at least triple that. But the way I saw it, if he was serious about having someone murdered he wouldn't go around advertising it to strangers in public. We call folks like him "AM Radio," because they're all talk, all the time. I told him that his Jets sucked and to email me if he ever heard from her.

After telling Carla and Craig the whole story they looked at each other and then back to me and nodded their heads sympathetically.

"Yeah, you can always stay with us, Norm," Craig said. And they meant it, too—I could have moved in right there and stayed with them for a year, eating their food and drinking their beer, and they never would have charged me a cent. That's how the Loonies rolled.

In fact, I'd met lots of incredibly kind, generous people while traveling. You might think that living in a little beach town in the topics is intellectually isolating, but it's actually a melting pot of dynamic, like-minded folks from all over the world. There were Loonies, Brits, Aussies, Kiwis, Boricuas, Mehicanos, Nicas, Dominicanos, Ticos, Ossis and Wessis, Argentines, Swedes, Nords, Fins, Italianos, Pinoys, Israelis, Yardies, even a few gringos, and on and on. The well-seasoned stew of language, ideas, art, culture, and music was breathtaking. I was exposed to the most amazing people on a daily basis, and whenever possible I exposed myself to them, too. Well, you know what I mean.

Sure, it had its challenges that kicked my ass on a regular basis, but that was also a good part of the process, of opening myself up to new experiences, dissolving the ego and assumptions that had crept into my thinking and calcified into rigidity. It kept my mind sharp, my spirit invigorated. I kept having these wonderful surreal moments that were so wild and random I couldn't have even made them up. If nothing else, it was unarguable confirmation that I was, indeed, alive.

"You sure you don't want a drink, Norm?" Craig asked again.

"No thanks, I'm cool. I have a lot of work to do with Pistol's stuff."

"Okay, let me show you." He led me to the supply room. "It's all been safe and sound in here. Gary brought everything the first day and we haven't touched a thing."

Craig opened the door. There was a mountain of suitcases, duffel bags, garbage bags, dirty clothing strewn about, car parts and pool toys, snaking cords and cables that'd lost their electronics, a half-deflated kayak, loose paperwork everywhere, and everything from socks to Q-tips. What a mess. It was going to take hours to go through it all.

"On second thought, I will need that drink. And make it a double."

I sat on an overturned five-gallon bucket and went through Pistol's things, recording them in a notebook. It's a strange thing to catalog someone's possessions, like cutting open a cross section of their life for scientists to examine. You can usually assume the worst; other than being in jail, or dead, I couldn't think of another situation where you'd need to do that.

I sweated profusely in the airless closet. It felt like it took forever, shrinking the mountain one item at a time and trying my best to pack it up neatly. Carla and Craig were nice enough to check in on me and keep refreshing my drink with rum and ice. Finally, three hours later, I emerged, soaked in sweat, drunk as skunk, but with all of Pistol's things packed and documented. It only took me nine trips to carry it all to the truck and pack it in the back until there was only one bag left.

"Does this go, too?" Carla asked.

"Nah, that goes into the trash! The *basura*!" I slurred. She looked inside and laughed. It was filled with bongs, pipes, rolling papers, ashtrays, a beach towel, mace, and a dozen empty lighters. I took out the beach towel and threw the rest in the trash.

"Before you go, let's do a shot," Craig said. "Here's to Joey. To health and good luck." How could I say no?

I was feeling pretty damn wonky, but it was time to head home. I hauled my *borracho* ass into the truck. Of course I shouldn't be driving, but I also shouldn't have been spending quality time in a Third World prison and crawling around the jungle with coke dealers. But no one cared about any of it in Tamarindo, where they could pull you over and give you a ticket just for being a gringo in a rental car. The roads were almost deserted, so I just had to drive slow and straight and if anything got in my way, turn.

Carla and Craig waved goodbye and I drove out to the gate. I got out of the truck and swung it open and then reached down to pick up the rock to hold it in place. I bent down and something stabbed me in the forehead. "ASS HAT!" that hurt. I put my hand to my head and felt a cactus thorn protruding from my skull. I pulled it out slowly, my forehead wet.

Dammit, I'd dropped the keys, too. It was pitch black out, only the headlights trained into the teeming jungle, so I scanned the ground for the keys but almost tipped over, then righted myself by taking a step back—into another cactus. I felt a stab into my leg and tumbled, my flip-flop giving way, sending me to the ground. Cactus barbs stuck into my cheek, the back of my neck, and two in my backside. I didn't even know where to start with the screaming, rolling around in a bloody drunken heap in the dirt. I didn't dare risk putting my hands anywhere to pull myself up, so I just belly-crawled across the dirt, through a puddle, one broken flip-flop dangling, to the front of the truck where I knew I was safe. I got up, slowly, and pulled them out one by one in the headlights, yelping with each self-surgical extraction.

This was certainly embarrassing, but at least no one saw—I was out of sight from the house, so Carla and Craig would never know that I almost impaled myself to death at their front gate.

"Are you okay out there, Norm?" Carla hollered. The front floodlights went on and the dogs started barking.

"Uhhh, no—I'm doing great," I said. "OUCH! GOD DAMMIT! All good. SHIT THAT HURTS! Thanks again for a great time! MONKEY FUCKER! I'll see you guys soon!"

Somehow I got in the truck and made it back to Tamarindo without driving off the road, my left flip-flop on my right foot so I could operate the gas petal. I drove toward Villa Verde and then stopped, put the truck in reverse, almost hit a cow that was leisurely crossing the road, then took the turn for Pueblo del Mar.

I fell out of the truck and walked at a 45 degree angle toward my apartment. A couple was out by the pool, relaxing and looking up at the stars.

"Hi, we're your new neighbors," said a young woman with white-blonde hair, approaching to introduce herself. "I am Louisa and this is my boyfriend, Thor. We're from Denmark and live in...oh gosh, are you okay? You're bleeding. Oh my!"

"Ighhh fell into the cactwus and bloke my flip fwop," I said.

"Here, sit down. Let me clean you up."

I woke up the next morning in the lawn chair by the pool with a Band-Aid on my forehead, Pistol's beach towel draped over me. My body felt like a used piñata, but at least I was home, MY home. I sat up to work the crink out of my neck and a piece of paper fell off my chest. It read: "Nice to meet you last night, neighbor! Let's all have a barbecue on Saturday! Come by # 17 and say hi to me and Thor. Cheers! –Louisa"

Ya gotta love the Danes. I dare you to try and find a mean Danish person—betcha can't.

CHAPTER 16

MY SCHOOL IS THE STREETS

I've never taken Spanish classes in school. I studied German in high school because it was the native tongue of my parents, but still I had to cheat my way to a D+ grade. I only knew a few words of *Español* from traveling through South America a decade earlier, so it was all a huge adjustment to move to Costa Rica.

The first weeks I stumbled through communication with simple phrases like "hello," "one extra raw shrimp ceviche, please," and "Oh dear God, please tell me you have a bathroom here." Every day I wrote down a few new words or phrases from a Spanish dictionary, but progress was slow. I felt isolated on a linguistic island, humbled that I couldn't just walk up to someone and express what was on my mind.

The problem with learning Spanish is the more you learn the more you realize you've been making an ass out of yourself all along. Without fail, any words that I misused I'd later find out had a lewd meaning.

When I went to the pool I asked for a *toalla*, what I thought was a towel, but in Costa Rica it's a sanitary napkin, and *paño* is a towel. When someone asked me how old I was, I said, "*Yo tengo 39 anos,*" which is "I have 39 anuses" if you don't put the proper accent on *a**ñ**o*.

I thought *excitado* meant excited, and even the dictionary said so, but in Costa Rica that word alludes to being horny-excited, not just excited-excited. So I was telling everyone that I was so horny to be living in Tamarindo, and horny to make their acquaintance, and horny for the weekend (which, coincidentally, was all true).

Gustar is the verb "to please," and if you want to say that you like something you say *"Me gusta"* or literally "It pleasures or pleases me." I was making the mistake of walking around town saying *"Me gustO,"* when I liked something, or "I pleasure myself." A proclamation of satisfying masturbation may technically be accurate, but it's nothing I wanted to advertise.

Even hand gestures weren't safe. I have plenty of friends with young children in the States and one of the easiest ways to make their little ones warm up was to pretend to pull their noses off. You know, the cute little thing to make them laugh where you hold your thumb between your first two fingers and wiggle it, saying "I got your nose! I got your nose!"? Well, I guess that same gesture means something different in Costa Rica, though I never got that memo. One afternoon Pistol's truck broke down out of town. Tania and I were stranded near the school where her sister worked, so we walked over there to use the phone. It was a kindergarten, and while I waited the kids came up to me and wanted to play, curious about the gringo. So I busted out the "I've got your nose" move to a couple of them, getting more laughs than usual. When Tania and her sister came back in the room, they rushed over.

"What the heck are you doing, N? Stop that!"

"What?"

"That thing you were doing with your thumb—why would you do that to the kids?"

"What?! I had their noses."

"Ummmm, yeah that means something else here." She took me aside and explained that that gesture means "fuck you" in Costa Rica, which I was wagging in their little innocent faces. Ooops. Those poor little bastards will never be the same because of me, destined to lives as sailors or truck drivers because of their early exposure to the F-bomb.

None of those mistakes could be worse than when I first stepped foot in the beautiful country of Costa Rica way back in 1999. I lived in San Jose and played basketball at the local park every day. When we finished hooping I'd walk up to the lady selling pineapple slices and baggies of coconut water by the court and order. *"Por favor, una pinga."* She looked me up and down like I'd just landed in a space ship, but then handed me pineapple. This went on for a month until I happened to order alongside a Tico friend who also spoke English well.

"Listen, Norm—I support your lifestyle choices and all, but what the hell did you just order?" he asked.

"Pineapple," I replied.

He looked around to make sure no one saw us together and lowered his voice.

"My friend, the Spanish word for pineapple is 'piña,' not 'pinga.'"

"Oh, okay," I said. I made about a thousand mistakes a day so it was no big deal. "So what does *pinga* mean, anyway?"

"Pinga is penis," he said. I'd been ordering penis from the lady for a month straight. Thank God she only gave me pineapple.

Then again, *Spanglish* was Tamarindo's official language. There were plenty of words that had Spanish translations that no one bothered to use, like "email." The Spanish name is "*el correo electrónico*" but everyone just said "*email.*" Or "beer" would become "*birra,*" even though "*cerveza*" is the correct Spanish word. Ticos said "*happy hour*" and couldn't get enough of "True Blood" on HBO, even though it was called "*Sangre Fresco.*" Many of the locals knew the basics of conversational English only because they made a living parting tourists from their money. The hotel clerks were fairly fluent. Waiters' vocabulary revolved around food items on the menu, collecting money, and explaining that the tip *was* already included but you were free to add more. The touts, hawks, and coke dealers actually spoke the best slang English:

"Hey man, what's up, man? Where you from? Ahhh, I love New York. Big Apples! Alicia Keys, bro! I have girlfriend in Ohios. Hey, man, want to buy some party favors? I got the best blow in town! You want to try surf? I give you lesson. You smoke da Mary Jane, bro? Hey, man, I have kind bud. Get you hiiiiiiigh! Good price for you. Local price. You come back and see me tonight!"

So the consensus on the street was that people used whichever word, in English or Spanish, was easiest—true *Spanglish.* In Tama the fundamental *concept* of language was butchered mercilessly on a daily basis. The French and Italians could speak Spanish fluently with ease; the Germans, Swedes and Danes spoke three languages since grade school; and the Canadians and Brits did a serviceable job of picking it up. But some of the gringos who relocated down there were shamefully unmotivated to learn. There were salty dog ex-pats who'd lived in Costa Rica for years and still knew only know a few basic phrases. I found that ridiculous and insulting to the local culture, but no one else seemed to mind as long as their money was green. Only a handful of Americans in Tama spoke Spanish well, like Rusty, who owned Rusty's Pizza. When I asked him how he learned Spanish he attributed his competence to the fact that he married a Tica, so if he wanted to understand what she was yelling at him he had to learn quickly!

The locals wanted to practice *their* English, so most conversations turned into a ping-pong volley of two or even three languages. When I passed someone on the street I always said "hello" but we often had no idea which language the other person spoke. It was a fun game to guess. Were they French? *Bonsoir*. A Tico? *Pura vida*! From Peru? *Como le va?* A Brit? *Cheers, mate!* A gringo from California? *What's up, dude?* Maybe an Italian? *Buon giorno*. Or an Israeli? *Shalom*. If I wasn't sure where the other person was from, then the default language was Spanish. I've had entire awkward, bumbling conversations with someone in patchwork Spanish before realizing that we were both Americans. I swear to God one time I found myself translating English to English for an American from Texas and a Brit from Liverpool. Sometimes it just became too confusing and we'd all say screw it and walk off.

If we didn't know a word we just made it up, taking the English word and adding an -O on the end to make it sound Spanish, like "where is the doctor-O?" or "How much does it cost-O?" Every blue moon we'd get lucky and it was the correct word, like *banco*. I found it helped to speak quickly, with ultimate confidence, and slur a little bit. Gringos spoke with such bad accents that they sounded like a motorcycle sputtering up a steep hill, but by speaking super-fast, even when my pronunciation and grammar were awful, I hoped they'd think I was speaking some Spanish dialect they weren't familiar with. Maybe I was from some lost indigenous tribe of albinos with big butts who lived deep in the Costa Rican jungle?

There was no way around it—my lack of Spanish would be a detriment to settling into my new life. It was time to take my mastery of the language seriously by enlisting the services of true teaching professionals. So I walked straight to the Wyra Language School…and then took a right and kept walking into town and sat down for a smoothie. Fedor and Repo magically appeared at the table next to me. They asked me where I was going and since it was only 9:00 a.m. and none of the bars were open, I figured it was safe to reveal the truth—that I was ready to study Spanish.

"*No problem, my friend!*" they responded. "*We will help you, man!*"

We sat at a table in front of the Wild Panda tiki bar and started my formal classes. It was a perfect vantage point for them to watch every girl who walked by and comment on her physique, reputation, and the probability of screwing her doggy style that very night like they were announcers covering the NFL combine. But I brought them back to the task at hand.

My one-day intensive language course began not with basic vocabulary or verb conjugation but pick-up lines in Spanish:

"*Tu con tantas curvas y yo sin frenos!*" translated to "You have many curves and I am without brakes."

"Hola soy ladron y estoy aqui para robar tu Corazon," meant "Hello, I am a thief and I'm here to steal your heart."

And *"Mi ropa interior es comestible,"* or "My underwear is edible," would always come in handy.

"Do any of these lines ever work?" I asked them.

"Sure, Repellito picks up fat drunk gringas all the time!" Fedor bragged. Wow, that's good stuff! All this time instead of getting Rosetta Stone, I just needed to go get stoned with Rosetta!

I figured the past tense would be next on the syllabus, but instead they tutored me on Tico curse words. Knowing those would give me the honor of speaking *Pachuco,* or Costa Rican street slang. Pay attention, they encouraged me, because this was very important. Soon Junior returned from running ten miles with his ankle weights on so he opened up Wild Panda and my instructors ordered cold Imperials. It was hot and the work was exhausting; we all grew frustrated with my progress but we pressed on, steadfast in our task. We worked all through the afternoon and late into the night, and for the price of only 31 beers I got a crash course in street Spanish like no other gringo ever has.

Fedor explained that speaking the Tico language was all about understanding their everyday greetings. The true *Pachuco* included a healthy dose of *"mop's"* (pronounced "mope") when addressing a young guy or a good friend. *Mop* was short for *"mopri,"* which is supposedly *"primo,"* or cousin, backwards, stemming from a fad in the 90s when everyone was saying words backwards to be cool. We had that same fad, only with overalls, I explained to them. Had they ever heard of Kriss Kross? No? They make you want to Jump! Jump!? No? Not ringing any bells?

Repo taught me to use plenty of *"mae's"* (pronounced "my") as well, which roughly meant dude or bro. I started working on balancing out my *mop* to *mae* ratio so I could achieve the perfect daily balance, approximately 347:296.

"Pura vida" was the Costa Rican national saying, which meant "pure life." It was a good-vibe expression used as a greeting, a goodbye, or a response if someone asked you how you were doing. If I was greeting someone from *el Caribe*, the eastern side of the country where the Afro-Caribbean population spoke an enchanting patois of Spanish and Jamaican English, I might say *"Wag gwan,"* or "What's up?"

I found out quickly that *"Un zarpe"* was the term for the last drink of the night, sort of like saying "Ah hell, let's have one more before we leave—why not?" Unfortunately, the *zarpe* would extend the night from 6:30 p.m. to quarter after four in the morning. The next day you would say, *"Estoy de goma,*" to let everyone know you have a hangover. "*Tuanis,*" meant "cool," an idiomatic expression for "too nice."

On the street I might hear "*cabron*" (bastard) or "*joder*" (fuck) or "*mierda*" (shit). The best curse they taught me was "*Me cago en la leche,*" or "I shit in the milk," which meant something along the lines of "damn, I have bad luck." I'd say you have HIDEOUS luck if someone is shitting in your milk, and you should renounce it immediately so it's no longer *your* milk. The most popular expletive was "*puta,*" which means "whore" or bitch." But *puta* was almost always used in conjunction with other expletives, like "ray-puta," pronounced with a huge rolling "r" like you are letting all of you life's frustrations out on that poor little letter, or "*hijo-de-puta*" (son of a bitch). You heard this constantly on the street in everyday life in Tama.

Whenever possible it was best to also bring someone's mom into the equation. The true magic to speaking Tico jive was how you combined those expletives, stringing them together like a maestro conducts a symphony.

Repo and Fedor told me not to say "*que tal,*" which sort of means "what's up," and is mostly used in South America, because there in Guanacaste Province it had a feminine or unmanly connotation. They encouraged me not to appear too friendly when meeting another guy—I was to keep my cool and only nod at him slightly, with the utmost indifference. After that, anytime I greeted a dude in town I'd squish up my face and squint, trying to look mean, though mostly I just managed to appear perpetually constipated. My new male friends grew concerned and advised me to try more fruit and maybe a fiber additive in my diet.

The local coastal community consisted of surfers and those who made a living off tourists, but inland Guanacaste was a rural province of ranchers and farmers. The old-school cowboys playfully called each other "*pegayeguas,*" or, literally translated, "horse fuckers," and that expression found its way down to the streets of Tamarindo. Calling someone a "*pegayegua*" was a good-natured insult among the rough working men, so I always yelled it at the squirrely parking lot attendant when he gave me a bad spot directly in the sun.

In the evening the lessons progressed from pure linguistics to learning the cacophony of whistles and hisses that those rude boys used on the street. There was a separate whistle when you were trying to get your friend's attention, a whistle to holler at a pretty girl on the street, and another whistle of indignation when she ignored you and kept walking. My head hurt trying to keep it all straight.

My tenured Tico professors even covered the three Great Costa Rican Lies, important because every Tico knew them. I'd heard bits and pieces, but finally I could piece this valuable information together. They were:

1. *El zarpe.* Just one last drink, before we call it a night. (I learned this one early on.)
2. *Te pago mañana.* I'll pay you the money I owe you tomorrow. (In fact, if someone owed you money, you'd never see a cent, which was consistent with what I'd seen in the States, too.)
3. *Solemente la puntita.* We won't have sex—I'll just put the tip in. (Ummm...no explanation needed.)

Around midnight, a Tico friend of ours, the good-vibe Row with his big afro, rode by on his Rasta-colored bike. In the past I would have said something fascinating, like, "Hi," but that night I turned to him and yelled, "*Hey, Mop! Pura vida, pegeyegua! Me cago en la leche, mae*!" with a couple of whistles mixed in—the ultimate verbal opus. Row almost crashed his bike off the side of the road but recovered in a cloud of dust and shaky knees, looking back several times to see if it was really me who had just yelled that.

With that they cracked one last beer to celebrate my graduation, telling me with tears in their eyes that they were proud. From that day on I walked around Tama cursing and yapping in the rawest of street *Pachuco* that surprised even the surfers and coke dealers. They'd given me the keys to the kingdom to become an authentic Costa Rican street hustler, just like them. That street cred would serve me well anywhere from the barrios to the bars of the prison, and when they asked me where I learned to speak Spanish I would say, "*Mi escuela es la calle*"—my school is the street, which was true.

CHAPTER 17

FLYING KAYAKS

We were all worried about Pistol. His mom hadn't heard from him in two days, unusual because he always phoned in at 6:30 a.m. and 4:10 p.m. promptly. I went to visit the jail to find out what was going on, and there was also something important I wanted to tell him. Hector, the bald-headed and bucked-toothed taxi driver from Tamarindo, drove me up there and waited. It was easier that way because Pistol's truck kept breaking down, and when you added it up, it was just as expensive. We got to the jail and as soon as I climbed out of his taxi I could feel that the vibe was different.

None of the visitors chatted or laughed while we waited. The guards were serious and searched everyone thoroughly, especially the women. By then the guards all knew me, but that day they didn't make eye contact or say "hello."

I was always courteous to them. Some of the guards were regular guys—portly and joking around as they did their jobs—but others wore mirrored sunglasses and didn't smile. Their shirts were tucked in and their combat boots were laced up tightly, shotguns resting at attention against their shoulders. That breed of guard did everything possible not to acknowledge my existence. My reflection in their sunglasses said, *"You're just a visitor, but we'd love to have you as a guest."*

Pistol was there to greet me at the gate into D2B. I don't know how he knew I was coming right at that moment. His shirt was dirty and his hair unkempt.

"Hey, what's happening, Normando?" he said, shaking my hand instead of hugging.

"All good, bro, what's new over here?"

"Same shit every day, Normando," he said with a smile. I was relieved to see he was in better spirits than the last visit, the wild desperation gone from his eyes. He took my grocery bags and we walked into the courtyard and sat down.

"Dude, what's going on? Everyone's been worried about you. Your mom said you haven't called in two days."

"I know, I know..." He pointed to the phone in the middle of the courtyard, or where the phone used to be. The stand was still there but nothing was left but some wires poking out.

"What happened?"

"Earlier this week two inmates got in a fight over the phone and ended up breaking it. So the guards ripped it out and haven't fixed it yet."

"Oh shit, that sucks."

"Yeah, tell me about it. They cut off the water the last two days to punish us. We've had nothing but a little water to drink every day—no showers, no laundry, nothing."

"Well, you don't take showers on the outside either, so you must be used to it," I said, gambling that he'd appreciate some levity at that moment.

"Fuck you, Normando!" he laughed.

"Oh, Joey, before I forget…"

"They just piss on our human rights and don't think anything of it. It's so corrupt here. But I'm going to expose it all if they aren't careful. You'll see. By the way, do you have money?" Maybe the water was shut off, but the marijuana pipeline must have been back on in the jail. I slipped it to him.

We caught up on a lot: correspondence from his mom and sister, happenings in Tamarindo, and how his trial was going. The Phillies had locked up the division with 102 wins and had World Series aspirations. It was completely irrelevant to his life in the joint, but I knew it helped him feel normal again, if just for a few minutes.

"Is it my imagination or are there less guys in here this week?" I asked.

"No, there are less. They sent a lot of them to solitary or a different unit across the way. There was a big riot in here the other day."

"What?! Are you serious?"

"It was crazy. Blood everywhere."

"Holy shit, are you okay?"

"Yeah, yeah, I'm fine. I was standing in my cell and all of a sudden all of these guys rushed in and grabbed the old Columbian man who slept in the bunk next to me and started beating the shit out of him. They ripped the wooden slats off the beds and smashed him in the head. "

"Jesus, Pistol."

"By the time the guards got in he was unconscious. I had blood splattered all over my shirt and my bedroll. They took him away, but all night people were yelling at each other across the cells. First thing in the morning, when the cell doors opened automatically, everyone rushed into the courtyard and started fighting. I had no idea how they knew something was going down but there must have been 100 out of the 140 guys in here going at it, pulling out blades and boards and all sorts of shit. But the guards rushed in pretty quickly and hauled a lot of guys away."

"And what did you do during all of this?"

"I just stayed in my cell. Some of my guys told me not to move."

"That's nuts, man. I'm glad you're okay."

"Yeah, me too," he chuckled. I was so relieved to see him safe and in a better state of mind. Damn, my man Pistol. As much as this all pissed me off, we'd had some good times, from Colorado all the way to Costa Rica. I'd be lying if I said I wasn't causing trouble right there with him for most of it. Hell, just the other morning I'd been thinking about the kayak.

"Hey, Joey, you remember the kayak?" I said. He threw his head back and laughed.

"Holy shit, the kayak! Too funny, Normando! What were we thinking?" When I was there on vacation, Pistol had me bring down an inflatable kayak. The thing was huge but folded up neatly in a case the size of a big suitcase. So I brought it down and we carried it up to his fourth-floor apartment. One morning he was high as shit, as usual, and we had the idea to blow it up and take it to nearby Playa Conchal for a nice paddle in the sea. Theresa was there and they were fighting like cats and dogs. So I told him let's haul it downstairs and blow it up out front on the grass, but he said no, it's too hot out, let's do it here and then carry it down.

"*It won't fit*," Theresa said, "*you can't blow it up here*."

"Sure it'll fit," Pistol said. "We can bring it down the stairs or even on the elevator."

Yes it will, no it won't—they kept going back and forth. Of course they were in a tug of war about their relationship and it had nothing to do with the kayak, but neither one of them would back down. I just sat back and drank my *café* and listened to the whole ridiculous thing.

Pistol insisted that it would fit, so we started blowing it up. It took us an hour of huffing and puffing to inflate the damn thing and it was huge. I kept looking at the size of the doorway and back to the kayak. Finally it was done and we were both exhausted and sweating. We picked it up and brought it to the door and…it didn't fit. Of course Pistol wouldn't admit it so we had to go through half an hour of trying to turn it at this angle, no this way, now put the back in first, no, maybe we can take off the door. Theresa loved it—it was her time to shine, so she did the whole play-by-play of how stupid and high we were. He got frustrated and said screw it, we'll fit it in the elevator (it was one of those fancy apartments where the elevator opens right to your apartment). So we went through another round of jamming and twisting, trying to get it in, but it was even smaller than the doorway to the stairs. At last it dawned on him that he was wrong. Pistol just couldn't fathom that he wasn't always the smartest guy in the room, so his ego was stuck.

You'll have to deflate the whole thing and bring it downstairs and blow it up again, Theresa said. No way Pistol was going to do that and admit he was wrong, so he looked around, his smoke-infused but razor sharp mind working overtime, and he came up with a bright idea: We would lower it off the balcony to the ground below.

We hauled it out onto the balcony and looked down four stories to nothing but jungle and a little pool below. It sure looked like a long way to lower it down. Pistol found some twine in the apartment but it was thin, not even rope. He assured us that it would work. We tied off the bow and the other end to the railing. Are you sure it's going to hold, Pistol? I asked. "

No way it's going to hold—you guys are stupid, you guys are high, you gringos are crazy," Theresa said.

"It will hold," Pistol said.

So we propped it up on the balcony and started lowering it down a little at a time and the twine was creaking but holding. Finally it was off the balcony and out of our hands and THWAK! the twine snapped and the kayak went falling down four stories, flopping and sailing in the wind. All three of us let out an "ohhhh shit!" at the same time and pressed our faces over the balcony to watch because we thought it would smash a window, a car, or land in a tree. Surely it would hit something sharp and pop on impact. It fluttered down in slow motion and, to my amazement…landed right in the pool. Perfect landing, no harm done. Wow. We just looked at each other and cracked up. Even Theresa was speechless.

That's Pistol. He did some reckless shit but somehow it all worked out for him. We laughed about the kayak and then both became conscious of where we were and tightened up. Damn, I really hoped he hit the pool on this one.

"Hey, Joey, why did they beat him up?" I asked.

"Who?"

"The old Columbian guy in your cell."

"Oh, I guess he was running a scam, defrauding pension checks from older prisoners or something. He told them that they were investing but he was really just taking their money. It's too bad because he was actually a nice guy. I talked to him all the time."

I nodded for him to go on.

"After the riot they put some of the guys in the solitary cells right here in the unit, but they wouldn't shut up. They yelled and banged on the bars all night long, keeping us up. So the next morning the other inmates rolled up newspapers and lit them on fire near the entrance to their solitary cells. It totally smoked them out—and shut them up the next night."

I guess there were ways of finding justice in jail, maybe even more so than on the outside.

The rest of the visit was uneventful. I got up and said goodbye when visiting hours were over.

"Take care of yourself, bro. I hope the phones get fixed soon. I'll tell everyone you're okay and why you couldn't call." Once again I had to fight the instinct to simply walk him out of there with me and go home. The guards would understand. The prison officials would understand. Of course, how could they not? Just let the poor kid go home. He didn't belong in there.

I got back to the taxi and Hector was waiting. We drove off down the potholed dirt road, shared only with a teenaged *Casanova* riding a bicycle, his sweetheart sitting on the handlebars.

I had no idea how to explain all to Pistol's mom without freaking her out. She had enough to worry about without envisioning her son in the middle of a riot. Maybe I would tell her about the kayak instead, with Joey and... shit! I'd forgotten to tell him.

Theresa was back in town.

"Que paso con su amigo? Esta bien?" Hector asked—What's up with your friend? Everything okay?

"Mas o menos, Hector," I sighed, more or less.

CHAPTER 18

THE SIDE DOOR TO HEAVEN

I heard it from Row, who said he saw her walking past Seasons when he was bartending the day before. That was about as reliable as information got in Tamarindo. Theresa was back in town.

I was surprised she was coming back after everything that went down—I assumed she would want to stay in San Jose to be close to her family and get a fresh start. There was a lot of heat on her in town. Everywhere she went there were rumors and whispers, like she was bad voodoo because of what happened to Pistol. The hustlers and dealers had her pegged as a snitch. That wasn't good for your health in Tamarindo.

Then again, there was some heat on me, too. No one really knew where I fit into it all. I didn't party and pretty much kept to myself, so maybe I was one of those Christian surfers? My hair was buzzed short and I was always working out, so I must be an expat from the army. But I was cool with all of the coke dealers, the Dominican working girls, the transvestites, the *negro* pot dealers from the Caribbean side, the *mariposas*, and even the Nicaraguan workers. I was driving Pistol's truck and people had seen me all around town drinking with him, yet I'd been seen with Lena, too. The rumor was out that he was in jail and people knew I was visiting him. My presence alone confused the hell out of people in Tamarindo.

The buzz about Theresa was true—a mutual friend ran into her outside of the market and talked to her for a while. She was back from San Jose. The rumor was that she'd left town immediately after Pistol got arrested and had a breakdown, ending up in the hospital. Damn, that was heavy. You had to take those things with a grain of salt in Tama, but, then again, I didn't doubt it the way Pistol and her were ripping each other apart. I was surprised she'd lasted that long—or that there was anything left to salvage.

I worried about running into her. The last thing I needed was another person coming at me with negativity for something I had nothing to do with, especially a Tica, who all seemed to have uncontrollable anger issues. After my vacation in Tamarindo, we weren't exactly on good terms. We all did have some nice times together and I'd tried to be cool with her, but she'd started taking her angst with Pistol out on me. Before my vacation ended she posted some nasty stuff on my Facebook wall about "lies that my whore attorney told me" (talking about Lena) when I wrote a blog about the drug trade in Tamarindo. But Theresa was the kind of person it was impossible to be mad at; deep down she was a big sweetheart. So I had no idea what to expect, but the gymnastics of avoiding yet another person in that tiny town made me squirm.

A few days later she added me on Facebook. I thought about it for a while and then accepted her as a friend. Sure, no problem—better to get it over with, and I'd always wanted to be cool with her. She hadn't exactly been a victim in her relationship, but damn she deserved better than Pistol had given her. We started a nice light chat about how I was enjoying Tamarindo and the rainy weather and how we should meet for a beer and catch up. We planned to meet at Kahiki's for happy hour the next day.

I waited at the bar and pressed a cold beer bottle against my forehead. What would I say? Gee, sorry your boyfriend left for another chick and then ended up in a Third World prison, which you might or might not have had something to do with, and hey, tough luck being run out of town and having a breakdown and all that?

I wondered if she would be all screwed up. I laughed at myself. What the hell did I expect? Lord knows I had been one step from a rubber room a few times in my life. Someone tapped me on the back.

"Hi, Normie!" she said with a big grin on her face.

I got up and hugged her and she kissed me on the cheek and we sat down. She looked good.

"How are you, my friend?" she asked

"Good, good. Just living the dream, you know?"

"Hahaha, sometimes it seems like a bad dream, no?" But there was softness in her voice. She looked different—thinner in the face. The stress of their tailspin had caused her to gain a few pounds the last time I saw her, but now it was gone. More than that, she seemed…like somehow there was more *light* around her.

"Yeah, I guess it's true," I said.

"And how about you, Normie? Are you happy to be living in Tamarindo?"

"Well, yeah, I love Tamarindo. The beach is so beautiful. But it's definitely been interesting moving here. I guess it's coming along."

"Do you miss the States?"

"I miss my family—my niece and nephews the most, but no, not the States. I have an older sister who has three kids and I just live for them. Actually, you remind me a little of my sis."

"Ahhhh, that's nice, Normie, thank you."

According to the politics of the jungle Theresa was considered different. Sure, she was Costa Rican, but since she was from San Jose she might as well have been from Mars to the people in Tamarindo. Those from San Jose were better educated, had better jobs, were more Americanized, drove nicer cars (or cars at all), and had lighter skin, their features more Spanish. On long weekends or holidays they came to Playa Jaco or Tamarindo to party on the beach, where they trashed the place and ordered people around without tipping. The Ticos from the mountains in San Jose looked down on the local dark-skinned Guanacasticans. Both of them looked down on the black Costa Ricans from Limon in El Caribe, the Caribbean side of the country. As a nation they looked down on the Nicaraguans to the north and feared the crazy Columbians to the south.

Theresa had pale skin like a gringa and was mistaken for one all the time. She had light brown hair and greenish eyes, more reasons for envy in Tama. She was pretty in a "young mom who takes great care of herself" sort of way.

"So, what are you doing now that you're back?" I asked. *"I've already been back for a couple weeks. I'm living with my friend, Grace, in Villareal and I got a job at Horizons—the property management company. I do all of their bookkeeping and accounting. They don't pay me enough but it's nice because I get to sit in the air conditioning all day and drive their company car, even when I'm not supposed to,"* she said.

"That's great, good for you. And good for me because now you can drive me around."

"Hahahaha, no, I make you walk so you get exercise!" she said. I was relieved to hear her laughing and talking about her new life. Seeing her again made me think of her story, *their* story:

> *She was only twenty years old when she first came to Tamarindo—just a kid—and met a charming, funny gringo nicknamed Pistol while working as a waitress in the casino. They were both new in town, both outsiders who had no one else. They grew close and*

dated for years. He met her parents and she went to the United States to visit his family in upstate New York. It was too cold and she didn't like the food other than the buffalo wings, but she took to his mom like it was her own abuela, grandmother.

But, like a lot of relationships, she was waiting for church bells and he was just enjoying the days. I guess it's like they say: "A man's love is life, and a woman's life is love."

"So, tell me, Normie, are you going out a lot?"

"Oh hell no. I have to be careful with my money, and I'm trying to be healthy."

"Yeah right, all of you gringos say that!"

"And honestly, I visit the jail almost every weekend so that takes a lot. Voy a el carcel," I said.

"*La. LA carcel*," she said, laughing." "*Oh my God—look at you trying to speak Spanish!*"

"Yeah, I mess it up on a daily basis, but I'm trying. I think I should be fully fluent by, like…the weekend."

"*Well at least that's better than Joey—he's lived here six years and speaks noooo Spanish!*"

"Yeah, that's true. I think he just didn't give a shit enough to learn."

It started to rain gently. She looked out at the orange angel's trumpets, glistening and sagging toward the earth.

"And what…how is Joey doing?" she asked.

She'd loved him and there was never anyone else. But Pistol was wild. To deal with it she became more like his mother, scolding and chastising. I think she was always waiting for the dream to come true, so she never let go.

"He's okay. Hanging in there. It sucks in there but he's safe so far—knock on wood." I tapped on the bar three times. She knocked on my head and I laughed.

"So, that's all we can hope for," I said. "I help out and talk to his mom all the time."

"I'd like to say 'hi' to Betty if you think it would be okay. I really love his parents."

"I think that would be nice."

Seven dry seasons and seven rainy seasons had passed since they'd met. They'd grown intertwined, like the roots of a twisted tree, but still there was no comfort for her, just his cold side of the bed. She

> *felt like she'd given him the best part of her womanhood and now there was less of her left. She was his media naranja, as they say in Costa Rica—the other half of his orange—forever tethered to Pistol's heart, but their days were defined by the disappointment of what had not come to be.*

"I wish I could to reach out to him. I do. I want to say 'hi' or visit him, but I don't think it would be good. My therapist says I'm not ready."

"Shiiiittt, nine out of ten of therapists agree that I'm not ready to walk around in public!" I said.

"Hahaha, stop trying to make me feel better." She slapped me on the arm.

"Well, look, you have to do what's healthy for you, so watch out for yourself first."

"I know, I do. I am. But it's hard, you know, because there are all these feelings. We have been together so long. Were together..." She looked down into her beer.

"I know, Theresa. But just promise me you'll protect yourself. Pistol is always going to be Pistol, and I don't know if he'll ever change."

> *Until finally it got really bad and she just couldn't take it anymore. He met a new, younger girlfriend and Theresa fell apart. I felt for her. Damn, we've all been there, sometimes the hammer, sometimes the nail. I wondered why she hadn't gotten out of the relationship sooner and found someone else, but of course love has nothing to do with the head. Furthermore, what the hell did I know about love? Most people weren't loyal at all and here she was, loyal to a fault.*

"I just have so much to say to him. But then everything got so crazy so fast. I have to get all of this out of me, but I don't want to start talking to him again or make him think I want to get back together."

"How about if you wrote a letter? Pour your heart out in a letter and then don't send it. Just write it and hold on to it."

"A letter. That's a good idea—maybe I'll do that," she said. *"You're such a good friend, Normie."*

Was I? I sure didn't feel like a good friend. I liked Theresa, but I wanted nothing to do with getting even deeper into the mess of their lives. I was too close to the whole thing already. I ordered another beer with ice, lime juice, and salt.

"Look at you—you drink a Michelada like a real Tico! Don't you want a gringo Budweiser?" she asked.

"Yuck. No thanks. I'll leave that for you stuck up Ticas from San Jose."

"*You're too funny*," she said. "*So, Normie, how was it living with Tania?*" She probably already knew the answer.

"It suuuuucked! I needed to get a place to stay and she was the only person I knew other than you and Pistol. To be honest, it hasn't been at all what I expected moving down here," I said, and I told her everything. I talked and talked—about my first days, how scary it was, how hard it was to handle everything by myself, but how I loved the ocean and the beach and how chasing my dream of writing my book kept me hanging on. I went on and on, like the rains opening up and clearing the sky. I hadn't realized until then how much I'd held onto everything inside of me. Theresa listened and I could tell she cared. She was the only person I had history with, who was so close to Pistol and his situation, who wasn't trying to get in my wallet, and who spoke English. I felt I could trust her, or at least more than anyone else around me. Maybe this meeting wasn't just for her, I thought. Maybe this was for me, too.

I told her about my challenge of trying to get my money back from Tania and the landlord. Theresa admitted that it was a Tico thing, to the point of being ridiculous. We joked that if a Tico pulled a knife on you and demanded your wallet, and you objected, they'd probably get upset for your display of bad victim's etiquette. "*Pura vida*," they'd say—my goodness, relax—and then proceed to stab you. But all the while you were expected to keep that smile on your face and that pura vida vibe! Pura vida—pow pow! They could shoot you, but don't be a gringo asshole and dare get angry about it! Theresa and I always shared that private joke when we talked—Pura vida, pow pow! Pura vida, boom boom!

We must have been talking for a long time because the band was setting up. Yazmin walked in with several friends and saw us together. She gave us a look but didn't come over and say "hi." I guess she thought we were on a date or something since we were sitting together in a bar. So that was going to be the latest rumor pulsing through the streets the next day—that along with everything else, I was hooking up with my friend's ex-girlfriend while he was in jail. This was more like a Mexican *novella* than a life.

"*Do you remember the langostas, Normie?*" Theresa asked. I almost spit out my beer.

"The *langostas*! Of course! I forgot about them."

"*I'm sooooo scared of them! They're coming again soon!*" she chuckled.

Once a year, right around Christmas, Tamarindo was besieged by insects nicknamed "*langostas*." They looked like giant flying cockroaches with sharp barbs on their front legs. They weren't really dangerous, but would dive bomb like little kamikaze pilots. All of the girls in Tamarindo were scared of them. She'd dreaded coming into Pistol's apartment because the open-air lobby had a bright light that attracted dozens of *langostas*. Once we entered all hell broke loose as they buzzed around and tried to fly into us, the girls screaming and crying. It became my mission to protect them from the *langostas*. I practiced my (nonexistent) kung fu skills on the insects, jumping around like an idiot throwing kicks and chops and knocking them out of midair. Theresa would run behind me as all of us made a break for the elevator and close the doors and fall into relieved laughter like children.

"Wow, that's too funny, Theresa. The *langostas*. Man, those were some good times," I said. They were and they weren't, but looking back, they sure seemed like simpler times.

"Seeeee...you have to be my friend in Tamarindo—who else will kung fu the langostas and keep me safe?" She had a point there.

CHAPTER 19

THE LETTER

Theresa wrote a letter to Joey and never mailed it, just like I suggested. Instead she handed it to me to deliver.

It was against my better advice. I was pleased that our meeting had gone well but I also wanted to be careful to avoid any more drama. She often Skyped me to say "hi" while she was sitting at work or if she had a question about how to get in touch with his mom, Betty. At first I was hesitant and ignored some of her messages, but she was persistent in her kindness and suggested we meet for lunch, like any friends would.

Things were feeling much better for me since I'd moved out of Tania's freeloading burlesque lair. I missed Disco but I loved the privacy of my new place, where I could shut the door and enjoy some peace. But there was still a sliver of sunlight under the door where the jungle vines of Pistol, Lena, Tania ripping me off, and the scoundrels of my past life threatened to tendril under the crack and spread across the room, entangling my leg, up my whole body, dragging me outside where they could all get at me. I kept the door closed tight.

Maybe Theresa was different? It seemed like surviving all of that pain made her hold her head up higher and take better care of the precious things inside. Still, she seemed fragile, like the wrong word or the wrong news about Pistol and she might break in two and be back where she started. I agreed to have lunch.

"No, I don't want to go to the Estrella, Normie, too many people talk there. Let's go somewhere else." So we sat at Nibbanas on the beach, eating fish tacos and looking out at a rare blue and gold day. The boats washed up and unloaded their catch, so fresh from the sea that the fish flopped and gasped for life.

"It's just so difficult. I want to help him, but I don't want him to think we're together. She handed me the letter. *"I just needed to get it out. But I wrote in here that I don't want him to write me back."*

"Okay, I'll give it to him," I said. I took the letter and folded it up in my pocket. It wasn't sealed—she trusted me. "Just be careful, kiddo. I care about him but I don't want to see you hurt, either."

"Oh, I know, Normie. I don't want any contact with him; I just had to let him know all that I felt. And that I forgave him."

"That's really cool of you. I don't know if I would be that forgiving. I think he's self-centered, and I'm not talking shit—but I don't think he's a bad guy, either. I don't know, he just lives in Pistol Land and he can't see anything else other than his way."

"Hahaha. He's the king of Pistol-landia. Exactly," she said.

"And you were the queen."

She looked out at the ocean. Tears welled in her eyes. She pushed her plate toward me, her tacos half eaten.

"I'm not feeling like eating. Do you want it?" I got it wrapped up to go and we paid and walked out.

The gypsies selling homemade jewelry in the roundabout looked at us, then looked away.

"Get in, Normie, I'll drive you home. It's hot out and I know how you gringos sweat too much," she said.

"Nah, it's okay, I can walk. You have to get to work."

"I don't mind—get in." She drove me up the road to my place and let me out. I handed her a CD that I'd burnt for her. Theresa always liked my hip hop music.

"Thanks, Theresa."

"Thank you, Normie! I'll listen to it at work on my computer. Pura vida, pow pow!"

"Boom boom!"

The next weekend, I brought the letter to Pistol in jail.

His case was not going well. His mom relayed information to me every day and she was often frustrated to the point of panic. Pistol took his angst out on her, yelling and cursing because she wouldn't follow one of his commands or even hanging up the phone. I didn't think that was cool, no matter how stressed he was. She had too much around her neck already.

Pistol's father was sick, so Betty had to take care of him. Her granddaughter was battling thyroid cancer, so she didn't want to burden their other children. They never had enough money, but every day Pistol needed something else—the truck broke down and needed repairs, his attorneys needed money to pay for a court appearance, he wanted more money in jail. All she could do was put on another sweater and turn the thermostat down.

Every day, Betty grabbed her shovel, trying desperately to dig out her suffocating child, her family that was being buried alive. I tried to help but most days it felt like we sank deeper. She had strength that only a mother could muster, but no human could take that alone. So I tried to be there for her, the person she could vent to and count on. I ended every email with encouragement like, "One day soon this will all be over. I'll come visit you in New York with Joey and I want you to make me homemade lasagna!" I almost even believed it.

I didn't have the heart to tell her that he was using the money to still smoke pot in jail.

Lena messaged me again and said she NEEDED to talk. It never friggin' ended. She'd never come back to me with a number to help Pistol, so I knew she just wanted to "dance" again. I was pissed off that she'd accused me of having something to do with the weed and lying to her. Kiss my gringo ass. I patted myself on the back for resisting temptation and being such a loyal friend to Pistol, but deep down I knew that if she looked like Salma Hayek I'd lose that ethical battle more times than not.

I didn't message her back but the next day she saw me walking on the road to the gym and swerved over, pulling her behemoth black Mercedes beside me in a cloud of dust.

"Hola, Norm! I need your help. I have this bill from Joey from my house. The electric bill and the damage from the police when they broke down the door. He never paid and still owes me $1,100."

"Okay, so did you ask him for it?"

"Yes, I ask his mom. I email her but she says they have no money. She said not nice things to me in her email. I don't understand these people, why they are mad at me—I just want my bill paid and my house fixed."

"So what is it I can help you with?"

"Can you give me money for the bill?"

"Wait—you want ME to give you money?"

"Yes, can you? I need to pay it soon or the bank takes my house. I still don't have a new renter in there."

Was she serious? She looked serious. You nasty soulless monkey shit of a human being. But, of course, I didn't say that.

"No, Lena, I'm broke. But even if I did have money, why would you want ME to pay? It's not my bill."

She took off her designer Gucci sunglasses and rubbed her eyes.

"Okay, well, I ask because you are his friend and you can ask him. I need that money, so let me know when you have it. Or talk to his mom again. I am afraid if I don't get paid things might be harder for him. You never know."

"Well then that's the way it's got to be, Lena, but it doesn't have a damn thing to do with me." I threw up my hands and shrugged.

"Okay, well, think about it and tell me. Come to my office on Friday."

"Yeah, right. I'll see what I can do."

She put her sunglasses back on and put the truck in drive and rolled away.

I kept walking up to the hill but my legs felt heavy. A conversation I'd had a few days earlier came to mind.

I was talking to Fat Doug, who was in the midst of one of his usual rants how he hated Tamarindo and all of the Critters in it. Some Tico had just ripped him off in a business venture and Doug was plotting his revenge.

"I'll call the cops and get his ass thrown in jail, and I have enough money put aside to pay off the Columbians in there for years. They'll beat him so bad and gang rape him every day until he can't take it anymore and he hangs himself!"

He was just fuming, but there was some truth to it. That could be done in Tamarindo, where it only took about $300 to have someone killed. Gang raped. Every day. Until he can't take it anymore and hangs himself. I couldn't get those words out of my head. I couldn't sleep when I thought about it, and when I did doze off toward morning, I'd wake up sweating. What kind of fucking world did we live in? It was that easy to ruin someone's life? Imagine what someone could do to Pistol—or to me, if properly motivated?

For the first time the question came to me, right there in the middle of the road when Lena drove away: *If I was in jail instead of him, would he do all of this for me?*

The answer was, "No, probably not."

I kept walking on to the gym. I worked out until I was dizzy, and then I worked out some more.

Of course I didn't tell any of this to Theresa, nor the part about the Columbians to Pistol's mom, but I did tell her about the electric bill and Lena hitting me up for money.

"What an evil woman," Betty said. "I don't understand who these people are. This would never happen in the United States. I don't know why he couldn't just stay here in New York with us." I told her I agreed, but in reality I sort of understood Lena's point of view on this one, though not her methods.

If Pistol owed her money for the electricity that he'd used then why wouldn't she ask for it? If someone rented a house from me and didn't pay the bill, I'd ask too. He threw around big words like blackmail and corruption, but in reality I couldn't get past the basic problem—he was illegally growing weed at a rental property. It wasn't a popular opinion in the Francesco camp, so I kept it to myself, but his mom saw the light too and negotiated with Lena. She agreed to pay the electric bill but not the damage from the cops and in exchange she would get a written full release of liability. She asked me to help her draft it. I did. She asked me to meet with Lena and broker the whole thing—I was the only person who had a shred of trust or credibility with both of them. So I had to go to the bank and wait in line to get the money, meet up with Lena, drive out to a remote department store where we could pay the bill, review the bill (in Spanish) to make sure it wasn't fraudulent, count out the money, get two copies of the release signed as I gave her the money, and hold on to one copy and scan and email it and then get the original back to the States somehow. I should have been a UN ambassador—I'd probably have that whole pesky Middle East thing cooled down by now.

Pistol relayed orders to all of us like an exiled general, twice a day via ten-minute phone calls. He admitted to me he was deciding which information to parcel out to whom and when, playing chess with all of us, setting up the board in his favor ten moves ahead. From there, everyone scrambled to make things happen.

I was consumed with concern for his well-being but still had doubts about my old friend's sanity. I feared that his synapses weren't connecting correctly after twenty years of smoking every day. Was he mad with the heat? Or maybe it was worse, some sort of schizophrenia, the jungle crawling up his spine?

One day he'd be in a good mood, the next day crying in the morning and then screaming and cursing in the afternoon, hanging up on his mom. He talked about how much he'd lost through this experience—tens of thousands of dollars, his house, his career—like it was someone else's fault.

He even managed to piss off his attorneys. The original deal was that they would get ten grand for all of his court appearances and negotiating a plea bargain. The prosecutor was proposing eight years, which meant, with time served and good behavior, he would probably have to do three more. Three more years was a long time, but the other option was to reject the plea bargain and go to trial.

A trial was the last thing he wanted. He'd be in a courtroom with a Tico judge and Tico jurors and Tico lawyers arguing his fate in a language he didn't even understand. I couldn't see a scenario where the jury would be even slightly sympathetic. If he lost—no, *when* he lost—the judge could give him the maximum sentence, twenty years. Twenty long years, that was just as good as a death sentence down there. The Tico news cameras would be on and I'm sure the judge would love to squash him like a bug to make an example out of the gringo that shit on their laws.

But Pistol didn't see it that way. He was on a personal crusade for justice, a glorious civil rights icon marching in a demonstration of one. I couldn't help but think of Don Quixote out there slaying dragons that were only windmills. He vowed to never accept a plea bargain, but to fight the charges tooth and nail until he was exonerated and released.

His family was in a frenzy of concern. What the hell was he thinking? They wanted me to give him a stern talking to the next time I was in jail and sort him out. "Talk some sense into him, Norm," his family said. I squirmed at the thought of having to look him in the eyes and confront him. Who the fuck was I to give anyone advice?

But I promised that I'd do my best.

Saturday morning, Hector picked me up nice and early. It was a perfect day, not too hot and not rainy.

"*Heyyyy, buddddy! Pura vida!*" he said, but I felt numb as we drove toward the jail, Theresa's letter folded up in my pocket. Half an hour later, as we took the sharp turn through *Veinti-Siete*, the little town named "twenty-seven" for some unknown reason, I cursed and smacked myself in the forehead. I'd forgotten my passport—we had to turn around. We went all the way back and I ran upstairs and grabbed it and then ran back and we took off again. I was sweating like a madman by the time I got back in the cab. So much for the early start, but Hector didn't mind. "*Tranquilo, amigo. Esta bien,*" he told me.

We drove on. My whole life felt like it was underwater, like I was a diver floating through the remains of a shipwreck. It wasn't real; it couldn't be. It was such a bad reality show that I couldn't help but look around for the hidden cameras. I could see the advertising executive in his black suit and black tie pitching it to the studio heads at a shiny conference table in a glass office overlooking Times Square:

"Okay, so let's drop a chubby, germaphobic gringo with an anxiety disorder into the middle of a Central American jungle with no friends, and he doesn't even speak the language, and no, NO!—this is even better!—let's force him to visit a Third World prison every weekend and see what happens?!"

"So it's like Survivor, but there's a 50% chance he might get stabbed or shot? I like it. Can we give him a dorky name, like 'Norm' or something?

That will score big with the 70-95-year-old demographic we've been trying to capture since Golden Girls went off the air."

"Sure, I don't see what not."

I was just an average guy from the States who couldn't hack it so I moved down to paradise for some sun and the simple life, but I was stuck. There was nothing else I could do but stumble forward and see it all through.

I put my thoughts to a better place: my only solace, the book. The *BOOK*. I could escape in there and control that world. Bad life made good writing, I reminded myself. It became my mantra, my purpose for enduring all that I was going through. I wrote furiously, like a soldier penning letters to his family the night before he stormed the beach. If I could only get the book done then there would be something I could leave the world, forever. Even when I was gone—if someone offed me or I got thrown in jail or the jungle swallowed me up over the years and I disappeared, there would be evidence that I once existed. My voice would be heard, and that's the only thing that seemed to matter.

Before I knew it, we pulled up to the jail.

CHAPTER 20

CANADIAN BACON

As soon as we pulled up to the jail I knew it was going to be a bad day.

An unruly crowd of women stampeded into the registration area. There was no line, they all just pushed and jostled to get closer to the door. I fell in and waited, too. Everyone tried to wait in the shade as long as possible, but soon wet patches emerged on their clothes. You knew it was damn hot if Ticas were sweating. The flies circled and landed on their foreheads, but they were packed in too tight to even lift their hands and brush them away, so they just left them. Someone bumped me from behind. An argument broke out when one mother stepped on another's foot and someone said, "*Hay dios mio!*" and made the sign of the cross.

Visiting hours were over at 1:00 p.m. and it was almost noon, and by the looks of it, not many people were getting in. The guard only opened the door every fifteen minutes to let a few women in at a time. When a visitor did leave the jail, they could barely push their way through the crowd to get out. One woman contorted her body to climb under a railing, trying to cut the line, but the others pushed her out, leaving her stuck under the railing with her back bent at an impossible angle, calling out in pain.

When the door didn't open for a while the women became agitated and yelled for the guards. An older Chinese couple slipped a guard money and he rolled opened up a fence to the side and let them in without waiting. That angered the wives, who cursed the guards about "*las Chinas*." Someone moaned in desperation, then others joined in until soon they all sounded like a pack of wounded animals. But just then a breeze blew and the crowd let out a collective sigh of relief. Someone told a joke and they laughed. But within minutes the crowd was tense and pressing again. The guard asked who was next and they all started calling to him. I understood enough of what they were saying to figure out that they were trying to get in for their conjugal visits.

I was one of the only guys, so once I got past registration it took me no time to get searched and stamped. I walked back to D2B. "*Hey, Canada! Throw a coin! Just 500 Colones!*" they yelled. When I got in the door, someone called for Pistol and he walked out of his cell and we said "hi." I knew plenty of the other guys, so I said "hi" to all of them too—Mike Tyson, Air Jordans, the guy who had his cousin in Tamarindo, and the lottery guy. But this time there was a special guest. I almost didn't believe my own eyes, but there was another white guy in the jail.

He walked up to me and held out his hand.

"Hey, Norm, my name's Ryan." He offered an easy smile and put a hand on my shoulder. "Joey's told me a lot about you." He was tall and thin, his ribs poking through his wife beater shirt, with sickly gray skin. He had a fresh shiner under one eye. I knew that look; I guessed he'd been in jail for a while, but I liked him instantly—he was one of those guys you couldn't *not* like.

"Hey, nice to meet you, Ryan. Well, not exactly 'nice,' in here…you know what I mean."

"Ryan just got transferred from another unit," Pistol said.

"There was a slight misunderstanding with some of the guys in my cell, so they moved me here."

"You guys just doubled the gringo population in the jail!" I laughed.

"Yeah, the other inmates tell us that if we're not careful we'll have a whole gringo soccer team."

"Here, let's sit," Ryan said and led us to a spot on the ground where two bedrolls were laid out. A very attractive and very young Tica in white shorts and a skimpy top lounged on one of the bedrolls. Ryan sat down next to her and they kissed. He saw me looking.

"Oh, this is Claudia. She's my girlfriend," he said.

"Do a lot of dating these days?" I laughed.

"More than you might think! She's the daughter of another inmate and I saw her visiting so we started talking. Now she visits me."

"Get the hell out of here," I said. This dude was pulling a hotter chick in jail than I could in a resort town by the beach.

"Oh yeah, there are all sorts of ways to meet girls," Pistol said. "Ryan wrote letters to all of the female inmates—every single one of them—and became pen pals with a few who wrote back. Tell him about that one chick, Ryan."

"So I wrote this one inmate and she wrote back, and we went back and forth and it started getting hot. She told me she used to win beauty pageants in Santa Cruz. It looked like we were going to get it on, so we arranged to meet."

"Wait, they'll just let you meet?" I said.

"Well, no, but there are ways to set it up. We planned to both complain about stomach pains on the same day so we'd end up in the nurse's clinic together, where we could meet face to face. We even made plans to get a minute alone in the bathroom."

"This is the best part," Pistol said.

"So I told the guard I had stomach pain and got to the clinic a little early. I was checking out every girl who walked in. "No, it's not her, no, it's not her, damn, I wish it was her,' and finally this chick walked in but she's ugly as sin and fat and nasty. I mean nasty-nasty. And she knows it's me because of course I stick out like a sore thumb because there are only two gringo prisoners. I'm praying it's not her but she walks right up to me and says my name and introduces herself."

"Oh no! What did you do?" I asked.

"I panicked and told her my name was Joey Francesco and I didn't know what she was talking about!"

"Oh my God, that's classic," I laughed.

"Now she's confused as hell every time she sees us!" Pistol said.

"Beauty queen my ass!" Ryan said.

"I'm just amazed that you guys get conjugal visits. I almost want to come here just for those."

"But you have to be careful," Ryan said. "You only get one conjugal visitor per year, though she can come a bunch of times. So if you piss her off or she breaks up with you, you're screwed."

"Or not screwed," I said.

"Exactly."

"They make them come to the jail three times for interviews and submit all of this paperwork and their passport, so it's a big process. You need the right horse in that race."

I listened, fascinated. I've always been a student of culture, how you could take any human being and put them in a certain environment and they will adapt to survive. And in prison there was no more urgent daily agenda than to survive.

Everyone has a story, and with a little incentive I got Ryan talking. It didn't take much—I just handed him one of the extra Whoppers I'd brought Pistol.

"Hey, that's mine, Normando!" Pistol joked.

"Slow down, gunsmoke, I brought extras." I even unwrapped one for myself as we all kicked it and chatted like old friends.

Ryan was from Toronto and had been arrested six months earlier for cocaine trafficking. He had a kilo of coke he was trying to smuggle back to Canada, so he'd emptied out two cans of black beans and put the coke inside and somehow sealed them up again. He went to the airport and cruised through security—everything was looking good. Then the dogs got him. They smelled the coke and ran over, barking. The cops took him into an interrogation room and picked up one of the cans and jammed a pair of scissors into the bottom of it. When they pulled the scissors out, they were covered in white powder, not *frijoles negros*. Busted.

He was using the public defender, who was actually doing a stand-up job. There were several technicalities they were arguing, so his sentence could be anywhere from getting out in a month to the full eight years. Despite their constant speculation, no one really knew what the hell was going on with their case in Costa Rica.

I looked at Ryan and he gave me a sheepish grin back. I liked the guy, but my first thought was, "What an idiot." First off, who the hell pretends to take black beans back to Canada as a souvenir? I could understand Costa Rican coffee or some woodcrafts or a stuffed parrot or some tourist shit like that, but black beans? That's like a European coming to New York and trying to fly home with a pack of Cony Island dogs loaded with crack. Furthermore, don't they have coke in Canada? Is it really worth years of your life in a Third World prison to bring some coke to Canada? That level of carelessness almost even trumped Pistol's story. Almost.

"DUDE!?" I said.

"I know, I know. You don't have to say it." That pretty much summed it up, so we went back to eating our Whoppers.

When we were done, Pistol cleaned up the napkins and wrappers and cleared his throat. Ryan excused himself.

"Well, I'll let you guys talk. Hey, real nice meeting you, Norm—and thanks for the grub."

"You got it, bro. Anything I can do for you the next time I visit?"

"Yeah, how about getting me the fuck out of here, eh?" he laughed.

"That's all? I'm on it. You guys watch out for each other, huh?"

He nodded and got up with his girlfriend, and they moved somewhere else to make out. I sort of wanted to go with her too.

I took out the letter and handed it to Pistol. "It's from Theresa," I told him. "We got together and talked."

"Oh wow, thanks, Normando. I appreciate that. How's she doing?"

"She's really hurt, but I think she's going to be okay. She just doesn't want to get caught up in everything with you, again."

"When's she going to visit?"

"Listen, Pistol, don't fuck with her. You've put that poor girl through enough. I know it's none of my business, but I care about both of you. It's not easy for her in Tamarindo, and to be honest, I'm surprised she even came back."

"I know, I know. Yeah. I'll write her back."

"She said not to. I really think you should leave her alone for now, Pistol. Maybe in the future..." A sexy Tica in heels and tight jeans walked by us, holding both of our gazes as she went by.

"I'll write her. Thanks for bringing this." He slapped the letter across his leg and put it in his back pocket.

I'd almost forgotten my whole point of being there—I was supposed to give him some big life-changing speech to straighten him out. Instead, I procrastinated by asking about his case, and he caught me up. I'd requested a Costa Rican criminal law textbook for him, and his attorney had delivered it. He went through it every day, picking apart the statutes for drug possession even though he didn't know Spanish. In typical brazen Pistol fashion, he said he'd figured it all out. The judges, the prosecutors, and his attorneys were all idiots and he'd found the phrasing that was going to make him a free man.

I looked into his eyes. Was he all there? He was incredibly intelligent and charismatic, but that didn't mean he was lucid. I'm sure he looked back and saw nothing but fear and frustration in my eyes. It scared the shit out of me that he was still looking to throw Hail Marys. I wanted to shake him—Jesus Christ, Pistol, twenty years! There was no way he could do that time. His mom couldn't do that time. And I certainly wasn't going to hang around that long.

"If I have to go to trial I'm taking everyone down. Believe me, they don't want that."

"You might want to think about laying low and just getting out of here first, no?"

"Fuck them, they're all going down. They'll turn on each other and sing like canaries and it will shake up all of Tamarindo."

"I'll let you know right now, Pistol, if you start taking everyone on I'm getting the hell out of town. There's no way I'm walking the streets with those people when you're trying to burn them. I'll end up in a ditch with my head cut off."

"If I get in front of the judge with all of this evidence of corruption against Lena and the OIJ and the prosecutor, they'll set me free immediately."

"Think on this one, Pistol. Please, please think. Take the plea, bro. Or do whatever the fuck you want, but you're the one who has to do the time either way."

He nodded his head.

"How long are you planning on sticking around Tamarindo?" he asked.

"I don't know, man, I just don't know right now."

A guard clapped his nightstick against the bars and yelled something in Spanish. Visiting hours were over. We stood up, along with all of the wives, mothers, and girlfriends. Damn, I was out of time, but I was supposed to get inside his head and figure it all out. The crowd moved toward the door, sweeping me with them. His family was counting on me to get his commitment to take the plea bargain, to unravel the cult of personality that was Pistol-landia, to get him to stop smoking pot, to promise to move back to the States and settle down into a normal adult existence the second he got out of jail, to accept the lord Jesus Christ as his savior and get married and have kids with a white picket fence. That was a hell of a lot. I didn't know what to say.

The guard walked up and pointed his nightstick at the door. Time was *really* up unless I wanted a much longer stay. The crowd pushed at my back. I didn't feel like I was moving my feet but Pistol seemed to get smaller, shrinking into the periphery of the cell.

"And Pistol..." I called out. He lifted his head to see me above the crowd. "You better be nice to your mom."

"I know, I know. I feel bad," he said. "I will."

When I walked out, Hector was relieved to see me. There was some sort of commotion with police around the front gates as visitors circled and watched, but I was just happy to get in the taxi and get the hell out of there for the day.

"*Hey, buddddyyyyy! Todo bien*?" Hector asked.

As we drove out, Hector told me why there had been so much commotion. While I was inside, a mother came with her eight-year-old daughter to visit her husband. The little girl was wearing her best church dress and a pink bow in her hair for him. Her mom put an eight ball of coke in a condom, tied a strong knot in it, and put it in her vagina. Their taxi driver knew she was carrying and warned her to be careful because the drug-sniffing dogs were out that day. She went on anyway; I assume she had no choice. The mother and daughter got out of the taxi and got in line with everyone else, but once they were behind the gates she saw the German Shepherds and her nerves betrayed her. She tried to duck out of the line, but it was too late, there was no place to go.

The dogs were all over her and the guards grabbed her roughly as she looked in panic for an escape but there was none. Her daughter started crying and yelling for her mommy because she didn't understand what was happening. They strip-searched the mom and found the drugs and threw her in a cell. She came to visit and ended up staying. They called child services and a social worker came and took the girl to a foster home. She came to see her father in jail and left without a mother, thrown into a jail for children herself.

We drove back toward Tamarindo. I rolled down the window and felt the wind. I couldn't figure it all out. Fuck, I was going to give up even trying.

A long time ago I saw some graffiti on the barrio streets of San Jose, red spray paint on a concrete wall under a bridge, so profound that it stuck with me through the many years. It said simply "*soy nada*"—I am nothing. That's it. I finally knew what the writer of that graffiti meant, felt what he felt: I am nothing, I don't exist. I am so small, so powerless, my life so inconsequential, that I don't even matter. I am nothing and I want nothing. And there are so many more like me. Our voices will never be heard no matter how loud we yell. In this life there is no comfort, no meaning, no justice. Love is just a song, but we all forgot the lyrics a long time ago. *Soy nada,* because that's just the way it is.

Eight years old. Dogs barking and guards ripping her mother away, the sound of her crying and a pink bow falling to the ground. Waking up among strangers to her new life in some dingy, state-run orphanage. I wanted to go back there and find that little girl, to save her, to tell her everything was going to be okay, but, of course that would be a lie.

CHAPTER 21

CASA LADRONES (HOUSE OF THIEVES)

In some cultures they believe that when you take a photograph of a person, you steal their soul. In Costa Rica, when you want to take a picture of someone, they've probably already stolen your camera.

Ticos will steal everything that isn't bolted down, and then come back under cover of night to liberate the bolts. Stealing and scamming is such a normal part of their culture that they'll actually get offended if you call them on it. See? I just offended 3,294 Ticos with that last sentence, and yet they can't deny it's true.

Thwarting the bad guys is big business in Costa Rica, too. I estimate that roughly 76% of the country is covered in barbed wire. Every window is crossed with metal bars, as are the front doors. Everything locks with a key from the inside, so if I were in my house and misplaced the key I wouldn't be able to get out. If there was a fire I'd deep fry like a redneck's Twinkie. Ticos love gates, razor wire, security doors, vicious guard dogs, and placed broken bottles into the wet concrete on the top of their walls, jagged edges up. Even with all of that, they still employ phalanxes of security guards.

There was a guard in front of every ATM machine, bank, apartment complex, car rental lot, upscale store, and bar. Every apartment had a night watchman. A little old man with a wooden pole and an orange vest patrolled every parking lot. Feel safe yet? Of course they weren't worth a damn because, assuming the guards weren't drunk or asleep, they were in on the take.

One time Pistol came back to his truck and his car window was broken, his paddle board missing from the rack on top. The guard just stood there and shrugged, like, "*Sorry, I didn't see anything.*" Sure you didn't, buddy. Forever after that, Pistol and that guard enjoyed a hate-hate relationship. The guard would yell and bang on his truck when he pulled in and Pistol would call him a *pegeyegua*—a horse fucker—and give him the finger. Then he would pay him a tip just so nothing else would disappear in the future and the guard would say, "*Gracias, jefe,*" like nothing ever happened.

When I lived in Villa Verde I had some serious security concerns, but there were a couple of things in our favor. Disco was a good-sized dog with some presence, even if she would only run into the wall headfirst if someone actually broke in. The bigger security deterrent was Tania, who would probably find a way to borrow money from any thief who crossed our threshold. Or she could always club them to death with a pink rabbit dildo. But I chose to be proactive and befriend the fat Tico night watchman. I'd say "hi" and bring him a can of beer or leftover pizza when I came home from dinner. He loved it and my place stayed safe, but I can't say the same for everyone else in *Villa Mierde.*

A brother and sister from Vancouver showed up for a week. They'd driven all the way down from Canada in a classic Land Cruiser, something straight out of an African safari. They'd passed through "dangerous" Mexico, Honduras, Guatemala, and Nicaragua without a single problem—*until* their stay in Tamarindo. They came out one morning and the back window was broken and a bunch of irreplaceable items missing. The security guard was there but just shrugged. He hadn't seen anything, of course. They must practice that shrug in grade school, a hundred times every morning in homeroom before reciting the Tico Pledge of Allegiance, starting 'em out early for all of the aspiring future security guards and parking lot attendants.

I came home from the beach one afternoon and there was a big commotion outside one of the other units. A tall, distinguished gringo and his wife and teenage daughter were arguing with the slovenly security guard. It looked pretty heated, the family yelling and waving their arms and the guard just shrugging, of course. I walked by, minding my own business, but the man soon came to my door.

"Excuse me, I don't mean to bother you. It's Norm, right?"

"Yup. What can I do for you?" I said.

"I was wondering if I can use your phone to call the police?"

"Whoaaa, slow down there, Andy Dufrain! The last thing I'm going to do is help sell out the locals—I'm no snitch. No WAY! I don't want to get involved."

"I'll buy you a six pack of beer."

"Come right on in, the phone is on the desk. Do you need me to dial?"

He called the cops but couldn't even get anyone on the phone, so he called the property management company, who promised to send someone over...*ahorita*.

He told me what had gone down. They'd arrived earlier that day and dropped their suitcases in the apartment and gone to the beach. When they came back the security guard was walking down the staircase inside of their apartment. They'd startled him, and when they asked what the hell he was doing in there he fumbled through some bullshit that it was part of his job to patrol the interiors of the units. He stank like booze. They argued and then the guard split. When they went upstairs to check what was missing, they found his daughter's suitcase opened and all of her panties strewn about. Pretty freaky, fat boy. The property manager showed up hours later and everyone argued some more but nothing happened. The wife and daughter were so rattled that they went to a hotel that night and flew out of the country the next morning. The poor husband stayed. I hung out with him at the bar that week and let him buy me multiple beers in exchange for the pleasure of my company.

I never saw that guard again, but I'm sure he's practicing his shrugs in the mirror somewhere in Costa Rica. He's probably been promoted to the chief of police.

My new apartment in Pueblo del Mar was safe by Tamarindo standards, but still I prepared for the worst. I hid all of my valuables. My passport went into a cleaned out jar of peanut butter, my extra ATM card taped to the back of the toilet tank, the external hard drive kept in the bottom of a cereal box. I hid my camera...where was my camera, come to think of it? I hid things so well that I hid them from myself. Within 3.9 seconds of not being able to locate any given object, I automatically blamed it on the cleaning ladies, an awful habit that left me feeling like a xenophobic bastard the moment it showed up. Where the hell was my left sock?! God dammit, those little smiling, hard-working, nice, brown ladies stole from me again! They're probably selling it on the black market for .0000000001 of a *Colone* as we speak. If there were police in this town, I'd press charge—oh, there it is. (Sorry.)

I couldn't help but assume that *ladrones* were right outside my door, hiding in the darkness, ready to come for me like pirates boarding a ship under cover of darkness. I'd be damned if I was going to make it easy for them.

Was I being paranoid? Was I some conspiracy-theory nut job holed up in his house with the curtains drawn, twirling his mustache at how to out-think the bad guys? Absolutely. But it served me well in Tamarindo, and I was one of the only long-term residents not to get something stolen. I had plenty of friends who came home to crack heads inside their apartments, ripping through their stuff. Even sealing up an apartment with security bars on the windows didn't deter change of ownership of choice possessions. A popular technique was to take a long pole, or pull down a tree branch and whittle the leaves off, and form sort of a Y on the end, then cut a little hole in the screen with a razor blade and poke the stick right through the gaps between the bars, into the apartment, and carefully fish things back out.

Ticos aren't known for being directly confrontational—instead it's the passive-aggressive capital of the world. A fair fight in Tama entailed three guys smashing bottles over the back of your head. Sometimes I think they *should* have an army so they'd experience a healthy distaste for violence. But now and again, brute force was the modus operandi for a robbery.

It was around 4:00 a.m. one morning in November and I happened to be out of town. My phone, sitting on the nightstand, started pinging like crazy. I picked it up and saw Facebook and Skype messages from someone I didn't know. He wrote that he was desperately looking for people who knew his son, Alex, a casual friend of mine in Tama.

Alex had been sitting in his apartment around 11:00 p.m. on a Skype video chat with his boss back in San Francisco. All of a sudden his boss saw three men in ski masks and machetes enter the apartment behind Alex. A scuffle ensued and then the screen went dead. The boss Skyped and called him repeatedly but couldn't make contact. Of course he was freaking out, so he called all of their mutual friends and everyone started reaching out for people in Tamarindo who might know him. They couldn't find Alex's address (there wasn't one), couldn't find a phone number to the police (totally useless), and he never got back online. Eventually they reached his parents in the New York, who went down the list of his Facebook friends and ended up messaging me. There wasn't much I could do, but we all spent an uneasy early morning on watch.

Alex emerged the next day and let everyone know he was okay. The *bandidos* broke in, roughed him up, tied his hands and his feet, gagged his mouth, and blindfolded him (it would be exactly at that point where I would freak the fuck out and start kicking and biting until I got away or they killed me). They threw him on the couch as they rifled through his apartment and stole his money, cards, computer, and camera, but they didn't hurt him. He was one of the lucky ones.

The grimy little *ladrones* even stole stuff right off the beach. It happened to tourists all the time, even when they were only 20 meters away in the ocean and turned their heads for a split second. Sure enough, my first months in town they nabbed my brand new flip-flops. I went for a long swim and when I came back, my shirt was still there but my nice green Billabong flip-flops were nowhere to be seen. It was a long, painful walk home. What was the world coming to if a local (sort of) couldn't even swim? Others shared my sentiment. Among the surf culture of Tama, a flip-flop-stealer was considered the lowest form of life, an amoeba slightly below pond scum. Their whole family was cursed to have itchy venereal crabs and Cee Lo Green arms for the rest of eternity. Breaking into a car was fine, an apartment was encouraged, and even mugging was fair game, but stealing flip-flops was condemned even by the Critters, the coke dealers, and other "respectable" thieves.

"Fucking putas stealing flip-flops. They give us a bad name with the tourists and then people won't want to come back," Fedor said, as he sized up a group of tourists he'd sell a dime bag of baking soda to later that night.

I learned to bury my stuff at the beach, digging under a log or beneath some sea grass where I could cover my possessions with sand while I was in the ocean. I put my house key and money into a plastic bag and buried them nearby. It worked like a charm and nothing was ever stolen again, though sometimes when I came back from a swim I had to dig up twenty holes before I found my buried prize.

It wasn't worth getting mad about larceny in Costa Rica because it wasn't personal, just a void in the moral code of the culture. But I could get even. Every morning I poured a big mug of coffee and Baileys and sat down to write. Well, one morning I took my coffee with me as I walked down to the beach with Disco. My main man, Kenny G, was lounging on a hammock under the lifeguard stand. Like many of those guys, his nightly accommodations were a work in progress. More often than not, he stayed up until 6:00 a.m. when Aqua closed and then slept on the beach for a few hours. I said, "What's up?" and chatted for a moment. I wanted to go running, but I still had half a cup of coffee so I gave it to him to finish, which he eagerly accepted (coffee with Baileys was a luxury). I took off for my run, and when I came back he was sleeping there in the hammock, snoring away with my empty coffee cup under his arm. Within view of all of the locals and surfers, I tiptoed up and eased the cup out of his grasp, leaving him snoozing. No one realized it was actually my cup, so they thought I was stealing from a local, beating a hustler at his own game. They loved it, and I must have earned 1,000 local points that morning. The next time I saw Kenny G I acted like nothing happened and asked him for my cup back. He bullshitted through some excuse about having it at home or something and promised to return it. I did the same thing for a month, tormenting him by asking him for the missing cup every time I saw him. Finally, I let him in on the joke and watched his face turn red with embarrassment because a gringo had outfoxed a Tico in front of everyone on the beach. The score was now Ticos 13,947, Gringos 1, but at least we were on the board.

During my time in Costa Rica I heard many stories of thievery, some tragic and some pure comedy, but there was one that stood out. George, the nice guy from Arizona who owned Kahiki's, sat down and chatted with me and my buddies, Kelly and Rafa, one night during the rainy season when things were really slow.

We got to talking about the usual—what business was closing, which working girl was the prettiest, and recalling the early 1980s Montreal Expos teams position by position, important stuff like that—when then the topic turned to robbery. He told us how he once dated a Tica from the Caribbean side of the country who took him back to her home town. It was a long journey by chicken bus through remote jungle to get there. In the afternoon the bus driver stopped among a few houses in the middle of nowhere, not even big enough to be called a village. Everyone got off the bus and bought Coca Colas and slices of coconut from the few locals who lived there. George strolled around as he waited and noticed that there were only a few houses in the hamlet, yet they were all reinforced with spiked fences, barbed wire, and barred windows. George asked a local guy why they needed all of that—were there invading tribes of indigenous Indians or something? No, the man said. In fact, there were only eight houses in town and everyone who lived there was related somehow. Then why the security? Because even though there were only eight houses in town and they were all family, they still constantly broke into each other's homes and stole things.

Oh, how we laughed at that one. *Pura vida, pow pow. Pura vida, boom boom.*

CHAPTER 22

BUZZARDS

One day in November the sun came out. I never thought I'd see it again in Tamarindo, but there it was, a clear, sparkling morning. Everyone who was left in town ran down to the beach. Mothers brought their children to the edge of the water where they splashed in, fully clothed. Everyone left work early and came down to the beach and put their arms around each other. They lit joints made out of cylindrical seashells and danced when the bartender at Nibbana's turned up the reggae music. The Rasta washed his locks in the ocean and threw them back against the setting sun.

"*No mas lluvia! The rain is over!*" people yelled to me as they passed. We were a ragged bunch—wet and torn clothing, skinny faces, tired eyes, like the crew of a ship cast ashore for the first time in months. But up and down the beach I heard laughter; the rains were over, the earth was new. The tourists would come again and everyone would eat. It was going to be all right.

I couldn't believe how beautiful it was—all of that sunlight, everything pure, blooming. Of course I'd seen nice weather plenty of times in Tama, but somehow it looked different. The sails were impossibly white on the wooden schooners bobbing in the bay, the hills glowing emerald green. Blue crowned motmots chirped and hung in the sky like shiny kites before dropping down to skim the water and snatch up their dinner in a spray of foam. The sunlight blessed it all. It seemed too good to be true, but I wouldn't see one more rain drop in all my time in Tamarindo.

Tania was down there with Disco. She was on the beach almost every sunset but usually left the dog at home because she had a new job working as a manager for the Estrella casino.

Disco played on the edge of the surf, retreating and barking when the waves rolled in. Her coat looked a little gray. I went over to her and she smelled me a few feet away and perked up. I gave her a hug as she licked my neck and face.

"*Disco, Disco, Discita*! What's up, sweet baby?"

"Hi, N! How are you?" Tania said.

"Oh, not bad. It's great to see the sun out, huh?"

"You should come by the casino. We're having a big party Friday night."

"Thanks, but I'm not partying much these days. No money."

I waited for her to respond to my hint but she just took a gulp of beer. Disco scratched at the fleas jumping off her hind.

"How's she doing?" I asked.

"I never get to see her. I leave for work in the afternoon and don't get home until 4:00 a.m. and then I just sleep all day."

"I hope you don't leave her..."

"No, no, I put her in the backyard when I'm gone. But she's a pain in the ass—my neighbors say she barks all night. And she keeps getting out of the gate. I lock it but somehow she still gets out."

"Well, take good care of her. Let me know if you want me to take her to the beach sometime."

"Ohhh, N, that's so nice of you! Now please come to the party on Friday."

I said goodbye, hugged Disco again, and shook her ears and head furiously. *Disco, Disco, Discita.* She tried following me when I walked away, but Tania grabbed her collar.

Damn, I missed that lovable bitch. Disco, I mean. She got me through some of the rough early days, when I had no friends and it all looked bleak. There's something about the unconditional love of an animal that warms my heart—it's just pure, I guess.

Disco may have been absent from my life, but I was feeling more comfortable in Tama. I enjoyed my daily routine and the warmth that comes with familiarity: saying hi to the same people, the smell of the tropics, walking those same dirt roads with the music of wind chimes always in my head. However, every visit to the jail dragged me back to reality, a humbling reminder of the shit show around me.

Pistol was convinced that a medical marijuana card from the States would help his case and set him free. Of course it had to be back-dated to be valid, but once presented to the courts it would prove that he was cultivating marijuana for personal consumption, out of medical necessity, and not intending to sell. That was THE pivotal point to his case because Costa Rican laws for possession of marijuana were much lighter than for trafficking. I did see the value in the card and thought it couldn't hurt.

Getting a card would be easy if he were living in the States—he'd just walk into his local doctor's office and say he had anxiety or headaches and the doc would write a prescription. As one could imagine it was a little more complicated when he was locked in prison in Central America. Pistol begged me to work my street connections to get a card. (Side bar: I just put that in to sound cool. Ohhhhh, Norm has *street connections*! How sexy and dangerous! It's really just a friend who runs a legit grow operation in San Francisco and has a doctor on the payroll. I didn't have to play Russian roulette in a dark alley in a seedy part of China Town or anything. Okay, we now return to the story.) I wasn't supposed to tell his mom about the card, or his sister, but I had to coordinate it with his brother, who would pay me for it. Oh boy.

I put the word out to my *STREET CONNECTS* and they did me a huge favor after I explained the situation. They would get me a medical marijuana card and back-date it…for $500. I reported this to Pistol and he was pleased. He told me to email his brother for the money. I paid the money out of my own pocket to expedite it and emailed my friends in the States with his legal name, DOB, and social security number. I emailed his brother and told him implicitly NOT to tell their mother. He sent me only half of the money back and promptly mentioned it to his mom. Well, just shit in my milk, why don't ya? That pissed me off. Here I was scampering around to keep his brother safe in a Third World country, when NONE of his family had even visited, and not only did he mess that up but then he started getting funny with my money? Oh *hell* nah!

It was time to put some red pants on the situation. I emailed him back and told him in no uncertain terms that paying me back was not optional. He hemmed and hawed and it took him a few weeks but eventually he got me the money. But the bigger problem was Betty. She flipped out when she heard about the medical marijuana card. She insisted that they'd have no part of it; there was absolutely no way she or her family was going to break the law, even if it helped Joey. Furthermore, there was no money in the budget to pay for it. She drew her line in the sand. I explained how big of a favor my friends had done for me, no, for *them*, and jeopardized their careers and livelihood just to help Pistol, but she wouldn't hear it. For weeks we had World War III between Pistol in jail saying he needed the card and cursing and hanging up on his mom and telling me to go ahead, and Betty telling me absolutely not, cancel the order, there's no more money. I emailed his attorneys independently to find out if it really would help his case:

Good afternoon XXXXX:

My name is Norm Schriever and I am a friend of Joey Francesco, and now a good friend of his family's. I have also been visiting him in jail most weekends. I had a question for you regarding his defense and plea bargain: Hypothetically, if he had a valid medical marijuana card from the U.S., would that help his chances of getting a lesser plea or help you doing your jobs arguing that the marijuana was grown for consumption and not trafficking?

Warm regards,

Norm Schriever

This is the response I got from his attorneys:

Good Morning Norman,

Thank you for your offer of assistance.

It does not help or harm his case.

Momma won, but they were still in a nasty tug of war. Pistol kicked and screamed and was adamant about going through with it—he needed it for his defense and it would exonerate him, couldn't we see that? Betty said absolutely not, it was fraud, and wanted nothing to do with it and told me to cancel the card and get my money back.

Get my money back? I didn't have time to explain the customer service practices of the criminal underworld to her, but there wasn't a very liberal return policy when you purchased illicit goods and services. This wasn't exactly Zappos.com. But she insisted, and I was still waiting for Pistol's brother to pay me back, so I thought that might be the only way I was getting my money back.

I called up *THE* guy, my *STREET CONNECTION*. A fly on the wall in my apartment in Costa Rica might have heard this conversation:

Ring. Ring.

"Umm, yes, hello, Mr. Do-Illegal-Shit Man? Yes, good day to you too, sir. Oh yeah, it is a kind day. I get it—KIND because you sell marijuana. Yes, legally. I know.

"Ummmm...yes, well the reason I'm calling you is because, well, I decided that NO, I don't want that THING that we talked about, after all.

"You know, the THING for the GUY about the STUFF who's in the PLACE? Yeah that. Well, I don't need it anymore. Sooooo...I guess what I'm asking is 'Can I please have a refund?'

"No, I didn't say I needed a REAL GUN. I'm all set with that for now. I said a RE-FUND.

"Yes, I'm serious. No, it's not April Fool's—it's November."

(I pull the phone away from my ear as he yells.)

"Yes. Yes. No. Yes. I understand. Yes. I'm sorry. I know. I am a jackass. An idiot, too. You're absolutely right. Of course you know you're right. I was just agreeing with you that you know you're right so you know that we both know.

"No, I'm not a fucktard. Yes, I'm pretty sure because I don't even know what that is."

"Okay, okay. Thank you. Thank you so much, Mr. Worthington. Ooops! I mean, Mr. Do-Illegal-Shit Man. Ohhh, I'm sorry—didn't mean to say your real name, yeah, now I guess they would know it's your real name because I just said 'real name.' To anyone listening, that is NOT his real name.

"No, no, my phone isn't tapped. Yes, I'm sure. How do I know? Because they can't even hook up my Internet correctly down here—it took them three weeks. It's a complete shit show, so trust me, we're good.

"Shit show? Yeah, I like that expression, too.

"Okay. Never again. I promise. I understand—I will never ever EVER contact you again. Okay, bye. Thank y—" *(He hung up on me.)*

(Something occurs to me. I call him right back.)

Ring. Ring.

"Umm, yes, hello Mr., Do-Illegal-Shit Man? Yes, it's me again. Yeah, shit show guy. I forgot to give you my PayPal address."

Luckily the guy took mercy on me because of Pistol's situation, though the doctor wanted to curse me up and down (and I don't blame him). I got half of the money back—the rest was a fee for their trouble. That's more than fair, so thank you, Mr. Worthington! Did you get my Christmas card?

Day by day, my resentment against Pistol and his family grew, but then I'd check myself. "Damn, Norm, cut him some slack. This dude is fighting for his life and under more pressure than you can possibly conceive." Well, I could conceive of it because I'd been in a very similar situation in the States—except I was innocent—and the anxiety had almost turned me into a blubbering crazy man. I could *empathize*, not just sympathize, and that's why the whole thing scared the hell out of me.

Helping him was a pain in the ass but I got to sleep in my bed every night and jump in the ocean and not worry about staying safe. What an asshole I was for getting cranky...but then again, I hadn't put him there. I wasn't the one who broke the law so egregiously and acted like a megalomaniac to Lena, practically begging to get caught. I didn't put him or his family in that position, but a lot of times it felt like I was the only one in the boat, bailing furiously to keep it from sinking.

"*You look sad*," Antonio had said, and now I knew his English was just fine. Deep down I just wanted the whole thing to be over with—one way or another. I hated the part of me that felt like that. I cared—of course I cared—but I was punch drunk with emotions from standing in lines in the hot sun half of my life.

At least Theresa was helping. Despite my warnings, I'd delivered her letter. He wasn't supposed to respond but he wrote a long letter back to her, and then they had a phone call, and then daily phone calls, and then a visit to the jail, and then regular visits. She swore that it was just as friends and there was no way she'd go back to a relationship with him, but he was pushing hard and I feared they were falling into old patterns. Shit, it was none of my business, and it was nice to have a second person to share my burden. Theresa prepared homemade stew and spaghetti instead of Burger King, and we coordinated our shopping trips and visits to the jail so I only had to go half of the time. It was nice to have a little space to breathe again, to focus on what I wanted out of my time in Tamarindo: my three goals before I turned 40, and now the sunlight to do it in.

The week after I saw Disco and Tania at the beach, I was headed to the gringo supermarket in Hector's taxi. We rolled out on the main road and saw Tania walking. She saw me and waved me down, so we stopped.

She had makeup running down her face and looked like she hadn't slept in days.

"Damn, girl, you look like a hot mess, what's wrong?"

"I...I can't find Disco. She's missing again. I've been looking everywhere."

"Oh no, that sucks. Where did she go? I mean...when did she get out?"

"I'm not sure—I haven't been home in a day and she was in the backyard but she always tries to come look for me. When I got back, the gate was open. None of the neighbors saw her and I've been looking around everywhere."

"Well, I'm headed to the grocery store now to get things for Pistol, but we'll swing through Villareal on the way out of town to look."

"Okay, thanks, N. I'm going to ask around in town. Oh my God, I...I just hope she's okay."

"Don't worry, Tania, she'll be fine. You'll probably find her soon. But we'll go looking right now."

"*Okay, okay, thank you*," and she scurried off, crying. I told Hector what she'd said.

We drove all around Villareal but didn't see Disco. I got home later and there weren't any Facebook message or emails from Tania so I thought everything must be okay. I made myself some food and took a siesta. There was a knock on my door. It was Tania.

She was crying hysterically. I brought her inside and sat her on the couch and calmed her down. Between sobs she told me what had happened:

Tania stopped in the pet store in Villareal. They told her that several people saw a dog running in circles the middle of the street that seemed to be confused, and later on someone came into the store saying a dog had been hit, though they didn't know if it was the same dog. They took Tania to the place where it was spotted, near the farmers market across from the Colombian bar Villa Costa. There on the ground was Disco, lying in a pile by the side of the road. A good chunk of the left side of her body wasn't there anymore, red, and insides everywhere. Disco had been hit by a car. No one knew if that killed her right away. I hoped it had because the buzzards had gotten to her and opened her up, even taking one of her eyes, and the hot sun did the rest.

"Why doesn't someone DO something?!" Tania screamed, trying to gather up Disco's limp body. It's amazing how much heavier things feel when they're dead.

"He's gone," they said.

"She!" Tania said. *"Disco is a she."*

"Oh. She's gone."

Tania sobbed there a long time then took off what was left of Disco's collar. They put the body in the back of a pickup truck and took it to the veterinarian, though of course there was nothing he could do.

She cried and cried on my couch and I put my arm around her. It wasn't all Tania's fault; I couldn't put that on her.

She planned a memorial for Disco the following evening on the beach. It was supposed to be at 5:00 p.m. but then she changed it to 4:00 p.m. I didn't go. I told her that I had to work and used the time change as an excuse. I didn't want to go. The last thing I felt like doing was being around her and her friends, listening to the same old insincere bullshit and using Disco's death as an excuse to party. Of course Tania would get mad at me, but I didn't care. Disco needed love and attention when she was alive, not a 21-joint salute and crocodile tears now that she was gone.

I stayed home. I closed the windows and sat in the dark. My heart wasn't into writing, so I just sat and thought. At one point I looked at my Facebook. A mutual friend changed her profile picture to a photo of Disco. Then another person did it, and another. One by one, people in Tamarindo paid tribute by putting her photo up. It must have looked so strange to someone who didn't know what was going on—one night when a whole village in the tropics claimed to be a blind dog named after a dance craze.

I looked through my pictures and found my favorite one of Disco, taken when I first got in town and brought her to the beach. She was frozen in midair, holding a huge stick in her mouth and springing off the sand into a big wave. I hit a couple of buttons and it was done: my Facebook profile picture was now a photo of Disco, too.

I put my head in my hands and cried.

CHAPTER 23

THE DREAM

I had a dream that I was sitting at a bar right on the beach. It was neither night nor day, the sun a black ornament hanging in a yellow sky. The waves of the ocean rolled backwards from the shore, out and in, out and in.

A Brazilian guy was with me, a scrappy dude with rotted sugar-cane teeth who didn't speak English. We talked about the trash pickers in the slums of Rio de Janeiro. I had something important to say that I wanted to write down.

There was no paper around and computers hadn't been invented yet, but it couldn't wait. I noticed a wooden beam above us so I stood on the bar and started writing with a pen. That didn't work because the wood was too hard, so I picked up a knife and carved the words. But the blade of the knife snapped, so I looked around and picked up a bowl of fruit. I mashed the fruit up into a black paste and started to smear the letters by hand with the mixture. The Brazilian guy laughed and remarked how resourceful I was. It was an important quote, about living life or something like that, and I just *had* to get it out before it was forgotten forever. I was almost done but ran out of the black stuff. I knew somehow that I would fade away if I couldn't get these words out, if I woke up and it was unwritten. Time was a boa constrictor slithering around my throat. The sun cracked in two and the Brazilian guy had turned into a pile of dust many years before. I started scratching the last words into the wood with my fingernails, clawing at them like I'd been buried alive, nails broken in half, harder, screaming in pain, harder, blood flowing from my fingers, raw bone, almost there, I had to write this everything depended on it I was almost done the last letter...

And then all the oxygen was gone.

I woke up gasping for breath. It was still black out and the howler monkeys were fast asleep. I sat up, looking at the tips of my fingers, and shook the dream from my head. I arose and walked downstairs.

It was 3:30 a.m., the time when drunks and robbers roamed Tamarindo. But the room was sweltering, airless, so I opened the front door, letting the night breeze find its way in. Leaving your door open at that time of night was just asking for trouble. I turned the coffee pot on and picked up the biggest kitchen knife I had, laying it on my desk within reach. I opened my computer and started writing.

I was ready. If someone stepped one foot into my door uninvited they were getting stabbed. That's when I realized how badly I wanted it—if I was willing to go to those lengths to get my writing done, to finish my book, then there was nothing that could stop me—at that point I became a writer.

CHAPTER 24

HAIRCUTS FOR HOMIES

In Tamarindo your karma arrived ten minutes before you did. Everyone knew everyone else, shared the same playground, tried to make a living off the same tourists during the high season on those few dirt roads. We were all like crabs in the same bucket.

Gringos, especially, had to navigate a fine line between friendliness and dealing with all of the vultures. Sometimes I thought it might be better to be standoffish in town; too much kindness in Tamarindo could be dangerous. I remembered that Pistol said "hi" to very few people and kept to himself. That's not a bad thing—he'd lived there so long he had to find a way to minimize the bullshit.

However, my tactic was to kill everyone with kindness, to be polite and always respectful no matter who they were. I said "hi" to everyone. At first a lot of people just looked at me crazy—who was this smiling gringo? Was he a little bit special? But then they'd see me day in and day out saying "hello," and they realized that I actually just cared.

Whenever Theresa picked me up she wanted to drive with the AC on, but I preferred to hang out the window so I could wave and yell to everyone we passed.

"Hey, mop! Pura vida, mae!" I'd yell.

"How do you know all these people?" she'd ask.

"*Tamarindo es mi gente, mi barrio!*—my people, my neighborhood!" I'd boast, pounding my chest, and I meant it.

"I'm a Tica and lived here seven years and you know way more people in town than me."

In Sacramento I'd opened myself up to just about everyone—giving unconditionally to my friends, in work, in my relationships—and been screwed over more often than not. So in Tamarindo I tried to play it cool. Sure, I said "hello" to people, but I was also careful who I *really* let into my life, always holding something back, giving them space to earn it. It may have appeared to people that I was too serious because I didn't bother faking my emotions on the outside, but what they didn't know was that as time went by I always held a smile inside, walked with a song humming in my head.

Everyone in town asked when I was going to get a local phone.

"Do you need a local cell phone? I can hook you up," Kenny G offered.

"Normmmmmmie, will you get a phone already? It's a pain in the ass trying to get in touch with you," Theresa joked.

"Hola, Papa Noel. Did you get a phone yet? Call me—I NEED to talk to you!" Lena Facebook messaged.

"Do you have a local phone number yet? Joey wants you to call him in jail because he has some things he wants you to do," Betty emailed.

Hell no—I didn't want one. I loved being less connected by technology, a relief from being available to everyone every minute of every day. And if I wanted to see someone I only needed to put them in my thoughts as I walked through town and, sure enough, I'd run into them. It worked every time.

When I moved into my own apartment it was a huge gift to myself—I finally had a buffer from people trying to project their bullshit on me, a slice of tranquil isolation that was heaven to a writer, or a guy with a lot on his mind. However, no secret lasts long in Tama; soon there were knocks on my door. I hadn't told anyone in town where I lived. No one. How the hell did they find out?

It could be Tania, stopping by to say "hello," still wearing a string bikini built for a smaller woman, her nipple peeking out but not noticing—or caring. I could only surmise that she was either coming straight from the beach or a furious gangbang. "*I'm headed to work at the casino*," she'd say. "*Do you have an extra beer in the fridge?*" I was angry about the money but at that point I figured, "Why bother?" There was no way I was getting a dollar back, so why allow her to take my money *and* poison me with bad energy? That was *my* choice. She'd helped me a lot with Pistol in the beginning and, honestly, she wasn't all that bad. But when she left my neighbors around the pool figured I'd gotten a hooker for a little afternoon delight.

There were more knocks on the door. I tried to be cordial to them all but really just counted the minutes until I could have my solitude back. The cleaning ladies knocked and needed to get in. The property manager had to show the place. Hector was just stopping by as he rolled through town. Neighbors and friends of neighbors and neighbors of friends wanted to chat. A man was going door-to-door selling that morning's catch of fish, but I politely declined (I'd learned long ago not to buy raw seafood out of a bucket that's been walked around in the hot sun). Then, a lady with bananas and mangos in a basket balanced on her head. Sarita was off work and needed someone to talk to about her relationship problems. Mishe, my cute bartender friend from Sharkey's, came by to say "hi." My busty alcoholic neighbor needed help turning on her barbecue. Actually, she could knock any time.

Thank God my door closed. Most of the time I pretended not to be home, but they'd keep knocking. I'd tiptoe to my kitchen for a glass of water and tiptoe back and tried to type quietly at my desk, slowing down to nine words per minute. Give them credit—Ticos are incredibly persistent when they know you're home but pretending not to be. They'll knock for hours and even sit on your front steps to wait you out like a one-person siege. After all, they already made the hot walk up to your place.

"Hola, Norm, are you home? Norm!"

"No, señor, it is not Norm," I responded in my best heavily-accented, high-pitched female voice. "Soy Irma, the loyal and lovable cleaning lady. I no steal nothing!"

"Open up, Norm! I can see you walking around in there!"

"Lo siento, señor, Mister Norm go Panama for weekend. He come back Tuesday. You need fresh towel?"

The problem with leaving my apartment was that someone was always asking for a handout. Why not? Think about it—if you did nothing else all day but walk around town and ask gringos for a beer, two cigarettes, a meal, or a dollar, the Law of Large Numbers dictates that you'll live like a king. U.S. corporations who want to train their salespeople should bring them to Third World countries for a weekend to observe the street hustlers. I'm serious—once they returned to work they'd be relentless closers, eating up the phones like hungry wolves. There were many nights I wanted to step out for a relaxing beer but weighed out the pain-in-the-ass factor of running into someone who would sit next to me and solicit. It sounds easy to say "no," but once you bought a beer even once it would be a personal affront not to do it again. I resented that guys like Fedor, Repollito, and Mauricio hit me up for a handout every day, even though I made the effort to be cool with them.

But as time passed, I came to understand those Ticos, or at least I understood that I would never fully understand them, and that was enough. Anything else would have crossed past empathy into arrogance.

The Ticos had anger. Slowly but surely, their town was becoming TamaGringo, a playground for the red, white, and blue. It was a localism thang. Maybe you can relate if you grew up in a college town, or have lived in Hawaii. I get it: Tamarindo was a tranquil fishing village until the early part of the millennium. Everyone knew each other, and the only tourists were surfers who wanted to respect the local culture, not buy it up. There was little economic stratification because there was nothing to own, no money to be made. People danced naked around bonfires on the beach and it was all good in their dusty sun slice of paradise. But the explosion of tourism and the international real estate boom brought in droves of investors with money to throw around. Grand construction projects popped up overnight with little care for fitting in with the culture of the town, whitewashed high-rise condos, White Elephants that blocked everyone's view of the beach. Trees came down and cell towers went up. In the span of five years Tamarindo went from a few hundred condos to 4,000. These units were overpriced to begin with, but once the real estate market crashed, shells of buildings and condo projects were left vacant for the jungle to overtake.

People came to Tama to make money, or get fucked up, or make money off those getting fucked up, but they came in from all over the country, and the world, with less-than-noble intentions. So there Tamarindo stood, a monument to decadence like little Las Vegas on the beach. But I've been fortunate enough to see its *real* soul and get to know its *real* people, and they hold my heart. It's just a crying shame it's been covered in seven layers of bad karma brought on by the wrong people.

However, if they had the choice, I don't know how many locals would go back in time and keep it a little surf village. It wouldn't be a tough choice to make—before tourism they were fishermen and ranchers and things were much harder. Ticos have been priced out of their own town but still it's a better quality of life working in tourism than swinging a machete in the sun. The unfortunate part is I don't think they've really gotten ahead. The rich—the international investors, gringos, and super-wealthy from San Jose—keep getting richer, and the poor are left in serfdom, just working a hotel instead of a field. I feel their pain, though their anger is somewhat misdirected at the U.S. It's not a country thing, it's a greed thing, and just as many Ticos are guilty as foreigners. Though they might not realize it, I think Ticos are most angry because they sold out their own country but didn't end up with a bigger piece of the pie.

There was no better example of the contentious love-hate relationship between the U.S. and Costa Rica than my friendship with Fedor. I genuinely liked the guy—I sensed that there was something in his soul that was worth redemption, just as he could tell that I wasn't the quintessential pompous American.

Except when he was drinking or coked up, then the switch flipped and I hoped he even remembered me. When he was on the bottle he was mean and nasty, and more than a few expats who saw me talking to him warned me about his mercurial temper.

Fedor hated that part of himself. He was smart and I could tell he had pride but, for whatever reason, he subjected himself to hustling. That made him mad, and it took a lot of alcohol to quench the fires of that indignity every day. Could I blame him? What were his other options? I'm not sure I would be so different if I were his age and in his situation.

When his dark wolf came out it wasn't pretty. He didn't need to jump anyone; he didn't need three brothers behind him. Fedor wasn't big but he had absolutely no fear. He was ready for a fight, the ecstasy of getting hit and the high of dominating another human being into submission would sate his demons for a short time. He didn't want to win—he wanted blood.

"So what? I don't care how big he is," he told me as we talked about a fight he'd had. *"It's simple—either I kill him or he kills me. There is nothing else."*

In some ways I think it was good for me to have the constant reminder of danger in my life. There's nothing that makes you appreciate peace as much as the threat of war. It humbled me, but I also understood that when it was "go time" I could throw hands and fight like a warrior, for my pride or my life—the outcome irrelevant.

I was sure that some sort of physical altercation in town was inevitable, but inexplicably, as the months went on, I never had a problem with Fedor, or anyone else. Instead, little by little, he opened up to me, telling me about his life growing up in the tough neighborhoods of Alajuela in San Jose, his love of soccer, and his dream of living a better life.

One day he was walking with a short, older lady. He saw me on the street and called me over.

"Hey, Norm, this is my mom," he said. I had no idea his mom lived there in town. Hell, I had no idea he even had a mom.

"*Mucho gusto, señorita, como está usted*?" I greeted her and smiled, making sure to use the more formal "*usted*" tense.

"She lives in Langosta and makes empanadas," he said. *"We sell them on the beach."*

"That's great—I'd love to try them some time."

"*They're the fucking best in Tama, man!*" he said.

"*Fedor!*" his mom scolded.

"*They're the best in Tama.*"

He reached into her bag and pulled out two, but she told him to switch those for two that were warm, and he gave them to me. That made me feel good—I think you really know a person once you've met their mom.

Fedor and Repo hung out and worked the scene together, but they couldn't have been more different. "Little Cabbage" was a predator—slippery and opportunistic, and everyone knew it. At least he was consistent—and entertaining as hell. But he went downhill as my time in Tamarindo progressed. His eyes grew even darker and sank further into his skull, like he hadn't slept in weeks. His skin looked terrible. He'd graduated from coke to crack, or maybe meth, but whatever it was, he was in a bad way. He used to be Fedor's road dog, but even he was at wits end.

"Have you seen Repo?!" Fedor said, still drunk from the night before at 9:00 in the morning when I went to play basketball in the park.

"No, I haven't."

"That fucking puta. He hit a girl last night. He was all fucked up on GHP and punched his gringa girlfriend right in the face. If you see him, tell him I'm looking for him because I'm going to kick his fucking ass." I didn't see Repo for a while after that; I think he skipped town to lay low, knowing that even Fedor had a code of ethics that wasn't okay to cross. But Fedor and I were cool.

One of the many things that was expensive in Tama were haircuts. There were plenty of fancy salons that would charge U.S. prices, but no real cheap barber in town. For those of us who had short hair and had to cut it every week, that was a real problem. Luckily, I'd brought a set of hair clippers with me from the States so I could cut it myself.

Fedor and I were talking over a couple of bags of coconut water one day when he said he was heading to get a haircut. He said that there was a barber outside of town but even he charged $7.00.

"No problem, Fedor, I have clippers. I'll do it for you."

"That's cool," he said, brushing it off like the typical bullshit people talked, his misdirected pride holding him back.

"No, seriously, mae. I can't guarantee that it comes out looking good, but I don't mind doing it."

"You really mean it, Norm? Okay, that's great. Gracias, mop."

"Yeah, no worries, come on up any time. I'm in #25 in Pueblo del Mar."

"Oh yeah, I know."

"How the hell does everyone know where I live?!"

He showed up that afternoon and knocked on my screen door, still sheepish. I invited him in and he took his shoes off at the door and washed his glass in the sink after I gave him some Fanta to drink. I plugged in an extension cord and the clippers and we sat on the front steps and I cut his hair.

"God damn, you hair is thick, Fedor. It's gonna break my clippers. How short do you want it?"

"Like yours, or shorter," he said.

"You sure? All right, here we go..." And I did the best I could, hacking and cursing as I went over it three times, but finally getting it looking somewhat respectable. Afterwards, he thanked me and brushed off the chair and swept the stairs before walking off, rubbing his head.

Those haircuts became our ritual. Every week or two he'd show up:

"You sure it's okay, Norm?" he'd ask, as if there were a part of him who wouldn't even invite his own bad wolf in.

"Of course. Why spend money when I can do it for free? I used to clip all my friends' hair in high school. It's haircuts for homies."

"Haircuts for homies. I like that. Gracias, mi hermano loco—my crazy gringo brother. Let's shave it all off, then."

CHAPTER 25

TAMARUMORS

One morning I watched a dog eat a dead iguana in the road. We all did—it was our morning entertainment. The crew at Sarita's Bakery sat outside and watched the mangy dog circle the carcass, ripping it apart. After it was done it rolled in its kill and laid down to sleep in the sun. When a car drove up, the driver had to swerve around because the dog was too lazy to move.

"Look at that dog. He's not even moving," Surfer Scotty said.

"Yeah," I said.

"It's going to be a hot one today," Salty Dog Rodney said.

"Sure is," I said. It always was hot so I don't know why we bothered saying it every day, but we did.

I liked the streets when it was early, sitting outside Sarita's when she first opened, watching the other shopkeepers hosing down the sidewalks in front of their stores, a deliveryman with bread steaming from the basket of his bicycle. Sleepy Nicaraguan and Dominican workers walked up the road toward the nice houses in white uniforms, their feet still hurting from the day before but smiling and thanking God just the same.

Sarita's Café was the center of the Tamarindo gossip exchange. Gossip, or "*el chisme*" in Spanish, was the central activity in town, the only currency shared by all. It was so prevalent that locals referred to our town as TamaRumor. We had plenty to talk about—there's nothing more dynamic than a small town in the tropics. In fact, the smaller the town, the more complex the relationships, the more the vines grow intertwined.

Information in Tama spread strictly by word of mouth. There was no local TV coverage, no local radio, no town hall I could see, no town meetings, and no community bulletin board. There was one monthly rag that covered local events and posted a surf report, called...*The TamaRumor*. The only daily newspapers were in San Jose, so far away in both distance and culture, it was like reading about another country.

It was easier to get our world news from Sarita's, and I liked it there. Sarita gave me a local discount so coffee was half price, only 400 *Colones*. To further entice me into her establishment she kept a bottle of Baileys behind the counter just for me. Where else in the world do proprietors in a café gladly contribute to your 7:00 a.m. alcohol consumption?

For a lot of us, Sarita's was our town center, our water cooler since we didn't have real jobs. There were five seats out front so the regulars joined me in our stakeout of the dirt road.

"Oh no, here comes Big Teeth," Rodney said.

"Ahhh shit, I can't stand this guy," Sarita said. "He's so rude."

"What's his real name again? Mike? Carl?" I asked.

"Who the fuck knows? Big Teeth," Sarita said. Big Teeth pulled up on his motorcycle in a cloud of dust, his German Shepherd running closely behind. He dismounted, took off his helmet, and started up the steps to the café. The dog followed, barking.

"Jesus, he's got some nasty choppers," Surfer Scotty said. "Those things could really do some damage if they got a hold of you."

"Yeah, and the dog does, too," I said.

Big Teeth ordered coffee and came outside. The rest of us just sat there and didn't say much. He hiked his khakis up to his chest, made some racist comments, and offended a passing girl before getting on his bike and driving away with the dog.

"He's always complaining about my muffins and my prices," Sarita said, smoking a cigarette.

"I like your muffins," Scotty said.

"We like your muffins, too," Rodney said.

"What about my prices?"

"I like your muffins a whole lot more than your prices," I said. She pretended to pour coffee on my head.

Sarita was from Rhode Island, a fiery redhead with the sass to match. Her real name was Sarah, but there were so many Sarah's in town I think she opened a café just to differentiate. It was nice to have a fellow east coast ball-buster in town. Every morning I looked forward to being lambasted with insults the moment I walked through her door.

Where I'm from everyone talks shit, whether it's puff-chested Italian bravado, mellifluous banter from the hood, or biting Jewish sarcasm. If your friends *weren't* talking shit to you then you knew there was a problem. Growing up in New Haven was like being at the Olympic Training Center of shit talking, and I was a prodigy fast-tracked for the gold.

That's why being a writer is my dream job—I get to talk shit for a living in a semi-socially-acceptable forum where I won't get beat up or thrown in jail. I can make people laugh and hopefully get paid for it one day. What are the alternatives for me? A used car salesman? A politician? An infomercial spokesmen? My God, those are some scummy vocations. No, I think I'll stick to writing.

Sarita had a first-class yapper on her, too; not quite on my level, but then again, who is? East coast shit talking isn't meant to be hurtful at all—quite the opposite; we understood that the frequency and viciousness of the verbal attacks actually corresponded with how much we cared for each other. So a typical east coast shit talking session at Sarita's might have sounded like this (with translation for the rest of you schleps):

I'd walk in.

"Ohhhhh nooooo! There goes my morning," Sarita would say. *(Good morning, kind sir. I hope you are well.)*

"Excuse me, I must be in the wrong place. I was looking for a café and this is obviously a shit hole." *(I wish you a splendid day too, fair lass.)*

"No, please, come in—you'll fit right in then. Wow, you look like crap!" *(So nice to see you. Did you sleep well?)*

She'd pour the Baileys and fresh café into my cup and hand it to me, noticing the t-shirt I was wearing.

"What's with you and yellow shirts all the time? You wear one like every day. Do you think you look good in yellow or something?" (*I like your shirt. You look good in yellow.*)

"Wow, that's a LOT of lipping you've got going on. You're at about an 11 and we can use you at a 4." (*Why thank you, I appreciate that.*)

"Oh, whatever, Norm. Why do you even come here? No one likes you." (*Thank you for coming. We really like you.)*

"Hey, if you prefer, I can leave and never come back." (*I like you too and appreciate your great café.)*

"Don't threaten ME with a good time!" (*Don't threaten me with a good time.)*

That was Sarita's favorite saying: "Don't threaten ME with a good time."

And so it went, on and on every day, a witty repartee amongst eastside friend-emies suitable for framing.

Sarita had an apartment near me in Pueblo del Mar. I helped her carry supplies to and from the café because she'd injured her foot. The first time I saw her apartment I was absolutely certain she was running a meth lab. White powder snow-flaked the countertops and it was approximately 187 degrees, even though the ceiling fans were working overtime. Everywhere I looked there were bins, tubes, and beakers containing spices, icing, and white powders of mysterious origin. I estimated the street value of her apartment to be $600,000 U.S. dollars, but she claimed it was just where she did all of her baking. Yeah, right.

She lived there with Jason, her gringo boyfriend. He was a personal chef who didn't have much work so he sat around the apartment smoking weed and watching Patriots games on his laptop all day. If I had to pinpoint his personal philosophy on life, I'd say that Jason was a follower of "I-Don't-Give-A-Fuckism." I respected him for that. We'd sit in front of the café in the afternoons, when he was watching the place for Sarita, and talk about old school punk bands, end-of-the-world conspiracy theories, and whether you'd rather get hit in the face with a lead pipe or a baseball bat—important stuff like that. I liked Jason. He looked a little rough around the edges, and suffered from crippling social anxiety that kept him from hanging out in public a lot, so we had more in common than he might have guessed.

Jason and Sarita were always on-again, off-again. Sarita would need someone to talk to at the café, or knock on my door to say "hi." It's useless giving relationship advice to anyone, but I did root for them so I just said "yup" and "I hear you" and shook my head in agreement every fourteen seconds, secretly wishing she'd brought over some of her famous meth cinnamon rolls. I liked them both but I wanted nothing more than to stay out of their relationship woes, though the human stain always seems to follow me.

Running a business in Tamarindo was a daunting task. Sarita had bills to pay and already had to work twenty hours a day trying to hold it all together. I don't know how she did it, but it didn't look like fun. She hired my neighbor's daughter to help, but that just created another salary to pay. Sarita was always exhausted and stressed, but to her credit she kept up her usual chipper, crappy attitude with us.

When tourists came into the café, us locals tried to put on a good show and watch what we were saying. The café wasn't like your neighborhood Starbucks back in the States. Every morning, tourists poked their well-shampooed and conditioned heads inside and asked for a *vente caramel Macchiato* or inquired if she served *Frappachinos*. No matter what they ordered we all just pointed to the big metal coffee pot sitting on the counter. We had coffee or more coffee—drink it and don't complain.

I think I speak for everyone who thinks a "*barista*" is just a dude who makes coffee when I say that the whole Starbucks thing has gotten a little out of control. It's to the point that the corporate coffee culture is gentrifying the last place I'd ever expect—the hood.

Before I left Sacramento, I was sitting in a Starbucks one afternoon on Stockton Blvd. For those of you who aren't familiar with that particular street, it rivals any avenue 'cross the country named "Martin Luther King Jr." or "John F. Kennedy" as ghetto-fabulous. So I was just sitting there, chilling, and this thug walks in with a gangsta limp—gold teeth, hoodie, jeans sagging. I figured he was there to rob the place, which was perfectly fine with me, but instead he walked right past the line of customers up to the register, leaned his tattooed forearms on the counter, and said:

"Yeah, like, ya know what I mean, yo yo—hook me up with some of dat...grande triple shot half-whip vanilla soy decaf mocha. Please."

I couldn't believe my ears. I wanted to shake him by his Sean Jean shirt and scream, "Really G?! Come onnnnnn, boo boo, you gonna go out like THAT?! That's not a coffee you just ordered—that's a Prince song!"

Well, I can promise you that you wouldn't find any of that same opulence, pretension, or insect-free cleanliness at Sarita's! But alas, she did need to cater to the tourists because us deadbeat locals weren't enough to make a living off. So we helped her out any way we could, even inviting them to sit down with us. You know me by now, I HEART tourists. I was more than happy to answer any questions they might have...about sharks.

The surf posers came right off the plane with legs so white they were unsuitable for public viewing, wearing Bob Marley t-shirts they'd just bought at Target, holding short boards they could never ride. They'd come into Sarita's for a quick shot of java on their way to the beach. Once they saw Surfer Scotty, Salty Dog Rodney, and me sitting outside, they'd figure it was a good time to ask some locals a few of questions. Which beach was best for surfing? When was high tide? What was a good place to buy a new rash guard? But most of all, they wanted to know about sharks before they jumped into the ocean.

"So, fellas, are there any sharks in the water down here? I mean, is it safe?"

"Oh yeah, perfectly safe. Nothing ever happens," I'd say.

"For sure, you're fine in the water. No worries," Surfer Scotty said.

"Yup, 100%," I said.

"110%!" Scotty chimed in.

"Whewww! Okay, cool. I was a little worried because I've never been in the Pacific before and before I left it was Shark Week on the Discovery Channel."

"Well...except for that guy last summer," I said. "Right, Scotty, remember him?"

"Oh yeah, of course. Except for the guy."

"Guy? Guy?! What guy? What happened? What happened last summer with the guy?"

"No one knows for sure," I said. "He was a local, a good surfer, too, out at Playa Grande with a couple of his friends. He got bitten by a shark and died. Does that about cover it, Scotty?"

"Yeah, but some say it was a crocodile. Not sure. But something definitely bit him on the leg and he died."

"You're not kidding?" the tourist said, looking over his shoulder to make sure his better half wasn't listening. "We Googled it but nothing like that came up. Please don't tell my wife—she wanted to go to Amish country instead."

"Ohhh, you have to be careful with those Amish, too," I said. "They're sneaky bastards once they get ahold of you."

"But, to be fair, he bled to death because they took forever getting him to the hospital," Scotty said. "He was only 200 meters away from the medical clinic but instead of putting him on a boat across the estuary they called a taxi. It took 45 minutes to show up and then they drove around for a while."

"Jesus, that's awful. Please—I don't want to hear anymore."

"So listen to this," I said. "I heard he bled out in the back of the taxi in a gas station parking lot across the street from the clinic."

"Big shark, too, from what his friends said. Ripped half his leg off. And once they get a taste for human blood, it's just a matter of time," Scotty laughed.

"Ughhhh, oh my God!"

"Hey—watch out, you're spilling coffee on my flip-flop," I said. "But really, don't worry about it, buddy. It's perfectly safe and I'm sure you'll be fine."

"Perfectly fine! Never better!" Scotty said. "But just remember if you DO get bitten by a shark, or a crocodile, just don't call a taxi! Hahahaha."

"Hahahaha, good point, Scotty!"

Bob Marley suddenly lost his appetite and left half of his banana bread on his chair for the ants to swarm. He looked a little green when he left, carrying that surfboard like a tombstone, heading in the opposite direction from the beach. Odds were they'd spend the rest of their vacation in the hotel pool.

The moment the tourists were out of earshot we started up our shit talking session right where we'd left off. Game on. From our chairs in front of Sarita's we had a perfect vantage point to watch people in town pass by. It was a great way of ascertaining everyone's personal business each morning, the perfect forum to judge without amnesty. It was immature, irresponsible, and borderline cruel, but hey, what can I say—you'd do it, too.

Big Chuck, the jolly personal chef, walked by. I liked Chuck—he was always cool to talk to as he smoked bud, wading in the pool at our apartment.

"Didn't he and Angela break up? She's been a hot mess at the bars every night."

"I don't know. I think they keep making up and breaking up."

"That's too bad, I like Big Chuck."

"It's too bad for her. I heard she borrowed money from Longboard Sarah and never paid her back."

My big-boobed alcoholic neighbor walked by, squinting against the sun. She wore the same dress as the night before and carried her high heels. She crossed the street before she passed us in a feeble attempt to evade notice.

"Hiiiiii there! How are you? Did you have a rough night?" we called out. She walked faster.

"You should have seen her at the barbecue the other night. She was sloshed! I think she hooked up with Grant."

"Your friend Gringo Grant? I thought she was a lesbian?"

"Your mom's a lesbian."

"Yeah, well, your dad is a lesbian."

"That doesn't even make sense." We all took a timeout, sipping our coffee.

"Didn't Grant's apartment get broken into? He lives in Langosta with that tall guy who plays online poker, right?"

"Yeah, while they were away doing their border shuffle someone broke in and cleaned 'em out: TV, laptop, nice camera—they got it all."

"Damn, that sucks. Who was it? A Critter?"

"Well, I'm not supposed to say anything, so you didn't hear it from me, but Grant thinks it was Tony Touch."

"Who's that? The crack head guy dating the waitress from Le Beach Club?"

"Yeah he works at Blue Turtle tours. I'm pretty sure he's clean these days, or at least off that shit."

"I heard he owned a gun."

I didn't say anything.

"I heard he beat her up."

I didn't say anything.

Lena drove by in her black Mercedes. I ducked down, but she didn't see me anyways because she was on her cellphone. I'd been dodging her for months and had no desire to deal with her ever again.

"Look at that one. Someone told me that she married a rich old gringo years back and took him for all of he was worth. That's how she got her money."

"Yeah, sounds about right. Chris said she ripped him off in a real estate deal and stole five acres of his land."

"I guess they're going bankrupt on those condos he was building."

"Oh, speaking of bankrupt…guess what I heard yesterday… "

It went on and on, all morning, talking about who was on a bender and who ripped someone off, who was acting like a prick, and where everyone was trying to put their pricks.

"Man, I saw Nayla, the yoga teacher/Spanish teacher/personal chef yelling at someone outside the market yesterday. She was really losing her shit."

"Yeah, I think she was yelling at Mack White. I heard he was sloppy drunk the other night and grabbed her ass, and she slapped him."

"He was at Casa Crack last week—I saw him walking out of that Dominican girl's apartment."

"Really? And what were *you* doing at Casa Crack?"

"Never mind."

Someone was going crazy. Someone else was pregnant. This one had a venereal disease, that one was broke and selling their surfboard to buy a ticket back to the States. Nothing was out of bounds and we didn't have to worry about being politically correct. That was Sarita's Café, the best source of information Tamarindo, excuse me—TamaRUMOR—had to offer.

"There are rumors about you, too, you know," Sarita said to me one day.

"What? Are you serious? Like what?" I said.

"I heard that you used to be in the army, but now you're ultra-religious and don't even curse."

"What the fuck? Who the hell said that?"

"You know, people talk. That's just the word around town," Sarita said.

"Jesus Christ, that's crazy talk! How do these rumors even get started? People should be more responsible with what they say."

Sarita, Rodney, and Scotty shook their heads in agreement, and we looked out at the road. The stray dog rose from the dirt, yawned, and started dragging what was left of the iguana down the road.

"Sure is hot today," Rodney said.

CHAPTER 26

POOR LITTLE WU FAT

There was a French lady living in Tamarindo who kept nine terriers and a pig as pets. The pig had its ears pierced for some strange reason. It was the queen of the litter and the terriers circled around her, snarling viciously at anyone who got too close. Those fuzzy brown terriers couldn't have been more than eight pounds each, but man they were nasty. Every day the French woman walked them on the beach.

I passed them when I jogged on the beach. I tried to make a wide berth but for some reason they hated me. Maybe they could smell fear, or tell that I was American and didn't think Jerry Lewis was all that funny? Perhaps they could sense that I loved bacon, I'm not sure, but all at once those nine little fuckers charged, showing their teeth and barking.

"Eeeeeyyyyattts!" I screamed, picking up the pace of my run. But they closed in and blocked my escape, snapping at my heels.

"Get back, you evil beasts!" I yelled. But these weren't your Grandma's poodles; those little mutated Ewoks were trained killers. I looked over to the woman for help, but she just stood there. How do you say, "Call off your nine psycho terriers, you horribly irresponsible woman!" in French?

"Hey! Little help over here!" I yelled to her, pointing at the carnage unfolding around me. But she just lit up a cigarette and stared off toward the sunset.

So I zigzagged up and down the beach with all nine of them giving chase, jumping around and waving my arms wildly like I was trying to cross a pit of hot coals. One terrier lunged at my testicles but missed. The other Ticos on the beach laughed hysterically, bent over holding their knees, but no one offered to help. So what if the little hairballs had pink collars—didn't they understand that this was a real emergency?

The leader of the terrier gang growled and took a step toward me. It was fourth and long, and coach was calling for a punt. I lined up…here comes the snap…laces out…I stepped into it and…. pulled back at the last moment because I didn't have the heart to kick him. I whiffed into bright blue air and went tumbling down. This would end badly, I thought. I was defenseless; surely they would rip me to shreds. Everything went dark.

I had so many questions for the lady. Maybe I could ask her once I was well enough to have visitors at the hospital, after the plastic surgeons pieced together what was left of my face. Of course I'd be in traction and a full body cast, the majority of damage to my man-junk region where the terriers were like little seek-and-destroy missiles. The French lady would visit me and put a box of truffles and an "I'm Sorry My Terriers Ate Your Penis" Hallmark card on my bed stand.

"Iiiiiii cwannnnt eat solwid fwood yet," I'd say, sipping my vanilla pudding through a straw. It was exhausting to speak. I was tired, so tired, but I had so much to ask her.

I took out my dry erase board and wrote in green marker: "Why earrings on the pig? And why the little fake diamond studs? Why not those Indian feather things that are in style?" And oh, there was one more small thing since we were having a nice pleasant conversation via dry erase board: "WHY THE FUCK DID YOU LET YOUR NINE TERRIERS MAUL ME ON THE BEACH? For the love of all that is holy…WHYYYYYYYYYY???!!!"

The machines that were hooked up to me would start beeping as my body went into convulsions. The nurses would run in. "We're losing him. Plug in those round things that look like the Perfect Pushup and get ready to jumpstart his heart. And give me 5,000 cc's of that fancy medical-talk shit and prepare him for surgery."

They'd turn to the French woman. "I'm sorry, but you'll have to leave. Your husband needs emergency surgery for a penis transplant," they'd tell her. "It's risky, and there are numerous better options, but it's up to you."

"Oh mon dieu pas, this man no is me husband," she'd say as she lit up a long-filtered cigarette with her white gloves, blowing smoke in the general direction of my breathing tube. "*But I will sign zee form, oui oui?*"

And she did.

"Mr. Scheeder, can you hear me?" the nurse would ask.

"Shhhhweeber," I'd say, trying to pronounce it right but the facial injuries and vanilla pudding getting in the way.

"What's that, Shweeber? How's that?"

"Sbweeber!" I'd moan.

"Fine then, Mr. Beaver, I have a very important medical question for you. The surgeon needs to know, how many times have you been sexually active—with your current penis—in the last six months?"

"With ah feemawle or my swelf?"

"Yes, Mr. Beaver, with a female."

"Inwooding dast weekwend?"

"Yes. Including last weekend." She took out her chart and her pen and waited patiently. I tried counting on my fingers, but I only had one big nub of a cast, so I tallied the figures in my head, carrying the one, and came up with what I thought was a semi-accurate number.

"Theeeerooowwww."

"Oh my, Mr. Beaver, did you just say ZERO?"

"Dwelllllll, gib oh thake?"

"Wow, never seen that before. Okay, zero it is," she said and wrote it down on her chart with raised eyebrows.

"Ighh whas twaking a bwreak end thworking on mythelf!" I said.

"Uh huh, sure you were. Now just calm down." She put the clipboard aside. "We've been trying to match you up with a suitable penis donor for the last two months but haven't had any luck. We need to match up the size and shape of your member exactly if it has any chance of functioning again. It's been a long, hard ...errr it's been a difficult task."

"Naht many pweople died?" I asked.

"Oh no, Mr. Beaver, we've had plenty of potential donors. Tons of them, actually. Just last week we had two Irishmen, a midget who died in a circus accident, and an adolescent Reggaton singer come through here, but they were all too large. But the good news is that we think we found a suitable donor for you!"

"An Iwishman was foo bwig?!! Are u shurre?"

"Yes, yes but we had a miracle last night. A ten-year-old Chinese boy died in a terrible scooter accident. Everything caught on fire. It was nasty business—his violin and his penis were the only things left intact. Congratulations, Mr. Beaver, you are going to have Wu Fat's penis!"

She opened a cooler next to the bed and there it sat, on ice in the middle of a bunch of vanilla pudding snack packs.

"Ughhhhhhh, whad dud pbuck!" I'd say.

Then it got really weird. The nurse ripped off her blouse and jumped on top me.

"Ohhh, Mr. Beaver, I can't control myself anymore." She licked my face. What the hell was going on?

"Oh, mon petit amoureux." The French lady started licking my face, too. *"Voulez vous coucher avec moi ce soir?"* They both were really going for it. Damn, they had some bad breath…

I came back to consciousness on the beach with a bunch of wagging terriers licking my face. The French lady stood above me, flicking her ashes.

"*Monsieur, are you okay?*" she said.

"Phhht phhht!" I spit out the dog saliva and pushed them away. "Whad whappened? I mean, what happened?"

"*My doggies wanted to play. You ran and fell down and hit your head,*" she said. *"Then you kept saying something about a Chinese boy's penis."*

"Dammit, you horrible frog woman, keep those rotten beasts on a leash! They could really hurt someone!" I got up and brushed the sand off myself and stumbled up the beach. "And leave poor Wu Fat out of this!" I cried. "That poor little bastard has been through enough!"

"*C'est la vie.*" She shrugged and lit up another cigarette and kept on walking down the beach with her nine terriers and a pig with an earring. I went in the other direction.

CHAPTER 27

THE STREETS ARE PAVED WITH HONEY

In Tamarindo the streets were paved with honey. Well it wasn't *real* honey, but sugarcane molasses that the locals called honey. Every year in early December, when the rains were gone, each day nicer and sunnier than the last, the whole town ramped up for the flock of tourists during the busy holiday season. The roads went from flooded slop to dust bowls, until early one morning a red tanker truck crawled through town spraying honey. It went on wet, like tar, and stank to high heaven. They covered every dirt road with it so for weeks we all trudged through carefully, our flip-flops sticking and tracking black footprints onto our floors. Flies circled and someone's flip-flop always got stuck and broke off in the black goo. There they'd leave it, hopping home to get another pair. But pretty soon the heat of the sun dried the honey and I was amazed to see it became a perfectly hard shell, just like someone had tarred the street.

This temporary pavement kept the dust from overtaking the town when rich vacationers from San Jose sped through town in their expensive cars and American college kids with surfboards crowded the streets. The business owners all chipped in to hire the molasses truck. If one person didn't pay, there'd be a gap in front of his establishment where the road was dirt and then it went back to honey farther on. I liked watching people wave to the driver as that red truck went through town—it was a symbol of renewal, hope for better times that the days of skinny cows were over. They'd certainly come a long way.

Twenty years earlier the only way to get around Guanacaste Province was on horseback or by walking. Most people farmed or worked with cattle, machetes hanging from their rope belts and necks permanently sun-leathered. Life was hard but the land provided plenty. There was coffee to sell and sugarcane to grow. Even when I first visited the country in 1999, they hadn't put in the modern highway from San Jose to the western coast yet, so making the short 300 km journey took seven memorable hours winding over mountain roads in a "chicken bus." They called it that because people would bring their chickens right on the bus, and buckets, and bags of bananas and machetes, roosters, and mean old nasty yard dogs that tried to bite the babies who cried the whole way. We squeezed in four to a seat or had to stand in the aisle with the animals, passing vomit bags to the front as we roller-coastered through the mountains. The road wasn't wide enough for two cars, so we swerved onto two wheels around corners, right on the edge of the cliff to avoid a head-on collision.

In the 70s and 80s, adventurous surfers flocked to Costa Rica's Pacific peninsula. They came down when Mexico got too crowded, following a postcard trail of surf legends like their cult leaders, Robert August and Captain Zero. They found epic waves and stayed. Gradually the locals got smart, laying down their ox plows and opening fish taco joints and *haciendas* where the surfers could crash by the beach for $1 a night. Every morning they rose at dawn, throwing off their mosquito nets, and shoveled down rice and beans, waxed their boards, and sprinted for the Pacific.

These days, tourism is the cash crop in Costa Rica. Well, at least on the coast, but you'll still see sugarcane fields stretching all the way to the airport south of Liberia. That airport has done wonders for the economy of Guanacaste province. No longer do tourists need to fly into San Jose, spend a night, and take a chicken bus to the coast. There are daily nonstop flights from Houston, Miami, and New York, and they've just opened up a sparkling new terminal. The government has done a great job promoting their country as a tourist haven. Let me say it again, because you'll almost never hear me give credit to any governmental agency in Costa Rica: The government has done a great job promoting the country. Some of their elaborate PR campaign is even true.

PR: Costa Rica hasn't had an army since 1949. True. That's actually pretty cool, though the UN has to step in when they have disputes with Nicaragua to the north over the San Carlos River. They desperately need some sort of military presence to help with the unchecked flow of cocaine coming in their borders by sea. Costa Ricans should be proud that their country always ranks at the top of Latin nations for democracy and human rights.

PR: Costa Rica is a true Green, eco-friendly country. True, sort of. The biodiversity in Costa Rica is mind-boggling: 25% of the country is protected national forest. It's one tiny country out of 194 in the world, covering only .03% of the earth's surface, yet it contains more than 5% of the whole world's flora and fauna. An almost prehistoric display of monkeys, turtles, birds, big cats, iguanas, crocodiles, fish, rays, spiders, insects, and sloths are on display, attracting biologists and naturalists form all over the world. But someone got smart and realized they could monetize the hell out of that green designation. So if you know someone and pay someone, you're officially a certified eco-friendly business. But, from what I saw, they don't even recycle—everyone just throws bottles and cans in the trash.

PR: Costa Rica has a 96% literacy rate. Not really. There is no accurate way to even take that census in the barrios and jungle interior of the country. But they do a better job than most developing countries of providing education and progressing social initiatives. The Costa Rican government has free educational radio programs, so just about any child in the country can go to school by listening to their AM receiver if they don't have other access. In many rural communities, people got cell phones and Internet before indoor plumbing. Other than a smattering of tourism, all of the good jobs are in San Jose, where many American corporations have set up shop, including Wal-Mart, Home Depot, and Hooters.

Other than that, it's a comedy of errors. Everything that should be simple is buried in mountains of red tape. Many Americans who are looking to retire in the tropics and open a little business have left Costa Rica for Panama, who make it easy to do so.

A Costa Rican friend of mine saw a bumper sticker the other day that he thought should be their national slogan:

Costa Rica. We make EASY shit HARD.

I couldn't have said it better. As far as I could tell, there was no one running the show in Tamarindo. They certainly didn't have much use for national politics and big ideas like in the capitol. The real movers and shakers headed into San Jose every week to do business, but in Tama it seemed the conglomerate of power was reserved for attorneys, female attorneys, fat lesbian female attorneys, and ex-gun runners who liked Nutella and wore black socks with sandals.

I was sober more than anyone in Tama except the rehabbed smack addicts and ex-alcoholics, shaky and 100-days proud, but still I couldn't figure out how it all *ticked*. I had no idea how the town didn't fall into complete chaos every morning: looting and Nazi surf gangs, hookers offering two-for-one hand jobs so they could pickpocket wallets, coke zombies dancing Thriller in the streets taking tourists hostage to line them up and kick penalty shots at their heads. How was it not all dogfights and chlamydia? That Broadway show seemed far more likely than the incredibly fragile ecosystem that existed. It defied logic, yet somehow it all stumbled forward to another day, and another. But at first the lack of any visible authority disturbed my *boughie* U.S. sensibility.

Most towns in Latin America are set up like this: a big central square with a fountain and nice shade trees sits right by the church, both crucibles of community life. The streets around the park are filled with quaint cafés, bars, and restaurants for all to enjoy. Tucked further back are the neighborhoods of houses and the schools, then they reserve the dirty business of cemeteries, the town hall, and the police station for the outskirts.

Tama had a church by the hardware store on the way out of town, but it looked more like a roller rink from the outside. I never saw anyone in it, though I heard masses were at 6:00 p.m. on Sundays. There was no town square or even a designated center of town. They had a small school with a brightly colored mural near the skate park, but I never saw any evidence that it was functional. If there was a town hall, a mayor, or even a hall monitor, I never saw one.

The police station used to be in town, on the hill toward Lookout Point, but it was donated land so years ago the owner kicked them out. They moved to a one-room station in a private home outside of town, but that led to one small problem—they didn't have any vehicles. When the police were needed in Tamarindo, they had to hitchhike into town. They had guns, but no one had money to buy ammunition.

As the town grew, a real police force was needed to protect the tourists, so between private donations and municipal funding they managed to put enough together to buy the police force its first car. What a proud moment indeed, to have a shiny new vehicle for the police, but there was one glitch: cars need gasoline. The closest gas station was in Bellin, 20 km away, and petrol was over $6.00 a gallon. So the cops started a fuel fund by collecting donations from local restaurants and hotels. When they kicked in enough to buy a tank of gas, the police force were mobile, agile, and hostile once again...at least until they got down to "E."

By the time I got there, they'd graduated to motorcycles and bulletproof vests. I saw police in town sometimes, when it was sunny out but not too hot and definitely not raining, between the hours of 10:00 a.m. and 2:00 p.m., except during siesta time or on the weekends. They'd park in the shade of the palm trees in the roundabout and hang out. Thank God they were serious about stopping all of the crimes that occurred under those conditions. But they sure put on a good show of it every time you drove by the station, congregating in front for flag raisings at 6:00 a.m. and lowerings at 6:00 p.m. like clockwork. Between all the fundraising and the flag raisings, they appeared to be more of a Girl Scout troop than a police force. You might as well have put them in little brown skirts and unleashed them on the good citizens of Tama with boxes of Thin Mints.

They were such a joke that one time the cops actually got robbed at gunpoint by *bandidos*. Robbing the cops! I'd love to see how *that* went down:

"Hey, you! Freeze!" the policeman says, pulling his gun.

"Whoaa, *cabron!* No, *you* freeze!" the *bandido* says, pulling his gun, too.

"*Mae*, I'm serious now! Freeze or I'll shoot! Don't you see my gun?!" the policeman says.

"Well...*I've* got a gun, too!" the *bandido* says.

"This is your last warning! Don't try me!"

"Ha! If you were really going to shoot you already would have. You probably don't even have bullets in your gun."

"Yes I do!" the policeman says.

"Then shoot."

(Pause.)

"Yes I do!" the policeman says.

"Ha! Okay, that's it. Hand over your gun!" the *bandido* says. The policeman hands his gun to the *bandido*. "Now, hands UP!" The policeman puts his hands up.

"Wait a second, do *you* even have bullets in *your* gun?" the policeman asks.

"Of course I do!"

"Show me!" the policeman says.

"Shut up! Or I'll shoot!" the *bandido* says.

"Liar! You don't have bullets either! I *knew* it!"

"Well...so what? Neither did *you*!"

"Enough of this—hands up!" the policeman says. "Give me your gun or you're under arrest!" The *bandido* puts his hands up.

"Be careful threatening me, cabron!" the *bandido* says. "If I had a bullet right now I'd *shoot* you!"

"Well, if I had a bullet right now I'd shoot *you* in your *FACE*!" the policeman says.
"Yeah? Well I'm going to buy a bullet next week and come looking for *you*!" the *bandido* says.

"Next week?! Unlikely, *puta*! Everyone knows you can't afford a bullet! You can't even afford the *bus* to Liberia!"

"Liberia? Is that where you buy your bullets? They're pretty expensive there, no?" the *bandido* asks.

"Yes, they really are."

"I find they're usually on sale up in Santa Cruz."

"Santa Cruz? Really? I'll try that next time, thanks," the policeman says. "There's a little frozen yogurt shop I just *adore* up there, too."

"Oh, you mean Heladeria Ricardo? Ohhh, I just *love* that place!" the *bandido* says. "I always get the strawb…"

"Strawberry!" the policeman says at the same time. "Hahahahaha."

"Hahahahahaha."

(They just stand there and look at each other.)

"Sooo…what do we do now?" the *bandido* asks.

"I don't know."

"Do you think it would be all right if we put our hands down, now?"

"Yeah, that would be okay, I think," the policeman says.

They both put their arms down.

"Okay. Whewww…my arms were getting tired. So…how about you give me my gun back and just keep yours?" the *bandido* asks.

"Well…"

"Come on…it's hot out here, and it's almost lunch time. "

"All right, I guess that's okay," the policeman says. "Here you go."

"Thanks. Wait…no, that one's yours."

"Oh, yeah. Here."

"Great, gracias," the *bandido* says. "Well…I guess I'll just go now?"

"Yeah, me too."

"I'll see you next week, *amigo*."

"You too, hermano. *Pura vida*," the policeman says. "And enjoy the strawberry at…"

"Ricardo's!" they say at the same time.

"Hahahahaha."

On the highways, the police force's main mission was to issue tickets for indecipherable infractions and then collect bribes. The average policeman probably made about 300 USD a month, so they found creative ways to subsidize their income. The going rate to pay them off and be on your way was usually $40 per officer.

I had to pay off my share of cops while driving with Hector. He didn't have a registered taxi, just a gypsy cab, so we tried to time our runs to the jail or the grocery store when it rained, or right at 6:00 p.m., because we knew the cops would be busy with their flag. But one time on the way to Liberia, we came around a blind turn too fast and there sat a roadblock with four officers stopping cars and giving tickets to everyone for no apparent reason. Hector freaked out because his registration sticker was past due and he couldn't get busted operating a taxi, so he kicked the car into reverse and drove backwards as fast as he could, weaving through traffic. We thought we were safe, but an officer saw us and took chase in his car. We had a good head start, but since we were driving backwards, he closed in fast.

Hector passed a billboard then swerved sharply down a dirt road into the jungle, the car bumping and kicking up dust. He backed right into the parking lot of a zip lining park. We jumped out and ran into the bathroom and hid in the stalls with our feet up. I heard the cops pull up and ask questions outside. The bathroom door opened and an officer walked in…and took a piss in the urinal. Apparently he'd had a lot of pineapple juice. The officers poked around but couldn't find us, so they eventually drove off. My ace, Hector.

Everyone drove drunk. The jungle and the coast were their backyard—driving drunk was like having a few beers and then cruising around on your riding lawnmower. There wasn't much to it—there were few cars and most of the roads were only one lane, only some of them paved, with no stop signs, traffic lights, or few intersections of note. But even drunk people paid better attention and used more common sense than most of us in the States.

The roads had no sidewalks or breakdown lanes, so pedestrians got clipped all the time. On Sunday afternoons I'd see old men stumbling and falling all over the street, hammered on their way back from the bars, and think, "There's no way he's going to make it." A pickup truck with a dozen kids sliding around in the back caromed by, barely missing a motorcycle with the father driving, the mother on back with a toddler, and a baby in his lap. The father was the only one wearing a helmet. They swerved to avoid the Italian guy who rode his unicycle every morning. Add a few ranchers on horseback, stray dogs running out at them, delivery trucks behind schedule cramming to get through, quads carrying expats, and surfers bicycling with their boards under their arms, and you have a picture of the roads around Tama. I felt alive in the thrill of it all.

Most bad accidents were fatal, only because it took the ambulance an hour and a half to get there from Santa Cruz. That's where the fire department was too, *los bomberos*. Fires were a real problem in the dry season in Tama. In March and April the whole town was like a tinderbox in the 100-degree heat. A tourist casually tossing a cigarette butt or a local burning garbage produced embers that carried in the wind. Most of the bars, restaurants, and hotels had thatched *palopa* roofs, beautiful handcrafted cones made out of woven palms, sometimes 40 feet high. But when those embers hit 'em, they became torches. When there was a fire, everyone in town ran out and threw buckets of water and turned hoses on it, but usually it was too late and they could only watch as the whole structure burned. The roof of Kahiki's went up and had to be rebuilt before I got there, and the old Sharkey's and an adjacent surf shop went up, leaving only a bombed-out concrete shell. They'd just received an order of 100 new surfboards and insurance was nonexistent.

Yup, life was short and hard, but equally happy for the locals. Survival was a daily reality for *all* of us living there, and there's really not much else to say. We were on our own and no one in authority was around to solve our problems. But you know what I learned? You exercised caution when caution was required. In Costa Rica if there's a hole in the road, people walk around it until the locals fill it with dirt themselves. In the U.S. when there's a hole in the road, you'll have twenty ridiculous lawsuits from people who supposedly fell in and have emotional damage. Their work order to pave over that hole has to get approved by ten officials and pass a budget allocation meeting and then they dispatch a crew of five overpaid road workers to take coffee breaks and sit on their asses all day because they're union. It's not always easy in Costa Rica, but I think I prefer the former. Faced with necessity, the best of mankind's innovative nature emerges.

My Loonie friend's maintenance man, Merle, was originally from Nicaragua, where he'd spent the last ten years crawling around the jungle shooting at Contras and dodging landmines during their civil war. He was one of the sweetest guys you'd ever meet and fiercely loyal to the Loonies, who supported his family and gave them a better life in Costa Rica. He lived close by in a humble concrete home within earshot of their beautiful compound. One time they were out of town and left me to watch the place and take care of their dogs. Merle took me aside and told me if there was ever a robber or any problem at all to just ring the brass bell they had hanging on the porch. Don't call the cops, don't try to do anything myself, just ring the bell. He would come running and take care of them. Locals take care of local problems, he said. That's what's up. There used to be a time in the States when people had pride in their neighborhoods and solved their own problems, too. They sat on their front porches and said "hi" to people and watched after each other's children. If a kid was being bad, they were spanked by the nearest adult, who would be thanked, not sued. Locals took care of local problems, and I dare to say it was a better time.

At Christmas time they put a pine tree up by the bar in the Estrella, decorated with ornaments and tinsel. Blinking white lights hung from palm trees and front doors all over town. Someone hung a stocking from the lifeguard tower. The local schoolchildren even put on a Christmas pageant on a stage built by the pool, complete with a Santa Claus, who was sweating his north pole off in that heavy suit.

They even brought out a local musical act as a special treat, though I think it was more of a treat for him than the audience. He introduced himself as "Tico Hendrix" and sported a jerry-curl and buck-teeth. Tico pawed at an electric keyboard and howled out Christmas songs and bad jokes into the microphone.

"It's *so* great that they give special needs people a chance to perform in public," I told my friend, who corrected me that Tico Hendrix was fully-functioning, and not even on the spectrum, but just *really* bad. During the merciful breaks between bad songs, he told bad jokes:

"Thank you ladies and germs, your applause is underwhelming. Excuse me, folks, but my English is not so good. And neither is my Spanish..." Crickets. I don't think I've ever heard Tamarindo so quiet.

I spent Christmas Day in the prison with Pistol. I didn't mind—it actually meant a lot more to those guys. The prison had a relaxed, festive feel, like all of the craziness was suspended for one day and everyone honored that silent treaty. They even collected enough money from the inmates to roast a pig that night. I gave Pistol the cheap white watch off my wrist as a present and busted his balls that he hadn't bought me a gift. When I got home, I sent an email to my family telling them that I loved them and things were going well and I was enjoying Costa Rica. This time, I wasn't lying.

Tamarindo bustled with visitors around Christmas. I knew the first names of the workers at the restaurants, and they nodded to me and served me first, even when there was a crowd of tourists. They were exhausted and sleep-deprived from working 14 hours a day, but at least they were making money. They smiled the best they could, and I smiled back, knowing that we'd made it that far. I was filled with a strange sense of warmth, a pride in our little *pueblo* that I hadn't anticipated.

So what if the banks ran out of U.S. dollars during the high season, and then ran out of money altogether? Who cares if the restaurants ran out of food sometimes? No cops, no fire department, no ambulance? We'd make do. The Internet went out? Congratulations—your work day was officially over, so go hit the beach. The power went out? Light candles and practice making babies. Got beef with someone? Figure that shit out in the daylight so it won't be settled with bottles and fists on the dance floor. So what if the bars ran out of booze? Well, actually that was unacceptable. But other than that, we made do, as a community, together.

I grew to love strolling the roads of Tama. I laughed with the taxi drivers and yelled, "*Bailar*!" as they salsa danced outside of their cars in the mornings, when it was otherwise quiet. The sleepy Nicaraguan workers said, "*Buenos dias*" to me as they went to their maintenance jobs for $10 a day. I offered the French photographer Bernard a ride because he had a bad leg from his time in the French Foreign Legion. He said he'd rather walk and enjoy the day, but thanked me. Hey, Row, hitting reggae night tonight? "*You know it.*" Kenny G, where's my coffee cup? "*Hahaha, you got me good, bro, pura vida*!" Hey, Sarita, need me to go grab some more milk at the store for you? Sure Theresa, I'll help you with your flat tire. FIRE, Rasta Mon! *Jah Love, seen?*! How are the waves, fellas? Shred one for me out there! "*Hola, Papa Noellll!!!*" "Hey, Pepito! It's almost Christmas, huh?" "*Si! Y tu eres un chico mallllooooo!*" There was nothing that filled me up more than walking those roads when the sun was new, waving to my new *familia* and playing catch with words of kindness. I picked up a beer can that a tourist had dropped the night before—the honey trucks were coming, and the roads needed to be clear.

How did it all work? Shit if I could figure it out, but it sure felt right.

On the last day of the year I walked all the way up to Lookout Point. I stood on a big rock and looked out over the town, the hills, and the ocean meeting the sky, larger than anything I've seen in my life. Down on the beach, they were releasing paper kites, a candle lit in each one to give them flight. I watched them rise toward me, dozens of them, globes dancing in the sky like molten balloons. It was beautiful beyond words, and I finally understand what it was all about: It was the beach, the ocean. Each day that surfboards outnumbered cars in our little banana republic, we were part of something special. It soothed even the most savage, fucked up soul—including mine. I understood that *ahorita* meant that I never had to rush around and stress, like back in the States, and *un zarpe* meant I could spend a little longer in the warmth of my friends. I didn't even need to wear a watch. It would take three of us chatting in the middle of the street to figure out what day of the week it was, but anyone in town could tell you what time high tide was, down to the minute.

There would always be problems, so why bother stressing over them? As long as there was sunshine and waves and we all faced west together at sunset, Tama would be our paradise. Together. A paradise where you had to navigate the quicksand, but a paradise nonetheless. Maybe *pura vida* really *meant* something.

It didn't matter if the outside world knew it or not, because they could never *understand* it. The tourists only saw the façade, like a Hollywood set. The rest of us had to earn it. You had to pass through the magic waterfall and climb over the impassable mountain to get to the *real* place. For those brave or crazy few, who'd left it all behind and set out on foot for the long, unknown journey, fueled only by rumors and the desire to fall off the edge of the world, they'd found their secret city of gold. In Tamarindo, we'd found our *El Dorado*.

CHAPTER 28

PISTOL SCORES A GOOOOOOOAAAALLLLLLLL!

Theresa and I grew to be close friends. Of course there were whispers among town, but we didn't care. No one else understood what we were dealing with. I'd bring her a smoothie at work when she was too busy to take a break. She introduced me to her friends and sometimes they'd drag me out for a beer or to go dancing. Otherwise, she knew I'd just stay home in my apartment.

"You need to go out more, old man," she'd say. I did and I didn't, but I took it as a compliment. What I used to see as pressure to please everyone I began to realize was a gift; my presence in peoples' lives seemed to give them some sense of comfort, even joy.

"I see they look up to you in town," Row said as we sat and talked on the basketball court one morning. "You are like a father figure to these younger ones, a...what is the word? Roles model?" Wow, I hadn't realized that. Maybe my karma of giving respect and saying "hi" to everyone was starting to pay off? I'd try my best to live up to that responsibility.

Sometimes Theresa picked me up and we'd go grab dinner and talk. I always tried to have a new CD burnt for her. When she needed someone to talk to, I listened. There wasn't a whole lot more I could do to help solve her problems, so I tried to make her laugh.

"Normie, I always think of you when I see the silverware," she said.

"Oh God, you'll never let me live that down, huh?"

"No way! That was too funny!"

When I first got to Tama I had to adapt to a thousand little things that were different in a foreign country. The cultural differences even extended to the dinner table. The restaurants put their silverware on the table sealed in clear plastic sleeves to protect them from dust and flies. I ripped open the plastic to take out the knife and fork and start eating. But it was tough, the plastic was strong, and I struggled to push the knife through and even used my teeth, as I cursed and sweated. I did that in front of Theresa when we ate and she just looked at me funny. Finally one day she asked me, "*What are you doing with those?*"

"I'm trying to get the damn silverware out of the fucking plastic thing!" I yelled in frustration, thrashing around and knocking over a glass of water.

"*No, No!*" she said. "*Look, it's open at the bottom,*" and she pulled hers out of the bottom of the plastic easily. It was only sealed at top, but I never realized it and was going to battle shredding the plastic apart at every meal.

I still did it once in a while just for her benefit. She needed the levity in her life. Theresa and Pistol were talking every day again, so sometimes she'd cry to me at night after visiting him in jail.

"*It was so hard seeing him in there. He was like a different person, Normie. I was so sad when I left.*"

She was helping out with his affairs, and I welcomed her to take as much off my to-do list as she wished. She started talking to his mom every day, a support network that would be good for both of them.

"Why can't they just let my son go?" Joey's mom emailed me. "Why can't he just come home?" I could almost see her tears falling on the keyboard. She seemed on the verge of falling apart. I had no idea how she was holding up under all of that pressure—she was definitely stronger than I was, but I began to question their decision-making process.

It got to the point that everyone was asking me to omit information from everyone else, so I had to tell certain people certain things. Pistol didn't want his mom to know he was smoking in jail. His brother didn't want his mom or sister to know where the money was coming from to pay for the medical card. Betty didn't want me to give his ATM card to his ex-girlfriend, Veronica, but Pistol insisted for some odd reason, so I was asked to lie to him about that. Elizabeth, his sister, tried her best to help, bless her soul, by corresponding with me about his defense, but it amounted to just another person giving me contradicting orders from their Stateside perch. She wanted me to hold certain things back from their mom to protect her feelings, and at the same time her mom asked me to do the same thing with the rest of the family. What a friggin' mess.

Part of me thought, "Get your asses on a plane and come visit Joey." He had four siblings, and surely between all of them they could afford to put *one* person on a plane. But, when I penciled it out, it just didn't make sense—there was missed work, airfare, a week of hotels, food, a rental car, and still they could only see him twice in a nine-day span, because they could only visit one day on the weekends. That $4,000 could be better used on attorneys and getting food and money into the jail every week. It was a Catch-22.

But the requests went from just inconvenient to downright dangerous, especially with the latest one Betty emailed me. I told her I'd do it, but from then on my efforts would only focus on ensuring his health and safety. I had to draw the line somewhere.

On Saturday morning I headed to the jail, a visit I dreaded. I'd received an email that Joey NEEDED me to go to the jail that day and bring him a sizeable sum of money. Apparently he'd borrowed money from another inmate and promised to pay him back. He was expecting a package to arrive from the States that contained money for him, but it didn't. The other prisoner was giving him one more chance to come up with the funds that weekend. If he didn't have it then, the other prisoner was going to stab daylight into his stomach. That's how scores got settled in there. I don't know for certain what Pistol had used the money for, but I could guess.

So Pistol was panicked to get the money into the jail because he knew they meant business. The problem was that prison regulations only allowed a visitor to bring in 30,000 *Colones*, $60, at a time. Any more than that was considered illegal contraband. But I HAD to get the money in—Pistol's very life might depend on it. I'd feared for my safety before, but now I was on a slippery slope, taking huge risks to help him and for the first time even breaking the rules myself. But there was no other choice; I couldn't say no.

Hector drove me to the jail and I waited in line, but this time I didn't mind the delay. A lot could go wrong. Sometimes the guards searched me thoroughly, sometimes I could have brought a bazooka in there and they wouldn't have cared. The rules changed every weekend depending on who was working and what drama had gone down that week. There were even times when it was just too crowded to get inside and I had to turn back. Or what if I forgot my passport again? I touched it in the pocket of my shorts and wiped the sweat from my brow.

I thought it was best to keep 30,000 *Colones* in my wallet, the legal amount that was allowed in. The rest I folded up in the pocket of my cargo shorts. They were more likely to search my wallet. I got through registration, got stamped, surrendered my passport, and headed back to the cramped hallway where they would search me. There were three guards working—not a good sign. I said "hello" and tried to act casual as they looked through my bags and started patting me down, my arms reaching for the sky and my legs spread. The guard asked me to take everything out of my pockets. I took my wallet out and handed it to him. He took it and asked me again to empty all of my pockets. Feigning not understanding Spanish wasn't going to work.

I reached into my pocket and pulled out the money but it fell to the floor, loose bills fanning out. I scrambled to grab them before they blew away or disappeared under a guard's boot sole. This didn't look good for me. He took the money and counted it.

"*Es mi dinero, es para mi taxi y comida y otra cosas. No es para mi amigo en la cárcel,*" I said—it's my money, it's for my taxi and food and other things. It's not for my friend in jail.

"No, you cannot bring it in," the guard said. *"Only 30,000 is allow."* He motioned to my wallet.

"Okay, okay, I understand—*yo entiendo*—but this money isn't for my friend. This is my money."

"No," he said, stern faced, *"es illegal."* It's illegal. I was on his radar now. I didn't know what to do—I had to get it in to Pistol or he was going to get fucked up. My face turned flushed and I grew agitated. "What am I supposed to do? What?!" I asked. He just shrugged. "If I take it outside, can I come right back in?" I asked in rudimentary Spanish.

"*No, you wait at line again.*" Damn.

I walked out dejectedly, left the building, and walked back to the taxi. I told Hector what happened and about Pistol's dilemma. He whistled.

"Es malo suerte por su amigo," he said—that's bad luck for your friend. *"Que vas a hacer?"* What are you going to do?

There were only 45 minutes until visiting hours were over, and I had to start over in the back of the line. I sat there on the edge of the taxi and thought. There was no way I could leave him to get cut up inside. I had to try again. The guards would be waiting for me, and if they found the money on me, there was a good chance I'd end up in there with him.

"Yo voy un otra vez," I said to Hector. *"Si no regreso en dos horas vas a Tama y habla con Theresa."* I'm going again. If I'm not back in two hours, go back to Tama and talk to Theresa.

Where should I hide it? I thought for a long time, and then I hid the money. I got up and said goodbye to Hector, handed him the keys to my apartment, and walked into the jail again.

I got past the lines and now there were only 30 minutes to spare. I walked back to the guards. They did a double take when they saw me.

"Okay, no mas dinero—trente mil solemente," I said. Okay no more money—just 30,000.

They took hold of my shoulder and spun me around. I prayed as he started to pat me down, once, then again. Nothing yet. They made me turn my pockets inside out. I only had my wallet on me. They made me take off my shoes. They made me take off my socks. Nothing. One guard made me take off my belt and searched the inside of it. He looked inside of the waistband on my shorts. Nada. They searched and searched but came up with nothing. He looked at me in the face. I looked back at him straight in the eyes and didn't blink, stone faced—*la tabla rasa.*

"*Okay, you can go through,*" he said. I walked in.

I went back toward the cells with several groups of people, all rushing to get in before visiting hours were over. But a guard stood in our way and put his hand up when we reached the big blue basketball court, diverting us off the sidewalk and onto the court. There were five other guards and they organized all of us into a row on one sideline. One guard held back a German Shepherd on a leash. They told us to put all of our possessions—the bags we'd brought in, food, and contents of our pockets—on the ground in front of us. We did so, and then one guard walked down the line with the dog sniffing our belongings. Another guard filmed the whole thing with a video camera in case it had to be used as evidence later in court. Even though I knew I was fine, because the dog was looking for drugs, it still felt unnerving. Everyone watched carefully when the dog got to me because I was the lone gringo and they half wished that I got caught with something. I had apples in my bag and the dog rooted his nose into them.

"*Yo pienso el tiene hambre,*" I said out loud—I think he's hungry. It broke the tension and everyone laughed at that, including the guards. They finished our search and asked a couple of people into a separate room for more thorough searches. I was allowed to walk on and go into D2B. I was down to minutes before visiting hours were over. I exhaled.

The money was in my wallet—all of it. It never occurred to them to look there. I would have to be incredibly stupid or unbelievably ballsy to put all of the money back in the one most obvious place. They'd searched everywhere else but never opened my wallet.

Pistol and the Canadian, Ryan, rushed toward me when I walked in. I was pissed, wrung-through with adrenaline from the whole thing. I didn't know whether to punch him or hug him.

"Hey, Norm, guess what happened?" Ryan said, almost out of breath. "You're never going to believe this!"

"What, what?" I asked, bracing myself for more bad news.

"Pistol scored a goal!" he said.

"What?"

"Yeah, I scored a goal!" Pistol said.

"A goal?"

"Fuck yeah! You know, gooooooaaaaallllllllll!"

"Come on in and we'll tell you about it."

Pistol had taken my advice and started getting more exercise than just walking circles in the courtyard. When the prisoners were good the guards let them exercise on the blue courts. There wasn't a chance in hell they were playing basketball in Costa Rica, so they played soccer. Pistol jumped in the soccer games a couple of times, mostly standing around racking up red cards because he couldn't coordinate his gringo feet with the ball if his life depended on it. He wore his trusty Birkenstocks, and when the action came near him, he flailed away at the ball or got juked so hard he wiped out.

"And then, yesterday, I actually scored a goal!" he said.

"How the hell did that happen?" I asked, caught up in their enthusiasm and already forgetting about the money.

"I don't know—the ball got kicked my way out of a scramble and I found myself in front of the net in perfect position. It was just me and the goalie."

"Holy shit, so you scored on him?"

"Uhhh, no, not quite," Ryan said. "He wound up and took a big kick at it and....missed the ball completely. I mean really whiffed and fell flat on his back."

"Yeah that sounds about right," I laughed.

"I didn't even see where the ball was, but I got up and it rebounded my way and hit me wham! on the chest and bounced off right into the goal!"

"So you didn't even kick it?"

"No—it went off my chest!"

"Without even meaning to do it!" Ryan said.

"That's hilarious! What did everyone do?"

"The whole place went crazy," Ryan said. "I mean, all of the other prisoners, even from the other teams, started cheering and laughing. Even the guards ran over and slapped him on the back. I thought they were going to lift him up over their heads and carry him off the court. It was quite a moment, man."

"The gringo scores a goal – amazing," I said. I realized how big something like that was for them; something small that I took for granted would help them do their time, a small flash of hope in an otherwise dark place.

I asked Ryan to describe the part about Pistol getting hit in the chest and falling down again, and Pistol to tell me how all of the prisoners and even the guards celebrated his success. The guards! I had tears in my eyes when he got up and acted it out.

Only a few minutes had passed but a guard yelled that visiting hours were over. I handed Pistol the money but was so distracted I forgot I was supposed to be mad.

"Okay, bro, I've got to go home now," I said. He nodded and looked down at his shoes.

"Airplane or taxi, Norm?" he asked.

"What's that?"

"You said that you're going home now. Do you mean in an airplane or a taxi?" His question took me by surprise. I thought about it for a second; nothing had gone as planned in Costa Rica. I didn't have any money coming in, nor a social life or even a girlfriend. I missed my family and didn't feel particularly safe. I was committing career suicide—most people thought writing a book was just a nonsensical whim and almost everyone told me it was impossible to make any money at it. It would be easy for me to leave Tamarindo, to go back to the States, or even to move on to another beach town in Panama or Nicaragua, where I could still write my book but I wouldn't have to deal with Pistol. But I couldn't do it.

"Taxi, Joey. Taxi." I smiled.

"Okay, good."

CHAPTER 29

THE SCORPION DANCE

I couldn't believe it was already January—seven months into my time down in Costa Rica and a brand new year. Where had the time gone? It seemed like only yesterday that I was new in town, struggling to figure it all out. In that short time, I'd survived the rainy season, weathered the big Pistol shit show, made some good friends, and grown to love Tamarindo, despite all of the obstacles. My fortieth birthday was fast approaching—February 9—and with it the three goals I'd set for myself. "What do you want for your birthday?" my mom emailed. "Nothing at all," I told her, for this year I was the only one who could give myself a gift.

On second thought, it would have been a nice to have some new clothes. I was sick of wearing the same six t-shirts in such heavy rotation that people knew what day of the week it was by whether I was wearing yellow, blue, or green. The good news was that I had a friend coming down to visit soon, Big Mike, so I got online and ordered a bunch of items, including workout clothes, socks and underwear, new shorts, a George Foreman grill, and a pull-up bar. I had them sent to my buddy to bring down for me. I'd also left a few boxes of winter clothes with him in California for when I visited in the future.

I was going to be plenty busy when Big Mike visited later that winter, entertaining him but still carving out time to write every day. The book was coming along—I was up to about 150 pages—but as I wrote I had no idea if it was the best book ever written or if it sucked so bad that I'd be laughed out of Barnes and Noble. It was all new to me. I found that when I *tried* to write well, it came out only marginally better than refried dog shit. So instead I attempted to stick to this formula: If I was sitting next to my best buddy in a bar and told him the story, what would I say? I built it up from there. Each chapter was going to be about a different country I'd visited. I hoped that was the right way to do it. I had no idea, and little guidance other than occasional words of encouragement from the self-publishing house I'd committed to, Authority Publishing. I emailed Stephanie my rough drafts as I went and hung on every word of her reply. She said she liked it so far and I had a gift for writing comedy. I hoped she wasn't just being nice.

Surely I should I be writing more though, spending more time at my desk. Didn't real, professional writers sit down and hammer out twelve hours of work a day without more than two bathroom breaks, or unnecessary scratching? Did Hemingway take three naps a day? He was bare-knuckle boxing and drinking wine at bullfights while I drank orange Fanta and wasted time on Facebook. I wasn't exactly impressing the hell out of myself, but somehow the chapters were still piling up faster than I expected.

My only shot of getting something done was early in the morning, when I rose before dawn and indulged in coffee and the tranquility of my thoughts with my laptop open. In between afternoon siestas, or during the still nights, I tried to put in a few more hours, but it was really hit or miss—by then my mind felt like an overripe mango that had been dropped on the hot pavement.

It seemed to me that I was spending more time by myself to summon the introspection to write. I had a whole world in my head, and I was responsible for giving them love and hate and hope so they didn't shrivel up and die. That was a tricky thing, for being in your own head is like holding up a mirror to a bigger mirror—your reflection bounces on forever. "*Stare into the abyss long enough and the abyss stares into you,*" they say. I was so consumed with the 90,000 needy citizens of my literary nation that I put my shirt on inside out and walked into trees in broad daylight. Eventually I grew exhausted to my bones—I had nothing left to give them, so I settled on just getting the main character to the story's finish line. That's exactly when the best writing began.

Damn, I needed a break from people. I actually enjoyed my own company and didn't really need a lot more in my life. Sure it was lonely at times, but I reminded myself it was all for the greater good of achieving my three goals. This book better work out, I thought, so I'm not living the life of a psychotic expatriate in the jungle for nothing. It's called "crazy" if you're a nobody, "eccentric" once you actually achieve something…

"You are SO lucky!" people messaged me on Facebook. "You get to live the PERFECT life in PARADISE! I wish I had YOUR life!"

Really? Perfect? Paradise? They had no idea what I had to deal with.

But I could always go to the beach and take a long swim and everything would be right in the world; floating in that water had a way of recalibrating my spirit. So I just kept to my routine. That was the only way to ensure I was going to be productive. Each day I prioritized what energy I had into writing, then working out, then everything else.

One day after New Year's I trudged back to my apartment after working on my manuscript through a lunch of rice, beans, and fish. I walked slowly in the sun, but still my shirt was wet by the time I got back to my apartment. I took it off and hung it on the bannister behind me and sat down at my desk to write. Here we go—time to really turn this thing around and crank out a few chapters. Focus time! I turned the fan on and sat down, shirtless, and started beating up the keyboard.

Twenty minutes passed and I figured my shirt must be dry. I grabbed it off the bannister, put it on, and kept writing at my desk, facing the open front door. I typed a few more lines and then felt something tickling the underside of my wrist. Whatever it was moved toward my forearm. It must be an ant or a fly, I thought, so I finished typing the sentence and then turned my arm over.

A scorpion sat on my wrist—a big one, jet-black with nasty looking pinchers bigger than its head and a barbed tail perfectly coiled to strike.

Let's FREEZE it right there, with me sitting at my desk, my wrist turned over and eyes bugging out of my head at the scorpion in mid-step, a weird noise about to come out of my twisted face.

Would it sting me? I guess that was the big question. And if it did, would it kill me? I think scorpions only kill old people and infants. Then again, I was turning 40 soon—was that considered old enough? Probably not. Everyone knows you aren't *officially* old until you eat dinner at 4:30 p.m. and watch reruns of Murder She Wrote. I ate at 5:00 and only got Spanish soccer on TV, so I was still scorpion-proof.

Since I've conveniently frozen time, let's sneak a quick peek again. Oh damn, that's a nasty sucker! They must be dangerous because they were in Indian Jones and the Rock made a whole movie based around them, the Scorpion King. Did you know that he went to my junior high? The Rock—not Indiana Jones. Yup, Michael J. Whalen middle school in Hamden, Connecticut. Rough place. Saw my first gang fight there. Then he moved to Hawaii for high school. I didn't know Dwayne Johnson, but odds are he stuffed me into a locker at some point. You should have seen me in middle school—I was such a dork. I had a big mouth full of shiny metal braces with little rubber bands and night guards and retainers and all sorts of medieval torture devices attached to my face. I was in my heavy metal phase so I had a jeans jacket with Mötley Crüe patches and a Captain 80's feathered haircut with a rat tail in the back. My God, why did our parents let us leave the house like that? I think I also had Hammer pants. Okay, I know I did.

But I digress. Let's get back to the present situation of the scorpion sitting on my arm. Once I unfreeze time, I'm going to have a big decision to make. Do I hold still and wait for it to crawl off? Do I play dead? It's not a bear, for Christ's sake. Do I call out for my neighbor to come and get it off with a spatula? Someone usually knocks on my door every 17.9 minutes, but where are they all now, when I really need them? Chillax, Normando, breathe. Now's not the time to panic—only a cool head and remarkable bravery will get you out of this one.

Well, I guess there's no more delaying the inevitable—it's hero time.

But I just want to say, in case it stings me and I start foaming at the mouth and my head turns purple and I croak, it's been nice knowing y'all. Well, most of y'all, anyways—some of y'all are highly suspect. Why did I start speaking with a Texas accent all of a sudden? Okay, so please tell my momma that I love her and donate the contents of my entire financial empire ($47.10 in my checking account) to my nephews and niece. And to my best friend, Mitch—yo dog, wassup homie? Do me a favor and grab my hard drive from the bottom of my sock drawer. There's some freaky stuff on there that I don't want my family to see. Dude, you're not supposed to look at it, either. Okay, so I went through a kinky phase where midgets wrestling in baby oil turned me on. Stop judging, bro.

Okay, ready folks? Here we go:

One,

Two,

Three,

UNFREEZE!

I screamed like a little byyyyyyyytttttchhhhhh. Like a curly-haired six-year-old girl at her first sleepover. "Oh my God, oh my God, holy sweet, bald-headed baby Jesus, get it off get it off get it off!" I jumped up from the desk, knocking over my chair, and danced around wildly, shaking my arm like it was on fire. I had no idea if the scorpion flew off or if it fell somewhere else on my body or if there were more of them, so I ripped off my shirt and shorts and boxers in wild convulsions. "Ughhh Ughhh Wughhh!!!" I was completely naked, dancing around like, well, like MC Hammer in the 80s, gyrating and convulsing to extricate the little demon(s) from my body. Hopefully, they couldn't touch this.

Then I saw it—the scorpion launched from my wrist and landed on the tile floor ten feet away. I was safe. I gave a sigh of relief. Ahhh, I would live to write another day. And my hard drive was safe and no one would know about the midgets in the baby oil. Well, of course, except Mitch. And you guys.

I looked up and realized I was standing by the open front door, in full view of all my neighbors out at the pool. They were lined up with mouths agape, just having watched my fully naked scorpion dance.

"Howdy! How y'all doing?" I waved, but they didn't seem to share my enthusiasm.

CHAPTER 30

RUNNING IN DREAMS

I had an image in my mind of what I looked like that was hard to shake, even as I shed the pounds. The perception of my dimensions remained like the phantom limbs of an amputee. I'd see my reflection in a store window or in a photograph and do a double take at the lean, healthy guy looking back at me.

But I couldn't deny that most of the clothing I'd brought to Costa Rica didn't fit anymore. My size 38 waist shorts went on like I was stepping into a burlap bag. My XL shirts were now uncomfortably loose, draped halfway to my knees. Did I really wear those snuggly only a few months earlier? I donated them to charity.

It was more than just losing weight. I realized that in my life the memory of my victories always faded faster than the defeats lingered, and that's what I needed to change. The mental belief of my un-health was harder to change than the physical manifestation.

Every morning I weighed myself on a scale that I'd bought in Liberia and recorded the number in a spreadsheet. That may seem obsessive but, quite the opposite, it kept me from falling victim to the stress and assumptions that allowed negative thinking to sabotage my fitness goals. I consistently lost a pound or two per week, a lot more in the beginning when I was sweating it all out. Most importantly, I could breathe again.

I discovered a secret weapon, which made it so easy to shed pounds it was almost unfair. Right here and now I'll give you that secret, which even the gazillion-dollar diet and fitness industry can't figure out. I've got two little words for you that are going to change your life, my friend: *Gringo Stomach.*

My first month in Tamarindo I drank the tap water. Everyone said it was *pretty* safe, which is really like saying your vest is *sort of* bulletproof. It looked okay, but the quality of the tap water depended a lot on where and when you drank it. When it rained, garbage and crap washed down the river into the bay and mixed in with the aquifers. But even when the water was clear my body was always fighting to adjust to the foreign bacteria.

I soon caught a case of Gringo Stomach. For those first weeks, I couldn't leave the bathroom for more than 37 minutes consecutively. If I'd brought a set of Encyclopedia Britannica in there with me, I'd be somewhere between *Sacajawea* and *Syphilis* by now. Thank God it was only a mild to extremely mild case, but it was great for weight loss. I dropped eight pounds just from Gringo Stomach.

It gave me a genius idea (if I do say so myself): "*The Tropical Vacation Weight Loss System*." This package will include two weeks on the beach in a beautiful tropical resort AND all of the good food you can eat, including deserts and second helpings. The kicker is that you're still GUARANTEED to lose twenty pounds in two weeks or you'll get a 100% refund. This package only costs…let's say $10,000. We'd have a plane full of rich Americans coming down to the tropics, eager to make out with French fries and pizza while lying around the pool like pregnant harbor seals and STILL lose twenty pounds. The reservations would come in so fast that my credit card machine would start smoking and probably explode.

Oh, and one last small detail I forgot to mention: Upon stepping off the plane, each guest will receive a nice cold glass of water before heading to the hotel. They won't realize it at the time, but this will be "special" water, not because it was hand carried by eunuch Sherpas from of a sacred waterfall in the Inca mountains, but because I scooped it out of a green-ish puddle behind the bus stop. Those cherubic gringos will be sprinting for the commodes by the time they reach the hotel. Of course, I'll spare no expense—the luxurious restrooms, lined up twenty deep, will be equipped with flat screen TVs and free wi-fi. It will be easy to honor the twenty-pound guarantee; by the time they're able to crawl out of their stalls they'll be pleasantly emaciated, unable to stomach more than Gatorade and half a Ritz cracker. Cha ching! Another round of satisfied customers!

The culture in Tama also made it easy to lose weight. People enjoyed the quality of cuisine and the social aspect of dining together, not quantity. There were no all-you-can-eat buffets, no insatiable lust for excess where everything is fast, big, cheap, open all night, frozen, easy, two-for-one, microwavable, and super-sized. The little things added up to a much healthier relationship with food.

Everyone walked, everyone rode bicycles, and everyone worked out, no matter how young or old. Going to the beach to play for a few hours was about the best thing you could conceive of, and it was free, so why not? People walked to the local market to pick up food every few days. The refrigerators were smaller, the plates and glasses were smaller, and so were the portions.

When it's so hot out you don't have huge cravings anyway, but food was also expensive in Tamarindo. Prices were the same or higher as in the United States because just about everything had to be imported and it was a tourist town, but unlike the U.S., going to the grocery store wasn't a cheaper option.

Thankfully, the cheapest meal I found in Tama also happened to be the most healthy: *Casados,* the typical Tico lunch or dinner consisting of *gallo pinto,* rice and black beans, a gelatinous hunk of cheese that I never ate, vegetables, salad, plantains, and a meat—chicken, beef, or fish. I ate at least one fresh *Casado* per day, and because most of the ingredients were local (the fish pulled right out the sea), it was usually around $7. I tried to eat fish as a first choice and veggies instead of fries when I was ordering off a menu. My go-to snack was a spoonful of peanut butter with honey. Other than that, it was pasta twice a week and scrambled eggs every day.

I can't forget the smoothies—they were bomb.com, and I had at least one a day. For only a couple of dollars at the local smoothie stand (the tourist stand was twice as expensive), I could pick from 25 different fruits and vegetables, blended with ice or yogurt. My favorite was a coconut, pineapple, banana, and mango smoothie with granola on top.

The food was healthier in other ways, too—there were less empty starches, breads, and carbs; few processed or packaged foods; no fast food (except Burger King for Pistol, which I tried to avoid); and less chemicals or additives in the food.

Glen had given me a few tactics to use on my weight loss journey, one of which was to do two-a-day workouts. By doing something in the morning and then the evening jumpstarted my metabolism, never giving it a chance to slow down and rest, even while I slept. It worked like a charm. I also set positive goals, a big change in my mindset. This allowed the momentum of my beliefs to move toward the positive, away from the darkness of judgment.

By mixing up the workouts I never got bored: running on the beach, swimming daily, lifting weights, mountain biking, boxing, and hiking up a steep set of stairs that wound up the hill at El Tesoro. Toward the end of my time in Tama, Row even collected enough donations for us to get the basketball hoop fixed at the skate park. We nailed the wooden slats on the backboard and he got a local welder to make us a regulation rim. There were intense hoop games in the heat with Row, who was surprisingly strong and took it to the rim with fierce abandon, and Gringo Grant, who had a smooth game from playing on his high school team. Our hoop battles in the hot sun thoroughly kicked my ass into shape.

Tamarindo even had its own gym. It was the size of a Starbucks on the second floor in the little shopping center up past hostel row. You could find it easily because it was right next to Gil's Place, a Mexican restaurant with Nicaraguan workers run by a Puerto Rican from New York living in Costa Rica. Only in Tama. The other residents in the plaza were a day care center for rich gringos and a few one-bedroom apartments occupied by Dominican prostitutes. The curvaceous Dominican girls stood in their doorways half-dressed, everything hanging out, whistling and calling to the guys who were headed to the gym. More than one guy abandoned their workouts and succumbed to their invitations, though, technically, I guess they did get some sort of exercise.

The gym was air conditioned, which was a big deal. People came in off the street just to cool off by the front desk, even bringing in a cold beer to crack open. Shirts were optional, and everyone wore flip-flops or went barefoot, even on the treadmill.

I loved that place; lord knows I put in enough work there. It was my evening entertainment when there was nothing else to do except go to the bars or sit at home. During the rainy season I'd throw on flip-flops and put a plastic bag over my head, my sneakers in my backpack, and hike up the muddy hill, showing up soaking wet but excited to spend a couple of blissful hours at the gym. I didn't care about lifting a lot of weight or getting bigger—I did everything to try and get lean and balanced. At first I had no idea how much weight I was lifting because everything was in kilos and I was too lazy to do the math. So the dumbbells I lifted said twenty kilos—was I incredibly strong or a big pussy? Who knew?

There was a great vibe to that gym. Everyone—Tico, surfer, local, young and old—encouraged each other and shared ideas and techniques. There was a lot of laughter and respect in there, a sense of community that was a reflection of the best parts of the streets outside.

The gym was great but I preferred to swim in the bay, and soon the ocean became my best friend in Tamarindo. I went for a long swim every day in those rolling waves, any worries from my life on dry land evaporating as I floated along. Every now and then I'd look up to take in the panorama of coastline, the smoky rolling green hills and big sky. Hot damn, I was swimming in the *ocean* in the *tropics* and this was my *life,* not just a quick vacation—I was one lucky bastard.

What we dislike the most is usually best for us, and for me it was running. I'd rather do just about anything other than run, including putting a live stingray in my board shorts.

Most mornings I'd take a break around 8:00 a.m. after writing for three hours for a run on the beach. I'd have to pass the beachside bar, El Pescador, and on the weekends the Columbians and Ticos were still out partying from the night before. They'd be blind drunk and coked out of their heads, arguing and fighting with the music still blasting. The path to the beach went right by them, a chain link fence on the other side. I'd look for a broken beer bottle to pick up, concealing it behind my back. I'd walk through to the beach without incident and then chuck it in the trash barrel. Life in Tamarindo.

I'd started by walking on the beach every day, which was about three-fourths of a mile. It wasn't much, but I did it either first thing in the morning or at sunset. Then I progressed to a jog, but the first time I only got halfway up the beach before I had to stop. I huffed and puffed but didn't seem to make any progress. Everything hurt—my lower back was on fire, my ankles throbbed. The sand felt like it was trying to swallow up every footstep. An old lady walked past me. I felt like collapsing and screaming to every passerby, "Go on! Just leave me! Save yourselves!" which, of course, they would because A) they didn't know who the hell I was or why I was rolling around on the ground in pain, and B) I was still in the parking lot, only 30 seconds into my run.

Running on the beach was a hell of a lot harder than running on the treadmill, but I stuck with it, stretching my personal goals further each week—just get to the tree, just get past the rocks, I'd tell myself. At least I could look at the ocean. How could I complain? But by the time I left Tama, my daily run was an incredible fitness experience.

Fast forward seven months to January and I was running with a backpack for wind resistance and to hold my goggles, flip-flops, and keys. I added a water bottle to my pack. Then two, then four. Then I filled water bottles with sand and ocean water for my own version of a fifteen-pound weight vest.

I ran barefoot in the sand. The part that was still wet was firmest so I chose my path through the sharp pebbles and sea shells, zigzagging to avoid the incoming waves. I ran through tidal pools, and then I got to the vast stretch that went all the way up to the estuary, so open that I had to reassess my sense of distance because there were few landmarks.

In the past, I had to stop near the volleyball courts because the sand was too soft, but the deep sand posed no problem anymore. I found that by picking my feet straight up and down, like a high-knees drill in football, I could keep from sinking in. I'd watched how the Brazilians ran through sand and how powerful and well balanced their legs grew.

I broke into a sprint as the beach curled down to the estuary, faster, faster still, chasing the birds. Out of breath, I reached the shore where the boats were anchored, waiting for passengers. I threw my backpack in a boat and helped push the bow off the sand bar and climbed in. I remembered the first time I came aboard one of the boats; I'd hopped on when the boat's captain was unprepared, looking down at his cell phone, and the boat rocked so violently that he was thrown into the water, soaking wet all the way up to his chest. The other boat captains laughed and laughed but I felt bad that I was too bulky to even be seaworthy.

It took us only ten minutes to reach the other side, plodding along at the outboard's slowest pace, just enough time for the thick and shoeless man, 35 but looking 55, to tell me how he got drunk the previous night and his old lady kicked him out of the house and that there were a lot of crocs floating that day. He was a jungle person, not a beach person, and the distinction was clear to me. He steered us around back of a protruding sandbar where the currents and the depth were predictable, sliding the boat in just enough for me to jump off into a sandy-floored thicket of mangrove. I flipped him a 500 *Colones* coin and headed off again. Playa Grande was wilder than Tama so at most I'd see a dozen people on the whole two-mile stretch, surfers or locals with their families on wind-blown blankets, and maybe a few leatherback sea turtles if I was lucky. Grande formed a gentle crescent so you could see the whole span of beach from any vantage point, and then it ended and disappeared behind a huge rock formation, Playa Conchal to the north.

At high tide, I ran in water as deep as my knees. I'd pass the occasional tourist venturing out from Tama and they'd smile, assuming I was in military training, with my backpack and army-green sunhat, doing my own Tough Mudder.

Playa Grande sloped sharply up from the water into sea grass and patterns of sand vines and then the jungle. Every eighth of a mile was marked by a red wooden post sticking out of the sand. I usually made it to #125, which meant nothing because I had no idea where they started or finished, before I decided it was time to take a little swim.

I found a good spot to bury my key and cover my backpack with sand, under a burnt-out piece of driftwood from an old bonfire. Caution was a habit.

I jumped into the sea and started kicking. The waves were unpredictable out there, the currents dragging you back into churning foam with a vengeance. There were no lifeguards, no one to help me if I couldn't make it. I loved it like that, fighting for my breath without room for weakness, and I emerged from the water forty minutes later breathless, dizzy for a few moments until my wave-vertigo subsided. I grabbed my possessions and brushed the sand off, gulped some water and started the whole run in reverse, headed home.

By then there was no fatigue, just a feeling of warm energy shooting effortlessly into my limbs, filling my lungs and mastering my breathing. I ended at the same spot—where they rent the jet skis by the Columbia restaurant—and took the path up into town and to my apartment. Then, at night, I would go to the gym. No wonder I was in great shape.

I wish I could tell you that it was all heroic jaunts across the seascape like this, epic and effortless, but there was a lot of mud and frustration and gasping progress. Being in shape felt wonderful, but *getting* in shape was the real source of pride—I'd earned every bit of it. What felt like an excruciating chore when I first moved down there gradually became my savior.

Would I reach my goal to be in the best shape of my life by my fortieth birthday? I still had months to go, but I realized that the answer wasn't as important as the pursuit of the question.

CHAPTER 31

DON'T FALL ASLEEP UNDER THE MANCHINEEL TREE

On the south end of Playa Tamarindo, where the sands narrowed into cliffs of black rock, impassable except by crossing the sharp crags at low tide, stood a lone tree. Nothing else grew out there, where the ocean blew relentlessly without the bay as a buffer: neither savannah oaks nor coconut trees. The Manchineel tree was the only one that could survive, its deep roots acting like a windbreak, keeping the sand from eroding off the beach.

That tree was the perfect shelter on a scorching day: an umbrella of waxy green leaves and spiked flowers with small gray apples. I walked down there when I wanted to be alone, and think.

"*Whaa gwaan mi breddah*!" the Rasta called out to me on the way, emerging barefoot and shirtless from the jungle. He greeted me warmly and made sure I didn't get tangled in his fishing lines, strung taut into the sea from bamboo sticks stuck in the sand.

He asked me where I was headed and I pointed to the Manchineel tree at the end of the beach.

"*Ahh, mind yah don't fall asleep under dat Manchineel tree*," he said.

"Why's that?" I asked.

He told me that the Manchineel was perfectly safe to sit under it when it was sunny, but when it rained the water filtered through the leaves and the apples and became poisonous. They called it *manzanilla de la muerte*, or the "little apple of death," in Spanish, and it was so poisonous that the Carib Indians used to dip their arrows in its sap. More than one drunk fell asleep under the Manchineel tree, the Rasta explained, and woke up with horrible blisters on his face like acid burns. If you got too much of it, or inhaled the smoke when it burned, you could go blind or become paralyzed, even die.

I thanked him and wished him luck with the fishing.

"*Jah provide*," he said.

I walked on toward the tree, my footsteps disappearing in the sand with each wave that rolled in.

I'd read somewhere that there are 422,000 species of plants in the world, 1.7 million scientific names to label them all. Each of them have unique characteristics, benefits to the ecosystem they exist within, and natural defenses. Every one of them has a role in nature, a reason for existing that isn't just a divine accident.

422,000 types of plants in the whole wide world, so much natural beauty in Costa Rica that it was like strolling in Edenic prehistory, and yet there were so many problems around this one little plant that some botanist named "marijuana." How arbitrary it seemed that the Manchineel tree wouldn't be just as shunned. After all, it could make you blind, or even kill you.

It sure seemed like a lot of people were smoking marijuana, no matter where I went in the world. It appeared to make people happier, to pacify their spirits a little bit. Maybe I was missing something, but I didn't see the evil with people getting high. We all were trying to get high in some way, weren't we? Through meditation, yoga, exercise, religion, chasing success, money, or pulling love toward us. And if that didn't work, we went to our doctor and got permission to take a little pill, designed to do the exact same thing, albeit with the small disclaimer that they "may cause anxiety, dizziness, vomiting, diarrhea, irregular heartbeat, blood spouting out of your ears, yellow fish eyes, six types of rectal cancer, and death in some cases." Wasn't it all the same endorphins? What was the alternative, trying to get LOW?

Just like the Manchineel, when you used everything in nature for its intended purpose, with balance and prudence, the ecosystem worked just fine. So why could you get thrown in jail for just touching that one species of plant, when you were perfectly welcome to fall asleep under the Manchineel tree? Or, if we're making everything that could be bad for us illegal, why are so many things left off the list?

I didn't have a dog in that fight either way; even though someone offered marijuana to me daily in Tama, I rarely smoked, and if I never touched that one particular plant again for the rest of my life it wouldn't really bother me. When I was younger I'd tried just about every substance under the sun (though I never put a needle in my arm), but once I reached my 30s do you want to know what my recreational drug of choice was? A few beers. I know, not very sexy, but a couple of beers and a 10:00 p.m. bedtime suited me just fine, maybe a puff every blue moon.

But Pistol was suffering in Babylon because he'd emulated nature and grew some plants for his own use. Sure, he got stupid. Okay, very stupid, and then he got caught, but he should have been scrubbing toilets and cleaning litter off the beach, not fighting for his life stuck in a Costa Rican prison with no hope of getting out for a long time. It felt so out of control, but there was no one I could go to and just say, "This is way out of hand and someone is going to get hurt. Please stop it." Anything could happen to him in there.

And me? That desperate rush of entropy was all too familiar—I'd been thrust into a similar situation seventeen years earlier in Colorado.

I was hanging out with my roommate and our female neighbors after the bars on a Wednesday night, smoking a bowl. They were throwing a football around, being goofy, and it broke a window by accident. Someone called the cops and they came in without a warrant. There was a little weed on the table, but I didn't think it would be a big deal. "Whatever you find is mine, but let the girls go," I said, thinking I'd take one for the team. Little did I know but my roommate had a pound of mushrooms hidden in a golf bag and eighteen marijuana plants growing in his closet upstairs. The police ripped our apartment to shreds and then woke up the judge and got a proper warrant. We were stuffed and cuffed, brought down to the station separately, and coerced into writing statements without an attorney present. From there, they brought me to the county jail, where I woke up sleepless on a metal bench in a cold concrete room. The fluorescent lights were on 24 hours a day, reaching into my eyes like hot fish hooks. I was allowed to make phone calls but I couldn't remember anyone's phone number. I was processed, strip-searched, and given an orange jumpsuit to wear. They guard took my shoelaces, a standard precaution, he explained, so that no one would try to hang themselves.

#96CR275. That was my new identity. I was thrown into general population and assigned the top bunk in Pod #2A, just like Jerry Seinfeld's apartment number on the show, I remember thinking. There was one small window facing east, a metal toilet with no seat, and a Bible. I was given a bologna sandwich, a mushy apple, and a carton of expired milk on a plastic tray. I got started on the Bible.

Reilly bailed me out on a Friday afternoon, only minutes before the cutoff time when I'd be stuck in there all weekend. I got home thinking it was just a bad dream, but when I listened to the answering machine it was my boss at the town community center firing me from my job.

I didn't tell my mother I'd been arrested. To be honest, I was more afraid of her than going to jail. I had no money and now no job, but everyone told me that using the public defender was suicide, so I scrounged together my last remaining credit cards and made a down payment for a solid criminal defense attorney who took pity and let me pay in installments.

The next six months were a hellish waiting game to learn the fate of my life. It wasn't looking good—they were trying to pin me with trafficking for the mushrooms and the marijuana that was growing, even though I'd had nothing to do with it. The prosecutor was pushing hard for four years in Federal prison with no chance of parole, and a felony on my record.

Still, I was one of the lucky ones, a white boy with a credit card, but there were plenty of others who went through processing with me who got denied bail, received stiffer sentences because the judge didn't like how they looked, and had to walk the plank with the public defender. They were guilty just for showing up, for being born. At least I got to stress on the outside. But I found out quickly that when you're in the system everyone has their hands in your pocket.

The only one who would give me a job was a drug dealer, a huge Mexican ex-felon named Jorge who ran a house painting company as a front for his other activities. He walked with a limp, courtesy of a baseball bat to the knee, and wore his sunglasses indoors. I woke up at dawn and worked all day outside in the winter, my fingers frozen from washing out buckets and cleaning brushes. Jorge bounced checks all over town, including to his employees, so the only other worker who stuck with him was a guy named Eric, a high school dropout who sported a bowl haircut and wore tight white pants. Eric talked incessantly about the time he was abducted by aliens out of his front yard. He didn't mind as much that Jorge wrote us bad paychecks because he wouldn't need money anyway once the aliens came back to take him to their home planet, but I sure needed Earth currency. On a big Saturday night I'd get a 99-cent bottomless cup of coffee and read at the local café. At least it was warm in there, and sometimes people left half-eaten pastries on their plates when they left. Don't get me wrong, I was incredibly thankful just to have a job because no one would hire someone with my criminal record, but still, my seven dollars an hour didn't cover court fees, attorneys, and rent and living expenses.

Sometimes I was hungry, but I refused to go on welfare or food stamps. There were more than a few nights that I had pride for dinner. One day I looked in the phone book and got a ride to the Blood Center, where they let me donate plasma twice a week. They'd stick a three-inch-long, alarmingly thick needle into my arm and draw out my blood for 45 minutes, spinning it through a centrifuge and injecting my own blood back into my veins, devoid of the valuable white blood cells and platelets. For that I got $15 the first time I donated in a week, and $12 the second time because my blood was so depleted.

That was my grocery money, $27 a week. I waited for my orange juice and a cookie after I was done and then I shuffled straight to the grocery store. Everyone looked so happy, so clean, but I didn't feel so good, sick to my stomach and about to fall over. I put things in my cart and added them up twice in my head and then brought them to the register. I waited with the other respectable people, but when everything was scanned and bagged my card bounced. "Maybe it's just your card, try again," the checkout girl said. "Do you have another one?" I didn't. I had to put the things back into the cart, one by one, and then leave them.

The shame made my cheeks red, the only color in my face. I wanted to cry. The gal working felt bad for me, and she wanted to cry. Some of you are shaking your heads because you've been there, too. You'll never forget that feeling, huh? "Just leave it, sweetie," she said. "I'll put it aside and have it ready for you when you come back," but we both knew I wasn't coming back. It was cold outside. I walked back home, past the college kids eating pizza and spilling beer on their front porches, making noises that I remembered as laughter.

When I got home I dialed the Blood Center. "The soonest you can come back in is Tuesday," they said.

That winter I shaved my head. I lived in my attic bedroom with the door shut. I did more pushups and pull-ups than I'd been able to do before, extra sets out of fear. I shouldered weights that I couldn't lift. I read 800-page books by Dumas and Dostoyevsky and actually understood them—*"It is not possible to eat me without insisting that I sing praises of my devourer?"*

My one pair of jeans sagged from my bony ass like a potato sack so I poked a new hole in my belt, then another. I waited months for a court date just to show up and they'd set another court date. The prosecutor was unrelenting.

I've never wanted so much in my life to get the fuck out, to just run and keep running. But if I bolted then there was no going back. My eyes bounced off the attic walls and then looked down at my shoelaces. I started considering options that weren't on the table before.

Four years in Federal prison—what would they do to me? I couldn't sleep. Every night the wolves howled louder. I dreamt about their snarling pack chase and woke up with the taste of blood in my mouth.

My sentencing hearing was on the fifth of July. My attorney did a bang up job and got them to accept a plea bargain for of a couple misdemeanors and suspend the felony, a four-year sentence hanging over my head if I got into any trouble at all. That meant I could only get sentenced to up to six months in state prison—a huge victory. Still, no one in my family knew.

The judge was bored and ready to give me the full sentence, and asked if I had anything to say as a formality. I spoke from my heart. He lifted his head for the first time that day, actually *looking* at me like a person, and sentenced me to the mandatory minimum, fifteen days in county.

They said I could turn myself in the following Monday but I told them I'd rather get it over with, so I was handcuffed and put in the back of a sheriff's car in my borrowed suit. "Sitting on the Dock of the Bay," by Otis Redding was playing on the radio, and right there I decided to move to San Francisco once the whole thing was over with.

We got to the Larimer County Detention Center and I went through processing again and got thrown in.

"Do you know where you are?" the guard asked. I assured him that I did.

A menacing prisoner with a square head and knuckles like hams approached me.

He looked at me. "Sit down," he said, motioning to a metal table where other menacing prisoners were sitting. I did, and he dealt us all cards. "My name is Metro," he said. "Two's and dirty Jacks are wild."

"What's up, Metro? I'm Norm," and we were all friends by lunchtime. Most of the guys weren't bad at all, just rough around the edges, in for fighting, small time possessions, or parole violations. There were a few guys who were in for check fraud or smacking their wives around, but we avoided them.

It was a vacation for me on the inside. We had cable TV and I got to play ping pong and cards.

Our first night we all watched a new movie on HBO, *Mr. Holland's Opus*. By the midway point the guys were all bored and wanted to change the channel, but I was so touched by the movie's emotion that I had a tear in my eye. Yeah, probably not the best time for that.

I did pull-ups on the shower bar and hung out with my homies, Metro, Gus Lee, a tall, athletic hippie from North Carolina who got pinched with mushrooms in his VW van on his way through town, and a Mexican teenager with a broken arm. I never asked him how his arm got broken. Gus kicked my ass at ping pong, but I could beat the kid playing with the cast most of the time.

We were given three meals a day, the same bologna sandwiches and spoiled milk, but I didn't care. On the weekends we could have visitors, and Reilly came to see me. I desperately needed him to bring me some toiletries because when I came straight from sentencing I didn't have a chance to bring any possessions. He brought me a toothbrush and deodorant and more clothes. He also presented me with soap on a rope. I'm not making this up—that horse fucker thought it was funny. But he also brought me lasagna, so I forgave him and we laughed about it.

I reached the Manchineel tree at the edge of the beach and sat in the sand beneath it, enjoying canopy from the midday sun. Imagine someone being *against* a tree, I thought. I knew if it rained I shouldn't be there, but of course I didn't have any bad *feelings* toward it for that. That's the same reason I'm not pro-marijuana. How can I be *for* a plant? That's almost as ridiculous as being *against* a plant. But do you want to hear what's even funnier than soap on a rope? As I sat under the tree in Tamarindo and contemplated these twists of fate, almost two decades after my own incarceration, marijuana had just been legalized in Colorado. I never thought I'd see that in my lifetime. It begged the question, was *I* immoral back then, or was the *law* immoral? Or does morality have nothing to do with the laws of man?

On the day of my release, I was twisted, jumpy. I threw all of my things in the trash and wished Metro and Gus and the Mexican kid with the cast good luck.

"Do you have someone picking you up?" the guard asked me.

"I don't know," I said, but when I walked out of the metal door and it buzzed and clicked behind me, there was Reilly's blue Escort, parked with his motor running. I looked over my shoulder and then walked across the parking lot, squinting against the sun. Everything felt different, though I couldn't explain why.

There was a guy in the front seat, so I jumped in the back and we drove off. "Norm, this is my new roommate, Joey," he said. The handsome, smiling Italian guy in the front seat turned around and shook my hand.

"Nice to meet you, man—you can call me Pistol. How was it?"

"It wasn't too bad. But no place you ever want to go, believe me."

"Yeah, I hear ya," he said.

"So, where do you want to go?" Reilly asked as he turned onto North College Street, into the real world again. "Are you hungry? Where are you staying?"

"I…I don't know," I said. "I haven't thought about it at all. I don't really have any money."

"Ahhh, don't sweat it," Pistol said. "You can stay with us. Right, Reilly? Now, let's go get a burger in Old Town. It's on me."

He reached into the back seat and handed me a lit joint. "And here—smoke one for freedom."

And I did.

CHAPTER 32

SIGN HERE

Pistol had a decision to make coming up soon—to accept a plea, thereby sealing his own fate locked in a cell in the jungle for half a decade, or to roll the dice with nothing less than his life with a jury trial; freedom or twenty years. He was up against a deadline because after January 20 any plea arrangement would be off the table. It was a choice he had to make alone, no matter how we urged and advised.

As for me, the shadows were growing long on my time in Tama. I only had a few weeks until my birthday, and once the book was finished I needed to head back to the States to handle its release. The first draft was rounding up and I only had three chapters left to write, though I learned there is no real finish line with the literary vocation, only mile markers. After that, there would be rewrites, cover layout, press releases, and decisions of my own. I didn't want to leave Tamarindo. Maybe you look at something differently when you know it will be gone soon, but I'd fallen hopelessly in love with that beach, the glowing comfort of midday sun on my face, the sand in my bed sheets. I felt the waves roll on inside of me long after I got out of the ocean. My spirit was emboldened by the company of good people. Theresa visited Pistol almost every weekend, and I saw him less and less. She was falling in love with him again.

The days before his deadline to accept the plea we all sat on eggshells, nerves frazzled as we waited to learn his fate. Everything stopped for one afternoon. Pistol was meeting with his defense attorney, the prosecuting attorney, and the judge in Santa Cruz at 1:00 p.m. We got word that the meeting was on as scheduled, which was incredible considering the number of times similar meetings had been cancelled because the judge was on vacation, the defense got bogged down in San Jose, or the translator didn't show up. No one knew what Pistol was going to do.

His mother and sick father sat by the phone in their little house in Rochester, where the screen door needed fixing and the fridge was almost empty. They waited. Theresa sat by her computer at work, biting her nails and hitting refresh on her email. She waited. Reilly emailed me and asked to keep him posted. I waited in my apartment, my computer open. I tried to write, but it was no use. So I just sat there with the fan trained on me and waited.

It was the longest three hours you can imagine, but finally, at 4:30, I heard something. Pistol managed to get back to the jail in time for his daily phone call. He called his mom and told her. She had to sit down at the kitchen table when he was done talking, her body shaking and tears streaming down her face. She called her daughter and her other children and told them. Then they emailed Theresa. Betty, Elizabeth, and Theresa all emailed me at once:

"*Norm—Joey accepted the plea bargain. They offered him 5.4 years and he took it. He signed the papers right there. They're allowing him to stay at the jail in Liberia. We didn't have much time to talk, but he thinks that will be better. He knows people in there now and is close enough for you and Theresa to visit. Okay, I have to go but will message later when I hear more. Oh, Norm, this will be a joy when it's all over. I just pray we all get through this.*"

5.4 years. I didn't know whether to write back words of congratulations or express my sympathy. That sounded like a long time now that it was official, but considering the alternatives, I knew it was best. Compared to the eight-year minimum sentence they wanted to slap him with, or the twenty years he'd be facing if he went to trial and lost (which he most definitely would), a cool *cinco* didn't seem like much.

I tried to calculate when he'd get out. Pistol told me there was approximately four months knocked off every year for good behavior, meaning you had to serve 1 year out of every 1.8 years, and then you got time off if you got a job, and I wasn't certain but I thought he got credit for time already served, which was rapidly approaching 1 year, and...ah hell, who really knows in Costa Rica. But my best gut guess was that he'd probably have to do another two years before he got out. At least he could stay in Liberia where he was safe and knew everyone.

I wondered what it was like for him signing those papers, handcuffed at a big table in a courthouse in San Jose, surrounded by people who didn't care one ounce of shit what happened to him. Poor guy. I prayed for him to stay safe and do the right things in jail. A two-year sentence was possible. He'd be out by his forty-first birthday. I'd be forty-two.

And Theresa? Would she still be waiting for him? I typed her a quick message:

"Hey, *chica*, thanks for the news. Are you okay? I think this is the best we could hope for. He'll be fine—it will give him time to get in shape and learn Spanish! Hey, let me know if you need to talk or get a beer tonight. *Pura vida, pow pow*!"

She typed back. "*Oh, thank you, Normie. I just want to be alone right now. But thank you. I know it's best, but I feel so sad for him. My boss let me go home. But I will be fine. We are going to the rodeos this weekend for the fiestas. Come with us, gringo! Pura vida, boom boom!*"

I was relieved—at least we could all move forward now. He would be transferred to the permanent housing cells, and that meant he could get a job and start knocking off his time. Every day would be another slash in red on *his* calendar.

I went to the fridge and pulled out a beer and cracked it open. I exhaled for the first time in months. Okay, Pistol, you finally made a good call.

CHAPTER 33

MALACRIENZA, THE BADDEST BULL ALIVE

"*Come onnnnn, Normie, you have to go with us,*" Theresa pleaded. "*The fiestas in Santa Cruz are going to be the best of the whole year. We neeeeeed you to go.*"

"I don't know, I have a lot of work to do. I'm way behind finishing the final two chapters of the book."

"*Oh, who cares, you can't work all the time. Come!*"

"Nah, but thanks—and I'll let you know if I change my mind."

"*It's just going to be me and a bunch of my girlfriends and you.*"

"I'm in. When do we leave?"

"*Hahahaha, crazy gringo. It's Thursday night. We'll drive up at 5:00, right after work.*"

It felt nice to be wanted, but I had no desire to party in Tamarindo. It was too much damn work trying to keep up with those twenty-something-year-old kids all night. I usually only went out on Friday nights to El Garito's, where Cristiano worked, my chummy Italian friend who was known for his creative use of Tequila, Jagermeister, and Red Bull in one horrific shot called a Hand Grenade. I passed on those, but they had a DJ spinning hip hop so we could all sit outside and groove to the music.

Other than that I preferred my nice and boring in-bed-by-nine routine. I felt lazy, but looking back I realize why I was so spent—I was waking up before dawn every morning, working out hard twice a day, entertaining my assorted friends who came to Costa Rica on vacation, dealing with Pistol, and, oh, in the midst of all of that, somehow writing an epic 250-page coming-of-age travel memoir. At least, I hoped it was epic. Or at least not dog shit.

I just didn't know anymore—some days it felt like I struck oil with my pen, meaningful prose and witticisms gushing skyward, but lately it all felt uphill. I sat down and fiddled at my desk for three hours with little more than reshuffled notes and a few paragraphs to show for it. My brain just went to blubber in the heat. I thought maybe something was wrong with me.

All I wanted to do was curl up on the couch with the fan on, but there was always so much more to do. More, more, more, my master summoned me every waking moment. At night I half-slept and dreamt about plot lines and word choice. I was stumbling toward the finish line, and if I crossed it at all, it would be crawling on my hands and knees.

I didn't want to go to the fiestas with Theresa and her friends. "I shouldn't," I told myself, "I have a ton to get done to finish the book on schedule. I need to be responsible, right?" Maybe I could weasel out of it.

Theresa messaged me on Wednesday to remind me: "*Don't forget you're going with us. Do not even think of cancelling or I will beat you up! Pow pow!*" She knew me all too well.

She picked me up on Thursday afternoon and we drove to her house in Villareal to pick up her roommate, Grace. They lived down a dirt lane with concrete structures with washing machines and broken-down motorcycles in the side yards. I knew it would be humble because the average Tico made about $800 a month and paid half of that in rent, not leaving much for food. It seemed like there was always more month than money in Tama, but I also noticed a certain appreciation, a sunny simplicity of character, that grew from overcoming life's cruel deficiencies. Grace came out with her dog, Roxy, and said "hi." She was always sweet to me, which I appreciated because I knew I wasn't exactly the popular candidate for Tamarindo Socialite of the Year.

Their friend, Magally , pulled up on a moped, a slender, athletic gal with big black eyeglasses. She was really cool and spoke good English. They said goodbye to Roxy and we piled into Grace's pickup truck.

"I'll drive so you guys can drink," Theresa volunteered.

"I don't mind driving," I said.

"No way—the cops will pull us over left and right with a gringo driving!" they said.

We stopped at the local market to pick up beer. They skipped through the aisles, grabbing me by the arm to point out their favorite drinks. "So, why don't we get that for you?" I asked, but they said it was too expensive so we ended up getting a case of Imperial Light. I paid for the beer, despite their protests. The other Ticos in the store looked at me funny. This wasn't Tamarindo, where they were used to gringo tourists. Let 'em look.

We got back into the truck and headed toward Santa Cruz, the main city in the province.

"Do you have enough room back there?" I asked the girls, who were pinned in the back seat.

"*We are great, thank you. Here, have a beer,*" Magally said and handed me an iced cold *cerveza*.

"*Turn up the music, I like this song. Do you know this one?*" Grace asked me.

I bopped my head to the beat and chuckled. It was Pharcyde's "Back in the Day," a song I'd put on one of the mixes I burnt for Theresa.

Back in the day, when I was young, I'm not a kid anymore
But sometimes I sit and wish I was a kid again.

"Watch out, Theresa," I said, as a car started to pull out in front of us. She smiled but didn't protest that I sounded like a concerned big brother. I couldn't help it—that's how I felt. I cared about those girls unconditionally, the same as most people in Tamarindo, although many of them didn't suspect it. Despite my best efforts to stay detached, to play it cool, the urge to protect them had blossomed within me. Sure, I'd had my frustrations, but when push came to shove there wasn't one person in Tama who I wouldn't have picked up and carried through the fires. And especially Theresa and her friends. These girls were so young, so full of bubbling positivity, their whole lives ahead of them. But what could I possibly do to protect them? Life would test them for sure, but I hoped they never lost that spirit of youth. When I looked back on my life it always seemed like things were so simple, so much more carefree, even if there were hard times. What happens to people when they get older? What had happened to *me*? Had I forgotten how to be young?

I sang along to the chorus and they laughed.

"*Norm thinks he can rap!*"

"Oh, I *know* I can! I've been rapping since y'all were just an itch in yo' daddy's pants. Let me show you how it's done:

"*...It's true, you don't realize what you got 'til it's gone*
and I'm not gonna sing another sad song, but
Sometimes I do sit and reminisce then
Think about the years I was raised, back in the day."

They laughed and patted me on the shoulder and tried to give me a new beer, though mine was still almost full.

Three Imperial Lights later, we rolled into Santa Cruz. It was weird to see the city after living in the tiny fly-speck of Tamarindo, but there it was—paved streets with stoplights and three-story buildings. Strands of golden lights hung across the rooftops. The night was filled with carnival neon and honking horns. We stood in line with all the other cars as we inched into the heart of the city and finally entered a fenced-in lot on the side of a bus station, where we could park for 4,000 *Colones.*

"Hurry up, I need to pee!" "Oh my God, me too!" they begged from the back seat. The moment the truck stopped we all threw open the doors and bolted for different spots in the bushes to relieve ourselves, not caring if people were walking past. We finished and paid the parking attendant and unloaded the truck. We were hemmed in by a tall chain link fence, the exit to the street a city block away.

"I don't want to walk around. Let's just jump the fence," Magally said.

"Yeah right, just hop right over it," I said, assuming they were kidding. But that's exactly what they did, one by one climbing up in their nice skirts and flip-flops and vaulting over. Damn those girls were down! I couldn't remember the last time I jumped a fence.

If you ever want to know how long you've officially been "old," just plug into this complex algorithm. The answer will not lie:

> *(Your age) – (Your age when you last hopped a fence) = (How long you've been old)*

"I'm just going to walk around," I said. But they cheered me on to jump over, too, so finally I succumbed. I got to the top okay, but the transition over the pommel horse and my dismount were shaky. My 200-pound bulk wobbled the fence for half a city block.

"Whoooaaaaa," the girls said, six little hands grabbing my ass to keep me from falling down backwards. But I did it. My new Effective Fence Jumping Age = 0.

I put the cooler up on my shoulder and we walked into the festivals, block after block.

"We can help you carry that, Norm," they said.

"It's okay, it's not that heavy," I said, switching sides because it hurt my shoulder.

"Okay, let's go this way, the bullfights are near the park," Theresa said.

I'd been to a bullfight before—at the little dead end pueblo of Santa Barbara a year before around Christmas. Every town, no matter how big or small, had their own fiestas. Residents far out in the country would talk about it for months with excitement. The bull ring was thrown together on the south side of town square facing the church, wooden planks held together with rusty nails. It looked like a good foot stomping by the audience would send it splintering to the ground. The grass in the square was worn thin. The girls dressed nice and the old men wore buttoned-up shirts and cowboy hats. Plump woman tended to their toddlers from their seats on plastic chairs. We'd run into Pistol's friend, Fabio, who dragged us around to meet all of his cousins. He introduced us to a pretty lady in her mid-twenties, a teacher at the local school who was looking to hook up with a gringo to make extra money. "She was my teacher when I was in grade school—she's an important person in town," he said, with no inkling of shame or judgment.

The bull ring in Santa Cruz was nicer, made out of metal scaffolding and hand-cut wooden planks. People filled in, climbing onto the sides of the rodeo ring after the seats filled up.

"*Hurry up, let's get a good seat before it starts,*" Grace said. The girls pulled my arm and pressed into the crowd.

"*Venga abajo, señoras y caballeros, agárrate el sombrero y cubrir los ojos de sus bebés, de pronto usted podrá ver los más valientes hombres y bestias metería el en todo Costa Rica!*" the announcer yelled into his tinny sound system. The crowd rose in excitement that the next fights were starting. Fathers lifted their baby daughters onto their shoulders. Packs of teenagers climbed and straddled the wooden arena wall to get a better view. We were right over the gateway when the bull came out.

In Costa Rica the bull is released into the ring with a brave cowboy on his back, holding on for dear life. He rides the bucking beast as long as possible. It usually only lasts a few seconds until he's thrown to the ground, and then rodeo hands swoop in and distract the bull so the cowboy can scamper to safety, the crowd offering their polite applause. That's when the real fun starts.

Unlike bullfighting in Spain, where the whole ceremony is little more than a one-sided slaughter, the real sport in Costa Rica is watching the bulls chase down and abuse the humans in the ring. The bull ring is open to any grown man who wants to get inside. They run around tormenting and teasing the bull, getting as close as possible to demonstrate their bravado. When the bull becomes enraged it chases them down, disbursing bodies like bowling pins.

"Holy shit, that bull is gonna kill someone!" I said. "Is it always like this?"

"*No, this bull is tranquilo. But with some bulls it is bad, especially Malacrianza.*"

"What's a Mala Empanada? I think one of those made me sick once, but I'll spare you the details."

"*Noooooo, tonto, MalaCRIANZA.*"

The scene was equal parts chaos and orchestrated adrenaline. There'd be a period of inactivity as the small-brained bull watched the ring in front of him, the men regrouping and catching their breath, taking advantage of the lull by running across its line of sight and yanking its tail. I was impressed by the camaraderie of the men in the ring, the primal bond of men versus beast (but I was sort of rooting for the beast).

"These guys are lunatics!" I yelled over the din, but the girls were cheering so loudly they didn't hear me.

All of a sudden the dormant bull came to life, charging with its head leveled, razor-sharp horns in line for their chests. The brave men were instantly rendered cowards.

Most of the time the bull lost interest once it charged, but sometimes he locked in on a young matador like a guided missile. In a microsecond the man sensed that he was the lone target and sprinted for his life toward the side of the ring, where he would spring high onto the stadium wall and scramble over to safety. He couldn't replicate that jump with one hundred tries on a pogo stick without that extra jolt of fight-or-flight adrenaline. The girls told me that it wasn't uncommon for a bull to jump right into the wall or even get over it, spilling bloodshed into the stands with the violence of a rogue NASCAR crash.

You can't outsprint a bull, so if you don't have an angle he'll catch you in the straightaway and gore you. If the matadors knew they were going to be caught, they hit the ground in the fetal position, covering their balls and heads. The bull would run them over, but they were betting that it wouldn't be able to get the tips of its horns low enough to snare them and toss them into the air.

I'd watched some bullfights on TV, a welcome change from the twenty-five channels of soccer matches. Every bullfight someone got trampled, gored, kicked, flipped fifteen feet in the air, crushed against the wall, their shirt tattered, pants ripped off (this happens more than you think, leaving the bullfighter bare-assed in front of all), bloodied, skulls cracked, lungs crushed, ribs broken, shoulders dislocated, or legs snapped in two. Or all of the above.

If they manage to survive they'd win the adulation of the crowd and glory in their hometown. They might even get on television when the carnage of that day's bullfights was highlighted on shows like *La Torra*. But more often they were dragged out of the ring and thrown in the back of a waiting ambulance.

I'd heard that a tourist was gored at the fiestas in Villareal the previous Saturday night. He was Canadian and, not surprisingly, quite drunk, jumping into the ring with the bull like the locals. This particular tourist thought it was all fun and games but didn't know what the hell he was doing, which could be argued is fairly important. In the provinces no one was going to stop him if he wanted to entertain them with his life. When the bull charged the tourist didn't hit the ground, but kept running and tried to swerve. The crowd let out a gasp of collective horror at his mistake, and sure enough, the bull caught up and gored him, ripping open his back like a white-hot knife into a tin can, snapping through his ribs and piercing his lung. They dragged him out of the ring, but he died in the ambulance on the way to the closest ramshackle hospital.

It was more organized in the cities; in San Jose you had to fill out paperwork and go through a sobriety test before getting in there. At the big venues the Red Cross was present to assist the fallen and injured. You could even buy life insurance right there before you got in the ring.

At the televised bullfights the guys in the ring dressed up to add to the pageantry: funny wigs, masks, clown outfits, sporting flowing capes like super heroes. But my favorite display of showmanship was a twisted game of chicken called "*La Mesa*"—The Table. They'd run out into the ring with a wooden table and chairs and plop down in the center. Several guys sat down, crossed their legs, and poured themselves beers. When the bull came out they tried to remain seated at the table as long as possible. The showmanship was to act casual, like they were just four guys drinking beers in a café, until the bull crashed the party, sending men, beer bottles, and the table splintering into the night. That's why Latinos make the best bullfighters and boxers—all heart and *cojones*.

That night in Santa Cruz no one was injured badly, though there were a few close calls. Eventually, the bull got tired and lost its aggression, and then gauchos on horseback rode in with lassos to lead it out. But the crowd never lost its bloodlust, drunk and frenzied in the streets until dawn. After a few bullfights we walked around Santa Cruz.

The smell of death was in the streets that night, the scent of men's bravery wafting up to my nostrils and....oh no...actually, wait, that's...ewww... okay, that's the smell of that huge pile of horse shit I just stepped directly into. Never mind.

"So, Theresa, what were you saying about Malacrienza?" I asked when it was finally quiet enough to talk.

"He's the most famous bull in Costa Rica—big and mean as Diablo. Already he's killed three people. Everyone knows him in the country, so his owners get up to $60,000 U.S. dollars for bringing him to the big fiestas."

"Damn. So he's sort of the bull version of me."

"Yeahhhhh right, Normie. You couldn't hurt a fly," she said.

"What does it mean, anyways?"

"Malacrienza is slang—it sort of means a spoiled or rebellious child, like one who throws a tantrum."

We walked by a vendor, who was grilling meat on an overturned hubcap over a wood fire.

"Oh, Normie, Chicharones! You have to try one of these."

We ordered a few, grilled pork on a stick, and I liked them so much that I dragged the girls back for another. The four of us stood in the town square, eating our food and craning our necks to see the band that was playing. I was getting sleepy and ready to get back to Tamarindo, but of course the girls wanted to stay out. Someone shouldered me from behind, hard, with an extra push at the end so I would know it was intentional. I whirled around and there was a skinny teenage kid, drunk and red-eyed, buzzing with adrenaline. He'd bumped into me on purpose, but I couldn't figure out why. I was twice as big as him and could easily snap him in half, not that I ever wanted to fight.

I was about to say something to him, just to make peace and make sure he was okay, when I glanced behind him farther into the square. There was a line of guys—at least a dozen of them—yelling and making gestures. They'd sent that little scrappy youth to bump into me on purpose and hopefully start a fight, and then the rest of them would charge over and jump me. He turned in a wide circle and came back at me to make another pass, but I walked with the girls in the other direction.

It happened often like that, and Theresa told me and the previous year at the same festival she'd seen some guy hauled away in an ambulance with his face completely mashed to a pulp after being rolled by five guys. I picked up a beer bottle and kept it in my pocket as we ducked into a bar, just in case they all followed their new gringo friend.

The place was playing some good reggae so the girls coaxed me out onto the dance floor. They laughed when they saw I could boogie, the last thing they expected out of a gringo almost old enough to be their dad. After a few songs we headed back out into the festivities.

"Come on, come on, Norm, we need to go on the rides," they said, each pulling me by an arm and ignoring my protests that I was too old and drunk and tired and needed to go home. We came to a carnival set up in a vacant field, with a ferris wheel and rides for kids. The girls bought our tickets and then pushed me toward the bumper cars. We each got into a car, though my legs barely fit. When the music started all eyes turned to me, my three friends and twenty mischievous Tico kids all taking great joy in hunting down and bumping the paint off the lone gringo's car.

I looked at their faces as we whirled and collided and gave each other minor concussions; those little hundred-pound, fence-jumping, Guaro-drinking dance machines were having the times of their lives. Magally had told me that she was leaving to San Jose to follow her dream of being a goalie for a woman's professional soccer team. I wished her luck. Things seemed so hard in their lives, but they took comfort in each other in a way that had been missing from my life.

Was I that happy about anything? Sometimes we can have too much in our lives, I thought, too many choices, and it leaves us imbalanced. I knew all too well when you get everything you want it just leaves you wanting more. I remembered when I had the big house and the cars and all of the bullshit, surrounded by people who always wanted more, it seemed more like a prison than something to be happy about. My God, that seemed like such a long time ago. I didn't have much in my life now—the sunshine, some good friends and family, and the sun rose and set with my passion to share my book with the world, but it felt, I don't know…clean.

But here they were, spinning around and laughing like children on the bumper cars. I understood—this is what *they* had: fiestas and music and dancing and each other. They weren't worrying about tomorrow because tomorrow would be just as hard and there still wouldn't be enough money, just like today. But their courage, to face it all with a smile, inspired me. I had a lot to learn. I hoped that Magally made the soccer team. I hoped that Theresa and Grace and all of them would be free to chase whatever it was that made them happy.

We grabbed the waiter and had him take a picture of all of us. Some of those moments you remember, and that was one of them.

By the end of the night I was faded, covered in sweat, and yawning. It was almost 4:00 a.m. when I begged them to take me home, and we found our truck and hit the streets back toward Tamarindo. The girls seemed fine—where the hell did they put all that booze?

Theresa drove down the empty road, with Magally and Grace dozing in the back seat, heads resting on each other's shoulders.

"Stay up with me, Normie, I need someone to keep me awake while I drive," Theresa said.

"Okay, I'll try."

"So, did you have a good time?"

"Yeah, I sure did. Thanks again—I'm glad you guys dragged me out."

"Well, there are more festivals in the next weeks in Heredia and Nicoya coming up if you want to go."

"Oh hell no, I'm partied out for a while. I can't keep up with you crazy *chicas*! But it was really nice to see you having fun."

The truck cruised through the ink-dark jungle, our whole world reaching only as far as the periphery of the headlights. I shook myself to keep my eyes open and rolled down the window.

"You girls are nice people, Theresa. You're a good person."

"Hahaha, you aren't bad yourself, Normie. We'll all go out this weekend if you want to dance again."

"No, I mean it. I know this whole thing has been hard on you. But I want you to know that I'm proud of you. And I'm glad we became friends."

"Ahhh, Normie, you too. Thank you for saying that. I just wish things..." She went quiet.

"I know," I said. "Believe me, I know. Just promise me that you'll look out for yourself. Whatever happened in the past, it's all right to let go."

"I will...I am. And you too, Normie. I know you came to Costa Rica for some reason, but whatever it is just remember that you have people who love you here."

"Where—in the back seat?" I joked.

"Shut up, silly gringo! I'm being serious!" she said.

"I know, Theresa, and you, too. I guess we all just do the best we can, huh? And tomorrow is always another day."

"Si, es verdad," she said. *"But, Normie, look—tomorrow is already today,"* and she pointed to the softening sky in the east, the moon and one last star hanging above the horizon, brightly dying as our world went from night's-felt to purple, then pastel streaks of orange.

We looked at each other and smiled and laughed, both wiping our eyes.

"Are you crying?!"

"NO! Of course not!" I said. "My eyes always tear when I'm sleepy."

"Yeah, right..." she said. *"Ahhh, you have a big heart, Normie."*

I put my head back listened to the sound of tires on the road, soft breathing from the back seat, the lullaby of sad Spanish radio.

"No way, not me. I'm mean and tough, like Malacri...Mala..." and then I faded off to sleep.

I was hungover later that day; I slept all day on the couch. I didn't even leave my apartment except to grab a pizza and Gatorade. I didn't write and never caught up on my schedule to finish the book. I didn't exactly reach my goal of publishing it by my birthday—I was a few weeks off. And you know what? Who cares? Sometimes it's worth it.

CHAPTER 34

GOT LOCAL

I know exactly the time and place I became a local. It's weird how it works like that because so much had gone into earning membership in that club, but then one day, in late January, it just happened. And I knew.

It was at Aqua on a Tuesday night. Earlier that evening, I'd stopped by Seasons to say "hi" to Row, who was working behind the bar. I liked going there because it was *tranquilo.* I'd hang with him and his sister, Sandra, and their sweetheart friends, Dayana and Marcela, while they all worked. On Friday nights my former neighbor, Avellino, played Brazilian music at Seasons, singing anything from samba ballads to Guns N' Roses alongside congas and an acoustic guitar. At the end of the night I helped them put the chairs up on the tables and close up. We walked down to Aqua together, where Kenny G got us in for free. Inside I bought the first round of beers.

The vibes were tight, and the DJ was playing my jam, "Hold Yah" by Gyptian, so I went out to shake my thing thang a little bit. The Critters were in full effect—the three bad brothers with surf fros and a couple of their friends drunk and sizing up victims. They got into it with a skinny tourist wearing a purple polo shirt who was standing right next to me. I don't know what he'd done—probably nothing—but the oldest Critter was in his face, telling him to watch himself and putting his fist to his chin to let him know what was next. The other brothers stood behind him. Purple Shirt knew he was in trouble but had no idea that he was close to getting rolled from behind, but he did the right thing and apologized and scampered off. Close call.

Still jacked with adrenaline and wanting to fight someone, the Critter scanned the room. His gaze came to me—another white boy standing right next to where Purple Shirt had been. Uh oh, did he think we were together? He walked right up to me, and I prepared for the worst.

"Pura vida, mae, que tuanis?" he said to me with a smile on his face, a warm *Pachuco* greeting among friends. *"Hay muchas chicas esta noche! Okay, ciao, hermano!"*—There are a lot of girls here tonight, see you later, brother—and he slapped me on the back and walked off.

Damn, that was cool. I didn't really know that guy, never said "hi" to him actually, but apparently he knew me, knew I'd lived in town long enough and what my karma was about, and that gave me enough cred in his eyes. Local cred. It felt good. I walked to the bar and told Row it was his round—if I was a local, then someone was buying me a beer, dammit!

There it was: the Tribe had spoken. There was no more use questioning it than there would have been lobbying for it. I'd like to think that I was a special case because I didn't earn it by surfing or partying, but instead I was the outcast who managed to fit in perfectly.

I was a completely different person than the day I arrived. Sure, I was tan and in good shape, but more than that, I'd adopted the aura people carry after living in the tropics long enough, a naturalistic but no-nonsense energy: survivors in sync with their environment. It was the little things that I looked at instinctually, like what a fisherman sees when he peers at the sea.

When it rained and the road was muddy, I walked over the patches with little white pebbles because they were firmer.

At restaurants I asked for "*la cuentita*" instead of "*la cuenta*" (the "little check" instead of the check), which always made the waitresses laugh.

I knew to watch out for jellyfish when the current brought cold water from the north.

We called goose bumps "chicken skins."

It was easy to tell that a Tica was from Guanacaste and not San Jose; her feet were dirty and she had a big outline of a tattoo on her back, but couldn't afford to get it colored in yet.

It became apparent that mayonnaise was the catsup of the world.

I shook out my shoes for scorpions. And my shirt. And then shook them out again.

When someone said "cheers" and we touched beer bottles, I looked them directly in the eyes. It was a Tico superstition that if you didn't, you'd be cursed with a bad sex life for seven years. After I learned that, I stared holes through people like I had x-ray vision, but it didn't seem to help.

I drank refrigerated red wine out of the box.

After a while I could tell where a traveler was staying by how bad their bug bites looked—the red welts clustered on their feet and ankles.

I had an Orange Fanta addiction. I was like a crackhead with that stuff, cowering in a dark alley with orange teeth, shivering and yelling at people passing:

"Yo man, I'll suck yo dick for a Fanta. Just one sip…ONEEEEEEE SIPPPPPPPPPP!?" Thank God you could just buy it at the store, instead.

I could open up the milk, which came in a plastic bag, without making a mess. The first few times it exploded all over my kitchen, and I was left dripping and sticky.

To avoid getting zapped by a stingray when I walked in shallow water, I slid my feet, not step directly down.

I could smell a tourist. Their American soap, their shampoo, their cologne, their deodorant. It was chemical and sickly sweet. I preferred the natural smell of sun and ocean.

I could tell where a male tourist was from just by the length of his shorts. The U.S. guys had long, flowing basketball shorts like skirts, two sizes too big for the tropics. The Loonies were above the knee, the Brits mid-thigh and tight in the seat, the Aussies even smaller to show off their rugby legs, and the Italians wore white shorts that were too diminutive even for pockets. Finally, there were the Frenchies, who wore double-stitched dental floss up their cracks, impossibly tan but hairy. I'd always get caught in line at the grocery store behind THAT guy.

We called sex "boom boom."

If the mosquitos got too bad, I could burn coconut husks and the smoke would keep them away, but they bit me less and less.

I didn't freak out anymore when I lifted the toilet seat and saw a frog in there.

Us locals could have a whole conversation just with a look and a nod.

A plastic bag filled with ice made a great beach cooler.

I understood why the locals moved at a certain pace, which I'd mistakenly judged as laziness. If I walked and moved at that same pace I wouldn't break out in a full sweat, just shine a little, as usual.

Pulling your shirt up over your stomach wasn't a display of sloth, it lowered your body temperature nicely, the breeze drying your whole torso.

My stroll through town was always on the shady side of the street, without even realizing it.

I could sense when the town was getting too hot and something was going to happen.

I tried to help locals whenever I could. When I saw Tico Jorge riding his bike on the road in Huacas on his way to work in Tama, I pulled over and threw his bike in the back and gave him a ride. I often passed Isabel on the sidewalk in front of the Estrella, the sweet young Tica who scraped together a living selling jewelry. I'd mention to any tourists within earshot that she had the nicest stuff and the best prices in town. She appreciated the backup—not many people knew yet but she was pregnant, way too young to be a single mom, and desperately needed money to eat.

One time I went running and passed two older gringo gentlemen standing on the beach, watching the surfers through a fancy camera with a long-range zoom. I saw an empty Corona bottle near their feet so I ran up and grabbed it, said, "B*uenos dias*," and ran on to a garbage can to throw it out. One of them gave a nod of acknowledgement. "That's what I like to see, thanks for keeping our beach clean," he said.

"Gotta do it," I said, huffing, and ran off. Only when I looked back did I realize that he was Robert August. I'd shared a moment, a connection honoring our beautiful beach, with a surf legend.

It was all of those little things, good and bad, that added up to warm nostalgia for me. I realized that my journey in Tama wouldn't last forever and it had been such a special time in my life, of struggle but also of healing. Even walking down the street in the sun, saying "hi" to everyone, filled me with appreciation, a blessing of nostalgia like thumbing through old photographs on a rainy day. I know, I know, I'm growing way too sentimental in my old age.

I may have finally belonged in Tama, but I noticed a growing distance from my past life in the U.S. I could relate less and less. When I saw people's Facebook statuses: "Fuck my life, I'm stuck in traffic," I couldn't understand where they were coming from. It seemed like the biggest concern was having the newest phone and the nicest car. Everyone was calling everyone else an idiot, complaining about how terrible they were being treated. They all seemed so angry, so hyper-intense, running in circles but going nowhere, 300 million people yelling, "What about *me*?!" What they considered problems would be seen as luxuries by the people I was living with.

When the TV was on CNN at Rusty's Pizza I watched those aliens with the sound off—morgue-white skin and comically fat, wearing suits that cost more than some people made in a year. Silk nooses were knotted tightly around their necks as they yelled at each other and pounded their fists, red-faced and trying to convince the world that they were right. The politics and banter seemed to be getting angrier in the States, everyone screaming at the top of their lungs but just drowning each other out. What did these creatures have to do with *people*? With *real life*? Had it always been like that, and I just hadn't noticed? Or was I the one who was changing? I couldn't figure it out, but I didn't like watching; that whole damn country needed a siesta and a big hug. But either way it dawned on me that I was now out there alone, somewhere in between two cultures, a citizen of only the World. I might return in geography one day, but I didn't think I could ever go back to *that*.

But don't worry, even though I now had the attitude for the latitude, I still managed to fit in some quality time with our tourist friends. It was way too much fun to watch them squirm and stumble, exactly like I had not so long ago.

The tourists were über-environmentally conscious during their one-week occupations of Costa Rica, before going home to their regular existence of Hummers, over-watered lawns, and vacuum-sealed plastic packaging. To do their part to help the planet they bought t-shirts with cool eco-friendly slogans and vowed to name their next child "Sierra."

I was having dinner one night at Pepperocino›s when the fat Italian waiter came out to take our order, the remnants of coke still on his nose. He kept sniffling but explained that his allergies were acting up. "Sure," I told him, "a lot of people around town seemed to have those same allergies, especially on the weekends." A *langosta* buzzed down at us and the waiter waved and flailed at it but couldn't get it to leave us alone. Finally, he took off his flip-flop and swatted it out of midair. It landed on the ground nearby, so he crunched it again then threw its body out in the road.

Two tourists walked by, eco-hippy trustifarians from the U.S.

"Oh my God, look—the poor little creature is hurt," the girlfriend said, tossing aside her cigarette and Styrofoam to-go box and dropping to one knee.

"Oh nooooooo!!! It looks like he's been attacked," her long-haired boyfriend said, straining to bend down because he was wearing tight cutoff jean shorts.

Captain Jean Shorts managed to pretzel to the ground, laying his head against the dirt and looking into the squashed *langosta*'s eyes.

"Is it alive? Is it still breathing?" she asked.

"I don't know," he said and put the tip of his finger on its chest to try and feel if it had a heartbeat. I'm pretty sure the anatomy of an insect is quite different, so he was probably feeling its second stomach.

"Poor, poor thing. I hope it's not suffering," she said, tears streaming down. "Maybe we can nurse it back to health?" She tried to straighten out one of its six twitching legs, but it broke off in her hand.

"Ugghhhaaaa!" she cried. "Baby, save it! Save it! It has a soul!" So Captain Jean Shorts and his girlfriend set up a little mini medical triage operation and tried to resuscitate the squashed critter, propping its head up and trying to give it mouth-to-mouth into what was probably its little insect anus. They even tried to use a nearby matchstick as a splint, but it wasn't looking good for the bug. They were about to airlift it back to their hotel when a garbage truck roared up the road. Captain Jean Shorts and his girlfriend scattered to avoid being run over, but the *langosta* was left defenseless, and the massive, smelly machine finished the matter *SPLAT!* once and for all.

I couldn't help but laugh. I know, that's bad. But Captain Jean Shorts & Associates were just *so* ridiculous. And if reincarnation IS real and you end up coming back as an oversized cockroach, then my guess is that you were probably either Hitler, Stalin, or Kim Kardashian in your past life, so you're getting what you deserve.

Hanging with tourist couples at the bars was the best. After a long day in the sun, they washed off the monkey champagne and parrot shit and put on their fedoras for a big night on the town. They wanted some *real* conversation with a local, a trophy they couldn't find in their guidebook, a *story*, dammit.

They always started with, "Can I ask you something, it looks like you live here?" How the hell did they know? Did I look *that* wild? I swear I just showered last Wednesday. Or had they spotted me around town wearing my yellow shirt five out of the past seven days?

Next, they'd introduce themselves—a short elevator commercial on who they were, where they were from, and their life story in fifteen words or less:

"Ron Stonelicker. Terra Haute. I sell fertilizer. Recently married for the second time."

But I never remembered any tourist's name. To do so would have been an admission that they were actually human beings, a grave violation of my Tourist Abuse Policy. I did remember their faces and every other factoid, but I never used their names; that was just too personal, like a hooker kissing on the lips.

Instead, I christened them with their very own special Tamarindo nickname, based on what they were drinking, the city they were from, what sports team they liked, a medical deformity, or what sexual piccadilly they confessed to.

That's how I met my dear, sweet, lifelong friends: "Red Wine," "Brooklyn," "Dallas Cowboys," "One Nut," and "Puck Fuck."

At first they'd order Pina Coladas, but I couldn't tolerate that level of foofiness if they were going to sit anywhere in my vicinity, so I'd suggest they try my drink—a *Flor de Caña* and ginger ale with lime, a deceivingly strong aged Nicaraguan rum. That stuff was like truth serum for yellow bellies.

After the second drink, the husband would loosen up a bit and start having fun, but his wife chided him for drinking too much and cursing in public. After the third drink wifey was plastered, snorting when she laughed. They were so happy to be in the tropics and sharing time with a salty dog local. I'd tell them all sorts of stories about my time in Tamarindo, scaring them with boogie man tales of coke dealers and crocodiles, charming them with local traditions and sayings, revealing local secrets and warning them not to fuck with drugs down there. My poor friend Pistol had become a cautionary tale, but I'm sure it kept more than one tourist safe.

By the fourth *Flor de Caña*, the bartender gave me a look that said, "If they puke I'm not cleaning it up." Wifey threw her fedora in the fountain and hiked up her skirt to show us her tan lines. She started talking out of nowhere about how many times a week they had sex. Hubbie rolled his eyes and ordered another round.

The tiger was out of the cage—I was no longer in control. They were finally free, for the first time in decades, and all of the dirty laundry was coming out. I was their therapist, but we had barstools instead of a leather couch and I only charged two drinks and hour. They proceeded to have two separate conversations with me, even though they were sitting right next to each other. He used to love punk music and missed playing guitar. She complained that his idea of romance was Applebee's with a coupon. He resented that she made him sell his jet ski. She didn't want him to know that she'd slept with the whole hockey team in college. He still wished he'd proposed to little Jenny Applewhite after high school instead of meeting *this* one (nod, nod) freshman year in college. Jenny had the best tits and her dad owned a chain of hardware stores. It really doesn't get better than that, I sympathized.

Wifey was so drunk that she thought Costa Rica was an island, but still wanted to go dancing. Hubbie just wanted to go back to the hotel to watch SportsCenter in the air conditioning and order room service. They argued for a while and then came to the same compromise that every married couple does: they'd go dancing.

"Okay, but before you go, we have to follow the Costa Rican tradition and have *una zarpe*, one more drink," I said.

We drank more. I'd hear the damndest things, and soon I'd be the one snorting laughing. To be honest with you, I met some of the coolest and most interesting people that way. Most of them matched me wit for wit, and I learned far more from them than they ever did from me. I am lifelong friends with many of them (though I still don't remember their names).

At some point their curiosity would get the best of them and the conversation turned personal: What was I doing down there? How long would I stay? How could I afford to live in paradise? And did I still pay taxes? "It's always been my dream to be a writer, so I just said 'fuck it' and sold everything and went for it. Maybe a year? No, there's no money in it. And 'not if I can help it' on the taxes."

"A writer?!" she remarked. "Wowsers, what are you going to do when you're famous?"

Good question. I'd daydreamed about that for hours while I should have been writing.

Most likely it won't happen—there are over 200,000 books published every year, and even the established authors with big publishers have a tough time making a living at it, BUT…let's just fantasize for a second and say that lightning strikes and my book hit it big. Here's how I see the whole thing going down:

Have you ever heard people say that when they get rich or famous they won't change? Or lottery winners who keep their jobs and remain the average Joe? Not me. I'm going to turn into a completely self-absorbed asshole. The second I sign with a publisher I'm going to transmogrify into a totally different person, leaving behind everyone who's been good to me. Let's just say that my first book hits it big and does end up on the *New York Time's* Bestseller list. The critics will probably call me "Raw and refreshing, with prose as smooth as a $50 cigar. The best underground American writer since Bukowski." The royalty checks will start coming in faster than I can take them to the bank. First off, I'm going to start wearing leather pants, put product in my severely-thinning hair, and don gaudy fur coats (made out of *real* baby marmot) while walking down the street. Actually, I won't walk anywhere, but hire someone like Turtle to drive me around in my Bentley (leased).

It's important to me that when I get famous I forget all of my old friends. Every chance I get I'll "Big Time" the *compadres* who supported me through thick and thin. I'll hire two super model assistants to screen my calls, until even my mom can't get through.

My new friends will all be shallow pretty people who leech off my fame. I'll buy a mansion in the hills that used to belong to Dave Chappelle and decorate it all in white leather. I'll have a huge "N" tiled onto the floor of my massive swimming pool. I'll buy a rare white-striped tiger cub that I'll walk around on a diamond-studded leash, and develop a huge coke habit. My old friends and family will shake their heads and try to talk to me about their concern for my behavior, but delicately so I don't go into one of my raging tantrums where I curse them out and throw escargot and fire the super models and have them all forcibly removed from my estate.

My publicist will make it known that I'm available for talk shows and radio interviews as the world's most renowned Humility Expert. Surprisingly, no one takes me up on this. As a rich and famous *artiste,* I'll try to sprinkle words like "*aesthetic*" and "*sensibility*" into my interviews, even though I have no idea what the hell they mean. If someone calls my next book a "book," I'll remind them, with all the snobbery I can muster, that it's actually still a "*manuscript.*"

Then my next book will come out and the critics will turn on me. They'll call it "self-indulged drivel, a soggy excuse for literature," and publicly question whether I plagiarized the first one. By then my spending habits of $20,000 a day will be impossible to maintain. I'll have to return the Bentley and donate the white tiger to the Los Angeles zoo. The pressure of my poor-me existence will be so overwhelming that I'll snort twice as much coke and start brushing my teeth with Jack Daniels. My finances will go into a tailspin and even the mansion will be up for sale. But all of the potential buyers will be named Justin or Kanye or Ahmed, so no one will want an "N" pool. Soon, the bank will foreclose. All of those fair-weather friends will disappear when I can't afford limousines and VIP bottle service anymore. I won't be able to sleep, little Norm won't work right, and, worst of all, I'll suffer from a horrible case of writer's block.

I'll lose it all and be resigned to the life of an average drunken bum, sleeping under my fur coat in the dumpster behind a vacant Borders. I'll live off discarded McDonald's French fries and rant and rave to anyone I pass how I used to be a *somebody.*

Eventually my true friends will hunt me down and drag me out of there and set up an intervention at the local Knights of Columbus. I'll have a complete emotional breakdown and cry like a little bitch, realizing the error of my ways, and vow to never be an asshole again. My mom will take me home and tuck me into the twin bed in her guest room, where I'll sleep for three days straight. Over the months, I'll clean out my body and rebuild my constitution, until I'm gulping down raw eggs and doing one-handed pull-ups in her basement...and writing again.

The ensuing book, "*White Tiger Dumpster Fries: My Life from A-hole to Amen,*" (Random House, June, 2016) will be such a testament to the resiliency of the human spirit that it will shoot me right back to the top. "Bravo, a fete de accompli! Our generations *Siddhartha*!" the critics will applaud. But this time I'll donate all of my royalty checks to children's charities. I'll be invited to the Ellen show, take public transport to the studio, and we'll laugh and hug like old friends, even doing a little victory dance together before commercial break.

But I haven't put a lot of thought into it or anything...

"So, what are you going to do when you're famous?" wifey asked again, snapping me back to reality.

"Nah, not my thing—it actually sounds awful. I'm just going to keep writing."

CHAPTER 35

BLUE, GREEN, BREATHE

The proper word for "the sea" in Spanish is *"el mar,"* a masculine-gendered noun. However, the fishermen call it "*la mar*," making it feminine, because they believe that the sea is a woman. She'll take care of you, provide for you, even give you life, but if you ever cross her she can unleash a tempest so furious that you might disappear forever.

The fishermen had it right—the ocean was to be respected, and I called her *la mar* as well, even though my Spanish-speaking friends corrected me. She was my refuge, my loving *esperanza* whom I could spend a few eager hours with every day. The thrill of her company never once diminished.

I wasn't a fast swimmer and I certainly wasn't graceful, but I plodded along, steadfast, unsinkable, like a tugboat. When I was out there no one could bother me, no one could reach me; it was just me and my thoughts. I've never felt as good as the times I was swimming in the ocean.

On the surface the water was blue—a thousand points of light reflecting off every crest, blinding if you looked straight at it like trying to count diamonds. But once I dipped my head underwater everything was green—the color of shiny apples.

Blue. I took a deep breath.

Green. I plunged beneath. Eyes open because I wore goggles, I could see my hands, my arms, and the periphery of my shoulders as I paddled, frog-kicking easily. The sea floor wrinkled like wind patterns in the desert. I could see shells and the horseshoe outlines of flounder hiding on the bottom.

Breathe. I came up and took in air, the one and only biological imperative at that moment.

Blue. And then back in, timed perfectly as the crest of the next wave swelled.

Green. When the sun was overhead rays of light pierced the water, reflecting off the bottom, an explosion of glass suspended in time.

Breathe.

The sheer magnitude of the ocean was hard for me to comprehend. It went on and on forever. And the waves? Where did they originate? I guess the technical answer is off the coast of Japan—the Kuroshio Current swirling counterclockwise south of the equator, pushing up against the cold water Aleutian Current from the north. The result is that the water off the Nicoya Peninsula, where Tamarindo sits, is an average of 82 degrees year-round, bathwater. As long as I kept moving I wouldn't get the slightest chill, even if I stayed in there for hours.

Blue,

Green,

Breathe.

I thought about how human beings have explored the cosmos even more than the depths of our own oceans, and yet water covers 71% of the earth. The Pacific Ocean alone covers a third of the Earth's surface, far greater than the size of all the continents jammed together, with an extra Africa to spare.

Blue,

Green,

Breathe.

The deepest point, the Mariana Trench, is 6,000 fathoms deep, over 36,000 feet. If the Mariana Trench were a mountain, instead of at the bottom of the sea, it would be on the edge of where the troposphere turns to the stratosphere—what we call "space." Unbelievably, there's life down there, somehow able to withstand the massive pressure and live in an environment where a beam of light has never once penetrated.

Blue,

Green,

Breathe.

Zoom upwards at 1,000 miles an hour to the surface and my act of swimming was basically skydiving into liquid sky, a subtle tweak of elements the only difference between liquid and gaseous form. When I floated on the surface, it was like I was suspended somewhere between free-falling out of a plane and the ground far below. I was swimming in sky, or flying in water, depending how you want to look at it.

Blue,

Green,

Breathe.

There are enough natural resources in our oceans—food, minerals, and energy ready to be harnessed—for every human being on Earth. It's teeming with life, an energy force so big and ancient that it's hard to deny that the ocean isn't just a host for organisms, but an organism itself, possessing a soul. Why not? If a 300-year-old tree in the rainforest has a soul, if something as small and fleeting as a human being has a soul, then who can deny that *la mar* possesses a universal spirit that we can't even comprehend.

Blue,

Green,

I tried to wrap my mind around the idea that the wave coming toward me was all the way on the other side of the Earth just a week ago. It traveled all that way just to meet me, at this very place and time. Or maybe *I* spent *my* whole lifetime getting to this exact point so we could come together. Did I create that destiny? Or did something else?

Breathe.

I put my warm and fuzzies on hold because I was in the kill zone, so I needed to focus. I'd learned to duck-dive the waves—paddling straight into them and diving into their face, cutting through them to negate the tons of kinetic energy that each wave was eager to deliver straight down on my head. I knew that coming back through the foam in the kill zone would be harder; sometimes the tide turned against me or I'd be fatigued, so the same swim to shore would feel like twice the distance.

If I mistimed a wave I'd find myself paralyzed in the trough, staring straight up at a curling wall of water. If that happened, I knew what to do: 1) form a cannonball, protecting my head and the back of my neck in case I get dragged over rocks or a sharp reef, 2) take a deep breath, 3) pray.

So to get through I looked for the *sets*, groups of waves that came in sevens, according to an old surf legend, but in reality the number of waves depended on the storm that formed them. When I saw a break, a temporary calming in the sea, I swam hard, abandoning my breaststroke for freestyle to gain speed, hoping that my timing was right and my shoulders were strong enough to make it through.

When a big set came in I swam straight up the pitch of the wave and did a barrel roll at the top, like an aikido move to diffuse all of that force, just enough to let it spin me skywards. I had fun, flip-kicking like a dolphin and swimming along the exact parallel where the waves broke so I was continuously high on their crest. I even tried doing flips off the back of the waves, but usually I got only halfway around before performing a comical wipe out, straight down into the valley of the next wave like I was jumping into an elevator shaft. When the wave broke and crashed it sent a mist of sea into the air, falling back down on me like drops of rain.

Past the kill zone I paddled in another world where it was tranquil, the horizon rising and falling gently like the belly of a sleeping dinosaur. Everything was still. It was nothing but me and the sun and a gentle wind stirring big blue. Pelicans swooped down, snapping at the flying fish that broke the water's surface, unbothered by my presence. The bigger the waves, the more determined the pull of the current, the more I'd feel at home once I'd earned my place behind them. No matter how many times I swam out there a jolt of electricity pulsed through my body, appreciation so vivid I had to suppress a yelp.

Surfers waited in the lineup around me. They sat on their boards, gazing west to assess the incoming sets, perfectly balanced so the tips pointed out of the water. I imagine that those times were golden for them. When they saw the right wave starting to form farther out they began the instinctual paddle and effortless spin to gain velocity. As the giant awakened beneath them, there was a perfectly choreographed dance, lasting only a second or two, where they paddled hard, sprang into a crouch like a jungle cat, and dropped in at exactly the right time and speed—in perfect control to take the ride.

There were no other swimmers out there with them but they didn't seem to mind my presence. Surfing is a closed culture, but a single loco swimmer is no threat, and a rare site. I might recognize a friend from town and say "hi," and they'd flash me the shaka sign. Still, I gave them space, circling far enough around and conscious if the curl was going to carry their next surf left or right.

I left the surfers behind and swam into the school of fishing boats, vacated for the afternoon and anchored in a floating ghost yard. It was silent except for the sounds of rope straining and water lapping against the peeling hulls.

I tried to count my strokes as I swam farther out past the boats but lost count after a hundred. I stopped and treaded water, looking around and realizing where I was: completely helpless, defenseless, and almost immobile, having to keep moving to stay afloat. There wasn't another person within earshot. What I'd basically done was take myself out of my natural habitat, where evolution gifted me with natural faculties to aid my survival, and fully immersed myself in an opposite habitat—traded oxygen and dry land for suspension in unbreathable liquids. I was, so to speak, a fish out of water. It was one of the worst physical predicaments a human being could put themselves in, so why did it feel so damn good? About 257 things could go wrong and only one thing could go right—I made it back to shore safely—so why did every pulse of my nature call me out there?

I shared the Pacific with countless life forms: whales, eels, crocs who'd wandered out, stingrays, barracuda, poisonous jellyfish, seas snakes, turtles, and every kind of fish imaginable. But I thought about sharks. It wasn't a matter of IF they were there, but HOW CLOSE they were. Every time I swam out into the ocean I voluntarily inserted myself into the food chain—and unnervingly low on the ranking.

Big White, the Landlord, the Man in the Gray Suit, Greg Norman, the White Death, Mac the Knife. Sharks. I was out there in the open like an unsuspecting white mouse dropped into a boa constrictor's cage. The thought tensed me with fear, bringing fatigue to my shoulders and neck as I treaded water.

I kept swimming. I was just being silly, I tried to reason. Cramping or being smashed by a rogue wave in the kill zone, drowning only meters from the shore, were far greater risks. The chances of getting killed by a shark were infinitesimal, only 1 in 11 million worldwide. But then again, that statistic factored in people who lived in Kansas and never even saw the ocean, and there were seven shark attacks for every death. What were the odds for people who lived in Costa Rica, on the beach, who swam deep into the ocean, by themselves, every day, and who'd had fish sticks the previous night for dinner? And how many of those attacks were never reported, either because there wasn't enough of the victim left to confirm or because they were locals so no one bothered? Gulp.

There was nothing to do but surrender. I loosened up and kept paddling, calming my breath. If a shark wanted me there was nothing I could do to stop him from biting me in half. Anyways, it would be sort of cool to have a little run-in with a shark, to get a tiny nibble and end up with a scar. Just an itty bitty one, in a convenient place, like on my upper thigh, so it would give me yet another excuse to take down my pants in front of girls in bars. If I could arrange to get bitten by a very mellow vegetarian shark with a massive overbite, that would be ideal. It would be just a scratch really, but instantly I'd be part of the Shark Attack Survivors' Club United (Against Sharks), an esteemed fraternity if there ever was one. My SASCU(AS) card would even get me a discount at sushi restaurants. I could get down with that.

Surrender. There was no way to hold onto my fear, my anger, and swim long distances at the same time. The tension in my body, in my mind, would turn it into a mechanical struggle. But if I loosened up and just concentrated on the few things I could control—my breath and the consistency of my stroke—then I relaxed into it, acceptance washing over me.

Blue,

Green,

Breathe.

Acceptance. I reflected on that word and deepened my breathing. I was so tired of fighting against everything in my life, always swimming against the current. When I was younger I felt so trapped, alone, like I was born into in a red room with soundproof walls. None of it made sense to me—the pain, the injustice, the random dice game of suffering in the world. I so desperately wanted to reach behind the clouds and shake sanity into God, but no matter how hard I looked, I couldn't find him.

Blue,

Green,

Breathe.

Sometimes I swam so far out that the beach looked like a postcard, the people little flecks of a severed former existence. As the sun neared the horizon, the sky folded over itself like a mural on fire, pink and orange and purple melting around me, sagging toward the contour where the ocean met the heavens. I wanted to keep swimming out, to go deeper, swim until I couldn't see land anymore. How far? How far was too far to get back? I'd just keep going and let the sunset take me. That is how I wanted to end, to go to my peace.

Blue,

Green,

Breathe.

But if I could manage to collect enough moments like these, then life might just be worth living. Maybe, if I could learn to surrender, and accept, I might open up my soul, and then the whole ocean could drown within *me*. Then it would be all right. Yeah, I wasn't ready yet. I turned around, the sunset at my back, and headed in.

Blue,

Green,

Breathe.

I had a long way to go to reach the shore. By then I should have been fatigued, but the swim back was effortless, like *I* was holding still while the earth was spinning toward me, fate's gentle conspiracy to bring me home. The dying sun felt good on my back.

Blue,

Green,

Breathe.

I realized that most of the problems in my life were from going too fast. Most of my defeats occurred only within my head. I'd stir up the waters, looking furiously for something, and then gaze down in frustration, wondering why it wasn't clear.

Blue,

Green,

Breathe.

But if I'd been my own jailer, then only I possessed the keys to my liberation.

Blue,

Green,

Breathe.

So with each headfirst plunge into the next wave I released the flotsam and jetsam of my negativity, the hurt and anger and guilt that had been my anchors to drag for so long. Each breath was a silent prayer of healing, cast adrift, like a message stuffed into a bottle and floated into the endless ocean.

Blue,

Green,

Breathe.

I imagined all of those bottles floating behind me, drifting in the presence of that silky mistress, the ocean, night and day, thousands of them, more than one could count. Eventually, they'd wash up on an uncharted tropical island, thousands of miles to the east, clanking and shimmering onto the beach where a man had been shipwrecked, living wild and alone for almost 40 years. One by one, he'd collect them and pull out the messages, unfolding and reading each one. At first his face would register confusion, but as he read on he'd form a serene smile, then throw his head back and laugh, tears of joy in the presence of God, whom he'd finally found: that mother, *la Mar.*

For they all read, every single one of them, going on forever:

I am free. I am free. I am free.

CHAPTER 36

THE BIRTHDAY

Before I knew it my big birthday was only a few days away, February 9, 2012. My friend, Big Mike, was coming down from the U.S. to visit for a couple of weeks.

"Do you want a big party for your birthday?" Theresa asked. *"Maybe we can rent out the catamaran and go on a booze cruise?"* But a big celebration was the last thing I wanted. Some peace and quiet sounded best to me—and anonymity from the party hounds in Tama.

So I called Hector and he drove me out of town on the down-low to the airport, where I met Big Mike as he got off the plane. We found a hotel in Liberia and threw his suitcases in the room. I was excited because one of them was for me—I'd had a few boxes of things sent to him to bring down, desperately needing new clothes because most of mine were too big for me, and a few t-shirts that weren't yellow wouldn't hurt. He handed over the suitcase with my things and I ripped through it.

"What the hell is this?! There must be a mistake," I said. He looked into the bag.

"No, that's the stuff you sent me." It contained two pairs of khaki pants, a leather jacket, and a business suit. Dammit, I'd sent him the wrong box. I'm pretty sure I wouldn't need those things in the 100-degree heat in Tama.

The next morning we grabbed a taxi toward the border, but first we had a surprise stop to make: the jail. I wanted to drop off some food and a couple of bucks for Pistol since I was going to be out of town during visiting day. I made Big Mike get out of the car and walk into the front registration area with me. He didn't want to go but I urged him in, just so he could say that he'd been in a Third World prison. I talked to the guards and gave them a few shopping bags of food and a book with money hidden in the binding to deliver. That done, we made the tranquil ninety-minute drive to *La Frontera*, the northern border with Nicaragua.

The border crossing was a chaotic three-hour affair of dust and crowds, hot sun and flies. We bribed some kids to bribe a policeman to bribe the officials to get us to the front of the line and get our passports stamped. Once we crossed over to the Nicaraguan side, the conditions were infinitely poorer. They make $6,000 a year on average in Costa Rica, but only $360 a YEAR in Nicaragua; 80% of the people in the country live on less than $2 a day. Big Mike tapped me on the shoulder and pointed to a man handcuffed to a flagpole, half-conscious in the blazing sun. He was slumped over but forced upright because of the metal cuffs pulling at his hands. He had no shirt or shoes, and only filthy rags for pants held up with a rope belt. He was covered in dirt and obviously hadn't cut his hair or bathed in a very long time.

"*Ughhhhhh,*" he moaned in pain. My best guess was that he'd been caught trying to sneak over the border or stealing something from a tourist and the border police were making an example out of him for all to see. Point taken.

Crossing over from Costa Rica to Nicaragua was as prolific a change in economics as someone from Beverly Hills wandering into neighboring South Central LA. Teens and men in fake Hollister t-shirts filled the shanty marketplace, all hustling to change money, sell homemade leather goods, or divert me to their taxi driver. I asked for a Coca Cola and six people got involved to make sure I got one, and share in the 40-cent spoils.

A friendly driver in a rusted '87 Corolla, held together with duct tape and twine, eased us north through green fields. He would take us all the way to San Juan del Sur for $20, he said, eager to make such a huge fare. He apologized that the air conditioning didn't work, the windows only rolled half down, the stereo was broken, and the floorboards were so rusted out that we had to watch our footing. I complimented him on the little stuffed animals he had lined up on the dashboard and he took one and offered it to me as a gift.

People in Costa Rica always talked about how dangerous and terrible Nicaragua was, but I saw nothing but pretty green countryside filled with cows and their farmers, all with decent faces. We passed a lake, far off across the water an island with two mountains rising from it. Our driver told us that it was a place called *Ometepe* and those were two active volcanoes on the island. He stopped at a ranch in the middle of nowhere so we could buy beers out of a *pulperia*, a dirt-floor market converted from someone's living room.

San Juan del Sur was completely different than Tamarindo. It started as a fishing village as well but became an under-the-radar surfer hotspot, the best kept secret on Central America's backpacker scene. Everyone raved how mellow and inexpensive it was, with only two bars and a handful of restaurants. It had wide, cobbled streets that ran into a boardwalk on the beach. Little kids kicked a soccer ball back and forth, avoiding horse carts clopping past.

A full meal was about $3 and a beer only 80 cents. It was so poor they had to employ security guards in bulletproof vests and shotguns to guard the meat trucks, but I found the people to be as warm and amiable as their lives were humble. The bay in town was nice enough, but within twenty minutes there were numerous deserted beaches that were a surfer's paradise; *Remonso, Maderas, Yankee*, and *Hermosa*. A sun-washed turquoise church sat in the middle of town. At sunset, young parents walked their toddlers around and grilled chicken out in front of their brightly painted clapboard bungalows.

"Revis, Revis, Revis. Granada!" the bus drivers yelled, trying to fill up with passengers before they departed. I felt the breeze rolling through those streets from the sea. What a magical little place, I thought.

I met up with my friends Trevor and Blake, surfers from Austin, Texas whom I'd met in Tama. I used to see them every day at Kahiki's but then one weekend they went on their visa run to Nicaragua. Once they saw the little sunny pueblo of San Juan del Sur they never came back, leaving all of their possessions behind in Tama. I could see why.

We ate a dinner of grilled seafood wrapped in banana leaves by the beach. I met their friends from Canada, England, the Canary Islands, Nicaragua, Costa Rica, Panama, Australia, and the U.S.; international businessmen and hippie backpackers together, all cool people I could vibe with. I hadn't told them that it was my birthday but somehow Blake found out, so they bought me dinner and took me out for rum and dancing at the Iguana Bar.

I woke up early the next morning to roosters and church bells. Mike and I set out to explore the town, but it didn't take long because it was only about six streets wide. We settled into brunch at a café sitting right on the sands, overlooking fishermen at work and the statue of San Juan up in the hills, the town's protector watching over us. We watched lithe, sun-browned teenagers playing baseball on the beach with a broom handle and a rubber ball, their center fielder standing ankle-high in the ocean.

Big Mike was perfect company—it was easy to relax around him without feeling like we needed to talk just for the sake of talking. It was his first time even leaving the USA, and he'd been to the jail, Costa Rica, and dirt-poor Nicaragua within 24 hours, but just took it all in stride. As we sat there by the sparking bay I had one of those surreal "Oh my God, this is my life" moments. Less than a year earlier I'd fled the United States in a flurry of turmoil, along the way setting some big goals for myself: to be in the best shape of my life, to be happy, and to write a book. The ensuing journey had stripped me of everything that was comfortable and normal in my life. I couldn't even have written the last 10 months as the wildest fiction.

It was finally my birthday, THE birthday, so how had I measured up? Well, I was in incredible shape, feeling the athletic self-confidence of a soldier coming out of boot camp. I'm sure there were times when I was younger and lighter when I could run farther, but what I could now do in the beach and the water, in the hot sun and then the endurance to perform in the gym, was remarkable. I'd completely transformed my physical shell—I'd lost those thirty-to-forty pounds that Glen stung me with and added muscle. I weighed in at less than 200 pounds consistently, the least in almost a decade.

I could breathe again. My allergies were gone, not even a sniffle, and the growing asthma that haunted me in my old life, leaving me coughing in the shower until I puked, had disappeared. I wondered how much of it was just stress-related. I had more energy, I slept better (when the howler monkeys let me sleep), and I felt so clear-headed—almost *pure*.

But most importantly, I had the mental health to maintain it. It was a choice. No, it was a thousand small choices, and that way they were achievable. I didn't need to win them all, just most of them, and keep it all heading in the right direction.

How about my second goal, to write my book? I was a little behind. Obviously it wouldn't be in print by my fortieth birthday, and after all it was only self-published, but who the hell cared? I had no negative judgments about missing that day on the nose. After all, there was finally proof of my existence, something that would be around long after I was gone. I'd taken out an essential part of myself and put it on the page to share with the world for generations, rooting me in the soil of eternity like a humble seed. Now I could finally just *be*.

Of course I hoped it sold well, but even if sales were humble, let's say 500 books in the first year, then I'd still be able to reach 500 human beings that I couldn't before. I'd be able to broaden their world, to help them *feel* something, to feel more human.

My third goal was to be happy, an elusive one to gauge for sure. Had I done it? That was a hard question to answer.

To be *truly* happy? What did that even mean? I saw a lot of people happy in their relationships, hormones and chemicals pumping through them temporarily, calling it love. I saw people happy with their job or their new car or when their football team won, but I didn't subscribe to the idea that happiness was a glowing light that washed over everything in our lives. That was for the movies, for fakers, for *Leave it to Beaver* reruns. That wasn't the shit we had to deal with in real life, or at least not my life.

I knew it was the *journey* that mattered, in the kung-fu-flick-fortune-cookie sense of the word, but a journey where? What was I supposed to be chasing?

I guess my whole life I'd been searching for meaning. If I didn't have a purpose to my existence, something bigger than myself, then I was just falling with nothing to grasp onto. It had to be my *true* purpose, and its pursuit would make it all worth it. Anything else would have been less than golden.

So what was that purpose for me, that *real* meaning of my life?

I once read an interview with the Dali Lama where a reporter asked him, "What's the meaning of life?" He asked the question tongue-in-cheek, not really expecting a serious answer, but the Dali Lama replied that he thought *happiness* was the meaning of life. For human beings to pursue true happiness was to pursue their higher selves. If we were all happy then there would be no fear, no hatred, no wars, no greed, and therefore no suffering. But then he thought about it for a moment more and corrected himself. He told the reporter that instead *hope* was more important than happiness. With hope one can go on despite their current circumstances; hope for a better life, hope for health, hope for safety, hope for *happiness.*

Wasn't that amazing? You didn't need the real thing, the current experience of that emotion, you just needed the *hope* of it to embolden your spirit and go on—the flicker of possibility. Happiness. And if you couldn't have that, then hope for happiness. That was the meaning of life.

"So happiness is what makes the world go round?" I contemplated after reading the article. "Well then, wouldn't we all be nihilistic pleasure seekers with no sense of responsibility, or cares beyond ourselves?" Not at all. People get the word *happiness* confused with *pleasure*. It might be one of the most important distinctions you could make.

Pleasure is the temporary state of feeling good. Pleasure means that you're enjoying comfort and money and alcohol and drugs and nice cars and sex and plenty of fun. Too often I see people of all ages pursuing pleasure as their life's purpose. It's fun for a while, and everyone gets jealous when they see the pictures, but there's no substance—it's all frosting and no cake. The feeling is short-lived and then you're left empty, with only a painful hunger to eat at that table again.

Happiness is so much more. Like love, it's one of the only commodities you get more of by giving it away to others. So that which made me happy was the purpose of my life? Easy to say, but what did that look like?

A long time ago, I was walking in the botanical gardens in San Francisco's Golden Gate Park. It was a Sunday, so young couples strolled around and lounged on blankets, reading the newspaper with a cup of coffee.

I found myself wandering down a path into a grove of redwoods and eucalyptus in the south end of the gardens. Sunlight filtered through the leaves just right, shooting down beams so clear that I could see the dust dance in each one, illuminating green ferns and flowers on the forest floor.

Coming my way on the path was a man with a shaved head, neither young nor old, his clothing worn but not neglected. He wore a necklace of round wooden beads and carried a book in his hands. He strolled through easily, watching butterflies in the stalks of sunlight, enjoying it all. He was Buddhist—I don't know how I knew this; I just knew. We passed each other.

"How's it going?" I asked. He didn't answer me with words but smiled with his eyes. He lifted up his hands, palms opened to the sky, motioning to everything that was around us, but didn't need to speak. I saw something in his eyes—something peaceful and pure, like still water. We were both part of it, abandoning our pretenses of direction or control in our lives, our legs moving in whatever direction we willed them but really just floating through our existence like cosmonauts in outer space. That moment stayed with me.

Fifteen years later, as I walked down the streets of Tamarindo, I finally knew what was in his still-water eyes, what the grand cosmic joke was. I felt pure acceptance, a connection to all. There had been bits and pieces of it in the past—scattered, inspired moments: summers in the White Mountains, a few weeks in Ecuador, perfect autumn weekends at college, bits and pieces with loved ones, but never like this. Those were beautiful vistas that I'd stumbled upon by accident, but this feeling sat with me always; I now had a roadmap how to get there.

Of course it wasn't perfect. Quite the opposite—my life was mired in rain and heat and a jungle of confusion, loneliness that cut like frozen steel, and a lot of things that scared the shit out of me, as well as many blessings. But I realized that it was all essential, all fundamentally part of the same cosmic swirl. Nothing was separate. There was only one energy. Of course there were bad things in life—people did terrible things to each other—but that was part of it all too, the darkness that was essential to light. My body was just a shell that would be ashes soon enough, but my soul was untouchable once it was plugged into all of that energy. I was both ancient and omniscient, yet so finite that I was nothing more than a cell in the thumbnail of a giant. I was in on the joke.

"I like it here," Mike's voice broke my meandering thoughts. "What would you think about spending an extra day?"

"Fine by me, bro," I smiled.

How had I changed in that year? I tried to pin it down. I could tell that I'd evolved to a higher plane of consciousness because I could identify a new emotion within me; I felt genuine empathy for people. I felt happy when good things happened to others *exactly* as if they'd happened to me, or better.

When I saw an old couple walking hand in hand, I could feel their tenderness. A father picking up his baby daughter filled me with sunny vibes. The warmth of wisdom radiated from an *abuela* sitting on her rocking chair on the front porch. I truly rooted for people—all people. I felt perfectly fulfilled seeing others experience joy, because of course there was no difference at all between "them" and "me" if I zoomed out far enough.

I needed nothing for myself, just air and some food and water—that was all. I desired nothing more than what I already had. It actually felt great to give my things away to those who appreciated them, a gift to have less. Being on Earth as a witness was more than enough for me, to be an open vessel for the universal energy to surge through me and reach others. The *hope* of it all was good enough. Wow, when you feel empathy, when someone else's happiness makes you happy, then the whole world is your palace.

Have you ever heard a song that starts out slowly in the first verse, with only the lead singer and an acoustic guitar? It's pretty subdued and you think that's the whole song, but then all of a sudden the second verse hits and the rest of the band comes in—the drummer, horns, electric guitars, backup singers, all at full pitch. The whole band is playing and it's alive, remarkably rich in contrast. That music just owns you. I don't know if there's a better answer to my own question, "Was I happy?" than to say that, for me, the band was finally all playing.

The consistency and clarity of this emotion was startling to me. But man oh man, how I'd earned it. Most of my life I'd wrestled with my condition as a human being, shredding at my own skin, but you know what? I wouldn't change a thing. I was lost on the map in a place called San Juan del Sur, my life as south of normal as you could get, but the band was all playing.

So, after four decades on Earth, if I could go back in time and give my younger self any advice, what would it be?

I chuckled. Where to begin? I'd made so many mistakes, fucked up royally too many times to count. Hurt others and myself. Thrown away love. I thought for a long time, watching the sun casting longer shadows across the shore, sailboats bobbing like toys in a bathtub. People came and went around me, and then I finally had it.

It came down to only two things:

"Always believe in yourself,"

and

"Laugh more."

That was it. If I could step in a time machine I wouldn't give my young, angry, confused self any other advice.

Laugh. Believe. That was all I needed to get through life, my sexton's point to keep me facing *my* true north. The rest would work itself out. I knew I had a good heart; I wished nothing bad on anyone; I cared about everyone; I didn't want anything else for myself.

There was no way of telling how many more birthdays I'd be around. Maybe a lot, maybe a few—either way it was okay. But my three goals? Yeah, I'd done just fine with those. Most importantly I'd given myself another gift, one I hadn't even anticipated or asked for: I'd saved my own life. Happy fortieth birthday, Norm.

CHAPTER 37

'GONE SURFING

I finally went surfing, though for some reason I waited until my last month in town. There was always some excuse to put it off—I wanted to wait until I got in better shape, the water was too dirty in the rainy season, or around Christmas and New Year's it was too crowded with tourists. I kept putting it off until February, and then it was now or never.

A friend of mine was in town from Sacramento, Sugar Ray. Actually, he was a friend of a friend whom I'd never met before, but I offered to show him around when he was in Tama. That happened a lot, as people back in the States came to associate me with Costa Rica. I'd get emails on a weekly basis saying, "I have friends coming down to Costa Rica on vacation. Would you give them some advice where to go or what to do?" or even people who said they were thinking about doing what I'd done, selling everything and moving out of the country, and wanted some guidance. I was happy to help, and I've met some amazing people that way.

Ray wanted to go surfing and asked me where was the best place to get a lesson. I connected him with my Loonie buddy, Kelly, who owned a surf shop. Ray asked if I wanted to go with him and I realized that I was out of excuses.

We put our things in a locker and grabbed surfboards at Kelly's. First-timers used longer boards, and from there they got smaller as the surfer's skill went up; in surfing, lack of size matters. The good ones carried waxed-up shark's fins no bigger than five and a half feet long, but my board was a twelve-foot foam battleship, rounded and softened for beginners so I wouldn't split my head open. I feared it would be a lightning rod of embarrassment among the crowd on the beach, but, of course, no one cared.

The wind was really blowing that day, so we held onto our boards tightly so they wouldn't fly away like kites. Our surf instructor, Jonathan, a small-framed Tico with indigenous roots, put us through drills on the beach, explaining how to paddle, jump up, and hold the correct stance. Then it was time to hit the water. We strapped on our leashes and waded out then dove on top of our boards and paddled. When the waves crashed down we had to pull up the nose to launch over or grab the side of the board and roll to avoid getting tossed around.

Finally, we paddled far enough out to float without interruption. Jonathan helped us get lined up and gauge the right wave, told us when to start paddling, and sent us off with a push. Ray went first and got up easily and rode the wave right in. I went next and jumped up awkwardly, my weight too far on my back foot, launching me backwards and splashing in. But I'd felt it.

We took turns paddling out and jumping up, usually with the same result. Finally, on my fourth wave, I caught one, crouching with a stable stance, one arm facing perpendicular to the board and my front arm pointing to the beach. I rode the crest of that wave all the way in and it felt amazing, like riding a giant carpet of water being unrolled down a long hallway. I was so excited that I paddled out again before Ray or the instructor had a chance to get back in place for the next waves.

"Squat down lower, it will help with your balance!" Jonathan shouted. I did, and it allowed me to stay square in that critical first moment when I got up. I caught five or six more good waves in, wiped out dozens of times, and even managed to catch one on my own. *"Crouch deeper! Down!"* he yelled.

Ray surfed most of the waves like a champ, but on adrenaline alone I paddled out twice as fast. This was so cool! I pictured myself one of those put-together Hawaiians, shooting effortlessly through the barrel, one hand trailing to touch the water. In reality, I was riding four-foot waves on a twelve-foot board, but hey, it felt great anyway.

After two hours Jonathan signaled us to head to the beach. I was exhausted, every muscle in my body spent. The constant paddling was the hardest part, probably about 90% of the effort. Damn, no wonder those surf bums were so shredded. But I felt exhilarated, finally getting a taste of that drug they called surfing. I'd really done it!

I said goodbye to the fellas and grabbed my gear and sauntered back through town toward my apartment. But this time it was different; I had a swag in my step. "Man oh man, guess who's king of the beach? Surfer Norm!" I thought to myself.

"Hey, bro, the waves are good today—they're not closing out too fast!" I hollered to a tourist who hadn't even asked, mimicking what I heard every day.

I strutted through town in my wet board shorts, a surf god in the making. Maybe I would start smoking weed again and try to grow dreadlocks? Did Rogaine have a special dreadlocks formula? I'd Google it when I got home. People stopped and stared. That's right—get a good look, ladies. I'm a rad surfer and I know it. Just for effect, I dropped my tube of zinc oxide and bent down slowly to pick it up.

"Oops...dropped my sunscreen. Just went surfing and it sure was hot out there today!" I hollered to the small crowd that was gathering behind me.

"OhhhhhhhhUGHHHHHH!!!" they said.

"Yeah, I hear ya," I stood back up and stretched. All that crouching and squatting took its toll.

I walked up to my apartment as the sun was setting. There was a wonderful breeze out. I turned on the garden hose and put my leg up to wash the sand off my flip-flops.

"Just went surfing!" I waved and yelled over to my neighbors by the pool.

"Looks like you sure did!" they yelled back, laughing. It was good to have such positive people in my life.

I turned off the hose and went into my apartment, grabbed a glass of water and opened my computer—Facebook needed to know about my surfing accomplishments immediately; it would do wonders to perpetuate the whole "nature-boy-living-in-the-tropics-cool-alternative-writer-white-Rasta" thing that I was going for. Hey, it was a lot better than telling everyone the truth—that most of my time was spent sweating in jail and embarrassing myself with the language barrier.

I sat down at my desk but jumped right up. I thought I just felt cold wood. I sat down again, slowly. My bare ass pressed against the wooden chair. What the fudgesicle?

I got up and tried to peer at my own backside, but it just twisted me up like a dog chasing his tail and I almost fell over. So I undid the drawstring of my board shorts and carefully took them off, holding them up to the light. Daylight came through; there was a six-inch rip up the back—the hem line along the ass had blown right out.

I put my arm right through it and looked at my hand, as if to make sure it was real. Dammit, that was my best swimsuit! Of course it must have ripped while I was surfing—probably all of that crouching and squatting and jumping up. But wait, I'd also walked all the way across town like that. No—I'd PIMPED across town like that, peacocking my ass around like Lil' Wayne.

The truth hit me; I was a clown, a moon-white, bare-assed poser. I was no surfer. Dare I say it? I was…a TOURIST! Gasp!

Oh well, if you can't beat 'em, join 'em.

I went to my computer and typed a message to Sugar Ray. "Hey, bro! Fun day. Let's go out again tomorrow."

One of my neighbors in Pueblo del Mar was a young couple with two little kids. She was a gringa from San Francisco, him an Argentine surfer named Francisco. He had a blondish surf afro and a 70s porn mustache that together made him look like a cross between Ron Jeremy and Krusty the Clown. He was always running around between his three jobs. Francisco was friendly, but I could recognize a man with places to go who didn't have time for bullshit. I respected that. I'd see him early every morning, hustling off to his first job working for his mom's hostel, Botella de Leche, a stone's throw down the hill from our apartment.

"*Buenos dias, Noel! Have a great day writing, mae! I'm off to work now,*" he'd yell over when he saw me outside the apartment, and scoot off just as fast.

In the heat of the afternoon, when I was eating an ice cream bar and winding down for my third siesta, he taught surf lessons. At night he bartended at Bamboo Sushi. Some nights I'd go in there and sit at the bar and chat with him when he wasn't too busy. Francisco loved surfing and punk music. We talked about bands like Manu Chao's Mano Negra and compared notes on all of the stupid and wild things we'd done when we were young. He was only 28, so his party days weren't that far behind him, but once he'd met his wife and become a father, he'd completely changed his ways. Now he was a family man, rarely drinking and working so much that his wife had to order him to chill out and take a day off. That's how you do it, I thought: all in—give your best no matter whether you're partying, working, or committing to a relationship and family. That's how I wanted to be.

"*So, me and my buddies partied all night and then drove our van to the coast, near Punta del Diablo in Uruguay, where the waves were epic,*" his stories would start. He told me about wild adventures surfing with his legendary board, the Black Mamba, and how he'd been jumped by five Columbians in Tamarindo just a few months prior.

"*The guy owed my mom money for the hostel and wouldn't pay. I saw him at the bar and asked him about it and he said 'Fuck your mother,' and I hauled off and clocked him. I got a good one in and he fell, but there were five of them and they dragged me outside and beat the shit out of me. I woke up in a ditch with blood everywhere. They broke two of my teeth. I'm lucky that people were watching because otherwise they would have killed me.*"

I asked him if we could go out surfing some time.

"Okay, we go out tomorrow at noon, Noel," he said. *"Now here, try this drink."*

We departed from Bottella de Leche with boards strapped to the roof of Francisco's SUV, adorned with a "Keep Tahoe Blue" sticker in Spanish. The parking lot attendant waved and gave him a good spot in the shade under a tree. He took the boards down and gave me one. I put it on my head and walked across the white sand. It was hot as fire, scalding the skin on the bottom of my feet.

"*Run, Noel, run!*" Francisco yelled.

'Cisco and I waded out and dove headfirst into the waves in perfect synchronicity. We paddled out to where he could still stand and we turned and watched west to gauge the waves coming in.

"See, Noel, that one has white water. You don't want that because it closes out too soon. Look for one that's big but doesn't have white water."

"What about this one?"

"No, that one is too small. Be patient. The best surfers are always patient."

"Hey, look at that one."

"Yeah, that's it. Good. Okay, now go Noel—paddle, PADDLE! Faster! GO!"

And I was up, the momentum of the wave spring-boarding me out of the water and into the blue sky toward the beach.

"You did good, Noel! You really rode that one!"

It was fun going out with 'Cisco—he pushed me athletically, like a tough-love coach. He kept the pace up but it was still relaxing, like two old surfing buddies paddling out for another go around into the horizon, not a lesson.

My last two weeks in town I went out with him almost daily. I'd walk down to Botella de Leche and find him eating a meal with his family. He'd put food on his mustache and make funny faces at his kids to make them laugh. He put his oldest, his girl, on his lap as he wolfed down his lunch.

"You always eat so fast," his girlfriend said. "Slow down. Norm will wait."

"Sure, no rush," I said. His mom offered me a plate of food.

"Muchas gracias, pero estoy lleno," I said—thank you, but I am full.

And then, out of nowhere, I only had a few days left in Tama. People wanted to take me out for beers, but I only wanted to surf, to spend as much time as possible in the ocean. My last day going out with 'Cisco felt special; I could see every spot of light off the waves as if in slow motion and took it all in because I wanted to remember. I brought my underwater digital camera and he shot some footage of me surfing. I didn't think about anything—my mind was clear. I just paddled and splashed and swam and fell and got back up and surfed.

There were plenty of other surf camps out there with us, dozens of tourists. They had expensive rash guard shirts and waterproof hats and colorful zinc oxide. We were just two dudes, shaved head and surf fro, enjoying the pure experience without any of the fancy shit.

One of the girls from the other camp ran into some trouble with her leash when she fell. She was fine, just a little tangled, so 'Cisco swam over to help her, only about five meters from where I was floating. He talked to her for a moment and helped her reattach her leash, but suddenly yelped and jumped right up onto her board with her. What the hell? Something was wrong.

"*Uhhh…we paddle over here. It's better surf,*" he said to her. "*Hurry, paddle now so you don't miss this next set,*" and he pointed her board in the opposite direction and they churned away sloppily. That wasn't like him. He turned to me and gave me a nod and a serious look so I followed.

About twenty meters away he stopped and climbed off her board. She thanked him and went off to rejoin her surf mates.

"What's up?" I asked him.

"*Well, Noel, I was standing there and something bumped my leg. I looked down and saw a fin.*"

"A fin? Really? So it was…"

"*Yes, I think so,*" he whispered, turning his head around to make sure no one was listening. It's bad luck for surfers to even talk about *los tiburons*, sharks, an old superstition passed down from fishermen. Everyone made their living off the sea one way or another in Tama, and if word got out that there were sharks in the bay, even one official report on the Internet, then the whole tide of tourism could turn and everyone would lose money. The locals understood the risks and made their living in that water with a healthy respect and a cautious eye.

"Seriously? What kind was it, Francisco?"

"*I don't know, but it was about two meters long, so I don't think it was a nurse shark.*"

"Damn, bro."

"*Yeah. Don't say anything. I will signal to the other surf instructors. But here's my question: We have one hour left on our lesson. We can go in if you feel unsafe and I can give you your money back. Or we can stay out and surf.*"

"Well, what's the smart thing to do?"

"*Honestly? Go in.*"

"And what would you do?" I asked. He looked at me.

"I'd surf," he said. It didn't take me long to think about it.

"Okay, 'Cisco, let's surf."

And we did. Man, it was fun, the danger adding a little hustle to my paddling. He must have let the other instructors know with a look or a whistle because the other surf camps found an excuse to end their lessons a little early, and we had the ocean to ourselves. When I caught a wave I sprang right up—I wanted to be ON that board a lot more than floundering around in that water, which would look like a seal from below. Francisco even grabbed the Black Mamba and surfed right along with me. I tried to follow him and watch how he did it—silky smooth and driven by an instinct that I couldn't yet access, but I was lucky just to stay up.

After an hour we got out and ran across the hot sand back to the truck. I went to pay him.

"Don't worry about it, Noel."

"Ahhh, man, you don't have to do that."

"It was fun. You did good for beginning," he said. *"I think you could get good with a lot of practice."*

"Thanks, man. Well, here, let me at least pay you a tip."

"No, Noel, we surfed as friends today."

"Okay, 'Cisco. Thanks again, bro."

We got back to Botella de Leche and I helped him wash off the boards so he could get back to his family. They asked how it was and we said great, of course leaving out the part about the shark. I walked back to my apartment and checked my swimsuit—no rips. After I drank a half-gallon of water, I plugged my camera into my laptop and started downloading the pictures and videos we'd taken. There were a lot of them to go through, most of them blurry or mistimed, but a few came out. We even had a video of me paddling like a maniac and 'Cisco yelling encouragement as I got up and caught the wave all the way into the shore.

I flipped through all of the pictures, then stopped. One caught my eye. I enlarged it and sat back. I was floating in the water beside my board, my arm extended over the board so it wouldn't drift away. I don't know if I had just ridden a wave or was about to jump on and paddle out or what, but there were green hills behind me and a mural of blue sky, the ocean all around. I was smiling. I looked happy, as happy as I've ever felt.

"That's how I want to remember my life," I thought, "with that smile. I want that picture on my tombstone. Or maybe if I ever write a book about Tamarindo..."

CHAPTER 38

THE BOOK ARRIVES

One day I stopped writing. I hadn't planned on it, I didn't even know it was coming, but I just stopped typing because there wasn't anything more to say. By sticking to my routine of writing in the early mornings the pages had added up—70, 120, 200. By the time I got to the end I reread my earlier chapters and almost didn't recognize the newly born writer who'd penned them.

The book may have been rounding into shape but I still never thought I was doing enough. "I should be writing much more, working harder. I should be running an extra mile or doing more pull-ups. My Spanish is falling behind," I'd think.

When that little voice popped up, which was often, I stopped and reminded myself to breathe. Slow. Down. Enjoy it. That primal instinct from my reptilian brain to move and hustle and achieve was still with me from my past life, and every day I had to make a conscious effort to slay it. And then train myself not to stress about not stressing. It's okay, Norm, you can relax. You're doing fine.

But was I? The truth was that I was limping to the finish line. Each day felt one degree hotter than the last—I couldn't escape it. I never got a full night sleep. My stomach was sick. I was constantly worried about Pistol and stressed about money. People back in the States still thought I was crazy to give up my cushy past life to write a book.

"Estas cansado, buddddy?" Hector always asked—are you tired?

"No, of course not," I'd lie, straightening my posture and smiling. I pushed forward on faith alone.

But wasn't I a *Writer*? Didn't that mean something? I sure didn't feel like anything special. I was documenting some stories but jumping around from idea to idea with no clue what the hell I was doing. I put in the funny or wild stuff I would want to read if I bought the book, and tried to hit some high points of emotion. Some mornings the writing rushed out of me effortlessly, but toward the end it was mostly just a trickle.

As I worked, I discovered what the *true* story was—about my exploration of life and the world we live in, the metaphorical journey to consciousness. Cool. A few stories I'd thrown in as afterthoughts, just so a certain region of the world was represented or I could touch on themes surrounding my family's origin, but to me, those turned out to be some of the best in the book (*The White Ghost, For Sunflowers and Survivors*). By the time I finished the first draft in late January, I had a bloated manuscript. Some of it was way too wild, too likely to offend, unorganized, repetitive, or basically just sucked. To be honest, I just wanted the damn thing to be over with, to have it printed and in my hands already.

I asked my publisher a million questions, forgot some of the answers, didn't like others, wrestled with the costs, and asked the same questions again. They were always patient and took time to answer thoroughly—more patient than I would have been with myself.

I emailed the rough draft to the publishers and Stephanie emailed back with her congratulations. Next came the editing process, they told me. No sweat. Three days later, they emailed the manuscript back to me with approximately 10,427 errors that needed to be addressed. "Not bad," she said. "Most first-time authors have more."

The editing process was excruciating. I wasn't fully prepared to roll up my sleeves and dig up every theme, every character, every plot line. I didn't understand that less is more, that the story plays out in the reader's head, where you need space and air for their imagination to flow, not on the page. Hell, I didn't even have ANY dialogue in the damn thing. Imagine that, a year around the world and two people never said anything to each other! The mechanics of grammar, sentence structure, and tense drowned me. I opened my toolbox but nothing was in it, so I patched the story together with duct tape and bubble gum and hoped it would hold together, at least long enough not to fall apart in the reader's hands.

I must have read each of those words twenty times. Or tried to, because I'd move to the couch to get more comfortable while I read and soon would be snoring, the pages fanned out on the floor. I couldn't look at it anymore; it made me dizzy. After the tenth reading, the lines all blurred into black spots on white cows. I had WAY more important things to do, like talk about it on Facebook and start casting for the movie. Let's see, Johnny Depp would play Shane, and Dylan Bruno or a young Woody Harrelson would be perfect for my character. Other than that, I spent most of my valuable time working on the dedication of the book, trying to cram every single person I've ever known in there. If someone was included in the dedication, then *of course* they'd buy at least one copy of the book, and maybe three. I wrote in people who I hadn't talked to in decades but stopped just short of Googling the most common Chinese surname in the world and adding it.

As I hacked away at the big tree of editing with a small axe, I was also up against the clock to come up with the cover art. The publishers had an artist on staff who drafted several concepts. They were awful—figures on the tops of mountains with arms outstretched or footprints in the sand. I might as well have titled the book *My Cliché*. We went through my idea, too, like a suitcase or passport with stamps that were my chapter titles, or a rough drawing of the world on a bar napkin next to a beer, but I wasn't feeling any of them.

This was going to be on people's shelves, lined up in the literary pantheon with others. I didn't want the other authors to look over and turn their noses up at how amateurish the new book looked.

J.D. Salinger: "Who's the new guy over there? Looks like a phony to me."

Kerouac: "I guess he hit the road and traveled around the world or something. Been there, done that. And look at that horrible cover!"

Hemingway: "Awful! And this guy fancies himself a drinker?! If he comes any closer, I'm going to challenge him to an arm wrestle."

Kesey: "Let's drop acid."

Didn't the publishers realize this was my *book*, my contribution to the *world* for time eternal? For Christ's sake, people would be doing lines of *coke* off this book and reading it on the *shitter*. It was *that* important! Nothing short of breathtaking would do.

I found "it" after dozens of hours of tinkering. Everyone advised me not to have a black book cover, but I loved its elegance. I found an old movie poster for "Death in the Afternoon" by Saul Bellow and loved the font and the colors, so I adopted those and that set the tone for the Rasta-like vibe. I chose a star for the main image, slightly off-kilter and stretched from front to back of the book jacket. The star could be a universal symbol of consciousness, for man's search for meaning in the universe, *blah blah blah*; I liked it because it looked cool. Let the reader figure it out—that wasn't my problem.

Hunkering down to focus on all of those edits and loose ends took every fiber of my patience. My eyes bugged out and my head was ready to explode.

But there it was—finally done. I emailed it to them again. They emailed back within a day; I'd whittled the errors down to 4,286; a lot of our corrections needed to be corrected. My God, was it too late to say forget it to the whole thing? On it went for a few excruciating weeks after my birthday until finally we both thought it was right.

They would print up one book and FedEx it to me down there in Costa Rica for final review before it was officially unleashed onto the world. I waited.

A week later I'd just come in from playing basketball with Row and Grant and Big Mike and saw an email from Theresa. FedEx was waiting at her office with a package for me. Big Mike and I rushed back out the door and walked down there.

"Slow down, we just played five games and my legs are killing me," he said. But I couldn't—I was practically floating. Outside of her office, the FedEx man was leaning against his truck, looking bored and a little pissed off that he had to wait so long. He told me that there was a 10,000 *Colones* import tax still due. I knew it was bullshit because everything had been prepaid in the States, but at that point I didn't care. I gave him a $20 bill and he handed me the package and I signed for it.

We walked back toward my apartment, slower this time. I didn't want to open it up until I got home. But halfway there, I couldn't take it anymore, so I ripped the box to shreds. Big Mike helped and picked up pieces of cardboard from the ground. Inside was a glossy black book, the title in red, green, and yellow, with a cool image of a star on the cover. It said *Pushups in the Prayer Room.* The book was by "Norm Schriever."

I didn't know what I was supposed to feel. To be honest, it seemed like a let down—it was just words on paper and a cover, something anyone could slap together at Kinko's in a long weekend with a case of Red Bull and enough unresolved memories of childhood angst. I didn't know what to do with it. I'd poured my heart and soul, all of my money, a whole lot of sweat, and even squashed a scorpion into that book. Now what? As far as I could see, nothing was different in my life. I took it home and threw it on the coffee table and we went out to surf.

Later that afternoon, I was taking a little siesta on the couch. The door was open and I could hear someone chuckling outside. I got up and looked out the screen door. Big Mike was sitting on a lawn chair by the pool. He had my book open and was laughing. No one was around. He read some more and then turned the page and laughed again. I didn't want to disturb him, so I walked back inside and sat down and listened. For an hour, his laughter floated into the apartment, and it was the best sound I've ever heard. *Then* it meant something.

I carried the book around town with me until the very day I left Tamarindo. I wanted to share it with all of the friends who'd been on that journey with me, who were a bigger part of that accomplishment than they'd ever know. Big Mike snapped photos of Row holding up the book behind the bar at Seasons, then Grant on the deck of his apartment, Hector with a look of pride under the shade of a tree, and Francisco with his surfboard. One afternoon, Theresa held the book up outside my apartment after lunch.

"Hurry up and take the picture, it's hot out here," she said, but held it high and smiled broadly, making sure the cover was straight. *"Take another one, just in case. And let's bring it to El Garito's tonight to show everyone."*

Now it was really starting to be fun, but there was still one more person who needed to see the book.

CHAPTER 39

FLOWER POWER

My last week in Tamarindo, Gringo Grant had everyone over to his apartment in Langosta for a barbecue. We went on the roof to watch the sunset. Playa Langosta was on the south end of Tamarindo and the view was spectacular. I'd never seen that vista of the coast line: a bird's eye view of the waves rolling in from hundreds of miles away, far off in the Pacific, and south toward Playa Avellana all the way down to Playa Junquillal. The breeze up there was a welcome respite from the merciless February sun, trade winds from the north known as the "*Alisios.*" They swooped through the bay and carried moist ocean air all the way up to the mountain ranges to form the enchanting Costa Rican cloud forests.

A lot of our friends were there: Grant, his tall roommate, Row, curly haired Yazmin, Sofia, and a few girls I didn't know. They were all drinking beers and passing joints as the sun went down, talking in English, and laughing as *Cultura Profética* sang to us over the radio.

I sat at a picnic table and talked to Sofia for a while in English. She introduced me to a girlfriend of hers named Bella who was from Puntarenas, a beach town four hours to the south. Everyone was chatting but Bella didn't speak English so she just sat there, smiling but keeping to herself. She was pretty in a simple, natural way, her big brown eyes almost making her look Persian. I felt bad that she was left out so I smiled at her and offered to get her another beer when I went inside.

I left a few hours later with Row, who had to go to work at the restaurant. I said goodbye to everyone, and then to Bella in Spanish, "Ciao y mucho gusto, Bella." I thought I saw something in her eyes, a glint of light meant to catch my gaze. I did a double take but she had already looked away. Was I just imagining it? I thought about her the rest of the day.

We saw each other the next night at El Garito's, where our group of friends sat out on the deck and drank Imperials and listened to the music. Bella was at one end of the table, wearing a white sundress with a white flower in her hair, her skin a delicious shade of caramel, her hair long and impossibly black against all the white. She looked as pretty as a country music song, and my pulse quickened when she smiled at me. I could live on the edge of her smile. I tried to sit down next to her but a few others sat down between us before I could grab the chair.

All I could think of was being closer to Bella, but she was too far down the table for me to talk to. Whenever someone got up I tried to move over without being too obvious. She urged me closer with her eyes. I grabbed at a chair next to me but two of our friends wanted to sit together because they were talking about something, and then a boyfriend and a girlfriend sat together, and then we had so many people that someone said, "Why not put another table together and, Norm, sit over hear on this end?" So, despite my best efforts, Bella and I were as far apart as when the night started.

Everyone spoke English and Bella didn't understand, but this night she wasn't bored. She chuckled at my failed game of musical chairs, tracking my progress over to her side, seat by seat, with anticipation.

I don't remember much else from that night other than Bella, and the trade winds that tossled her hair. It all glowed. Four hours went by like a minute, and eventually people left the table and started going home. I made my way over two more seats, and then to her side of the table, and finally, as the night was ending, there was a seat open right next to her. She picked up my beer and placed it next to her's, and I sat down.

"Hola, Bella" I said.

"*Hola, como estas? Todo bien?*" she said. Hi, how are you? Everything good?

"Bien, gracias. Que haces?" Well, thank you. What's going on?

"*Ummm...todo bien?*" she said, nervously.

Yes, Bella, we've established that I'm good.

We pulled our chairs closer and she was thrilled that I spoke some Spanish. It was so hard for her in Tamarindo, she confessed, because everyone spoke English and her Tica friends spoke English around the gringos so she felt left out. When they went to a restaurant or a bar it was like she was sitting alone, she said. I understood the feeling, I told her.

She got a kick out of it because I spoke some Spanish but looked like such a gringo. That was so funny to her, so she started calling me her *gringito* (little gringo) and asked me what slang words I knew.

I recited the three great Costa Rican lies for her and told her what Pachuco phrases I knew. She clapped her hands and laughed.

"*Mas, mi gringito, mas*!

"Do you want to hear the swear words I know?" I asked in Spanish.

"*Si! Si! Por favor!*" she said.

Then it was closing time. Everyone got up to leave and go home. Sofia said she was exhausted and told Bella, who was staying with her, it was time to go. Bella looked at me with big soft eyes, and I didn't know what to do. So we said goodbye and I hugged her and she kissed me on the cheek. She smelled like coconut lotion. I didn't want to let go. But they left and I got up to leave, too. A little white flower was left on the table. I looked around to see if anyone was watching and picked it up, and then walked on home.

The next day, Sunday, I was cleaning my apartment and packing when there was a knock on my screen door. It was Sofia, and behind her Bella, who looked as nervous as a kid on her first day of school. *"Hi, Norm,"* Sofia said in English. *"We just wanted to come by and say goodbye because Bella is leaving for Puntarenas this afternoon."*

I was completely surprised because Sofia had never had visited me before, but I asked them inside.

"Sorry, it's a bit of mess," I said and opened the screen door. I thought they would both come inside but only Bella walked in, and then Sofia said, *"Okay, nice seeing you. I'll be back in a while to pick her up,"* and walked off.

I asked Bella to sit down on the futon. I turned on the radio and pointed the fan toward us then sat down next to her. She fiddled with her hair and played with the hem of her skirt. I offered her a beer but she just wanted water. She looked down at my coffee table and smiled.

"*Que es eso, gringito*?" she asked, picking up the little white flower I'd brought home.

I still didn't understand why she was there and why Sofia left, but I made pleasant conversation. We talked about our families, where we lived, and what we did for work. She was in graduate school to become a psychologist. Her senior thesis was about helping indigenous people in Costa Rica, but instead of just writing an academic paper she'd gone to live with tribes in the jungle and counseled their children. There was no money to be made as a psychologist in Costa Rica but she really wanted to help children. She talked faster as she got comfortable, forgetting that I wasn't a native speaker. Soon I had no idea what the hell she was saying, but I could listen to her forever.

After a while it dawned on me that she'd come to my apartment to see *me*. She wasn't looking for the neighbor or needing to borrow hot sauce or asking me for rent money. It was hard for me to believe that a creature so beautiful would want something to do with me—she was a lot younger, naturally beautiful, incredibly smart, and obviously good-hearted. She was too good for me, I thought.

But there she was. Soon her water glass was empty and we'd chatted about every member of both of our families and went through every picture in our phones and talked about the weather in detail. I looked at her. Her body leaned closer and those eyes drew me in, half shut. She wanted me to kiss her, so I did. I leaned in and closed my eyes and our lips touched.

Those first moments are always the best, that promise of brown flesh miracles, better than religion, better than Sunday morning jazz, like hot angel curtains blowing on a Spanish afternoon. I kissed her neck and she moaned. There was no rushing, we let it all come to us. She put her hand on the back of my head and pulled her body into mine, those smooth brown legs intertwining with mine. When she kissed me I got lost within all of her hair, like tangled fishing nets. She didn't try to brush it out of the way and I didn't mind. She smelled so good I couldn't let go.

I kissed down her neck and along her collarbone. She was wearing a halter top, revealing the cutest brown stomach. I kissed it, around her belly button, and she giggled. "*Me encanta—I feel good*," she said and laid back. I kissed her stomach more. I laid my face on it and she rubbed her fingers through my hair. Her skin was so warm, like the sunbeams never left her.

My kisses got smaller and smaller. I closed my eyes and listened to the sound of her breathing, the music playing, the breeze rustling palm fronds against my window, her stomach rising and falling gently. I didn't want it to end. I didn't want to move in case that feeling went away. It all felt like... home. We drifted...

We woke up to Sofia honking her car horn outside, calling for Bella. We jumped up, disoriented, untangling ourselves and shaking half-asleep limbs. I'd fallen asleep on her stomach, and her cradling me in her arms. She scrambled to grab her purse and sunglasses, suddenly self-conscious.

I tried to figure out what to say, as did she, but we both just started laughing. We fell into each other one more time and hugged and kissed goodbye, laughing the whole time.

"*Return to Costa Rica soon, my gringito,*" she said in Spanish. "*I want to see you again and again.*"

"I will."

And then she ran out into the sunlight and was gone, the screen door left swaying, the sound of her laughter lingering in my room.

I sat down, watching the curtains dance to their own secret music. The apartment smelled like coconuts and the ocean.

CHAPTER 40

ORGAN DONORS

My last few days in Tamarindo, I didn't feel so well. My whole body ached like I'd been in a car accident and I couldn't even keep my eyes open. Maybe it's just the surfing, I told myself, or all the excitement of finishing the book and cleaning the apartment and packing. But I was drained.

Hector knocked on my screen door and I let him in. He sat down and I gave him a cup of water, with extra ice like he liked it, and fell back down on the couch. We both looked around the empty room.

"Estas cansado, buddddy?" he asked.

I perked up, ready to give him the usual bullshit positive answer, but then slumped back down and covered my eyes with my arm.

"*Si, Hector. Estoy muy cansado. No se porque.*" I am very tired, I don't know why.

"*Yo tambien, a vezes estoy cansado tambien,*" he said. Me too, sometimes I feel tired too.

He smiled and we just sat there, not saying anything, both enjoying the quiet and the cool shade of the apartment. Hector had been good to me. I don't know what I would have done without him.

"Okay, Hector, we should go. I have several stops to make. *Vámanos.*"

I didn't have much, just my backpack and a carry-on bag. I'd given most of my things away and was leaving a duffel bag filled with odd items with Theresa: my boxing gear, nice bed sheets, a few books and notebooks, and some clothes, for if and when I came back to Central America. Nicaragua was on my mind more and more, but who the hell knew?

I picked up my bags but Hector took them out of my hands and carried them outside and put them in his trunk. I recalled the day when I'd arrived and how important my luggage had seemed, as if the material things I had were my whole life. Damn, I couldn't believe I was leaving. In some ways it felt like it went by so fast, but it was also the longest year of my life.

"*Hector, primero vamos a Botella de Leche*," I said.

We rolled down the hill to the hostel and I ran inside to look for 'Cisco. I'm not much of a goodbye guy because it's pointless—you just stand there and fumble through it and say the same thing five times. It's not that I don't care—quite the opposite. I just prefer "see you laters" to "goodbyes" with the ones I love.

I went in and found 'Cisco's mom and girlfriend and children at the kitchen table.

"Hola, Noel. You just missed him—he went out to teach a surf lesson," his mom said.

"Okay. Just please tell him that…that…"

"Yes?"

"Well, just give him this." I handed her my camera case.

"What's this?"

"It's my underwater camera. We used it when we surfed together. I figured he could take photos and videos when he gives surf lessons and probably charge an extra $50. Maybe now he can work a little less and spend more time with you guys."

"Oh, wow. Are you sure? That is such a gift," his mom said.

"Of course. Francisco has been great to me."

They got up and hugged me goodbye.

"Are you sure you can't wait for him, or do you want something to eat?" his mom asked.

"*Muchas gracias*, but I can't. I have a plane to catch. He has my email—tell him to keep in touch," I said, though I knew he wouldn't, and that was okay.

I went back outside, got into the taxi, and sipped some water. I felt like I was coming down with a fever.

"A donde vamos, buddddy?" Hector asked.

"Seasons Hotel," I told him.

We stopped there and I grabbed something from my bag and jumped out and walked up to the restaurant. It wasn't open yet; the chairs were up on the tables like we'd left them the night before. A barefoot lady was mopping the floor, singing a song under her breath. Row was behind the bar, taking inventory of the bottles.

"Tuanis, mae! Como estas?" I said.

"Hola, Noel! You go today? To United States? When do you return?" Row said.

"I don't know. Yo quiero regresar pronto." I want to return soon.

"Well, I miss you, my brother."

"Yeah, me too. Here, this is for you." I handed him my basketball, the only one in town as far as I knew.

"That's for me? So cool!" He turned it around in his hands. Written in black Sharpie on one side was "Row" and on the other "Next."

We hugged and said goodbye and I ran back to the taxi.

"Okay, Hector, vamos a Liberia. Pero despacio." Let's go to Liberia, but drive slowly.

We cruised through town, my window open. I waved at people as we passed, just like I did every day. They waved and whistled back, not knowing that it was the last time we'd ever see each other.

I saw Fedor.

"Hey, hermano loco! What's up, bro?" he said.

"Nothing man. Todo bien! Hey, I have something for you." I gave him a plastic bag with my hair clippers in it. "These are for you, Fedor."

"Oh, thank you. But why for me?"

"No reason. Take care of yourself, man, and thanks for introducing me to your mom. And the Spanish lesson!"

"Pura vida, mae! Hey—can I buy you a beer?"

"You want to buy *me* a beer?" I asked, stunned.

"Yeah. I just got paid. Come on, the first round is on me."

"Next time, Fedor, I promise."

"Okay!" he shrugged. *"Hasta luego, mopri!"*

We went by Aqua and I gave a pair of my sneakers to Kenny G. He'd asked about them before and they were almost brand new.

We drove right by Theresa's office but I didn't tell Hector to stop. I couldn't do it. How do you summon the words to say goodbye to your little sister, someone who taught you so much about *feeling* your life again, even if she didn't know it? I just couldn't stand a tearful goodbye. Besides, I'd hung out with her all week, and I had a gut feeling that we'd see each other again soon, maybe even in upstate New York once Pistol was released?

Hector drove down the dirt road and turned onto the pavement on our way out of town. Everyone went about their day as usual—carrying their boards to the beach, parking cars, or selling necklaces to tourists. The beach was over my left shoulder, though I distinctly remembered rolling into town that first time in the opposite direction. I glimpsed the ocean through the breaks in the coconut palms as we picked up speed. The waves came in and out, in and out.

Goodbye, Tamarindo. The wonderful shit show would have to go on without me. I'll be back in a few months, I'd told everyone, but deep down I didn't know when I might be there again. I wondered what would happen to everyone.

I wanted to say goodbye to the Loonies Carla and Craig; Kelly Zak; and Rafa at the surf shop; Sarita and Jason; my surf instructor, Jonathan; Sarah Long; Mack White; Lt. Colonel Trapp; my neighbor, Sarah; Jaime Pelligro at the bookstore. I'd miss Tico Hendrix telling bad jokes; Snooky; Alyssa; Nayla, the yoga/Spanish teacher/personal chef; cute Mishe; Trevor and Blake; and the Buzz. I wanted to slap one last high four to Fausto, and wish well the old *pegeyegua* that parked cars; Big Chuck; Pepito the *mariposa*; Louisa and Thor, the Danes; Cristiano, the best bartender in the world; the Brazilian, Avellino; my good friend, Antonio; Row's sister, Sandra; and Dayana and Marcella. I'd cherished the memories of a blind dog named Disco, warm-hearted Magally, Grace, and Sofia; Gringo Grant; Bernard the French photographer; Marcello, who knew when the ships came in, and yes, even my misguided friend Tania. They were all a big part of my life, my family for that year, whether good or bad. We laughed and cried and drank and fought and loved together, but we'd been *together*, and sometimes that was the best thing.

I dozed on the way to Liberia. The sun felt good on my face. I perked up a few kilometers before the airport. "*Bienvenidos a Costa Rica!*" a billboard said, showing white people in white linen pants with perfect pearly white teeth walking on a pristine beach. I tapped Hector on the arm, signaling him to keep driving straight, into Liberia.

"No vamos a el aeropuerto. Ir al carcel," I said. We had one last stop on the way to the airport—the jail.

"*En serio?*" he said, but he'd already merged out of the turn lane.

"Si—una mas vez mi bueno amigo." Yes, one more time, my good friend. It was Saturday, visiting day, and I had one more important item of business with Pistol before I got on a plane.

I checked in at the jail. The line moved quickly and the guards nodded me through without any problems. For the first time they didn't even search me, though I only carried one item.

As I walked in a group of Tica ladies approached me, a mother and a grandmother and a daughter. They wore freshly ironed dresses and simple shoes. One carried a pillow, a bag of food, and a bundle of twine. The grandmother carried a bible and rosary beads, which she fondled nervously. Visiting a newcomer, I thought. They seemed frazzled, and asked me:

"Pardon. Where do us go D2B? Sorry—first time jail."

I told them in Spanish that I was happy to help and explained where it was. I invited them to follow me there.

"*Ahhh, gracias por Dios!*" the lady said. "*My son here and we come first time.*"

"It will be okay," I smiled softly. "It will all be okay. Just come with me."

They stuck close to me, taking my arm as we passed the permanent housing cells where the prisoners hollered. We walked back and I showed them D2B.

"*Gracias para su ayuda. Tu eres muy amable,*" she said—thank you for your help. You are very nice.

We got to D2B and I helped them inside. I saw Pistol and said "hello" and we walked to the back wall of the courtyard to sit down.

"Hey, Normando, what's happening, man?"

"Not much, just coming to see your ass one more time before I get on a plane."

"Yeah, you psyched to see your family?"

"I am—it will be good. They're going to pick me up at the airport. But, of course, I feel sort of..."

"I know, Normando. Don't even sweat it."

"Okay," I said.

We looked around at the prisoners in the courtyard and their visitors.

"You gonna take good care of yourself?" I asked.

"Sure thing. I'm excited to get over to the other cell soon. They're just processing my plea agreement, so it should happen any day now. I know plenty of guys over there so it will be an easy transition."

"Cool, I think that will be good for you. Of course, let me know if there's anything I can do to help. Your mom can email me any time, but I'll have my U.S. number again so her or Theresa can call me, too."

"I appreciate that," he said. "By the way, did they win?"

"Who's that?"

"The Phillies. You never told me if they won the World Series."

It took a moment to register. That was way back in October and now it was springtime, but of course he had no way of knowing in there—about *anything*.

"Nah, they lost to the Cardinals in the playoffs. Couldn't hit the ball worth a shit and Ryan Howard blew out his Achilles on the last play."

He looked disappointed. "Oh well, there's always next year."

"Next year, I promise."

Suddenly, I realized that we were missing a third of our gringo crew.

"Hey, where's Black Beans?" I asked.

"Hahaha, he got transferred to another unit. But he actually had a favor to ask you. His Canadian girlfriend is living in Manhattan now. He made something for her, and wanted to see if you could carry it back to the States and then mail it?"

"Yeah, sure. I can do that."

"He said to be careful because it's sort of fragile." He handed me a lump, wrapped in newspaper and heavily taped.

"And what about you and Theresa? What do you think will happen with her once you get out of here?"

"I don't know, but I love her, Norm. I have way too much time to think in here—there's nothing else to do—but she's the only thing in this world that makes me feel better."

"That's cool, man."

"Would you tell her I said that?"

"Nope—you tell her yourself. I think she needs to hear that from you."

"Okay, Normando, I will. Hey, you better get going—you're going to miss your flight."

"Yeah, I only have ninety minutes, but before I go, I have something for you, too. It's not much, but I hope it can make even one day in here a little easier."

I handed him the book—the one and only copy of *my* book.

"Well, I'll be damned. You did it," he said, turning it over and thumbing through. "I like the cover."

"Thanks."

"Yeah. You actually did it…"

We hugged and slapped each other on the back, like homies do, and I walked toward the door. I looked back and he was sitting on the concrete bench, already turning the first page.

I walked out of D2B, for the last time ever. I walked by the blue courts where Pistol had scored a goal and the German Shepherd had sniffed at me, the spot where the old man in the wheelchair usually sat. He wasn't there.

I asked the guard, who knew me by then, where the guy in the wheelchair was.

"Quien?" he asked.

"You know, the nice old man. The one in the wheelchair who sits here with his cup out?"

"I don't know who you talk about," he said.

"The wheelchair guy? I've seen him every time I've been here."

"Sorry, but no one wheelchair in this jail."

Maybe he misunderstood, or his English was bad? I couldn't figure it out, so I just followed the sidewalk. But his words echoed in my head, the voice of that friendly, crippled Svengali whose presence had made no sense to me, and now I was told didn't exist at all: *"Are you sure you're on the right path?"*

I left the prison and got in the taxi with Hector and we started rolling our way out of the potholed, dusty maze.

"Como esta su amigo?" he asked.

"Él es mejor, Hector. This time I actually think he's going to be fine."

We got on the paved road and drove toward the airport. I held the package wrapped in newspaper, weighing it in my hands. It occurred to me that I shouldn't bring something through airport security without thoroughly searching it. For all I knew, he was trying to smuggle drugs or something illegal and using me as the fall guy. I ripped the tape and paper off. The last thing I needed was to get involved with…

Inside was a heart, a wooden heart that he'd crafted out of popsicle sticks and glue, about the size of a jewelry box. It had an inscription on the top, crudely etched, like kids might carve into a tree: *"I love you, April. You have my heart."* There was a slip of paper with her name and mailing address in Manhattan.

I wrapped up the wooden heart in the newspaper and put it in my backpack, carefully. Hector sped on, checking his rearview mirrors. I closed my eyes and must have drifted off because I had the strangest dream: that I was living in a little surf town on the beach in the tropics, a place called *Tamarindo*, that was so crazy it couldn't have been real.

"We are here, buddddy," Hector said, startling me. *"Which airplane is yours?"*

CHAPTER 41

THE BEGINNING OF THE END OF THE BEGINNING

(APRIL, ONE MONTH LATER)

On the morning of April 18, 2012 I was in the United States, in California, visiting friends and ramping up for a book release party.

I got an email from Fat Doug:

> *Dude, I received the following email from one of the owners of Caracollas. One of their workers has a friend who is in jail, so maybe this is how they heard this.*
>
> *-Doug*
>
> Can you get in touch with Norm and ask him to call Joey's lawyers…he got into a fight and is in solitary. His lawyers need to help him. Gary said you might have Norm's number.
>
> Thanks,

I emailed him back immediately that I was on it, then wrote an email to Joey's sister, Elizabeth, with the information. I didn't want to shock Betty too badly so it was best that she tell the family. She wrote me back:

> *I just left you a voicemail. We have been working on it all day. We last spoke to him @ 8:20 a.m. today. He was extremely upset & said officials were not treating him well. Ever since he was moved to this building a couple of weeks ago, they have targeted him by threatening him, stealing his supplies & extorting money. If you hear anything else, please contact us immediately. My cell is 555-555-5555. Thank you!*

Later that day, I got an email from his mom:

> *Joey was moved to the other building and he has had all his stuff stolen and been threatened... He must have had enough... I have been trying to find out about him but have not been able to so I cannot tell you much...*

The next day, I got a message from Theresa. She asked me not to discuss it with anyone else. Of course I understood, I said—I'd just received the email and forwarded it. She filled me in on what happened:

Once Pistol was sentenced they'd moved him to the permanent housing cells. We were all relieved. There were four units where he could possibly go and he had friends in three of them. He applied to be put in any of those three. They put him in the fourth, where he knew no one.

It was a set-up, he knew it from the beginning. Pistol guessed it was the work of the prison warden, who hated him for the additional scrutiny and problems he'd caused. Or maybe Lena had something to do with it? Either way, they threw him in the worst possible unit with a bunch of crackheads.

The prison didn't deliver his mail for three weeks, then gave him everything the day before he was transferred, so he walked into his new unit with an armful of mail and packages that the crackies eyeballed. He put the things in his locker but he knew they could get in without a key—you could unscrew the whole locking mechanism easily.

There was a dreadlock from the Caribbean side that ran shit in there, a skinny rotten basehead. From day one he started stealing Pistol's things. Every time he left the cell something went missing. The other prisoners harassed him and even the guards threatened his life.

I'd given Pistol my watch for Christmas, just a cheap plastic white thing. One night he took it off and placed it next to him on the top bunk before falling asleep. When he woke up in the morning it was gone—the dreadlock had crawled over him during the night and taken it.

Joey snapped. He jumped down and pulled the guy out of bed by his legs and confronted him. The dread pulled a buck knife on him. Pistol backed up and then ran outside to tell the nearest guard. They saw the dread slithering off in the other direction to go hide the knife. When he walked back into the cell, Pistol charged and hockey-checked him into the concrete wall, rattling him semi-conscious to the floor. All hell broke loose and everyone started fighting. He got in two more good shots to the guy's face before he was pulled off.

The guards let the dread go with a warning but dragged Pistol to a holding cell, just a small room with a barred door where prisoners met with their lawyers. They left him in there for a while, but when they returned they wanted to throw him back in his same cell, with the dread and the others.

"No way, they'll kill me in there," Pistol argued, but the guards didn't care and went to enter his cell. Pistol refused their entry by blocking the door, wedging himself against a concrete half wall, feet braced against the door. The guards couldn't get in and rattled the bars and threatened him. "Hell, no," Pistol said. "Not until I can see my lawyer."

It was a standoff. They came back with more guards and tried to push their way in but couldn't. It was surprisingly easy for Pistol to keep them at bay with just his legs. He laughed at them, which only made them more furious. They would disappear for an hour or two and come back with more guards and try again. He stayed in there all night with no food or water and pissed in the waste basket. The guards came back and pointed mace through the bars and sprayed him. He held up his t-shirt over his eyes to block it. He thought it would hurt but surprisingly it didn't burn his eyes at all, though it did burn his skin. Maybe it was the adrenaline or that he was sweating so profusely, he thought. Either way, the guards were indignant and must have thought he was some sort of superman. They left him in there for another night. Another prisoner managed to sneak him in some water and passed a note to Black Beans, who got word out to Pistol's attorney to contact the U.S. Embassy, and then me and his family.

The next day, the guards tried to get him out again, this time with eight of them, but still Pistol held them off. They took out their nightsticks and whacked him in the legs. But he just pulled back one foot, still keeping the door closed with the other foot, and then switched when they tried to hit that one. They still couldn't get in. On the third day they both realized something had to give, so he agreed to let them in *if* they moved him to his original cell until he could see his lawyer, where he'd been safe for all those months, which he wanted in writing. They agreed.

The lawyer came and caused a stink and the warden had enough of the whole situation, so they agreed to have him transferred to another prison. He was being moved to *La Reforma* in the main city of San Jose, the biggest and baddest prison in all of Costa Rica. They handcuffed him and put him on a prison bus. He was going to a new prison where he would be the only gringo out of 1,600 prisoners and didn't know a soul.

God help him.

CHAPTER 42

ADVENTURES PAST MIDNIGHT

(OCTOBER, 2012, SIX MONTHS LATER)

I rose from a warm, fluffy hotel bed at 5:00 a.m. and left the light off as I packed my things, trying to be quiet as I slipped on my jeans. The room smelled faintly of coconuts and the ocean.

"Do you have to go, gringito? Es mu temprano. I no want you go," Bella said, stirring from sleep and rolling over into the indention where I'd laid.

"Yes, I have to go. You know—to see my friend."

"*Yo entiendo. I know. En La Reforma,*" she said.

"Yes. I…I'm a little nervous about it, to be honest."

"*Come here, come to me, gringito,*" she said, sitting up and patting the bed next to her.

I went over and kissed her on the forehead.

"*Let me tell you story from my hospital,*" she said. In the six months since I'd seen her in Tamarindo, Bella had graduated from the university with a degree in psychology. There were no jobs for her so she volunteered at a children's hospital for poor people. She had to take a chicken bus three hours each way from Puntarenas to get there, but she loved the work.

"*One day, playing with little boy, very sick, Norm. But he is happy when see me, he laugh a lot. 'I love you, Bella,' he say and forget he sick and pain. And he mother say, 'God bless you, Bella, thank you, he so happy.' I cry of happiness and hug him and tell him, 'Tu ocupas un lugar especial en nuestro corazon.'*"

"You occupy a special place in my heart?"

"*Si, almost. En 'our' hearts,*" she said. "*The next day I go hospital and they give me news that the little boy die in morning. I cry but I remember his laugh. I always keep him special in my heart.*"

I shook my head.

"God give us life, Norm. We know we here today but maybe no tomorrow. But there are good moments in life that cannot be erased, that will never go away. Remember those moments. Keep them special place inside."

I kissed her again.

"Thank you, Bella. That's good advice. It helps. *You* help."

She smiled and looked at me with brown eyes.

"Oh, do you want you shirt back?" she said, starting to take off my yellow shirt that she was wearing. *"I like—it smell good, like you."*

"No, you keep it."

"Mi gringito, it was too short a visit. Te extraño mucho—I will miss you much."

"Yo tambien, Bella. Take care of yourself."

I hugged her and promised that I'd message her later on that I was okay, and then I took my bag and I left, closing and the door behind me, softly.

I took the elevator down to the lobby and stood out front, waiting for Theresa. The hotel was in a commercial area with signs for the Home Depot, Denny's, and Subway, though this time I was in San Jose, Costa Rica. I was thirsty, but I didn't drink any water—you never want to have to use the bathroom where we were going. I wore sneakers and made sure my passport was in my pocket. The old instincts were back.

Theresa pulled up in her blue Volkswagen and I got in.

"So good to see you again, Normie! Give me a big hug!"

"You too, Theresa."

"We appreciate you coming all the way down here to visit. He's so excited to see you."

It had been a long trip from my new home in San Juan del Sur, Nicaragua—a taxi to Revis, a bus ride to the border, a couple of sweaty hours crossing over to Costa Rica, and back on the bus for an hour to Liberia. But instead of stopping there, where it all looked familiar and I knew the road to the jail, the bus kept going, four hours on the road through the mountains to San Jose, then an hour in the city and a taxi from the bus station to the hotel. I hadn't been to San Jose in over a decade, since '99, and it all looked Americanized and was super expensive. But at least I got to meet up with Bella and enjoy luxuries at the hotel I wasn't accustomed to: a fluffy bed, television, and a hot shower.

Theresa and I drove into the city. It was 7:00 a.m. on a Sunday morning so not many people were out, just security guards and mothers shuffling off the bus, their hair still wet. We pulled into a McDonald's and went in and bought breakfast for us and for Pistol.

"This prison is different. You'll see, but be careful because there are a lot of very poor people from bad neighborhoods who go there. It's really ghetto," she said.

Hearing that turned my stomach, but then I thought, "Ah, what the hell's the point?" I'd been through it all before and there was nothing to worry about, or if something went down, then worrying wasn't going to help. Besides, I'd been living in Nicaragua, the second-poorest country in the western hemisphere, in the toughest neighborhood in town, Barrio Chino, so I wasn't about to let those city Ticos shake me up.

We got back in the car and headed toward the prison. The neighborhoods blended together, storefronts locked behind metal grates and people hurrying to get off the streets. It was all so different than the jungle.

"After we get out, I want to drive you past my high school because it's not far off, and I need to stop by my mom's house to get some things so you can finally meet her! But she doesn't know I'm still talking to Joey or visiting him, so don't say anything," Theresa said.

"Of course. Yeah, that would be nice."

"Okay, this is it—we're here," she said, pulling up and parking in the dirt yard of an old man's house. He was lucky enough to live next to the prison so he made a living renting safe parking spaces for $3 a pop. I hid my wallet and iPhone under the floor mat and we got out. The entrance looked more like a bustling flea market, busloads of people arriving every few minutes, but there it was—"*Diez Puntas,* Ten Points," the medium security compound of *La Reforma.* I'd Googled it the night before and read a few articles about riots and guards abusing and killing prisoners before I shut my laptop.

"Come on down here, Normie, there are three lines and we need to get in the last one," Theresa said, navigating over a swampy ditch. I didn't see any lines—just people crammed in together trying not to fall into mud puddles.

We took our place and I looked around without making eye contact, instinctively scanning who might be trouble. But it wasn't so bad—the people didn't seem that poor or threatening to me. We waited along a chain link fence running the prison grounds. Inside, a hundred meters away, I could see boarded-up cabañas infested with brown prisoners in wife beaters, pacing and whistling.

We waited in line for an hour. I didn't mind because the sun wasn't so hot as in Liberia. In fact, I wore a light sweatshirt, and Theresa marveled at how I'd become accustomed to the heat. I hung our heavy shopping bags on the fence in front of us so we didn't have to hold them the whole time. Theresa snacked on her McDonald's but I wasn't hungry. More for Pistol.

We got to the front and Theresa split left into the woman's line. I gave them my passport and the name Joseph Francesco and they let me in. They checked the bags and patted me down in a long concrete hallway and then I was inside.

I was relieved to see how different this prison was; everyone could walk around outdoors, and only had to be locked in their cabañas at night. Theresa caught up with me and we walked inside another fence, and there was Pistol.

It was good to see him again. It felt different, more relaxed, and we were both such different people than only a year before, when we'd both sweated out our survival in the jungle.

"Hey, Normando, what's up, bud?" He hugged me and then gave a hug and a kiss to Theresa, putting his arm around her shoulder, pulling her close. I realized that it was the first time I'd seen them together since I'd moved to Tama. That blew me away.

"Let's go over here to the visiting area so we can sit down," he said. I walked behind them, watching their silhouette become one as Theresa rested her head against his shoulder. He smiled and looked into her eyes. "So *that's* why I've done all of this," I thought. Finally, I understood, and it was all worth it.

Pistol led us into a hangar-like building with open walls and a basketball court. People were everywhere, laid out on blankets, leaning against walls, and sitting at tables. The women were dressed like hoochies, handing their babies to the men, who held them up and marveled how big they'd grown. It was a Rorschach blot of bandanas, shirtless flesh, nice sneakers left unlaced, and faded tattoos: human beings who used to have names but now were all numbers. The whole thing looked like an emergency shelter after a bad storm.

Then again, it was nice to see families united, under any circumstances. They ate homemade meals, cuddled and chatted, and did something that involved hip thrusts under the blankets. Wait, it was happening over there. And over there, too. And that girl had her tits out, and everywhere there were stray hands working under the blankets.

We walked up a wide terrace of concrete steps and sat on blankets already spread out near the top. I thought about taking off my shoes so I didn't track mud onto them, but Pistol told me not to worry about it. We settled in.

"It's great to see you, bro. How's this place treating you?"

"Well, it's still prison, and it still sucks, but it's a lot better than Liberia. They're more organized here, there's more structure. The guards are really professional, unlike the last jail. Two years ago, there was a scandal here because the warden was selling conjugal visits, phone time, and visiting privileges to the inmates. They busted him and replaced his whole staff so now they don't mess around—they'll transfer inmates right up to general population if they fuck up, and no one wants to go there."

"That's good you ended up in here. What's the setup like? It seems less crowded."

"Not really, there are 1,600 inmates here, but there's more room to spread out—except in the cabañas, where we sleep. There are 78 inmates in my cell, and when I sleep, there are 20 people sleeping within a meter of me. But they only have five people on the floor, which isn't bad."

"Damn, can you transfer out of there to a good behavior house or something?"

"I can but I don't want to. I know everyone where I'm at and they treat me good. If I transferred somewhere new the guards might bust my balls or I'd get written up for smoking and either get sent to *La Reforma* or to a cell where I don't know anyone. So I'll just stick it out for now."

It was good to see him safe, but I felt a little guilty I'd left him alone while I was back in the States, getting lazy on sushi and beer on my book tour.

I asked him to catch me up on his case, and he was more than happy to fill me in. He delved right in, taking out a folder and a notebook jammed full of handwritten notes, translations, photocopied articles, and court documents. He flipped through them frantically, cross-referencing and reading heavily underlined passages like a mad scientist close to a discovery.

He went on and on for an hour, letting me in on the magnitude of his future civil case against the state, which would eventually set precedent and get marijuana legalized in Costa Rica and bring the whole corrupt judicial system in Guanacaste to its knees. He would sue those responsible for his demise, and the country of Costa Rica would end up writing him a huge check. I took notes and asked questions as he outlined the false testimony, contradictions, conveniently lost evidence, and forged paperwork the state had stacked against him.

I was hooked, the charmed snake rising from the basket. He didn't mean to do it, his passion was just contagious, and there's no one more passionate than a prisoner discussing his case. I'd had six months to think about the whole thing, the perspective of writing the first-draft about our journey together, 350 pages of snake pits and sunshine waiting for me back on my laptop, and I couldn't deny that he was being screwed—the OIJ, the police, and even Lena had broken more laws ensuring his arrest and conviction than he ever did growing marijuana. My old friend was a little crazy, but he also happened to be right.

"When my attorney got me transferred to San Jose, I was a more than a little scared because I'd heard so many bad things about *Reforma*. They handcuffed me and put me on a prison bus, and when I got off every single prisoner was at the fence yelling at me. Talk about intimidating, there are 1,600 prisoners and I'm the only gringo."

"Yeah, I'd say! Seriously, not one other gringo?"

"Just me. There was a crackhead white guy from Florida, but he kept getting beat up because he was borrowing money from people and not paying them back, so they transferred him. They assigned me to my unit and I was worried going in, but the guys were cool. They took me in and told me what's up. The big boss man was in my cell and getting released in a week, so they even gave me his bed when he left. I told them that I didn't mind staying on the floor, but they said it was no problem."

"That's pretty cool, actually. Damn, I'm glad to hear that. So, are there still a lot of problems in here?"

"It's different, because only one guy is allowed to bring drugs into the whole prison, an old timer that's in my cell. It all goes through him, so it's a lot more organized. But everyone smokes crack; that's the drug in here because it's cheap. It's crazy, but they all smoke it right out in the open. I play basketball with this Columbian dude—he's really cool and a great baller—and he smokes like five rocks right in front of me and then gets out there and starts hitting 30-foot jumpers. It's incredible."

"*You gringos talk way too much,*" Theresa chimed in, bored as Pistol and I bantered. *"Always it comes back to sports."*

"Well, we *are* sitting near a basketball court," I joked.

"*Noooo! It's for football—a real sport!*" she protested, and we laughed. I noticed a string of people shuffling up to a door on the side of the court, none of whom looked pleased.

"What's that line for?" I asked.

"That's the line for the bathroom. If you have to go, you might have to wait for a while, and I hope you brought your own toilet paper."

"Oh, I did," I said.

"*No you didn't! Really*?" Theresa said.

"Sure—I know how it works at these places," I said and pulled out five folded sheets of TP from my back pocket, waving them around.

"Wow, you came prepared! Well, that's good, because there's a big line for the bathroom and it's disgusting."

"*And that's also why I guarantee that Joey didn't take a shower today,*" Theresa said.

"Nope, no shower, you're right. On visiting day I don't even bother because everyone is trying to get in. Guys get up at 3:30 a.m. to get in line for the shower. By the time it's your turn, it's so dirty that you're better off not showering."

He looked good, healthy. He seemed to be in a bright mood and was clear-eyed. But as we talked more, I saw some lines around his mouth that hadn't been there before, maybe a little more hollow in his cheeks. Someone else meeting him for the first time might guess that he was older than just 39. I mean 40. His teeth looked a little yellow. I asked if they got free medical and dental care and he said yes, it was all provided.

"I brought you a bunch of clothes, but I guess they don't allow anything but food in on visiting day?"

"*Yeah, I have to bring it back another time,*" Theresa said.

"Okay, well, there's plenty in there. What do you need?"

"I need athletic shorts. And socks," Pistol said.

"Yeah, I have all of that. And tons of underwear if you need it. For some reason, my luggage was filled with nothing but underwear when I first moved down here."

"I don't even wear it most of the time," he said.

"Me neither."

"*But you're wearing some now, right?*" Theresa asked, noticing the waistband of my boxer briefs sticking out of my jeans.

"Well, *TODAY* I am!" I said.

"Of course, *TODAY* you are," Pistol joked.

"Yeah, when I visit the prison, I wear *three* pairs, just in case!"

Our laughter was interrupted only by guys trying to sell us stuff—wooden toy boats and homemade lottery tickets—just like in the last prison, but everyone in there had a city swag. Even though it was tough, it wasn't as chaotic and desperate as in Liberia. In contrast, I realized just how horrible those concrete jungle cages had been. Wow, had that really been less than a year ago? It seemed like a different lifetime.

Pistol nodded to a guy with a shaved head and gold teeth, wearing big construction boots with one pant leg rolled up. He climbed the concrete terraces toward us.

"He's a good guy, in for murder and got 30 years," he said. "Though it's weird—there are only thirteen Columbians in the whole jail. I don't know why."

He came up and we all talked for a while. It was good that he had guys like this looking out for him, I thought.

He said goodbye, but before the guy walked off, I noticed that his fly was down. Out of instinct I yelled, "Hey!" to him and made the international sign for "zip up your fly" with the corresponding whistle, meant to simulate the zipping sound. Or at least I thought it was international, but apparently it hadn't reached Columbia yet. Maybe they were one of those eco-friendly nations that went Velcro a long time ago? Or maybe he'd left it down intentionally, some sort of signal to the other prisoners that meant "Big Chooch sent a message—we're moving at midnight. Stay cool." I had no idea, but he sure was confused. I did it again, making the motion of someone zipping up and mumbled, "Your fly is down" to him, but of course he didn't get it and walked back over to us, thinking I was working out some new cool handshake.

Now I was committed to helping my brotha out—it was Man Code that I couldn't let him walk around like that, and unless I explained it, he'd forever think that Pistol had some kinky, deviant gringo friends. How exactly *does* one tell a Columbian murderer doing life in a Costa Rican prison that his fly is down? What would *you* have done? A wave of the absurd nature of my life washed over me. How the hell did I *get* to this place? Just two years earlier I was wearing a suit and tie every day and pulling down six figures ($23,198, just like it's listed on my taxes if the IRS is reading this). And now *this* was my most pressing dilemma?

I could keep telling him that his fly was down, but it would do no good because he didn't speak English. My Spanish had advanced nicely—I could use the preterite tense and conjugate irregular verbs, but my Spanish teachers hadn't prepared me for *this.* Should I point to my own fly? Hell no, my hand wasn't going anywhere near the vicinity of my man junk in that place.

I guess I could point to *his* fly? Ummm, no can do—likewise, he might take it as an offer for some "under the blanket" extracurriculars.

The best I could do was, again, simulate the action of zipping up a fly with a series of whistles, this time with English and Spanish in the mix and carefully orchestrated winks to clue him in to the private nature of the matter.

"Hey ,amigo. Perdón. Your (whistle) is (wink)."

What possibly could I mean? He went to shake my hand again, followed by a fist bump, but I pushed it away, clearing the air by waving my hands around like I was shaking up an Etch-a-Sketch. Let's start over.

"Lo siento, hermano, (wink) but your zipper-O (shrillllll whistle) is (slowwwwww whistle, double wink) down-oh."

Nothing.

He was past confused, and now we were in a bizarre game of charades. Did I want an AM radio? No. Okay, mayonnaise? I was hungry and wanted mayonnaise? That couldn't be it. Someone important was landing in an airplane? How many syllables? Sounds like…"your SKY is FROWN."

Nada.

Pistol and Theresa looked at me with blank faces, in shock that I'd chosen this exact moment to completely lose my gringo mind, scooting farther away in case my behavior started a riot.

I tried everything, but blank eyes just looked back at me.

"Que?"

I couldn't take it. It was driving me mad.

"No! No fistbump, God dammit! I'm not shaking your hand! *Su PANTALONES*! Your FLY-O is *abajo*! Your *WHISTLLLLLLEEEEEE* is *WIIIIINNNNKKKKK*!!!"

Finally, the light went on when he looked down, though it was probably to reach for the shank in his pants to shut me up. He half-turned and zipped up unceremoniously and all four of us exhaled. The Columbian murderer looked the most relieved out of everyone, his forehead beaded with sweat and his face a little pale. He gave a half-hearted goodbye, without shaking my hand, and ran back to his cell as fast as he could. Oh wait, his shirt was tucked into the back of his pants. Maybe I should….ahhh forget it.

We talked for a while longer. My legs were falling asleep on those concrete benches. I kept looking around, but it was the same prisoners, the same guards, the same people moving under blankets. I could only imagine the strain of that being your whole world.

Pistol sensed we were getting uncomfortable. "Let's go for a walk. I'll show you around the place," he said. We got up and stretched and walked outside.

There was a lot of open space in the prison. We followed a sidewalk past grass lots and clusters of buildings. He explained that it used to be a prison for teenagers and kids, and that's why there were jungle gyms and soccer goals.

"Over there is where I start work every day. I got a job picking up trash on the grounds. I like it because I get to just stroll around and keep to myself, but be out in the sun," Pistol said.

"That's great that you have a job to help keep busy."

"Yeah, it doesn't really pay anything, and I just give the money to some guys in my cell who really need it."

"That's cool of you."

"I could make more working in the shop, but I won't do it. They have a contract with a U.S. company, so a lot of prisoners assemble those phone adapters. You know, those little jacks you plug into the wall or your computer? I hate it because they pay the guys pennies compared to what they sell them for, but it's still a lot for the guys in here."

"Damn, so not only do they exploit Third World labor but Third World *prison* labor? That's shady as hell. They must have really bribed the right people to get that contract."

"I tried to organize the guys into writing a letter demanding higher wages and some sort of benefits, but they don't want to jeopardize their jobs. As long as the money keeps coming in, I guess..."

Pistol pointed out the other cells, the clinic, and the mess hall.

"One of the few funny things about this place is when they automatically unlock the cell doors every morning. All of the prisoners run to the mess hall to get in line for coffee. With so many prisoners, it takes half an hour to get our food, so they come charging out of the gate like it's a horse race, grown men sprinting in boxer shorts, wearing flip-flops, or barefoot, pushing each other out of the way to get to the front. I watch it every morning and laugh."

We swam through a sea of inmates, all staring holes into us. I reminded myself how to play it: keep your cool, relax your face so they can't see your fear, walk slowly, chill, but proud. Don't make eye contact but don't look away, either. Remember that you can take most of these guys one on one. Or even two. Let 'em try something—I didn't care. I knew that it was all just a game, that they were trying to punk me. Living in Barrio Chino in San Juan del Sur sure had changed me. Then again, I realized I wouldn't feel so tough up at *La Reforma*.

There were some rough-looking characters and Pistol gave us the play-by-play on all of them as we walked.

We passed a prisoner who had a big chunk missing from his nose. I mean, it was a *big* open hole in the flesh and you could see the red guts and bone inside of his nose. Pistol told me that he'd done so much coke that it had burned through his nasal passages, leaving him like that for life. He was shucking and jiving with a group of prisoners like everything was normal, but I wouldn't want to be around that guy when he sneezed.

A shirtless teen walked by. He was a cutter, dozens of horizontal razor blade slashes on each arm, fresh, open wounds. He seemed to be proud of them. Pistol speculated that he'd cut himself to get transferred out of *La Reforma,* knowing that they'd want to do a psychological evaluation at *Diez Puntos*. Easier time.

The cutter looked back at Pistol, said something to his buddy with a snicker, and then glanced back again.

"What the FUCK you looking at, Chino?" Pistol barked. I stood upright and got ready, fists out of pockets, but it was nothing. I was shocked by Pistol's hardness, the street chirp of his reaction. I hadn't seen that side of him before—he was getting used to life in there. What would he be like by the time he got out?

We strolled in a loop around the grounds, dodging prisoners and trying to stay in the shade. Pistol stopped when he saw yet another nondescript Latin youth in his early twenties, just a skin-and-bones kid, his hair freshly combed, holding a photograph. Pistol patted him on the back and introduced us. He had a smile on his face but was missing a front tooth. I don't remember his name, but Pistol said the kid was from Nicaragua.

"Si, el es verdad, hermano? Yo vivo en Nica—en San Juan del Sur," I told the kid. When he heard that I lived in his home country, he beamed from ear to ear, amazed that he was actually meeting some who lived in his homeland, and a *gringo* no less!

"He's a good guy, probably my best friend in here," Pistol told us. I understood that to call him "a friend" at all meant something. "But I feel bad for him. When he was a boy he snuck over the border from Nicaragua during their Civil War, and ended up living on the streets in San Jose. But he got arrested for stealing food and thrown in here."

"Damn, that's rough," I said.

"But that's not even the start of it." Pistol motioned to the kid and he handed me the photograph. It was faded and cracked, the edges worn by fingerprints.

"That's his mother. It was taken more than ten years ago, the day he left Nicaragua. After the war, he had no way of knowing where his mother and family were, or if they even survived. But just a few weeks ago he managed to track down his mom in Nicaragua. He finally talked to her on the phone and she even agreed to come visit. I've never seen him so happy."

A fresh-faced, skinny Nicaraguan woman stared back at me from the photograph, holding a toddler in her arms.

"But on the way to the prison that day she got in a car accident and died. When he found out he didn't cry at all, he just sort of blanked out. He's been wandering around in shock ever since, showing that picture to everyone at the prison, asking if anyone's seen her."

I went to hand him the photograph back, but he pushed it into my hands again, pointing to it as if to ask if I'd seen his mom in Nicaragua. I shook my head softly and put my hand on his shoulder, squeezing as I put the photograph back into his hands.

"It hasn't really sunk in for him, yet," Pistol said.

"Shit, Joey. Can I Western Union some money to the rest of his family in Nicaragua to bring to him?" I asked.

"No, he doesn't have anyone left. But I hook him up and he watches over me. He's never asked me for anything until the other day. He wanted me to send him $100 once I get out of here so he could get a fake tooth put in. That's what it costs, I guess—$100 a tooth."

"$100, huh?"

"Oh yeah. But he likes it in here, he's grown up in this prison. A couple times he was released and a few days later he wandered back to the front gates and begged the guards for leftover food. He has no idea how to adjust, what to do, how to provide for himself on the outside. But in here he has family. He gets three meals a day, a roof over his head, a bed, running water, and medical care. This is heaven to him."

Heaven. That was heaven to someone. When we said goodbye, I said, *"Dale pues,"* to the kid, a Nicaraguan slang saying. He loved it and left with an even bigger smile on his face.

As if by telepathy, everyone stirred from their blankets and their spots in the shade. A moment later the loudspeaker blared and the guards began rustling everyone toward the exit; visiting hours were over. Lines formed at the back of the registration building where people collected their passports.

"Well, you guys better get in line," Pistol said.

We got to the gate and once again I didn't know what to say. So I just hugged Pistol and told him to hang in there and I'd see him soon. It all sounded familiar, but he understood. Things would go on; I would live my life outside, press on with my next book in Nicaragua, and he would do what he had to survive in there. But I had a feeling that he was gonna be all right. I was touched by how most of the guys had shown Pistol compassion, taken him in when the obvious plot line would be to fuck with the one and only gringo in jail. There was mercy tangled somewhere within all of that razor wire, a ray of grace that reached into the darkest of places, if you just looked for it long enough. Somehow that trip to the jail renewed my faith in humanity, not subtracted from it. I wasn't expecting that.

Theresa hugged Joey and told him she'd be back in two weeks and we walked out. I waited in line in the registration building for my passport. I was almost to the end of the long hallway when I heard yelling, commotion from behind me in the prison. Out of the corner of my eye I saw prisoners running, maybe toward a fight. Who knows? I took my passport and kept walking, north, toward my new home, and I didn't look back.

EPILOGUE

I'd headed back to the States from Tamarindo as the book was released. The customs agent at the Houston airport didn't know what to make of me, tan as a Tico, my passport riddled with Central American visa stamps, but without any luggage.

"What was the purpose of your stay in Costa Rica?" he asked. Good question. I assumed he didn't have an hour to hear the real story, so I gave him the short version:

"A little vacation, a little business."

"It says here on your passport that you were there for almost a year. But you don't have any bags to check?"

"I travel light."

He nodded me through and welcomed me back to the United States.

I sold a few books, but the Ellen show never called. That's okay, the victory for me was in the experience, the learning. I guess you can't write your second book until you've written your first book. But writing the book also opened doors and gave me opportunities that I never in a million years would have anticipated. I've reconnected with old friends and made countless new ones, reaching many people with a message of *pura vida*. Whenever I'm feeling discouraged, I'll get an email from a complete stranger who says they read my book and are inspired, an alchemy that amazes me every time. My life isn't easy by any stretch of the imagination and "success" is still a distant and foreign concept, but I'm doing what's in my heart, so for me there is no other path.

I realize now that some people are put in your life to help you learn patience, tolerance, and understanding. For those of you who fit that description during my time in Costa Rica I say, "Thank you."

For those of you who showed me kindness and love without expecting anything back, I say, "Thank you."

For los Ticos, and Tamarindo, and Costa Rica, I say, "Gracias por todos."

I still am without a house, an apartment, a car, or possessions other than some clothes and a laptop. I'm not making any money, so once again I count change for cups of coffee. But I don't miss a thing and have no desire to get them back. You could hand me the keys to a mansion and a Mercedes but I wouldn't want them—I'd rather have the simple truth in the shade of the Manchineel tree on a sunny day.

I guess it's like the Rasta say: "*Wanti wanti, no get it, getti getti, no want it.*"

After throwing a book release party in my home town and hanging out with the mayor, who confessed he's also a Charles Bukowski fan, I headed out west to visit Reilly in Colorado. We drank beers and reminisced about the old days, as usual, and he asked how Joey was doing. It was a triumphant return for me—we drove right past the Larimer County Detention Center on our way to Channel 9 News in Denver, where they had me live in studio on NBC to talk about my book.

My next stop was in California. We had a great book release party in Sacramento, and people were just amazing with their support and friendship.

The time I spent in the States was comfortable and fun, but pretty soon I was squirming again, the big unknown world calling to me. So in July I moved down to San Juan del Sur, Nicaragua. My friend, Gretchen, found me an apartment in a local neighborhood, Barrio Chino, on a hill overlooking the church and the town. I rescued a puppy off the street and named him Panda. He slept at my feet as I wrote every morning, Baileys in my coffee and Michael Franti singing on my headphones, morning chatter and the smoke from cooking fires rising up to me on the breeze. This time I kept my door open, and my friends Blake, Trevor, Tommas, Meghan, and Adam all stayed with me at some point. I made some great friends, like Big Wave Chris, a Canadian expat surfer, who filled me in on the news of the U.S. elections every evening as we traded punches in the boxing gym. I befriended Gaspar, the toughest guy in town, who's finishing law school. I told him that when he runs for mayor in a few years I'll come back and work for him. My Spanish was still a work progress, so after a few beers Gaspar yelled at me that I spoke like a Tico. I just told him, "*La calle es mi escuela, mae*"

My favorite part of the day was strolling through the streets, saying hi to everyone. Pretty soon all of the families and the grandmothers knew me, and waved when I passed, the children running out to play with Panda. I lived there for six months writing this book, and when I left, I threw a pig roast on top of the hill as a "thank you" to the people in my barrio. The electricity went out, so we couldn't see and the DJ couldn't play. But we didn't care—we turned on flashlights and someone turned the stereo on in their car. Then it started pouring rain, but we didn't care—we still drank and danced and hugged each other.

Once this book is released I'm thinking about where to go in the world and do it again. It would be easy to go back to Nicaragua, but I'm not looking for easy—not yet, anyway. So I think I'll head to Southeast Asia, where I can find a little hut on a secluded, beautiful beach and live like a pauper and write my heart out. I plan on studying muay thai and volunteering at an orphanage. Next time I want to do a small book, maybe about the plight of children in the Third World.

What I am doing still makes no logical sense, to me or to anyone around me. People still look at me funny and question what the hell I'm doing. I don't know, exactly, but at least I'm doing *something*.

You should do the same. Go on a journey. Do something that rings true in your heart, even if it doesn't add up in your mind. It doesn't need to be a geographical journey, but a journey toward your dreams. Take one little step in that direction, that's all I ask. Oh, but remember to smile, and believe.

There's not much else left to say.

Lena: We never danced on her desk, nor did I talk to her anymore after. I heard she lost the rental house to the bank and moved to San Jose, but who knows? I've gotten a few random "hellos" from her over the past year, but I don't have any contact.

Pepito: Pepito is still living and working in Tama. I think he's the real "chico mallllooooo" these days.

Tania: We stayed in touch on Facebook, where she encourages me to come visit Tama and party with her. I politely decline. But I wish her the best, I hold no grudges, and would be happy to crack a brew with her one day and reminisce about the big shit show, pouring a little out for Disco. But when the bill comes I'll just shrug.

Francisco: I haven't heard from Francisco, but I'm sure he's working hard and riding a wave somewhere.

Kelly Zak: Kelly and I didn't hang out a lot when I was in Tama, but I can tell he's a good, honest dude, so we stay in touch via Facebook and sometimes talk baseball. Rafa is still working with him and their surf shop, Kelly's, just got voted the #1 in Tamarindo by Lonely Planet.

Carla and Craig: They're doing great and we keep in touch. Gotta love the Loonies! (Especially since I'm 3,000 miles away so they can't pour me a drink.)

Sugar Ray: Ray and I became good friends and we're plotting our takeover of the world.

Row: I don't hear much from Row, but that's just because he's not a Facebook kind of guy. His friendship and vibe, and the bruises from playing him in basketball, are still with me to this day. Whenever Theresa sees him around town, he tells her to say "*hola*" to me. I say "hi" to his sister, Sandra, and Dayana and Marcella, on FB as well.

Fedor: He's still doing his thing in Tama and living *la vida loca*. I say "hi" via FB every once in a while and root for the Alajuela soccer team, just for him. I heard he has a nice girlfriend who is calming him down a little.

Antonio: Antonio and Shannon got married in Nicaragua and then had a beautiful ceremony in the States as well. We all keep in touch, and Lori, Shannon's mom and Antonio's mother-in-law, invited me to visit them in California if I'm ever around. What nice people—good for them.

Magally and Grace: Magally did go to San Jose to chase her dream of being a professional goalie, but she didn't make the team, and I guess she's back in Tama. I'm proud of her for trying. Grace is as sweet as ever, and I still thank them for being so nice to me. They all go to the festivals in Santa Cruz every year, and I'm sure they're still jumping fences.

Sarita: Sarita eventually succumbed to the stress of working 20 hours a day for no money, so she gave up the shop but still baked for other cafés and restaurants. After a short-lived career as a Tamarindo karaoke star, Sarita came back to the States, to Rhode Island, but I bet she'll be down to Tama again soon.

Cristiano: Cristiano, the best bartender in the world, went to work for Gringo Grant at Bar One for a while. He's now doing some traveling of his own, including a cross-country trek in the U.S.

Big Chuck: Chuck opened a restaurant delivery service in Tama. I ran into him on the beach in San Juan del Sur when he was up there with a friend doing their border shuffle. They rented motorcycles and rode out into the country when a stray dog ran out at his friend. He crashed the bike and the dog attacked him. He was rushed to a medical clinic and survived, but has a hell of a Nicaragua/motorcycle crash/dog mauling story to tell. Good thing he didn't need a penis transplant, because Wu Fat's is already spoken for.

Fat Doug: Doug got sick of the Critters and the bullshit in Tama and relocated to Asia. He gave his dog, Pinta, to Theresa to care for, and I see pictures of them on the beach all the time.

Gringo Grant: Grant did buy Bar One, and it looks like he's having the time of his life.

The Danes: I became good friends with Thor and Lousia when I was living in Pueblo del Mar and keep in touch with them from time to time.

Mishe: We're still friendly and she's still working as a bartender at Sharkey's.

The Oyer Sisters: I keep in touch with Melissa, Monique, and Michelle, who return to Tamarindo often. Or is it Michelle, Monique, and... hey look, a rooster! They're great people who are going to achieve wonderful things in life.

China and her crew of working girls: They are still in Tama, working seven days a week. I wish them all the health and happiness in the world.

Black Beans: I mailed his wooden heart right when I got back to the States. He's still in prison in Costa Rica, but no one is exactly sure where.

Hector: I haven't seen Hector since moving to nearby Nicaragua, but heard from him once on Facebook, where he said "*Hola, buddddyyy*!" I gave Theresa a duffel bag of clothing to give to him when she saw him.

Trevor and Blake: Trev and Blake opened an awesome café in San Juan del Sur called Banana Hamacas (Banana Hammocks). You can check them out at facebook.com/BananaHamacas and say "hi" if you're thinking of heading down. Trev moved to Columbia for a while and Blake is back and forth between Nica and Austin, Texas.

Tommas, Adam, and Meghan: Tommas is in Moscow teaching English. Adam surfed and played guitar in San Juan del Sur for a long time and then headed back to England to regroup. Meghan was back in

Jersey when Hurricane Sandy hit and devastated the shore. I'm trying to talk them all into coming to Asia with me.

Stephanie Chandler at Authority Publishing: Stephanie was a rock star during the whole process. There are self-publishers out there for a buck less, but no one cares more or produces a final product better than her. Check her out at www.AuthoriyPublishing.com if you're ever thinking of writing a book. We just met for the first time when I was visiting Sacramento and had a nice lunch. I'm committed to using her for all of my books, well, at least until *White Tiger Dumpster Fries* comes out in 2016. But I haven't put any thought into it or anything.

The Phillies: I don't want to talk about it, but there's always next year.

Reilly: Reilly is still living in Colorado, and his wonderful girlfriend, Melissa, just gave birth to their first child, a daughter named Tatum. I visit them once a year and I can't wait to meet her. We often laugh about the old days and wonder how we survived.

The Francensco family: Over the last six months I've checked in with Betty several times, but they communicate less and less. I have nothing but the utmost respect and admiration for Betty, her husband, and Pistol's sister, Elizabeth. This nightmare is very much still with them every day, and their strength and love and commitment are awe-inspiring.

Theresa: She's doing great, just getting through the normal ups and downs of life, but always with a smile on her face. I keep in touch with her via Facebook almost daily. I still consider her to be my little sister, and one of the best friends I've ever had.

Pistol: From what I hear, Pistol is doing okay, still throwing punches and flying kayaks, plotting his big case against the Costa Rican government that will lead to his imminent release. Theresa still visits him every two weeks. I hope he's right, and wish him the best. But first things first, I pray for his safety, day by day. I'm looking forward to getting an email saying that he's been released.

Bella: Bella still lives in Puntarenas with her family. Things are hard for them. She still cannot find a job in her field, so she keeps taking the bus for countless hours to volunteer at the children's hospital. We talk all the time and she says I'm her toughest patient, and part of my therapy is to give her 1,000 kisses when I see her next. I hope that's soon.

hi@NormSchriever.com
www.NormSchriever.com
@NormSchriever